Naval Science 1

1

Naval Science

An Illustrated Text for the NJROTC Student • Fourth Edition

Cdr. Richard R. Hobbs, USNR (Ret.)

NAVAL INSTITUTE PRESS • ANNAPOLIS, MARYLAND

To

The Cadets of the
Naval Junior Reserve Officers Training Corps
*for whom the challenge of life is
leadership and citizenship
in a stronger America.*

"We need men and women who by their personal integrity, their sense of moral purpose and their acceptance of the requirement for hard work will exemplify the best in the leadership traditions of the Navy and of our country. . . . Through this program the already great strength of the Navy will be increased even more, and through it we will respond more effectively to the challenge which confronts our country."

—Adm. Arleigh Burke, U.S. Navy

© 1996
by the United States Naval Institute
Annapolis, Maryland

First edition by Capt. W. A. Sundt, USN (Ret.),
published in 1980.

ISBN 1-55750-634-5

Printed in the United States of America on acid-free paper ∞
03 02 01 00 99 98 97 96   9 8 7 6 5 4 3 2
First printing

Contents

Preface to the First Edition

Naval Science 1 is designed to serve four purposes:

- To introduce the beginning NJROTC cadet to the Navy and its program for youth in America's high schools.
- To stimulate an enthusiasm for scholarship as a foundation for higher citizenship and leadership goals among individual young Americans.
- To engender a sound appreciation for the heritage and traditions of America, with recognition that the historically significant role of sea power will be increasingly influential in America's future.
- To initiate in each cadet a growing sense of pride in his or her organization, associates, and self, which will translate into an improved, expanded NJROTC nationwide and a better America.

A thorough understanding of the total NJROTC program and its purposes by cadets, their parents, and school administrators is essential to the success of any unit. Only by an appreciation of these goals can the necessary support be aroused in the school and community.

The four-year NJROTC program is designed to build leadership and citizenship in participating cadets. This is intended to be done through (1) a broad social-science academic approach and (2) a practical, guided leadership experience in naval organization and administration of the unit. The curriculum emphasizes the relationship of the seas to American history, world geography, international relations, and economics, on the one hand, and the behavioral aspects of leadership on the other. Study habits, personal hygiene, conduct, and courtesy are covered in this first text in order to lay the foundation for sound leadership and citizenship growth of individuals. Initial information on naval organization, career opportunities, navigation, seamanship, and military drill introduces the cadet to the naval environment. While each unit in this and subsequent texts is designed to stand independently, there is a continuity of purpose throughout all texts in the series. Each year of the course assists in building a basis for more advanced study of the Navy and sea power as it relates to the nation.

It is the personal intent of the author to motivate each cadet to develop his or her potential to the maximum extent. Hopefully the NJROTC program, with these texts, will stimulate each cadet to seek worthwhile goals in high school, advanced education, and lifetime careers.

The help of many enabled me to pursue this text to its successful publication. Tom Epley, editorial director for books of the Naval Institute Press, has supported the Naval Science series from its inception. Dick Hobbs, acquisitions editor, has been very helpful as my principal working contact for manuscript review. Bill McClay has served with diligence and competence as the manuscript editor for this introductory work in the series. Ward Brown, educational specialist in the Navy Youth Programs, and his successor Joe Gilliam, Office of the Chief of Naval Education and Training, continued to coordinate the project effectively in Pensacola.

Patty Maddocks, director of the Naval Institute library and photographic service, again provided essential assistance from her extensive photographic files. Mr. Ed Wilson, publication officer at the U.S. Naval Academy, generously authorized use of recent Academy photographs which provide timely and meaningful illustrations throughout the book. Very helpful photos of NJROTC units were provided by Mr. Robert A. Carlisle, Head of the Still Photo Branch, Office of Information, Navy Department, and PHCS B. E. Long and JOC James Jones of the Atlantic Fleet Audio Visual Command in Norfolk.

Review of the material on drug abuse was generously done by Detective Ervin Burrow of the Jefferson County (Wisconsin) Sheriff's Department. Detective James Meyer of the department is gratefully credited with the photography.

It is with honest pride that I am able to continue my service to my Navy through the youth in the NJROTC. I remain convinced that the NJROTC program and its fine cadets represent an island of stability and potential strength within the too often turbulent scene in the nation's schools. Young people need and want guidance and leadership; they will respond quickly and positively in the environment of this excellent program. With this experience during formative years, their own lives will take on new meaning which will bode well for the continuation of democratic ideals in the nation. My hope is that the lessons learned in NJROTC, assisted by the Naval Science series, will provide the basis for a renewed spirit of scholarship and patriotism among cadets, and all with whom they associate, so the Navy and the nation will reap lasting benefits.

Finally, I pay sincere tribute to my wife, Jean, who has continued to encourage me in my endeavors as an author throughout the year of work which went into this text. Without her support, the project would not have been possible.

Capt. W. A. Sundt, USN (Ret.)

Acknowledgments

As reviser of this fourth edition of volume 1 of the Naval Science series for NJROTC students, I wish to express appreciation once again to Capt. W. A. Sundt, USN (Ret.), the original author of the series, and to the editorial and design departments of the Naval Institute Press for their many contributions to the successful production of the books.

Special thanks are due to the 1994–95 NJROTC Curriculum Review Committee and to Mr. Don Dorin and Mr. Mike Hendersen on the staff of the Chief of Naval Education and Training (CNET) in Pensacola, Florida, who made many valuable suggestions for this revision and who furnished many of the cadet pictures within. Thanks are also due to Mr. Hans Krucke and the other members of the CNET NJROTC staff for their able administration of the program and the superb support they provide to it.

Several references were consulted for various sections of this text. One that was particularly helpful in describing the attitudes of winners versus losers in the Introduction to Leadership unit was an older but still valid little pamphlet titled *Winners and Losers* by Sydney J. Harris (Allen, Tex.: Argus Communications, 1968). Much of the material in this unit was drawn from my thirty years of personal associations with young people in high school, college, sports, and business. Much of the information on the origins of naval terms in the appendix was adapted from *Naval Ceremonies, Customs, and Traditions* by Vice Adm. William P. Mack and Cdr. Royal W. Connell (Annapolis, Md.: Naval Institute Press, 1980). Finally, special thanks are due to Ms. Jill Grupski, RN, a high school and emergency room nurse who reviewed the material in the appendix on first aid and health education.

Naval Science **1**

1

The NJROTC Program

Chapter 1. Goals of the NJROTC

Welcome aboard! You have chosen to become a member of the Navy Junior Reserve Officers Training Corps (NJROTC). Your experiences in the Corps will make you a better student, cadet, and citizen.

By becoming a naval cadet, you have shown that you want to be a good citizen. You have indicated that you want to develop your talents more fully. By making this decision, you have shown that you are on the right track toward meeting your goals in life.

Your instructors look forward to teaching you, and learning with you, all we can about our United States and our Navy. We want our naval science program to help make you able to follow leaders, and able to lead others as well. Everything in this course should help you meet your highest goals. We hope your personal goals are the same as those of the NJROTC program.

NJROTC Mission

The NJROTC program was established by Congress as part of the Reserve Officers' Training Corps Vitalization Act of 1964. The program went into effect in high schools in the fall of 1966.

Congress created this program because they saw the need for informed young leaders who un-

NJROTC cadets do many exciting things. These cadets are learning shiphandling and seamanship firsthand on board a Naval Academy patrol craft.

derstand the duties of U.S. citizenship. They believed that youths with leadership ability should learn what it takes to keep our nation strong. Congress wanted these youths to understand that, as U.S. citizens, they must do their part to help their country.

The NJROTC emphasizes each person's responsibilities in society. The program includes classroom study, physical fitness, respectful conduct, good personal appearance, and leadership training. It also gives the student a look at the Navy's part in U.S. history.

INDIVIDUAL AIMS

The NJROTC program is based on the needs of today's high school student. But Congress also wanted a few other things such as history included. An understanding of the present or a guess about the future is not possible without some knowledge of history. History provides a record of humans' past deeds and mistakes, and helps us to understand ourselves, our government, and our world.

For each member, then, the NJROTC seeks the following:

- Respect for proper authority
- Patriotism
- A high degree of personal honor, self-reliance, individual discipline, and leadership
- Pride, self-respect, confidence, and the desire to do one's best
- Better information on matters of national security
- An understanding of the U.S. Navy's role in the national defense

U.S. NAVY SUPPORT

The Navy gives the NJROTC program good support. Naval science instructors (NSIs) are retired officers. Associate naval science instructors (ANSIs) are retired officers or senior petty officers. Both NSIs and ANSIs, therefore, have had many years of active duty in the Navy or Marine Corps. Naval science instructors normally have college degrees, and many have higher degrees and state certification in teaching. Many enlisted ANSIs also have college degrees, and all have had extensive training in their job specialty. Both NSIs and ANSIs have much experience in leadership, guidance, and training of young people.

The Chief of Naval Education and Training (CNET) in Pensacola, Florida, does the program planning and sets policies for the whole NJROTC program. The CNET staff manages the budget for uniforms and books and recommends to the sec-

retary of the navy which NJROTC units should be started or stopped. CNET certifies all NSIs and ANSIs before they may instruct in the program. CNET's staff works with educators, civic leaders, and naval personnel to develop the best possible naval science program. This program is always being updated and improved for the students in today's high schools.

The local responsibility for running your NJROTC unit rests with your school board and school officials. Your naval science instructors work for the board and your principal. They run the unit according to local school district rules. The NJROTC program must meet local rules for graduation credit, in addition to the goals of the Navy and the requirements of Congress. The NJROTC

These NJROTC cadets on a visit to the tank landing ship USS *Sumter* (LST-1181) are gaining practical knowledge about modern shipboard warfare.

is therefore a team effort by the local schools and the Navy, both of which want to make cadets better citizens and leaders.

The naval science program helps with other subjects leading toward a high school diploma. But it also provides other things that only those in the unit can get. You, your school, and your community all benefit from this extra learning.

After high school graduation, some cadets take advantage of the special benefits that they have earned through the NJROTC. These benefits include:

- Qualification to enlist in the Navy or other military service in a higher pay grade
- Help in getting Naval Academy and NROTC scholarships if the student is qualified in all other ways

NJROTC COURSES AND ACTIVITIES

The NJROTC provides a more complete high school education for cadets. It helps develop a concern for humanity and world affairs. This is done by showing how history relates to the present, how events around the world affect Americans, and how the problems of humans everywhere affect each person. Cadets are taught self-discipline in order to get more done. They learn problem-solving, research, vocabulary, and goal-setting. Cadets take part in various unit physical fitness training activities that add to the school's health and physical education programs. The result is a more alert and healthy person.

Military drill helps develop good personal traits. Such traits include self-discipline, self-reliance, honesty, pride, patriotism, and respect for authority. In addition to their normal military drill, most units also have a color guard and a precision drill team. These extracurricular (afterschool) activities give cadets a chance to compete in parades and drill meets.

The NJROTC program lasts three years in some schools and four years in others. Along the way, cadets will learn many skills, about equal to those a seaman in the Navy would have.

The naval parts of the NJROTC course should develop the following:

- An interest in the oceans and how they affect world affairs
- An understanding of world geography and politics, and how these affect the United States and its allies
- A scientific interest in the sea and space
- An appreciation of the history and traditions of the naval service
- An appreciation of sea power in peace and war
- Basic knowledge of the Navy and its ships, aircraft, and tactics

These matters are all discussed in more detail throughout the naval science course.

The subjects you will work with in your NJROTC program are varied and interesting. The course stresses the social sciences, including history, geography, international relations, political science, economics, law, and psychology. Scientific areas are also covered, including meteorology, astronomy, electricity, and oceanography. The rest of the course deals with naval subjects, career and educational planning, and personal health.

The total program gives you a great chance to build on what you learn in high school. In fact, your naval science units will help you in your other social science and science courses. Best of all, you will be a better citizen and leader, better prepared to enter the adult world because of your being in NJROTC.

Chapter 1. Study Guide Questions

1. What will experiences gained in the NJROTC do for you?

2. What can the naval science program help you become?

3. Why did Congress see a need for the NJROTC program?

4. What are the NJROTC program goals?

5. Why is the study of history an important part of naval science?

6. What kinds of backgrounds do NSIs and ANSIs have?

7. Who has the overall responsibility for the NJROTC program in the Navy?

8. Who has local responsibility for your NJROTC unit?

9. What are two special benefits available to an NJROTC cadet following completion of the program and graduation?

10. What personal traits does military drill develop?

11. What do the naval science programs give the NJROTC cadet?

Vocabulary

responsibilities	trait
self-reliance	guidance
honesty	extracurricular
budget	activity
self-respect	citizens
personal honor	citizenship
patriotism	self-discipline
certification	leadership
CNET	naval science

Chapter 2.   How to Study

To learn, a person has to study. To study well, a person must form good habits. Good study habits make it possible to remember and apply what has been learned. Studying is important if you want to be successful.

To learn how to study requires self-discipline. Self-discipline is often defined as "being able to control yourself." Self-discipline is also one of the keys to becoming a good leader. Since one of the purposes of NJROTC is to make better leaders, each cadet must learn how to study. By so doing, you will have taken a step toward academic success and leadership.

This chapter will give you some ideas on how to study. You can apply these ideas in all your courses. Give very careful thought to this chapter, because it will help make you a better student and cadet. If you are successful as a student in high school, you will become a happier and more confident person. Upon graduation, you will be able to look back on high school and NJROTC with pride.

Study Habits

The words "study" and "habits" go together naturally. In fact, getting good study habits started is the most important thing you can do to get off on the right foot in school. A proven way to study is given below. Your instructors and teachers may require or suggest some changes. But in any good study system a good *routine* is important.

First of all, study at the same time every day. Probably right after supper, from about 7:00 until 8:30 or 9:00 P.M., will be best. You may have to study a bit longer if you have a paper or report to write, but you should try to *start* at the same time every night. Usually you will be able to finish all of your school work within two hours, if you get at it. If you have good habits, you may be able to finish in even less time. That's one of the most beneficial results of good study habits—they save time.

Most books on how to study say that you should study some on weekends, as well as on school nights. The idea is to keep yourself on a *schedule* (routine), and to keep your mind fresh on the subject. You won't have to study as long on Friday or Saturday, but a half-hour might be just enough to keep your mind in gear.

You also must *organize* your study materials. You will have your text and the notes you took in class. You will have a notebook, neatly divided for the different subjects you take. You may have a separate notebook for some particular class, if the teacher wants you to. All materials you have should be well organized. You don't want to waste time looking for the right papers.

If possible, you should have a desk or table that is "yours" for studying. It should be in a quiet place, such as your room, or at least some place out of the way of others. Your family should not have to stop everything just because you have to study. In addition, you cannot do a good job of studying if you are always being bothered.

Classroom study about the Navy is an interesting and fun part of the NJROTC curriculum.

You can't study very well while watching and listening to TV. If a good program about important events is on television, watch it. But don't try to watch it *and* do your school lessons at the same time; that way, you will get little from either. Radio is another distraction, especially talk programs or loud music. Other people talking and children playing will also distract you from your studies. Find a quiet place by yourself where you can get at the job, and get it finished. Then you can join in family activities with a free mind, knowing that you've taken care of your school responsibilities.

Have a place for everything, and keep everything in its place. Keep your pencils, pens, paper, ruler, scissors, erasers, pencil sharpener, and other things where you can find them right away. Have a dictionary handy. If you have an encyclopedia, keep it nearby. Half the battle of good study habits is in setting up a good study area.

You may have figured out by now that good study habits are not a mystery. They are just common sense. The idea is not to waste time on other things, but to think only about the job at hand.

A STUDY SYSTEM FOR A READING ASSIGNMENT

To study well you must use a good *system*. Almost all school lessons include a reading assign-

ment. Many vocational courses have reading assignments also. Mathematics and physical sciences generally require less reading than do social sciences, but will often have problems, experiments, and formulas that take more time. The social sciences, English, foreign languages, and general sciences mainly require reading, remembering, and writing.

The study system below will work well for naval science or any other course that assigns reading. Your instructors may have other methods that they want you to use, or they may change some things here.

Keep in mind two things, however: (1) a study system must be used often in order to work; and (2) the "normal" or "natural" way of reading without a good study pattern will give you poor results. With that in mind, then, here are the steps for *studying* and *learning* a naval science reading assignment:

1. *Scan* or *preview* section titles and the first sentences of paragraphs before reading the chapter.
2. *Question* what you are trying to find out. This can be helped by reading through the questions at the end of the chapter. Also try thinking of questions as you preview the section titles and topic sentences in Step 1.
3. *Read* the assignment carefully, and as you do, think of your questions.
4. *Recall* and think about what you read after finishing the reading assignment. This can be done by going through the questions and the vocabulary list at the end of each chapter.
5. *Write* short answers to the questions at the end of the chapter in your spiral or looseleaf naval science notebook. With a neatly kept notebook like this, you can make a quick review before class and before tests or quizzes.
6. *Review* your answers to the last chapter's questions, and look over once more the major topics in this reading assignment.

The *recall* and *write* steps may be combined. Use of the vocabulary list at this point is also good. The naval science instructor may also make other assignments with the vocabulary lists. These lists help both in reviewing the chapter and in expanding your own vocabulary. The size of your vocabulary and your reading ability are important areas in high school achievement tests and college entrance exams. Now let's go over these steps in more detail.

Step 1. Scan or Preview. The *scanning* or *previewing* step of the study system means going over the reading assignment to find the main topics and subtopics. These are given in capital letters or italics at the beginning of each section. Your naval science texts generally have a topic sentence at the beginning of each paragraph. If a short summary or conclusion is given at the end of a chapter, it should be read during this step also. The important thing is to scan the material and pick out the major points. When previewing, look at all pictures and drawings and read their captions. They also provide useful information.

Scanning is like outlining the chapter in your mind. Therefore, it may be helpful to jot down major points, as you find them, in outline form. Scanning not only helps you pick out the most important ideas, but also shows you how the material is organized. This will help you see the "whole picture" of the chapter and make it easier for you to understand the reading assignment.

Step 2. Question. If you can think of *questions* while you preview, you will get a good idea of what you should learn from the assignment. The naval science texts give you special help with this. At the end of each chapter are questions that cover main points of the chapter. Usually these questions are in the same order as the answers in the reading; this helps make previewing and outlining easier.

The questions give you something to look for—to zero in on—so you can get the most out of your reading. Looking for the answers should help you to pay closer attention to what you are reading.

If you also think up questions of your own as you preview, you will soon learn to find the important points in the reading. These points are almost certain to be asked in class or on tests and exams. If you can spot likely questions for tests, you will do much better on such questions when they appear. Give it a try! It is an art that will take a while

to learn, but if you keep at it, you are bound to succeed.

Step 3. Read. If you have followed Steps 1 and 2, you are now ready to *read.* You have your mind in gear; you have a good idea of what you are seeking. Look for the major points again as you go along; the details will quickly fall into place and make it read smoothly. Check the section titles again before reading the paragraph, and try to remember what you are looking for in that section. You now have a purpose for your reading; you are looking for answers to your questions because you *want to find* those answers. And you will be able to read *much faster* because of your earlier preview.

When you are reading, don't become too comfortable and relaxed. Studying is different from reading for fun. The old saying about "curling up with a good book" doesn't lead to the best results when you're studying. You have to "attack" the material, seeking answers and making those answers fit into what you are thinking about. You need an alert mind—not a relaxed mind that wanders about the page, daydreaming about other things. You must concentrate. If you don't you may finish a page and not know what you just read.

Step 4. Recall. To *recall* you must be able to pick out the main points from the reading assignment and state or write the important subpoints under them. You may have to reread a section or two at first, but you will improve as you stick by the system. You must be able to explain the major points in *your own words* and *understand* what you are saying. When you understand the material, you can discuss it both in your own words and in the words of the author.

If you jotted down a brief topic outline as suggested in Step 1 as you previewed the assignment, this can help you recall and organize facts and ideas. What you are trying to do here is understand what you have read so that it is useful to you. Often, it is helpful to recall aloud to yourself in a low voice. This not only causes you to *think* about what you are saying, but also causes you to *hear* what you have said. Recall is a vital part of learning, for it causes you to *remember* what you have read.

Step 5. Write. At the end of each chapter you will find questions on the most important points covered. For the naval science course, it is recommended that you *write* answers to these questions after going through the first four steps of this study system. *Writing* is also a learning tool. All high school students and adults should be able to do it well. It is required if you plan to go to college or get into any type of management position. It is a must for a naval officer and a petty officer.

Writing may be considered a part of the recall process, for it requires you to remember answers. It can also be used for the sixth step in the learning process, called *review* or *test*. Writing, then, is an important part of the recall process and is necessary to organize your materials for review.

Step 6. Review/Test Preparation. *Review* may take place at any time—usually days or even weeks after you have finished the reading assignment. You may review to refresh your own memory. More often, you will review before a test or exam. If you have followed the above steps, you should be able to prepare well for the test. You can go through your notebook of questions and answers, your vocabulary drills, and the notes you took in class. You shouldn't have to reread the whole book again—and that's nearly impossible, anyway. With your materials in order, you can go over them, feeling sure that you know all the important points. Then you can go to bed early and get a good night's sleep, arriving ready for the test the next day. Others will be worried and tired after staying up late to cram, and won't do as well as you. Isn't it worth a try?

STUDY TIME

You may think that the study system above takes too long or is too hard. This simply isn't so. It has been proved with students just like you many times in the past. This text will assist you by giving topics and subtopics, key sentences, illustrations, end-of-chapter questions, and vocabulary lists.

One question you may ask is, "How much time should I spend on each of the steps outlined?" There is no hard and fast rule. In general, you should spend about half of your time scanning and reading, and about half on questioning and recalling (including writing). Using a one-hour study time, that would break down like this:

Step	Percent of time	Time in minutes
1. Scan/Preview	10%	6 minutes
2. Question	10%	6 minutes
3. Read	40%	24 minutes
4. Recall	10%	6 minutes
5. Write	30%	18 minutes
6. Review/Test	—	As required

But no study system can "give you learning" or give you the answers. It can help you learn if you put in the time and effort, and if you do your studying with the right attitude. But it is *you* who must do the learning.

CLASSROOM BEHAVIOR

Besides knowing how to study well, you also must be able to get the most from your time in the school classroom. Three things are very important here: proper classroom behavior, good listening habits, and good notetaking.

Classroom behavior means the way you act in the classroom. As in studying, you won't get much out of class if you let yourself be bothered or distracted a lot. You should be alert and pay attention to what your instructor is trying to teach. After all, if it weren't important, he or she wouldn't be spending time on it. Don't whisper or bother your classmates. Not only is it rude to talk while someone else is talking to you, but you might miss something. Sit up straight. Think about what is being taught, not about last night's date, tomorrow's game, or other things. Ask questions about things you don't understand.

Good listening is a skill few people have. If you can work on listening well, this ability will help you greatly, both in school and later in life. There is a difference between just *hearing* and *listening*. Hearing means you are aware of sounds being made, but are not thinking much about them—like having rock music playing while you are studying. To really listen means not just hearing the sounds, but also thinking about the meaning of each word, and what the speaker is trying to get across. Look at the speaker. Everyone appreciates a good listener. Try it and see.

Good notetaking is another handy skill, both in school and later in life. Good notes make it easier to review, one of the six steps of good studying. When you take notes in class, don't try to write down everything. Concentrate on the main points and subpoints, just as you do in a reading assignment. If taken correctly, your notes should almost look like those your instructor uses for teaching. After a discussion you might want to spend a few minutes jotting down some of the most important things talked about, to wrap up your thoughts on that topic.

Chapter 2. Study Guide Questions

1. To study well, what must a person do?

2. What is one sure way of becoming a more confident, happier person in high school?

3. What is one of the most beneficial results of good study habits?

4. What are some distractions to avoid when setting up a study area?

5. What are the six steps for studying a reading assignment?

6. Why are naval science notebooks a good idea for NJROTC cadets?

7. What should the *scanning* step do?

8. Why is an outline helpful?

9. Why should you try to identify questions when scanning a reading assignment?

10. Why is being relaxed and comfortable often not good for someone who is studying?

11. What should a student be able to do when he or she has understood a reading assignment?

12. A. What is the sixth step in the learning process?

B. How will your answers to the Study Guide Questions help you prepare for a test?

13. What are the important things to remember about good listening skills in the classroom?

Vocabulary

schedule	system
distraction	vocational
organize	scan
recall	summary
scholarship	topic, subtopic
outline	subpoint
study habits	classroom behavior

Chapter 3.   NJROTC Organization and Regulations

The goals of the NJROTC program were given in the first chapter of this unit. Chapter 2 gave suggestions on how to study. We will now talk about how NJROTC is set up.

Makeup of the NJROTC

The NJROTC program is made up of units in many public, private, and military high schools in the United States. A *unit* is made up of all the naval science students in the NJROTC program in any one high school. In order to qualify as a unit in good standing, a high school NJROTC program must maintain an enrollment of at least 100 cadets or 10 percent of the school's student population. There are currently over 400 NJROTC units authorized in the fifty states, the District of Columbia, Guam, Italy, and Japan.

Enrollment. To enroll in an NJROTC unit, a student must:

- Be a U.S. citizen or alien lawfully admitted for permanent residence in the United States.
- Attend the school sponsoring the unit.
- Be of good moral character. Students who have academic or behavior problems are not admitted.
- Be physically fit enough to take part in the school's normal physical education program.

- Agree to comply with uniform and grooming regulations.

Disenrollment. A cadet may be disenrolled by the NJROTC instructor, with the approval of the principal. This will be done by the standard procedures of the school, for any of the following reasons:

- Failure to maintain the academic standards required for enrollment.
- Lack of aptitude or bad character traits. The NJROTC is a special outfit in which cadets receive special instruction, privileges, travel, training, and leadership opportunities. Each person must be worthy of membership in the corps of cadets.
- Disenrollment from the school, for any reason. If a cadet moves to another school with a JROTC unit of the Navy, Army, Air Force, or Marines, the cadet can transfer to the new unit, getting full credit for the training already received (but not necessarily the same rank).
- Request of the individual cadet.
- Inability to take part in the school's physical education program.

UNIT ORGANIZATION

The NJROTC unit at any school will be officially called "NJROTC Unit, (name of school)." The head of the department of naval science is designated the NSI. ANSIs are retired officers or senior petty officers. They have teaching and other duties in the units.

Instructors will require you to conduct yourself in a military way at all times when performing NJROTC activities. This means when you participate in naval science classes, drills, social or parade activities, field trips, and cruises.

A typical unit of 100 to 150 cadets would probably be organized into one company containing three platoons. Each platoon would contain three or four squads, and each squad would be made up of eight to ten cadets.

The unit is set up so each individual knows what he or she is supposed to do. Each member has a place in the unit *chain of command.* Think of the people in your unit as being like links in a chain—a chain in which the top link is filled by the senior cadet officer. Each lower link in the chain is a cadet with slightly less authority and responsibility. A sample organization chart of a typical unit with 100 to 150 cadets appears on page 10.

A unit having 150 or more cadets is called a *battalion.* A unit with 300 or more cadets is considered a *regiment.* In the regiment there are two or more battalions, each headed by a cadet called a battalion commander.

All units have a color guard. Its size will depend on the number of flags carried. NSIs select the color guard commander. There also will be at least two drill-rifle bearers for color escorts.

Most units will have a drill team. A drill team commander will be named by the NSI. Some units have a rifle team for marksmanship competition.

The color guard and drill team often represent the school and the unit in public. Therefore, the cadets in these special groups must be dedicated and willing to work hard to perfect their routines. Membership in these groups is a high honor. The extra work will be more than repaid in fun, prestige, and learning. Many drill teams compete with nearby JROTC units of the other U.S. armed services.

NJROTC CADET RANKS

NJROTC cadet enlisted rates and officer ranks are based on those used in the U.S. Navy. The enlisted rates start with three levels of *seaman*—seaman recruit, seaman apprentice, then seaman. Then there are three levels of *petty officer*—third, second, then first class. If a petty officer is good enough, he or she can advance to be a *chief petty officer,* then *senior chief petty officer.* More about naval enlisted rates and ratings will be given in Unit 4.

Officer ranks start at ensign, then progress through lieutenant (junior grade), lieutenant, and lieutenant commander. In some big units a cadet may be able to reach the rank of commander. Next in the Navy come the ranks of captain and admiral, but cadets in NJROTC units do not have these ranks.

Normally, first-year cadets are nonrated seamen. Qualified second-year cadets may move up

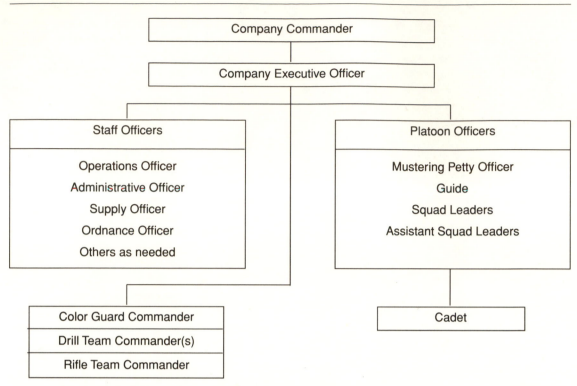

A typical NJROTC organization chart for a company-sized unit of 100 to 150 cadets.

to petty officer. Many third- and fourth-year cadets earn senior petty officer and officer ranks. The length of time alone that you're in the unit doesn't guarantee you a promotion, though.

Your NSI will make all officer promotions and petty officer advancements in rate on the basis of military and academic performance, ability, loyalty, and other qualities. The NSI can also demote or remove any cadet whose performance does not measure up.

Unit Regulations and Leadership

Policies and procedures for the unit are set by the NSI and by the *NJROTC Regulations* prepared by CNET. Each unit has a copy of these *Regulations,* so they do not need repeating in this text. But we will say a few general things about them.

The rules for the unit are passed down to the cadet commander and his or her staff officers. The cadet officers then manage the unit under the supervision of the NSI. This is a key part of the leadership training of cadets.

Leadership qualities of unit officers are similar to those of students in other leadership positions in the school—the president of the student council, class officers, captains of athletic teams, club chairmen, and editor of the school yearbook. One good thing about NJROTC, though, is that there are many more leadership positions at different levels than in most school organizations. This gives more students a chance to test their leadership ability.

Your school and unit leaders have qualities that you and other students should respect. Study their

This sharp young NJROTC cadet has her hair done in a style suitable for both officers and enlisteds.

approach to leadership and try to learn from them. That way, you will be a better leader when it is your turn.

The Naval Uniform

The *Uniform Regulations* of the U.S. Navy require people in the Navy to wear a correct uniform. The uniform makes it possible to identify on sight those belonging to the naval service. Anyone can see at a glance a person's rank, corps, or rating.

Boys and girls in the NJROTC must be neatly dressed at all times. Personal appearance is important to everyone. So, whether you're in your NJROTC uniform or civilian clothing, you should have a neat and clean appearance.

The military uniform has a long history. Early Greek soldiers wore uniforms with metal plates and plumed helmets. So did the Roman legionnaires. Each period in history made changes in uniform to adjust to climate, weapons, and battlefield tactics. Styles and colors of uniforms have also changed to meet practical needs.

Uniforms also improve the spirit of a fighting unit. At one time, it was thought that the brighter and more colorful the uniform, the better. Troops in the dust and smoke of battle could quickly tell friend from foe if uniforms were distinctive. But this caused problems. The British red coat, white breeches, and black leather headdress made British soldiers sitting ducks in the woods of America during the Revolutionary War. Britain changed the uniform.

Today, uniforms for the field are *camouflaged* (colored to blend with the background) to protect the soldier. On board ship, uniforms must be easy to clean, since laundry facilities are limited. Uniforms for liberty and shore leave are neatly styled and clean-cut.

Since World War I (1914–18), *decorations* and *insignia* have been worn on uniforms. The decorations are used to show the branch of service, the job specialty, and special qualifications. Other insignia show the rank and corps of officers, and rating and rate of petty officers and nonrated personnel.

NJROTC Uniforms

Uniform rules for cadets are given in *NJROTC Regulations* and the *NJROTC Field Manual*. The basic uniform in winter is the service dress blue, or winter blue in warmer climates, for both male and female cadets. In warm weather, uniforms are blue trousers with short-sleeved white shirts (summer blue). Working uniforms are sometimes issued for field trips and cruises; they are tropical khaki for both males and females. Caps, belts, ties, and insignia are issued to go with the uniforms. The first pair of uniform black shoes is provided. Cadets supply their own underclothing and socks/stockings. Winter overcoats and raincoats are issued if necessary.

NJROTC uniforms are worn by all cadets at least once a week and on other special occasions as

Keeping a proper military image is very important for members of NJROTC units. Your community and classmates form an impression of the Navy based on what they see.

This does not mean male cadets have to get a crew cut. But their hair should be neatly trimmed, off the shirt collar and away from the ears. Female cadets' hair should also be off the collar. This won't cramp anyone's style, and is much easier to keep clean and combed. It is much cheaper and easier to manage than most other styles as well.

In addition, NJROTC regulations require the proper wearing of the military hat—combination cap or garrison cap. A big mass of hair simply won't fit well under or around a military cap. So make up your mind to follow the regulations; be neatly groomed, clean, and comfortable—and in uniform!

Military image is very important for members of an NJROTC unit. The NJROTC represents the Navy in many schools and communities. Don't forget that the NJROTC has a responsibility to the Navy and to the public. The Navy has the right to say what the NJROTC's image should be. For this reason, NJROTC rules for personal appearance must be followed.

determined by the NSI. Special occasions may include Veterans' Day, the Navy Birthday, Washington's Birthday, Armed Forces Day, and Memorial Day, among others.

Uniforms are U.S. government property. Uniforms are clean when issued, but the cadet must clean and press them during the school year. If uniform clothing items are lost or destroyed, the NSI normally will require the cadet to replace or pay for the item lost. Uniform items that wear out or become too small are turned in to the NSI. The cadet supply officer will issue replacements.

NJROTC uniforms may not be worn by persons who are not members of the unit. Cadets do not wear incomplete uniforms or parts of the uniform with civilian clothes. The uniform should only be worn when you are taking part in some official NJROTC or school activity.

PERSONAL GROOMING

Personal grooming is largely a matter of personal pride. Long, messy hair simply does not "fit" well with a neat, clean uniform. A unit can't look uniform and shipshape if some cadets have their hair hanging over their eyes, ears, and shoulders.

Chapter 3. Study Guide Questions

1. What are the eligibility requirements for enrollment in the NJROTC?

2. What can cause disenrollment from an NJROTC unit?

3. What are the ranks of the company commander, executive officer, and staff officers of your NJROTC unit?

4. A. What are the qualifications sought for members of the unit's color guard and drill teams?

   B. What are the benefits from participation in these special teams?

5. What are the naval enlisted rates upon which NJROTC cadet rates are based?

6. Who determines promotions and advancements in the NJROTC?

7. Who and what determine the policies and rules for operation of the NJROTC unit?

8. Why is proper wear of the uniform important for NJROTC cadets?

9. What are the basic winter and warm-weather uniforms for the NJROTC?

10. What parts of uniform clothing must the cadet provide?

Vocabulary

regulations	petty officer	aptitude	chain of command
corps	personal grooming	performance	compete
enrollment	pride	prestige	rate
probation	military image	camouflage	rating
disenroll	cruise	insignia	rank

Chapter 4.   Military Customs and Courtesies

The military services have a long history, with many *traditions*. You will understand the military better if you know some of these traditions. These traditions can be broken down into various customs and courtesies.

A *custom* is a way of acting—something that has been done for so long that it has become like a law. A *courtesy* is a form of polite manners and behavior. Customs and courtesies help make life orderly, and are a way of showing respect.

Customs are regular, expected actions. They have been done again and again, and passed from one generation to the next. Courteous actions show your concern and respect for others. Courtesy also means respect for certain objects or symbols, such as the American flag.

Ceremonies, customs, and courtesies help keep discipline and order in a military organization. This chapter will discuss some of the customs and courtesies of the services, especially those you will need to learn and use as an NJROTC cadet.

The Hand Salute

The *hand salute* came to us by way of the British navy. The military salute, however, goes back to ancient times, when it was done by raising the right hand (the weapon hand) in a greeting of friendship (showing that no weapon was held). Courtesy requires the lower-ranking person to make the gesture first to the higher-ranking one. This tradition probably comes from the days when a knight would raise his helmet visor to show an

approaching senior who he was. In the British navy of the eighteenth and nineteenth centuries, junior officers lifted their hats to seniors. Enlisted men took their hats off as a mark of respect to officers.

Today the salute is an important military gesture. It is part of military courtesy, used whenever a junior meets or greets a more senior officer in every country, and shows respect and pride in the service.

Proper Manner of Saluting

Except when walking, you should be at attention when saluting. Your head and eyes are turned toward the person saluted. Your right hand is raised until the tip of your forefinger touches the lower part of your headgear, if a combination cap is worn. (The forefinger touches the forehead above and slightly to the right of the right eye if you are wearing a garrison cap or beret.) Thumb and fingers are extended and joined. The palm is turned slightly inward so that the person saluting can just see its surface in the corner of the right eye. The upper arm is parallel to the ground, the elbow slightly in front of the body. The forearm is inclined at a 45° angle; the hand and wrist are in a straight line. A person completes the salute, after it has been returned, by dropping the arm to its normal position at the side in one sharp, clean motion.

The first position of the hand salute should occur when you are about six paces from the person being saluted, in a normal meeting situation. Salutes can also be made at greater distances (up to thirty paces) if you cannot come within six paces. The hand salute, by naval custom, is accompanied by a spoken greeting. The junior, either standing or meeting, looks the senior straight in the eye and says, depending upon the time of day:

- From first rising until noon—"Good morning, (Sir, Ma'am, or rank)."
- From noon until sunset—"Good afternoon, _____."
- From sunset until turning in—"Good evening, _____."

Naval custom permits saluting with the left hand when a salute cannot be given with the right hand. (Army and Air Force custom permits only right-hand salutes.)

Naval personnel normally do not salute when "uncovered" (without hat on). Since naval personnel normally "uncover" inside, they do not usually salute inside. (Army and Air Force custom, however, require the salute when uncovered. Uncovered naval personnel should return salutes by persons in other services as a military courtesy.) In any event, a person who is saluted while uncovered acknowledges a salute by the appropriate words and a nod of the head if a salute cannot be returned. Enlisted personnel salute all officers, and every officer salutes his or her seniors.

If a junior overtakes a senior while walking and wishes to pass he or she will say when coming up next to the senior. "By your leave, sir (or ma'am)," and salute when alongside. The senior will return the salute and either give permission or say "Good morning." Male naval officers normally salute a woman during introduction, and when she boards a ship. During formal ceremonies inside a building, naval personnel remain covered when standing so they can give the hand salute if necessary.

All naval and military personnel stand at attention facing the colors when the national anthem is played at a formal or public ceremony. If the colors are not displayed, they face the music. If covered, they salute at the first note of the anthem, and remain at the salute until the last note. During parades, military personnel salute the flag when it is carried by in formation.

The hand salute is given by members of the color detail and all other persons in uniform

A person should be at attention when saluting, except when walking. The right hand is raised smartly until the tip of the forefinger touches the lower part of the cap brim.

nearby when the flag is raised at morning colors, and when it is lowered at evening colors. This ceremony is normally carried out by the NJROTC color detail in front of the unit's school building.

Military and NJROTC personnel in uniform stand at attention and give the hand salute at memorial services (Veterans' Day, Memorial Day) when "Taps" is sounded.

When boarding a ship in which the U.S. flag is flying, all persons in the naval service should face the flag and salute. They then salute the officer of the deck (OOD) and request permission to come on board. On leaving the ship, they give the same salutes in reverse order: first to the OOD, and then to the national ensign. These same salutes are also given on board foreign warships.

NAVAL ETIQUETTE

Etiquette means the manners that are normal or required in dealing with people. Military courtesy refers to the manners between officers, and between officers and enlisted personnel. Naval etiquette is similar in peace or war.

Military courtesy among officers depends on two things: (1) precedence, and (2) deference to seniors. *Precedence* has to do with having a higher rank and greater responsibility. *Deference* means that a junior must yield to a senior, out of respect for his or her authority. Officers take *precedence* according to their rank. This applies to both military relations and social life.

Naval courtesy demands that junior officers show their seniors deference and respect. Officers should respond with equal courtesy. This is a bit like the relationship between young people and their elders. It also is like the relationship between student and teacher, teacher and principal, or employee and employer.

Junior officers sometimes make mistakes in supervising their personnel. So do NJROTC cadet officers, in their dealings with other cadets. This is because of inexperience. They are learning to lead, just as you are learning to follow. Errors are made by both of you along the way. But you learn by experience. Sometimes you learn best by an error. An error can be a learning experience that you will never forget. And remember, you must be able to *follow* orders well before you can learn to *lead* and give orders.

In summary, personal relations in the military are based on mutual respect between fellow men and women. The amount of respect for an officer shows whether or not he or she is effective. And a senior will respect juniors who, when given a job, can be depended upon to do it right.

RELATIONS BETWEEN JUNIORS AND SENIORS

Here are some general rules of etiquette followed in dealings between juniors and seniors. These rules are carefully observed in the Navy. They should also be followed in your NJROTC unit. Of course, civilian life is less formal than military life must be. But these general rules of naval etiquette can also be applied, in many ways, to correct and polite manners in civilian life.

A junior approaching a senior to make an official report stays at attention until asked to be seated or to stand at ease.

Unless on watch, a person in the naval service uncovers when entering a room where a senior is present.

When a senior enters a room in which juniors

Good leaders know when to relax and be less formal with their subordinates. These NJROTC cadets share some observations during a break in a drill competition.

are seated, the one who first sees the senior calls "Attention on deck!" All present remain at attention until told to carry on.

When spoken to by a senior, the junior, if seated, rises and remains at attention. When personnel are seated, they need not rise when an officer (other than a flag officer or the captain of the ship) passes, unless they are called to attention or if it is necessary to clear a gangway.

The place of honor is on the right. When a junior walks, rides, or sits with a senior, the junior takes position alongside and to the left.

When entering an automobile or a boat, naval officers do so in reverse order of rank, from lowest to highest. In a car, the junior takes the seat on the far or left-hand corner, the senior sitting on the right side. When getting out, the senior leaves first. In entering buildings or rooms, however, the junior opens doors for the senior and enters last.

A junior does not offer to shake hands with a senior; the senior makes the offer.

A junior doesn't keep a senior waiting. It's important to be on time in the service. When called by a senior, a junior responds immediately.

In answering questions from a senior, a junior gives clearly worded answers. If the desired answer cannot be given, say "I don't know, sir/ma'am;

This NJROTC color guard presents the colors at many of its high school's sports events.

but I will find out and let you know." This is much better than giving a wrong answer.

A junior who has been assigned a task should report back right away to the senior after completion of the task.

Juniors must make sure they understand their orders. They should ask questions if they don't understand.

Juniors should not "jump the chain of command," that is, skip their seniors, in normal situations. If an emergency needs quick attention, the immediate senior should be told right away.

Sometimes an officer may not like orders that come from seniors. But the officer must follow these orders and see that they are obeyed anyway. An officer should never blame a senior for such orders, and should never question an order in front of his or her subordinates.

Excuses for failure are never acceptable. An officer should take responsibility and not make an alibi. If you're at fault, accept the blame.

"Buttering-up" or trying to get on the good side of your seniors is despised. Usually a senior will see what you're up to. However, an effort to be friendly and cooperative helps bring a junior success. A willingness to do any task assigned will give you a good reputation and make you popular with fellow officers and petty officers.

There is only one correct response to an oral order—"Aye, aye, sir/ma'am." This reply means more than "yes." It says "I understand and will obey." Don't ever say, "O.K., sir," or "All right, sir." You should say, "Yes, sir/ma'am," or "No, sir/ma'am" in answer to questions from a senior.

CONCLUSION

Matthew Fontaine Maury, an outstanding naval officer of the nineteenth century, said: "Make it a rule never to offend, nor to seek causes of offense in the conduct of others. Be polite to all, familiar with but a few." That is still good advice today.

Knowing when and how to do things is called *tact*. Tactful officers and petty officers know how to deal with their shipmates. Many otherwise good officers and petty officers have been less effective because they did not use tact on the job.

All organizations have customs and etiquette. These are very necessary when people live and work closely together, as they do on board a ship. If you don't follow the customs and etiquette, others will think you're careless or ignorant.

Every officer and enlisted person takes pride in naval traditions. They follow the customs and etiquette of the service. All cadets in the NJROTC should learn them.

Chapter 4. Study Guide Questions

1. Why are customs and courtesies important to military organizations?

2. What is the significance of the hand salute?

3. By naval custom, when do male officers salute women?

4. How is the hand salute rendered in boarding and departing a commissioned naval vessel?

5. Upon what two things is military courtesy among officers founded?

6. Upon what should personal relations within the military be based?

7. What military courtesies should be observed in the following instances?

A. Junior comes to a senior to make a report.

B. Senior enters the room where juniors are seated.

C. Senior talks to a junior who is seated.

D. Junior and senior enter and leave a boat or car.

E. Junior and senior enter and leave a building.

F. Junior is introduced to a senior.

8. How should a junior reply to a senior's question if the answer is not known?

9. What is meant by the phrase "jump the chain of command"?

10. What is the only correct response to an oral order?

11. What is *tact*, and why is it important in dealing with people?

12. Why should NJROTC cadets seek to learn the customs and etiquette of the Navy?

Vocabulary

tradition	precedence
custom	deference
courtesy	senior
ceremony	junior
salute	respect
memorial services	tact
etiquette	

Chapter 5. The U.S. Flag and National Anthem

The U.S. flag tells a noble story to the entire world. It tells how a free people became a single nation, one and indivisible. It tells of the spirit of liberty and the ideal of human freedom. It tells of a unique opportunity for life, liberty, and the pursuit of happiness.

The flag is a symbol of patriotism. It displays the spirit of the United States. Millions of citizens have fought under it, and heroes have died for it. It is the flag of all of us; so all U.S. citizens should treat it with honor and loyalty.

Many different designs of homemade flags were flown in the American colonies and over their armies and ships before the "Stars and Stripes" was made the official national ensign on 14 June 1777. This date is now called Flag Day. Tradition has it that the first foreign salute to the new American flag was made by a French warship. The French ship saluted the flag carried by John Paul Jones's ship the *Ranger* during a visit to a French port in February 1778. The nickname "Old Glory" was given to the flag in 1831 by Navy Captain William Driver, who carried it twice around the world. Later during the Civil War

when Union troops captured the city of Nashville, Tennessee, where Driver was then living in retirement, he raised it with his own hands over the state house.

The flag has had about the same shape, with thirteen stripes and one star in the blue field for each of the states, since the early 1800s.

MEANING AND DISPLAY OF THE FLAG

The colors in the flag each stand for noble qualities of our nation. The red is for valor and zeal. The white is for hope, purity, cleanliness, and honesty. And the blue, the color of heaven, signifies reverence to God, loyalty, sincerity, and justice. George Washington probably interpreted our flag best when he said, "We take the stars from heaven, the red from our mother country . . . and the white stripes . . . represent our Liberty."

There are clear rules about how to use or display the flag. We cannot go into all aspects of flag display here, but we will cover a few of the displays you will see in the NJROTC and in school.

Flag displays follow the rules of *heraldry*. These rules have been handed down since the days of knights in armor. According to heraldry, the right side is the position of danger, since it is the position of the arm which holds the sword. Therefore, the right side is also the position of honor. The blue field on the flag, according to these rules, must be displayed on top and to the flag's own right (the observer's left). A simple "rule of thumb" tells how to display the flag correctly, whether in a horizontal or vertical position: We always speak of the flag as the *Stars and Stripes,* never as the "stripes and stars." Therefore, when we look at the flag it should read "stars and stripes"; that is, the stars in the blue field should come first.

When the national flag is carried in group with another flag or flags, it should be on the marching right. If there is a line of other flags, it should be in front of the center of that line.

When the national flag is displayed with another flag against a wall from a crossed staff, it should be on the flag's own right (to the left of an observer). The staff should be in front of the staff of the other flag.

When a number of flags of states, cities, or schools are grouped and displayed from staffs with the U.S. flag, the U.S. flag should be at the center and at the highest point of the group.

When used on a speaker's platform, the flag, if displayed flat, should be above and behind the speaker, attached firmly and without sagging, with the blue field to the speaker's right.

When on a speaker's platform, as in a school auditorium, the flag of the United States should be in front of the audience and at the speaker's right. Any other flag displayed should be placed to the left of the podium (speaker's stand), or to the right of the audience.

When flown at half-staff the flag should be hoisted to the top and then lowered to the half-staff position. Before being lowered for the day, it should be raised again to the peak before slowly coming down. The flag should always be hoisted briskly and lowered slowly, with dignity.

CAUTIONS: HOW NOT TO USE THE FLAG

Do not permit disrespect to be shown to the flag of the United States of America.

Do not dip the national flag to any person or any thing. Unit colors, state flags, and organization or institutional flags will give this type of honor.

Do not place any other flag or pennant above or, if on the same level, to the right of the flag of the United States. The only exception is the church pennant, which is flown above the ensign aboard ships at sea when divine services are being held.

Do not let the flag touch the ground or the floor or trail in the water.

Do not place any object, emblem, or lettering on or above the national flag.

Do not use the flag as part of a costume.

Do not drape the flag on any platform or speaker's podium, or on the hood, top, or sides of a car. If used on a float or vehicle in a parade, it must be flown from a staff which is fixed firmly to the right fender or on the right, forward side of the chassis.

Do not use the flag for any kind of advertising.

School officials often ask the advice of the NSI and NJROTC cadets on displaying the flag. It might come up for displays in the auditorium, at athletic contests, in parades, and for school programs and parade floats. The color guard of the unit often presents colors during the playing of the National Anthem before football and basketball games. You will be able to think of many other places that the flag will be displayed in your school and by your unit. Render the flag proper honor, and display it correctly at all times.

DEFINITIONS FOR U.S. FLAGS

The flag of the United States is also referred to as the national flag, national ensign, and national colors. The term *national flag* can be used in any situation. The other terms have well-defined usages within the armed services.

National ensign indicates the national flag when flown by ships and boats. *National colors* refers to flags carried by dismounted units of a landing force. This flag is stubbier in size than the national ensign. The *union jack* is the blue field of white stars from the national ensign, flown by day from the jackstaff on the bow of U.S. naval warships at anchor or moored.

There is another type of U.S. flag sometimes flown by civilian boats and yachts, called the *yacht-*

Customary Personal Courtesies during the Pledge of Allegiance and National Anthem

All personnel stand quietly at attention facing flag if present, or music.		Covered	Uncovered
In civilian attire	Males	Remove hat, hold over heart with right hand, recite pledge/ may sing anthem.	Place right hand over heart, recite pledge/ may sing anthem.
	Females	Place right hand over heart, recite pledge/may sing anthem.	
In military uniform	Males	Remain silent, salute.	Place right hand over heart, recite pledge/ may sing anthem.
	Females		

ing ensign. This flag has a white anchor surrounded by a circle of thirteen stars in the blue field.

PLEDGE OF ALLEGIANCE AND NATIONAL ANTHEM

Another honor shown the U.S. flag is the Pledge of Allegiance: "I pledge allegiance to the flag of the United States of America and to the republic for which it stands, one nation under God, indivisible, with liberty and justice for all." When you pledge allegiance to the flag, you are also pledging allegiance to the Republic of the United States. You should never act in any way that would go against your pledge to the flag and your country.

Customs for the Pledge of Allegiance. When the Pledge of Allegiance is recited, it should be said in a firm voice, with personnel standing at attention and facing the flag. Males in civilian clothes, if covered, should remove their hat with their right hand and hold it over the heart. If uncovered, they should place their right hand over the heart. Females in civilian attire, whether covered or not, should place their right hand over the heart. All covered military personnel in uniform should remain silent, face the flag at attention, and salute. Uncovered military personnel in uniform should place their right hand over the heart and say the pledge.

Customs for the National Anthem. Another honor to our country is the traditional courtesy shown during the playing of the National Anthem ("The Star Spangled Banner"). When the anthem is played, all personnel should stand at attention facing the flag, if one is present, or facing the music, if no flag is present. All other customary courtesies are the same as those for the Pledge of Allegiance. Refer to the table above for a summary of the appropriate courtesies during the pledge and the anthem.

CONCLUSION

The U.S. flag brings pride to all Americans. It is this feeling that should become a part of every NJROTC cadet as he or she takes part in the naval science program.

Our flag is the symbol of our nation, carried across the high seas and respected in distant ports. It stands for the American people's honor and power. Naval men and women guard its dignity. To uphold it is a naval man or woman's special trust.

Chapter 5. Study Guide Questions

1. What message does the U.S. flag give the American people and the world?

2. How does heraldry influence the way the American flag is placed and handled?

3. On a speaker's platform or stage in a school auditorium, where is the flag placed?

4. What procedure must be followed in raising and lowering the flag on a day when it is to be flown at half-staff?

5. What is meant by the following terms used in relation to the flag of the United States?

    A. National flag.

    B. National ensign.

    C. Jack.

6. What do personnel in full uniform do during the Pledge of Allegiance and the National Anthem?

7. What do the colors of the American flag represent?

Vocabulary

symbol	pledge
indivisible	anthem
heraldry	dignity
national ensign	flagstaff
allegiance	

2

Introduction to Leadership

Chapter 1.   Followership and Leadership

Naval leadership requires intelligence, understanding of people, and moral character. Leadership is the ability to inspire and manage a group of people successfully. It is the art of getting people to work toward a goal. Leadership skills are similar in any situation, whether it is the classroom, community, home, NJROTC, or the Navy. We will discuss some of these skills in this unit.

FOLLOWERSHIP

Followership is the art of following. Everyone in the U.S. armed forces is in a position of followership. No matter how high you are in the chain of command, there is always someone above you. Even the president, as commander in chief of the armed forces, is responsible to the people. Therefore, a truly effective leader within the armed forces must also be an effective follower.

This is also true in the NJROTC. As a first-year naval science cadet, you are the *subordinate*—that is, the follower. You have everything yet to learn. You must be willing to follow and learn from your unit leaders and from your naval science instructors. Only by becoming a good follower and learning the requirements of the course and the corps can you move up to positions of leadership.

Although all good leaders must be good follow-

One of the goals of the NJROTC program is to develop leaders. This NJROTC executive officer inspects the personnel of his unit.

ers, not all followers become good leaders. If everyone did, the world would be full of good leaders. But many people simply do not become good leaders. Some would rather stay followers because they cannot (or will not) accept the duties that go with leadership.

Everyone, of course, has a responsibility for his or her ship or unit, the Navy, and the nation. In a ship or unit the commanding officer is responsible for everyone and everything, but the follower has a responsibility only to his or her leader. The leader has a responsibility to his or her seniors *and* juniors.

RESPONSIBILITIES OF A SUBORDINATE

The military person must be able to carry out orders. The mark of a true soldier and sailor has always been loyalty and obedience to leaders. It is the same for NJROTC cadets, who are learning to become better citizens and leaders in their schools, communities, and nation.

The person who is trained to follow orders is learning how to lead others. Leaders set good examples, which makes it easier to respect them. The smart and hard-working subordinate will get respect and cooperation from his or her leaders, and will get this same cooperation from his or her own subordinates when acting as a leader.

Be smart. As a subordinate, you must know your job thoroughly. If possible, you should learn the jobs of your seniors, even though you are not yet at that level of responsibility. By doing so, you can move up and assume the leadership role if the opportunity occurs.

A subordinate should point out to his or her immediate senior those things he or she knows will help make the command work better. All persons in the naval service benefit from the ideas of their shipmates. Leaders should always pass good ideas up to their own seniors, giving credit to the person who deserves it.

A subordinate must pay attention to his or her seniors when they outline plans or give orders. The subordinate should assume that seniors know more than he or she does, and work to achieve what the leader wants. The junior should want to complete the task as much as the senior does.

Honest disagreement may occur in the military, as well as anywhere else. A subordinate who thinks that he or she has a different idea that will help should say so, in the proper manner. Such ideas may be the source of healthy change. But differences of opinion shouldn't get in the way of obeying an order, once a decision has been made by the person in charge.

Be loyal. Among the traits of a good follower, *loyalty* is at the top of the list. This means loyalty to those above us in the chain of command, whether or not we agree with them. Stephen De-

Effective leaders must teach and instruct their subordinates. A first-class ordanceman shows a second-class petty officer how to adjust some equipment on a Navy F-14 jet fighter.

catur, a hero of the war with Tripoli, put it this way: "My country, may she ever be right. But right or wrong, my country."

So when the leader gives an order, everyone must carry it out in the best way possible. Each order must be passed down the chain of command. Each person gives the order as if it were *his or her own order.* One does not blame seniors by saying that difficult orders came from higher up. That is disloyal to the command and the commander when loyalty is most needed.

Show initiative. A good follower does not wait to be told what to do. The leader needs followers who plan ahead, see what has to be done, and then do it. Persons with initiative show that they are ready to assume leadership roles themselves.

This does not mean that one should go charging around like a bull in a china shop, doing things without permission. It is always wise to keep the senior informed. Given the go-ahead, the junior can show initiative and common sense.

Be dependable. The leader cannot carry out a mission alone, but does so *through* subordinates. The leader must be able to depend on subordinates to do their duties in the right way. If they cannot be depended upon, the job will not get done.

There is no point in giving an important job to an undependable person—and then following one step behind to make sure the job gets done. After training his or her officers and crew, the leader has to show confidence in them, and let them go ahead with their jobs. The leader can't check up on personnel every step of the way. The proper kind of leadership will encourage people to be dependable.

Subordinates should "grow" with training and experience. If they don't, they're not carrying their share of the load. Dependable subordinates can take some of the weight off the leader's back. This leaves the leader free to look at the overall picture. Undependable followers add to the leader's job, and hurt the efficiency of the command.

Chain of Command

We briefly mentioned the *chain of command* in Unit 1, when discussing unit organization. We should point out the purpose of the chain of command. Then you will understand why subordinates are expected to take orders from seniors.

The chain of command allows a good flow of information from and to the commanding officer. It works both ways, up and down the chain. It makes sure that there is communication at each level in the command. No one is left out; everyone will get "the word." This gets the job done better, because everyone can work toward the same goal.

As much as possible, information should flow up or down the chain without skipping a step. If, however, some person is not available, and the situation is urgent, a link may be skipped for a time. But the person passed by is told as quickly as possible, afterwards. If followed, the chain of command makes work go more smoothly and quickly.

Obedience

A good follower obeys all commands and orders given by those higher in the chain of command.

Obedience is more important in the military than in civilian life. Disobedience of orders in civilian life could mean the loss of a job, but in the military, disobedience might result in loss of lives. There is no room for disobedience in the military. The safety of many individuals, the ship or unit, and even the nation, may depend on following commands and orders.

With a *command,* there is no time to ask for a reason. Sometimes quick obedience is essential. One good example would be the helmsman at the ship's steering wheel. When given a command to turn to the right, the helmsman must obey instantly. The ship may be in danger if that command is not carried out right away. When the gunnery officer commands, "Commence firing!" one must obey immediately. Otherwise the ship may suffer damage from enemy attack.

An *order,* on the other hand, allows you some time to ask questions, and to use your own initiative in carrying it out. It gives the subordinate a chance to obey and learn at the same time. The more easily you can work and learn on your own, the more self-disciplined you become. This is a first step toward becoming a leader.

Self-disciplined people don't need much supervision. But most people need some supervision. This means that subordinates have to be checked by their seniors now and then to see that orders are being carried out.

As a beginning NJROTC cadet, you will receive both commands and orders. This will not be a new experience for you. You receive commands and orders throughout life. When your coach tells you to run around the track on the double, you do it without grumbling or asking "Why?" When your unit commander gives you a command to "Right, face!" or "Parade, rest!" he or she expects that you will do so, instantly and without question. When your parents order you to mow the lawn on Saturday morning, they expect the job done before noon. They don't say that you have to mow the back yard before the front, or mow north-and-south rather than east-and-west. When instructors and teachers make reading or writing assignments, they expect that those tasks will be done, on time.

A recruit training company at Great Lakes, Illinois, marches to its next training session under the command of the recruit petty officer in charge (RPOC), right.

WORKING TOGETHER

Followers expect certain things from their leaders. Among these are good manners, honesty, knowledge, judgment, firmness, and fairness. At the same time, the leader has the right to expect certain things from subordinates.

Enlisted subordinates must obey their officers and others in authority over them. Similarly, officers must show a good example and look after the officers and enlisted persons under them. Subordinates expect their leaders to be honest and sincere. It is just as correct for leaders to expect the same from their followers. Good manners apply to everyone.

The subordinate expects the leader to know his or her job and set an example. The leader expects subordinates to learn their jobs quickly and correctly, so they can be counted on.

Subordinates expect their leaders to have good judgment. But decisions are often made using information supplied by subordinates. Correct decisions depend on correct information. The leader is not a mind reader.

Followers expect their leaders to show courage and firmness during times of doubt, pressure, and risk. Followers should show their confidence in the leader and back him or her up. By helping each other, they will give each other confidence.

In the NJROTC unit, the naval science instructors expect these same things of all cadets. In return, the instructors must show good management and teaching skills, and loyalty. When everyone does his or her part, a unit is bound to be successful.

TRAINING FOR LEADERSHIP

To learn about how to be a leader, you must be in situations that allow you to lead. It is not enough just to have the right traits.

In order to become a good citizen and a leader of your community as an adult, you must practice your leadership skills as a cadet. There are many school activities such as sports and clubs that will give you the chance to do this. The NJROTC program can provide many situations in which you can act as a leader to improve your skills. You should take advantage of as many leadership opportunities as you can during your high school years. The experience you gain will be of great value to you later.

PERSONAL ATTITUDES

To be successful in any role in an organization, whether as a leader or a subordinate, a person needs to develop good attitudes both toward oneself and toward other people. In recent years much study and thought have been devoted to what constitutes such good attitudes on the part of people. Basically, it breaks down to developing a winning instead of a losing attitude toward life in general, ourselves, and others around us.

What is a winner? Everyone can probably think of many examples of people around us who are winners and, by contrast, some others who can only be described as losers. Winners see themselves, and everyone else around them, as important individuals able to contribute to the world. This is not to say that everyone is a gifted student, athlete, or popular leader. But everyone is *important* because they are individuals capable of making some contribution under the proper circumstances. One of the responsibilities of a leader, as will be enlarged upon in your other *Naval Science* textbooks, is to be sure to create the conditions under which individuals can make their contributions.

There are certain things anyone can do who wants to be (or become) a winner. Because so much of being a winner depends on one's attitudes toward oneself, probably the key thing is to avoid the temptation, very common in the teenage years, to put yourself down. Get rid of phrases like "I can't," "It's too hard," "I'm too dumb," or "I'm not _____ enough." These are for losers. Winners *do*. They say things like "I can!" "I'll do it!" and "Let's go!"

Below are comparisons that show some of the different attitudes between winners and losers. If you find that very often you think like the loser, try adopting the winner's attitude the next time these things come up. You'll find you'll like yourself better, and others will like the positive change they'll see in you.

- A *winner* makes commitments that are kept; a *loser* just makes promises.
- When a *winner* makes a mistake, he or she says, "I was wrong"; a *loser* says, "It wasn't my fault."
- A *winner* works harder than a loser and has more time; a *loser* is always too busy to do what is necessary.

Sometimes a leader must motivate and direct subordinates to action instantly. This realistic firefighting drill requires quick response and good organization.

The leader has the right to expect the subordinate to try to learn his or her job quickly and correctly, so he or she can be counted on. Here, a petty officer watch supervisor instructs a subordinate as they work together guiding an aircraft on an approach to a runway.

- A *winner* goes through a problem, a *loser* goes around it.
- A *winner* shows he or she is sorry by not repeating a mistake; a *loser* says, "I'm sorry," but does the same thing again next time.
- A *winner* would rather be admired than liked; a *loser* would rather be liked than admired.
- A *winner* says, "There ought to be a better way." A *loser* says, "That's the way it's always been done."
- A *winner* takes a big problem and breaks it down into smaller solvable parts; a *loser* always combines little problems into something too big to solve.

- A *winner* realizes how much there is to learn; a *loser* doesn't care.
- A *winner* isn't afraid to leave the road when not in agreement with the direction it's taking; a *loser* follows the road oblivious to where it's going.
- A *winner* dares to be different; a *loser* is always scared of not being the same as everybody else.

Many other examples of winning versus losing attitudes could be drawn from everyday life. But the important thing to remember is that everyone can be a winner in their own way. It's mostly just a matter of the attitudes people take about life. One of the major aims of the NJROTC program is to help young people discover that they *can* be winners, and in so being, make a positive contribution to their personal success and their unit, school, community, and nation.

Chapter 1. Study Guide Questions

1. What qualities does naval leadership require?

2. Why is it necessary to become a good follower before you can become a good leader?

3. What are the traditional marks of a good soldier and sailor?

4. Why should a subordinate learn the job of his or her senior in the chain of command?

5. If a junior has an idea to improve the command, what should he or she do?

6. Why is the "chain of command" necessary?

7. Why is obedience important in the military?

8. What is the difference between an *order* and a *command*?

9. A. What do followers expect of their leaders?

   B. What do leaders have a right to expect of followers?

10. How should the junior show initiative in carrying out orders?

11. How is the art of leadership learned?

12. With what attitude does a winner approach life, as opposed to a loser?

Vocabulary

goal
example
followership
subordinate
obedience

disobedience
supervision
regulations
loyalty

initiative
dependability
command
order

self-confidence
respect
judgment
management

Chapter 2.   Leadership in the Navy

Our Navy has one purpose: to defend our country and our way of life. This means that the Navy is a fighting organization. To be an effective fighting organization, the Navy must have discipline. Discipline is produced by the leadership of the Navy's people.

The Navy's purpose in peacetime is to be ready for war. Our being ready for war will make enemies think twice before attacking us. Without effective leaders, the Navy could not perform its mission. Therefore, it must always be developing new leaders at every level. This is a challenge for the present leaders of the Navy.

The rules of leadership in the Navy come from the U.S. Constitution, our nation's laws, the missions of our armed forces, and the customs and traditions of the Navy. Rules on conduct between superiors and subordinates were written into the Navy's laws and regulations.

It isn't easy to be a leader in today's Navy, but all officers and petty officers have to accept that responsibility. In an NJROTC unit, the tasks and responsibilities of leadership are the same. It means dealing with people the right way, so the unit will be successful. Individual cadets can become better citizens and leaders through their NJROTC experience.

GOALS OF NAVAL LEADERSHIP

Naval leadership programs have three goals:
1. Get the right people for the right jobs.
2. Put together a good team.
3. Inspire the team to do the job.

The leader must take part. He or she will set the tone for the command. There must be discipline and order for a leadership program to succeed. Discipline makes sure that the people of the command do what's needed.

Leadership training should include both reading and actual *practice* in solving problems and leading people. This textbook provides the reading material. The NJROTC program provides the "leadership laboratory" that gives cadets a chance to get leadership experience.

Each command should always try to get better in all areas. The leaders should look over their program, its successes, and its failures. In this way, they can work on those areas still needing improvement.

A good leadership program should make all hands—officers, enlisted, instructors, and cadets—realize why they are trying to improve their leadership skills. They must see that leadership makes a better unit or ship. Cadets will do better in naval science, and in all other classes, if there is good leadership in the unit.

LEADERSHIP DEVELOPMENT

Leadership is the ability to manage and inspire a group of people to work together successfully to achieve a goal. The leader directs the efforts of others to get the job done. To be effective, the leader must earn and keep the respect of his or her people. Leaders help guide their people to make the most of their talents and skills. They assist in setting goals. In turn, subordinates work better.

How does a leader earn the respect of others?

NJROTC cadets must be willing to accept the responsibilities of leadership. This requires good training, interest, and spirit.

Leaders must inspire and motivate their subordinates. This drill team leader is in charge of his NJROTC unit drill team.

We can all try to succeed in this goal. Let's discuss some of the traits a leader must develop.

The leader must *want* to advance in rate and rank. This desire is not just for the badges of rank or dream of "power;" it is in order to be able to take on more *responsibility*. Such an individual must feel that he or she can help the unit. He or she must want to succeed.

The leader must have the *ability* to succeed. The person must have common sense and intelligence. A leader must provide *inspiration* and *motivation* to subordinates.

A leader must have good *personal conduct* and *morals*. The Naval Academy Honor Concept defines these qualities well: "Midshipmen will not lie, cheat, or steal, nor [try to] mislead or deceive anyone [about] known facts. . . ." Subordinates will follow a good leader's personal example. Superiors and subordinates know that they can count on such individuals. Officers and leaders are expected

to be gentlemen and ladies. They willingly obey the rules of good conduct.

A leader must be a *good manager*. This means knowing everyone's jobs. It also means knowing what he or she can do and what his or her subordinates can do. It means knowing how to keep people on track to get a job done.

The leader must balance concern about getting the job done with concern for subordinates. This means caring about their needs, problems, and worries. It means taking responsibility for their well-being and being loyal to them.

The leader must work for *good morale* in the unit. When given good leadership, the members of the unit feel good about themselves, their unit, and their service. This spirit shows in the way they do their jobs.

A leader must be *dependable*. Seniors must be able to count on him or her to do an assigned task well, and on time. The good leader will use initiative to finish the job if normal ways do not work.

To summarize, the naval officer or petty officer must remember three things about leadership: (1) *command* is the authority that an officer or petty officer has because of his or her rank or rate; (2) *leadership* is the art of getting people to do a job; and (3) *management* is the science of using people and material in the best way.

Chapter 2. Study Guide Questions

1. What is the purpose of the Navy?
2. From where do the rules of naval leadership come?
3. What are the three goals of naval leadership programs?
4. To be effective, what must a leader get from his or her subordinates?

5. What are some of the traits a good leader must develop?
6. Why should a person want to advance in rate or rank?

Vocabulary

discipline	talent
morals	inspiration
morale	motivation
organization	responsibility

3

Naval Ships: Missions, Construction, and Damage Control

Chapter 1. Naval Ships and Their Missions

The Navy has many kinds of ships, smaller boats, and craft to perform its various tasks. Naval ships are classified as either combatant or auxiliary ships. *Combatants* are of three types: warships, amphibious warfare ships, and mine warfare ships. *Auxiliary* ships provide services to other ships and to overseas stations. Smaller vessels are classified as combatant craft and service craft. We will discuss a number of each of these types of ships in this chapter in order to give you an idea of what each is like.

IDENTIFYING SHIPS

Each naval ship is identified by a name, designation, and hull number. Let us take as an example the USS *Enterprise* (CVN-65). USS means United States Ship; *Enterprise* is the *name;* CVN is the *designation* for nuclear-powered aircraft carrier (CV designates carrier, N indicates nuclear propulsion); and 65 is the *hull number.* More about ship designations will be given in chapter 2 of this unit.

The size of a ship usually is given in terms of her displacement in tons. *Displacement* means the weight of the amount of water that the ship pushes aside when afloat; in other words, the weight of a ship by herself.

Armament is the offensive weapons a ship carries: guns, rockets, guided missiles, and planes. *Armor* is the protective steel built into a ship: special steel installed along the sides of the ship, on the deck, and on some gun mounts and turrets.

Ships are said to be of a particular *class*. This refers to all of the same type of ships having the same size, weight, armament, propulsion, and so on. For instance, there is only one *Enterprise*-class CVN. Newer carriers of the same size but with different power plants, either conventional (steam) or nuclear, are different enough to be in different *classes,* though all are CVs.

WARSHIPS

Warships are built to attack an enemy using gunfire, missiles, torpedoes, and other weapons. Presently in the U.S. fleet there are aircraft carriers, battleships, cruisers, destroyers, submarines, frigates, and patrol combatants.

Aircraft Carriers. The U.S. Navy has both nuclear-powered and conventionally powered aircraft carriers. The nuclear-powered carriers are the world's largest warships.

The giant nuclear-powered aircraft carrier USS *Nimitz* (CVN-68) drives through the sea, with some of her more than 100 combat aircraft visible on the flight deck.

The main job of the carrier is to carry, launch, and handle aircraft. She tries to approach an enemy at high speed, launch her planes for the attack, recover them, and get away before she can be found. She has fighter planes, antiaircraft guns, and guided missiles to protect her from enemy air attack. The planes of aircraft carriers do the following:

1. Scout to locate and observe enemy forces or to detect hostile aircraft.
2. Make long-range attacks against targets ashore and afloat.
3. Provide ships of the battle force with air protection against enemy airborne, surface, and submarine attack.
4. Hunt and attack enemy submarines.

The carrier has a large flight deck and a large hangar deck to stow planes. Elevators permit quick transfer of planes from one deck to another. There are repair shops, living quarters, and much electronic equipment. The huge power plant enables the ship to exceed 30 knots in speed, to help her planes take off and land.

The *Nimitz* is a good example of a modern nuclear-powered carrier. She is 1,092 feet long and has a displacement of almost 95,000 tons. At the heart of her engineering plant are two nuclear reactors with a fifteen-year life that can turn four giant propellers with 280,000 horsepower.

When the *Nimitz* has an air group embarked, she has about 570 officers and 5,720 enlisted personnel in her crew. From her decks she operates 100 aircraft—attack and reconnaissance planes, electronic warfare planes, fighters, and antisubmarine warfare and rescue helicopters. She carries missiles in addition to her aircraft for self-defense.

There are also several conventionally powered oil-fueled carriers in our fleet. They can carry as many as ninety aircraft. They have eight oil-burning boilers with a steam-turbine drive rated at 260,000 horsepower.

Cruisers. The Navy presently has about forty cruisers. All carry guided missiles, so have the letter G in their designation. Most are steam and gas turbine-powered ships (CG), but some have been built with nuclear power plants (CGN). The cruiser's main job is to defend the carrier task force from air or missile attack. Cruisers also can provide gunfire support during amphibious operations.

The newest CG is the Aegis guided missile

The first Aegis cruiser USS *Ticonderoga* (CG-47) is the most advanced ship of her kind in the world. The Aegis cruisers will protect the Navy's battlegroups well into the twenty-first century.

cruiser, named after the magic shield of a mythical Greek god that could protect him from all harm. The lead ship of the class, the USS *Ticonderoga* (CG-47), was commissioned in January 1983. These ships are among the most technically advanced ships ever built, a state-of-the-art blend of advanced computer, radar, weapons, electronic warfare, and gas turbine propulsion systems. There are presently about twenty-five of these ships in service.

The heart of the Aegis cruisers is their new computer-controlled *phased array* radar. It is totally electronic, with four octagon-shaped arrays fitted onto the superstructure, instead of the old-style rotating-dish radars. These arrays do the job of both search radars and fire-control radars, tracking and engaging more than 200 surface and air targets, all at the same time.

The latest Aegis cruisers are also fitted with a new *vertical launch system* (VLS). This system has a series of vertical launch tubes built into the deck, rather than being exposed single- or twin-rail launchers as in older missile ships. The tubes provide better protection for the missiles below the armored deck, and mean the missiles can be fired faster, since all can be fired together, rather than one or two at a time as with the older launchers. The VLS system can fire a mix of the Navy's standard antiair missiles, Tomahawk cruise antisurface missiles, and ASROC antisubmarine rockets. These cruisers are designed to provide complete in-depth protection to the carrier and battleship battle groups they will escort.

Destroyers and Frigates. The Navy has a large number of destroyers and frigates. Destroyers (DDs) are able to do many kinds of duties in almost any kind of naval operation. Frigates (FFs) are smaller vessels, but are able to perform many of the same duties. They have little armor; they depend upon their speed and maneuverability for protection.

The destroyer's job is to attack and defend against submarines and surface ships, to defend against air attack, and to provide gunfire support for amphibious assaults. It can control aircraft for antisubmarine operations, patrol, and search-and-rescue missions.

The newest destroyers in the fleet are members of the USS *Arleigh Burke* (DDG-51) class, the lead ship of which was commissioned on 4 July 1991. These ships have all-steel superstructures and are driven by four gas-turbine engines. They are fitted with the most capable weapon systems ever to be put on a destroyer, including a modified Aegis air-defense system, vertically launched antiaircraft missiles, a 5-inch rapid-fire gun, and the latest antisubmarine warfare (ASW) torpedoes and rockets. They also have a helicopter pad for ASW helicopter operations. Some thirty-five of these capable multipurpose destroyers are scheduled to be built throughout the 1990s.

Frigates are used mainly to protect support forces and shipping against submarines. Their most important task is to detect and destroy submarines—either by themselves or as part of an

A starboard side view of the guided-missile frigate USS *Oliver Hazard Perry* (FFG-7).

The USS *Arleigh Burke* (DDG-51) class is our navy's newest destroyer class. It is fitted with the most capable weapon systems ever to be put on a destroyer.

The *Los Angeles* (SSN-688) is our latest operational class of nuclear-powered attack submarine. Shown here at her commissioning is the USS *Jacksonville* (SSN-699).

ASW group. Newer frigates can launch cruise and surface-to-air missiles. They also carry rapid-fire, dual-purpose, close-in guns of the latest Oto Melara and Phalanx type. These weapons can "spit out" bullets at the rate of several thousand per minute. Frigates also carry the latest antisubmarine helicopters.

Submarines. The submarine has become one of the most important weapons in naval warfare. Originally, the submarine's main mission was to seek out and sink enemy surface ships using torpedoes. Now, their mission has become broader. By means of homing torpedoes or ballistic missiles, submarines can effectively fight enemy submarines or launch a missile attack against inland targets. The submarine has developed into a nuclear-powered, high-speed vessel that can cruise underwater for months without refueling. The U.S. Navy has two types of nuclear submarines: *attack submarines* (SSNs) and *ballistic-missile sub-*

marines (SSBNs). The United States has about ninety submarines, about twenty of which are SSBNs.

The SSN's main job is to attack enemy ships and submarines. It is the best weapon against enemy submarines. The SSN's weapons are the high-speed, wire-guided torpedo, an antisubmarine rocket, and on some subs, the Harpoon and Tomahawk cruise missile to hit surface targets. The latest operational SSN is the *Los Angeles* class (SSN-688), of which there will eventually be twenty-eight. It displaces 6,900 tons. It is the largest and most powerful of the SSNs, and can operate faster, deeper, and more quietly than any previous class. Speeds and operating depths of submarines are highly classified. This much can be said, however; they can go as fast as most surface ships when underwater, and can safely operate more than 400 feet below the surface.

SSBNs are the nation's main strategic (nuclear) weapon. They carry Trident missiles, which can be launched while the submarine is submerged. The Trident missile has a range of more than 4,000 nautical miles—far enough to put any place on earth within its range.

To maximize the time that SSBNs can stay on patrol at sea, they have two separate crews, called the Blue and Gold Crews. While one crew is on patrol, the other is ashore doing training, receiving medical and dental care, and taking well-earned rest and leave periods. The average patrol is about four months long. Most SSBNs are on continuous patrol.

A new class of attack submarine, the *Seawolf* (SSN-21) class, is being developed. The construction of the lead ship began in earnest in 1991. It will be quieter, deeper-diving, and able to perform missions ranging from land attack with cruise missiles to extended operations under the Arctic ice cap. For the next several decades, it will be the most advanced submarine in the world.

Patrol Combatants. The Navy has several types of patrol combatants. Currently the largest of these is the *Cyclone* (PC-1) class, 170 feet long, powered by four diesel engines capable of propelling the boats at speeds up to 35 knots. They are armed with 25-millimeter guns and a surface-to-air missile (SAM) launcher. Thirteen of these are scheduled to be built during the 1990s.

MINE WARFARE SHIPS

The Navy has only a small number of mine warfare vessels in commission in the active forces. Called mine countermeasure (MCM) ships, mine hunters (MHCs), and minesweepers (MSOs), they are made of wood, in order not to set off magnetic mines while sweeping. Other NATO navies have many mine warfare vessels in commission. Most U.S. minesweeping operations are now carried out by specially equipped helicopters using tows.

AMPHIBIOUS WARFARE SHIPS

To carry out an amphibious operation, personnel, equipment, ammunition, and supplies must all be landed on enemy shores. This is the job of amphibious warfare ships. Various types of ships have been designed to do this, and they have proved their worth many times—in World War II, the Korean War, Vietnam, and the Persian Gulf. There are about sixty active ships in the amphibious forces of the Atlantic and Pacific fleets.

Amphibious warfare ships are often referred to as the "amphibs" or "gators." They work mainly where the sea and land meet, and where assault landings are carried out by the Navy-Marine Corps team.

Amphibious Command Ship (LCC). The LCC serves as a floating command center for amphibious assaults. This ship has the best command facilities afloat. Elaborate communications equipment makes it possible to collect, process, and distribute intelligence information to all assault forces and their staffs. There are two LCCs, one for each coast.

Tank Landing Ship (LST). LSTs have a shallow draft so they can run up to the beach, lower their extended bow ramp, and unload vehicles, tanks, and personnel directly onto the beach or onto pontoon bridges leading to the beach. Vehicles and their crews are protected from light enemy gunfire right up to the moment they leave the ship.

Dock Landing Ship (LSD). LSDs have a well

The amphibious command ship USS *Blue Ridge* (LCC-19).

deck that can be flooded so that landing craft and amphibious vehicles can be floated out of the ship. The ship is like a self-propelled floating drydock, used to transport and launch landing craft. It can give limited docking and repair services to small ships and craft and has a flight deck for helicopters.

Amphibious Transport Dock (LPD). The LPD is similar to the LSD, but is larger and can carry more cargo, troops, and vehicles. It has a much larger helicopter deck for vertical-assault operations. The LPD makes it possible for first assault groups to carry their own vehicles and troops into combat. Like the LSD, the LPD also can have its amphibious craft and vehicles "swim" out of the well deck.

Amphibious Cargo Ship (LKA). LKAs carry bulk material, equipment, ammunition, guns, tanks, and vehicles. These are the heavy stores and supplies that must follow the initial amphibious assault. The ship carries only enough troops to help manage the cargo. Ship's personnel unload the cargo, using huge cargo booms that can lift as much as 70 tons. LKAs also carry amphibious landing craft, which are stored topside, offloaded by the booms, and then used to carry the supplies and vehicles ashore. The ship has a cargo capacity of more than 5,000 tons.

The cargo is *combat-loaded.* This means that cargo is placed on board in reverse order to the way in which it will be needed, so that the material that will be needed right away will be unloaded first.

Amphibious Assault Ship (LPH). There are seven LPHs of the 18,000-ton *Iwo Jima* class.

The tank landing ship USS *Spartanburg County* (LST-1192), mated to a pontoon causeway to a beach during an amphibious exercise. The ramp and causeway permit heavy vehicles to be driven directly onto the shore.

The dock landing ship USS *Portland* (LSD-37). Notice the stern gate opening of the well deck, where amphibious craft load to go to the landing area.

These are the world's first helicopter carriers. They were designed specifically for amphibious *vertical* (air) *envelopment* of enemy territory. The purpose of vertical envelopment is to airlift troops to strong points behind the beachhead where they can guard the routes to the beach area, preventing enemy reinforcement. The LPH can carry twenty large troop-carrying helicopters.

Another good thing about vertical envelopment is that it gives one the ability to land a force wherever it is needed, not just on beaches. Thus the large assemblies of personnel and equipment on the beach that often took place in World War II are partially eliminated by the LPH. Spreading out the forces reduces the likelihood of heavy casualties. LPHs carry the nearly 2,000 people and equipment of a Marine battalion landing team, along with a crew of more than 1,000.

General-Purpose Assault Ship (LHA). There are five *Tarawa*-class LHAs. They combine all the features of the LPH, LPD, LKA, and LSD in one large 39,300-ton amphibious vessel. The LHA can do both helicopter and landing-craft operations at the same time, for it has both a flight deck and a well deck.

The LHA also provides the commander of an amphibious squadron and the Marine landing force with communications equipment to support their operations. For self-defense against surface and air attack, the LHA is equipped with 5-inch guns and air-defense missiles.

Helicopter/Dock Landing Ship (LHD). The newest and largest amphibious warfare ship is the USS *Wasp*-clasp helicopter/dock landing ship. The lead ship, the USS *Wasp* (LHD-1), was placed in service in 1989. Additional LHDs are planned during the 1990s. Displacing 40,500 tons, they can carry either helicopters or vertical-launch jets such as the Harrier. They can launch landing craft from a well deck in the stern. They have ample room for amphibious assault vehicles and tanks, as well as accommodations for some 1,800 troops.

AUXILIARY SHIPS

A fleet at sea or at an advanced base must be supplied with fuel, munitions, food, repair parts, mail, and personnel. Auxiliary ships deliver these items. A combatant fleet depends greatly on these auxiliary ships. They back up the fighting forces with services and supplies that keep them ready for battle.

There are many types of auxiliary ships, so we will discuss only some of the principal types. The U.S. Navy has about eighty auxiliary ships, the largest group of which are the mobile logistic support ships. These ships are designed to conduct replenishment-at-sea operations. They can resupply the combatants while under way, at speeds up to 20 knots. Most new replenishment ships also have two large helicopters that can provide vertical replenishment (VertRep) so the ships will not even have to come alongside to rig for transfer.

Underway replenishment (UnRep) is done by having both the replenishment ship and the ships being replenished steam alongside on parallel courses at the same speed. About 100 feet of distance is maintained between the ships. Often the replenishment ship can serve ships on either side at the same time. Lines and special transfer cables are passed between the ships to haul over cargo or fuel hoses.

During the 1980s many older Navy auxiliary ships were transferred to the Military Sealift Command (MSC) and crewed by civilians to save the Navy money. The MSC ships carry the same designations as their regular Navy counterparts, except that a "T" is added as a prefix, such as T-AO and T-AE. Distinguished by a blue and gold stripe on the stack, these ships are often used to ferry fuel, ammunition, and stores from shore depots to fleet auxiliaries operating with deployed forces at sea.

Ammunition Ship (AE). AEs deliver ammunition and missiles to the fleet at sea. They have such equipment as elevators, forklift trucks, and other things that permit safe handling of ammunition.

Oiler (AO). AOs carry naval fuel oil, gasoline, and other petroleum products. They operate with replenishment groups and deliver their cargoes to ships alongside.

Fast Combat Support Ship (AOE). The AOE is the largest and most powerful auxiliary ship in the Navy. Unlike other replenishment ships, this ship is designed to operate as part of the combatant force. She can steam faster than 25 knots. The AOE also carries ammunition and other general and food stores. She has a cargo-fuel capacity larger than that of the largest fleet oilers, and more ammunition stowage than an ammunition ship.

Combat Stores Ship (AFS). The AFS combines a general stores ship, a refrigerator ship, and dry stores (food) issue ship, all in one hull. A helicopter platform and hangar for two large cargo helicopters add to the capability of the ship.

Tenders. There are two major types of tenders—*destroyer tenders* (ADs) and *submarine tenders* (ASs). These ships are among the largest auxiliaries. Their crews are mainly technicians and repairmen. Some submarine tenders specialize in supporting SSNs, while others support SSBNs.

Destroyer tenders can support a number of other types of ships; such as the latest Aegis cruisers, in addition to destroyers.

The tenders usually have medical and dental departments on board, to serve the needs of the smaller ships that come alongside. The AS also provides disbursing (payroll) facilities for submarine crews.

Repair Ships. Repair ships (ARs) perform repairs and maintenance that are beyond the capa-

The fast combat support ship USS *Sacramento* (AOE-1), the largest of all Navy auxiliary ships.

bilities of other ships' own facilities or personnel. They have skilled workers, in a wide variety of mechanical and electrical trades. Delicate optical and navigational instruments can be repaired. Underwater welding and cutting can be done; engine and hull repairs performed; machine work and electrical and electronic repairs accomplished. On board are foundries, forges, and machine tools of many types. There are instrument shops, carpentry shops, boat shops, and boat-engine shops. They have medical and dental facilities and laundry, tailor, and shoe-repair shops.

Repair ships have large crews of more than 1,200 personnel. They can go to advance bases and deployed stations.

Towing, Salvage, and Rescue Ships. The *fleet ocean tug* (ATF) is a powerful little ship equipped with automatic towing machines, booms, and firefighting equipment, including fire monitors. (A fire monitor looks like a gun, but it can pump water from the sea and shoot it out with great force.) These tugs can tow large ships all the way across the ocean. They have been used as patrol ships, laid smoke screens, and towed landing craft off beaches. These versatile ships were even used with convoys in World War II to pick up stragglers, and sometimes carried depth charges and operated with convoy screens.

Modern *salvage ships* (ARSs), *salvage and rescue ships* (ATSs), and *submarine rescue ships* (ASRs) are typical of the special auxiliaries needed by any large navy. Qualified divers are assigned to these ships. In wartime this hazardous work is often done under combat conditions. Sunken ships may have to be cut up, moved, or refloated. The ARS can support diving operations as deep as 200 feet, the ATS as deep as 850 feet. The *Pigeon*-class ASR was the world's first ship designed especially to rescue submarines. Though the *Pigeon* was retired, its sister ship USS *Ortolan* (ASR-22) is still active. It has a catamaran hull; this improves stability when operating equipment at great depths. It is the surface support ship for the *deep submergence rescue vehicles* (DSRVs) and is a control ship for salvage operations.

Fleet ocean tug, the USS *Utina* (ATF-163). She is a powerful little ship designed to tow vessels and perform a variety of other support tasks, including fighting fires.

Chapter 1. Study Guide Questions

1. A. What are the two broad classifications of naval ships?

   B. What are the three types of combatant ships?

The submarine rescue ship USS *Ortolan* (ASR-22). She has a catamaran hull, which increases her stability in rough seas. She can act as the base ship for submarine rescue vehicles (DSRVs).

2. A. What does "USS" before a ship's name mean?

    B. What are the identifying letters and numbers after a ship's name called?

3. What is "the weight of the amount of water that the ship pushes aside when afloat"?

4. What is armament?

5. What is meant by the "class" of a ship type?

6. What are the four main jobs of an aircraft carrier's planes?

7. How much does a *Nimitz*-class carrier displace, and how many aircraft does it carry?

8. A. What is the cruiser's main job?

    B. What is the newest cruiser class in the fleet?

9. A. What are destroyers and frigates designed to do?

    B. What is the newest destroyer class in the fleet?

10. What has become the principal mission of the SSN?

11. A. What does the designator "SSBN" stand for?

    B. Why does each SSBN have two crews?

12. A. What is the basic task of amphibious ships?

    B. What nicknames are often given to amphibious ships?

13. What is the main feature of the LCC?

14. How does an LST accomplish its mission?

15. What is unique about the LSD and the LPD?

16. What is meant by the term "combat-loaded"?

17. What is the main feature of the LHD?

18. What is vertical envelopment and what is its purpose?

19. Why do the combatant ships depend upon the auxiliaries?

20. What types of auxiliary ships do these designators identify?

A. AE	G. AR
B. AO	H. ATF
C. AOE	I. ARS
D. AFS	J. ATS
E. AD	K. ASR
F. AS	

21. Where do submarines and destroyers get many of their repairs and personnel services done?

22. A. What specially qualified personnel are assigned to the salvage and rescue ships?

    B. What is unique about the design of the *Pigeon*-class ASR?

Vocabulary

auxiliary ship	Aegis cruiser
designation	amphibious ship
hull number	shallow draft
displacement	pontoon
armament	debarkation
nuclear power	well deck
conventional power	cargo boom
aircraft carrier	vertical envelopment
cruiser	vertical replenishment
destroyer	underway
frigate	replenishment
submarine	helicopter
ASW	foundry
propeller	optical instrument
ballistic missile	fire monitor
attack submarine	catamaran
cruise missile	salvage
Trident	phased array radar
endurance	vertical launch system
minesweeper	(VLS)

Chapter 2. Ship Construction

Navy ships are very complicated. They have propulsion plants, weapons, store rooms, repair shops, offices, and operating spaces. They provide for the crew's living, sleeping, and eating needs. Large ships are almost like cities with their lighting, sanitary, communications, mail delivery, water, and power systems. Most have libraries and recreation spaces. All must be able to operate on their own for long periods of time.

The designer tries to put as many favorable features as possible into a ship, in keeping with its intended mission. All ships represent a compromise; not every desired feature can be put on or into every ship. Despite this, all ships have certain essential qualities. In this chapter we will talk of ship characteristics and construction and the nautical terms used in ships and shipbuilding.

SHIP CONSTRUCTION FACTORS

The major factors considered in the construction of any naval ship are mission, armament, protection, seaworthiness, maneuverability, speed, endurance, and habitability.

The *mission,* or main purpose, of a ship is the biggest factor in determining its design. The weapons systems, speed, crew size, and everything else are dependent on the ship's intended mission.

The *armament* consists of all the *offensive* weapons used to fight an enemy on or under the sea and in the air. Generally, we think of armament as being guns, torpedoes, missiles, and so forth. However, the term also includes aircraft used for offensive purposes (an extension of the ship's attacking capability) and landing craft used for amphibious operations.

Protection means *defensive* features that help a ship survive enemy attack. In addition to its weapons, a ship's sturdy construction, armor, and inner compartmentation to limit the spread of flooding make up its protective features.

Seaworthiness describes the ship's ability to operate in all kinds of weather, high winds, and heavy seas. Stability, size, and freeboard (the hull space between the waterline and the main deck) determine a ship's seaworthiness. *Stability* refers to the way a ship returns to an upright position after a roll in heavy seas. Stability also affects the value of a ship as a weapons or aircraft platform.

Maneuverability means the way a ship handles—in turns, in backing down, in going alongside another ship, or in evading enemy weapons. Combatants such as carriers and destroyers must be very maneuverable so they can change course and speed rapidly.

Speed is affected by the weight (displacement) of the ship, its underwater shape, and the power of its propulsion plant. Speed gets a ship to the scene of action quickly and enables her to escape a pursuing enemy.

Endurance is the maximum time a ship can steam at a given speed. It depends on fuel capacity, freshwater capacity, fuel consumption, and storage space and refrigeration for food provisions. Most oil-powered ships can steam for one to two weeks without refueling, while nuclear-powered ships can steam for years. Fresh provisions need to be replenished about every thirty days, but dry stores (including canned foods) may be kept much longer. Another term sometimes used for endurance is *cruising range.*

Habitability refers to the features required for the comfort and living conditions of the crew. Adequate heads and washrooms; laundries; air conditioning; and comfortable, safe, and clean berthing and messing spaces are important habitability features.

NAUTICAL TERMS

In civilian life you become accustomed to using terms like upstairs, downstairs, windows, floors, ceilings, walls, hallways, and so forth. In the Navy, you must learn to describe objects and places aboard a ship using nautical language. To use civilian terms aboard a ship marks you as a *landlubber,* one who knows nothing of the sea.

In some ways, a ship is like a building. Its outer walls form the *hull,* the supporting body of a ship. Floors are called *decks.* Inner walls are called *partitions* or *bulkheads,* ceilings are termed *overheads,* and hallways are *passageways.* Stairs are called *ladders;* an *accommodation ladder* is the stairs from the ship to a dock, and a *Jacob's ladder* is a portable ladder made of rope or metal used to climb up the side of a ship. The *quarterdeck* might be compared to an entrance hall or foyer in a building.

The lengthwise direction on a ship is *fore* and *aft;* crosswise is *athwartships.* The front part of a

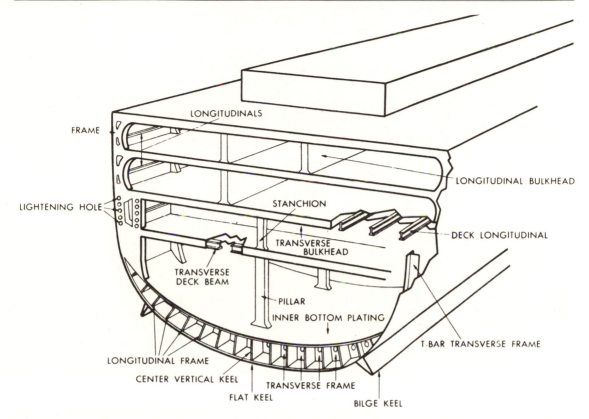

FRAME

LONGITUDINALS

LONGITUDINAL BULKHEAD

LIGHTENING HOLE

STANCHION

DECK LONGITUDINAL

TRANSVERSE
BULKHEAD

TRANSVERSE
DECK BEAM

PILLAR

INNER BOTTOM PLATING

T-BAR TRANSVERSE FRAME

LONGITUDINAL FRAME

CENTER VERTICAL KEEL

TRANSVERSE FRAME

FLAT KEEL

BILGE KEEL

Transverse and longitudinal structure of a ship. Note that transverse beams and bulkheads run athwartships, while longitudinals run the "long way," from stern to stern. See also the double bottoms.

ship is the *bow*; to go in that direction is to go *forward*. The rear part or after part of the ship is the *stern*; to go in that direction is to go *aft*. Back of the ship, in the water, is *astern*. The forward part of the main deck is the *forecastle* (pronounced (foc'sle), and the after part is the *fantail*.

A ship is divided lengthwise in half by the *centerline*. Everything to the right of the centerline is to *starboard,* and everything to the left is to *port*. The direction from the centerline toward either side is *outboard,* and from either side toward the centerline is *inboard*. The section of the ship around the midpoint area is called *amidships*. The extreme width of a ship, at the widest part, is the *beam*. Sightings by lookouts are noted and reported as being off the port or starboard bow or

beam, and off the port or starboard *quarter* (area aft of the beam toward the stern).

You never go downstairs in a ship; you always go *below*. To go up to the main deck or above is to go *topside*. However, if you climb the mast, stacks, rigging, or any other areas above the solid structure of the ship, you go *aloft*.

SHIP STRUCTURE

The *hull* is the main body of the ship. It is like a box. Its inner construction might be compared to the girders of a steel bridge. The *keel* is the backbone of the hull; it is on the centerline like an I-beam running the full length of the ship, with heavy castings fore and aft called the *stem* and *stern posts*. "Girders" attached to the keel called

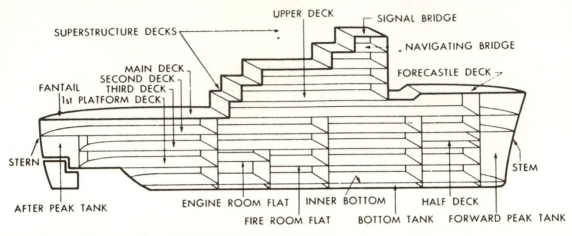

Decks are named by their position in the ship and their function.

transverse frames run athwartships and support the watertight skin or *shell plating,* which forms the sides and bottoms of the ship. Most Navy ships also have *longitudinal frames* running fore and aft. The longitudinal and athwartship frames form a honeycomb structure in the bottom of the ship called the *double bottom.* This type of construction greatly strengthens the bottom. When the honeycomb is covered by plating, the spaces between the inner and outer bottoms are known as *tanks* or *bilges,* which may be used for fuel and water stowage, ballast (usually concrete or pig iron), or as *voids* (air spaces).

The top of the main hull is called the *main deck.* The intersection of the main deck with the shell or side plating is called the *gunwale* (pronounced gun'el), or *deck-edge.* The joint between the side plating and the bottom plating is called the *bilge keel*; its purpose is to reduce rolling of the ship. (A ship *rolls* from side to side; she *pitches* when she goes up and down fore and aft; she *yaws* when the bow swings to port and starboard because of wave action.)

Most ships have unarmored hulls. Ships with armored hulls (the old battleships and heavy cruisers) have vertical armored belts of very thick steel running fore and aft along the sides of the hull to protect engine rooms and magazines from torpedoes, shell fire, and missiles, and thinner armor steel plates on other decks to protect against plunging bombs, shells, and missiles. The *waterline* is the water level along the hull of the ship. The vertical distance from the keel to the waterline is the ship's *draft. Freeboard* is the distance from the waterline to the main deck. The figure on page 43 illustrates some hull and deck terms.

DECKS

The "floors" of a ship are called *decks.* They divide the ship into layers in much the same way that floors of a building divide it into stories. Decks help strengthen the hull and protect the inner spaces. The under-surface of each deck forms the overhead of the compartment below. *Compartments* are the rooms of a ship. Some compartments are called rooms, such as the wardroom, officers' staterooms, engine room, and so on, but usually they are known as compartments. All spaces aboard a ship are identified by compartment numbers assigned according to a standardized system. *Deck beams, transverse bulkheads,* and *stanchions* support the decks and help strengthen the sides against water pressure.

A deck normally consists of steel plates,

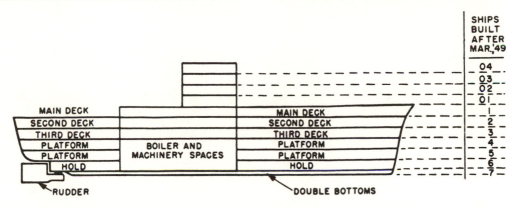

The deck numbering system of all U.S. naval ships built after 1949 has been standardized to the system shown here. The main deck is always numbered 1. Decks below are numbered sequentially 2, 3, 4, etc., while decks above are called "levels" and are numbered 01, 02, 03, etc.

strengthened by transverse deck beams (athwartships) and longitudinal deck girders (fore and aft). Decks are usually slightly arched from gunwale to centerline in order to drain off water and strengthen the deck.

Decks are named by their position in the ship and their functions. (See the illustration on page 44.) The *main deck* is the uppermost of the decks that run continuously from bow to stern. Decks are numbered to make identification of compartments easier. The *second, third,* and *fourth* decks are complete decks below the main deck numbered in sequence from topside down. The main deck and other decks that extend from side to side and stem to stern are also called *complete decks.*

In aircraft carriers, the uppermost complete deck is the *flight deck,* from which aircraft take off and land. In all other ships, the uppermost complete deck is the main deck; in carriers, the *hangar deck* is the main deck. The hangar deck is the deck on which aircraft are stowed and serviced.

A partial deck at the bow above the main deck is named the *forecastle deck.* Amidships it becomes an *upper deck,* and at the stern it is a *poop deck.* Main deck areas between the forecastle and poop decks are called *well decks.* Very few Navy ships have forecastle and poop decks today, but these are often built into merchant ships. A *half*

deck is any partial deck between complete decks. *Platform decks* are partial decks below the lowest complete deck.

The term *weather deck* includes all parts of decks that are exposed to the weather. *Bulwarks* are a sort of solid steel fence along the gunwale of the main deck, fitted with *scuppers,* rubber or metal drains that allow water to run off the deck during rain or heavy seas.

Any deck above the main deck, forecastle deck, or poop deck is called a *superstructure deck.* These decks are generally called *levels.* The first level above the main deck is the 01 (pronounced ohone) level, the second the 02 level, and so on. These decks may have other names related to their use, such as boat deck, signal bridge, and navigating bridge.

Watertight Integrity

In order to prevent the spread of flooding, watertight bulkheads are built in naval ships to divide the hull into a series of watertight compartments. This is called *watertight integrity,* meaning soundness or without leaks. The compartments of cargo ships, and main storage spaces of all ships, are called *holds;* holds are normally larger in merchant ships than in naval combatants or civilian passenger ships. The more watertight compartments a ship has, the more secure it will be from flooding. Watertight integrity is intended to limit flooding, which can cause a ship to *list* (lean) to port or starboard, lose *trim* (be "down" by the head or stern), *capsize* (tip over), or sink.

Watertight doors and watertight hatches allow access through bulkheads and decks, respectively. Any ship could be made almost unsinkable if it were divided into enough watertight compartments, but too much compartmentation would interfere with the arrangement of mechanical equipment and with the ship's operation. The double bottoms mentioned earlier that are used to carry liquids such as fuels, boiler-feed water, fresh water, or saltwater ballast are fitted with pumps. These pumps can transfer liquids from one tank compartment to another to help keep the ship on an "even keel." The tanks at the extreme bow and stern, called the *forward* (or *forepeak*) and *after peak tanks*, are used for trimming the ship.

A strong watertight bulkhead at the after side of the forepeak tank is called the *collision bulkhead*. If one ship rams another head on, the bow structure would collapse, hopefully, somewhere forward of the collision bulkhead, thus preventing flooding of compartments aft of it.

Maintenance of watertight integrity is a function of *damage control*. The purpose of damage control is to keep the damage, from whatever cause, from spreading elsewhere in the ship. All doors and hatches through watertight bulkheads or decks must be watertight. Wherever steam, oil, air piping, electric cables, or ventilation ducts penetrate a watertight bulkhead or deck, they go through a watertight *stuffing tube* (a cylinder plugged with watertight filler material) or other device to prevent leakage. All watertight doors and hatches carry markings that determine when they may or may not be opened.

SUPERSTRUCTURE

The *superstructure* includes all structures above the main deck. It will vary according to the type of ship, but most ships have a wheelhouse, bridge, signal bridge, chart room, combat information center, radio "shack," and probably a sea cabin for the captain.

The superstructure is topped by the mast. It will be at least one vertical pole fitted with a horizontal yardarm that extends above the ship and carries flag halyards and navigational and signal lights. The mast may also be in the form of a structural tripod. On most ships there also will be electronic devices, radar antennas, radio aerials, and meteorological instruments on the mast or the yardarm. Some Navy ships have only one mast, but many merchant and naval vessels have two. The one forward is called the *foremast*, and the one aft of this is called the *mainmast*; the mainmast is usually taller than the foremast, making it normally the highest structure above the main deck.

The top of a mast is called the *truck*. The *pigstick* is a slender vertical extension above the mast from which the ship's commission pennant or an admiral's personal flag is flown. The *gaff* extends *abaft* (to the rear of) the mainmast. It is from the gaff that the national ensign is flown when the ship is under way.

The small vertical pole at the bow on the forecastle and the slightly raked (diagonal) pole at the very stern are called the *jackstaff* and *flagstaff*, respectively. When a Navy ship is at anchor or moored, it flies the union jack on the jackstaff and the national ensign on the flagstaff from 0800 hours to sunset.

The *stack* of a ship supplies air to and carries off smoke and hot gases from the main propulsion engines. Nuclear-powered ships do not need stacks, since their reactors require no air for combustion and they produce no smoke or gas.

PROPULSION PLANTS

Today's naval ships are propelled mainly by conventional steam plants, gas-turbine engines, or nuclear power plants. A conventional steam propulsion plant consists of boilers, main engines (steam turbines), reduction gears, propeller shafts, and propellers. Nuclear-powered ships have steam propulsion, too, but the steam is produced in a nuclear reactor instead of in oil-fired boilers.

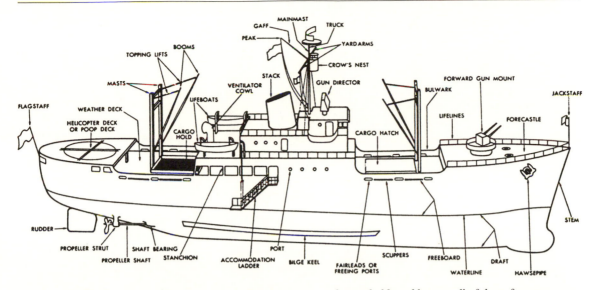

The principal parts of a typical auxiliary ship. With the exception of cargo holds and booms, all of these features are on warships as well.

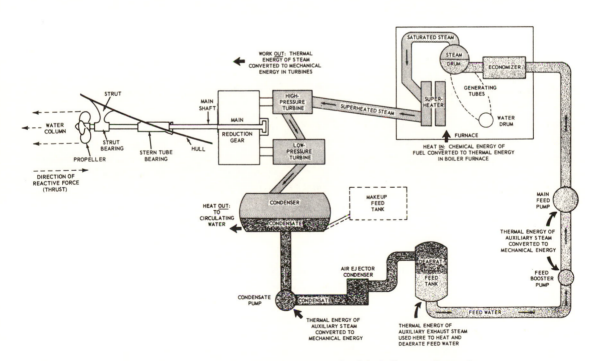

Principles and components of the basic steam cycle of a conventional (oil-fueled) steam-driven ship.

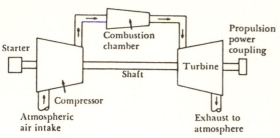

Basic parts of a gas turbine.

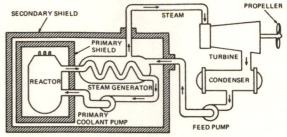

Schematic diagram showing steam flow from a nuclear reactor to the ship's propulsion unit. Nuclear fuel (uranium) heats the water to change it into steam, much like burning fuel oil does in a conventional boiler. The rest of the propulsion system, with turbines, condenser, and reduction gears, is essentially the same.

A *boiler* consists of a boxlike casing containing hundreds of water-filled steel tubes near the top. These tubes are arranged so that heat from furnacelike fireboxes beneath passes over them turning the water into steam. Fuel oil, sprayed into the fireboxes under high pressure, ignites and burns intensely, producing the heat. After being raised to high pressure and temperature in a superheater in another part of the boiler, the steam flows through pipes to turbines, called the "main engines" in this type of power plant. Fresh water used in the boilers is made from salt water by evaporators and condensers.

A steam turbine consists of a central rotating shaft, to which are attached several rows of movable blades, with stationary blades between. The shaft and blading are enclosed within a thick, airtight casing. As the steam passes through the turbine, it is directed through the stationary blades onto the rotating ones, causing the shaft to spin rapidly.

Reduction gears connect the turbines to the propeller shafts. Because turbines operate most efficiently at speeds of several thousand revolutions per minute (rpm), but propellers are not very effective above a few hundred rpm, *reduction gears* must be used to make the transition from the high speed of the turbine to the necessarily slower speed of the propeller.

In recent years the *gas turbine engine* has been developed for ship propulsion. This engine is now installed as the main power plant in *Spruance* and *Arleigh Burke*–class destroyers, *Oliver H. Perry*–class frigates, *Ticonderoga*–class Aegis cruisers,

minesweepers, PT boats, Coast Guard cutters, landing craft, and other craft.

Gas turbines are made up of three basic, separate parts: a compressor, a combustion chamber, and a turbine. The compressor draws in air, compresses it, and sends it under pressure to the combustion chamber, where it is combined with atomized (small droplets) fuel and burned. The combustion gases expand and flow through the turbine blades, producing energy to drive the shaft and propeller.

The gas turbine has several advantages over a conventional steam plant. It is more compact, lighter, and easier to maintain and repair. Because it has a spark ignition system—much like a car—it can go from "cold iron" shutdown to fully ready to turn the shaft in only one minute, in contrast to the several hours of warm-up time required to bring a steam engine on line.

With a nuclear reactor, the primary system is a circulating water cycle. This consists of the reactor, loops or piping, primary coolant pumps, and steam generators. Heat produced in the reactor by nuclear fission is transferred to the circulating primary coolant water, which is pressurized to prevent it from boiling. This water is then pumped through the steam generator and back into the reactor by the primary coolant pumps. It can then be reheated for the next cycle.

Large portions of ships are often built in subassembly bays away from the site where the main part of the ship is being built. Here shipbuilders at Bath Iron Works Corporation, Bath, Maine, position the 97-ton upper bow on a new merchant ship, SS *Argonaut*.

The generation of nuclear power does not require oxygen. Because of this, submarines can operate submerged for extended periods of time. Because there are high levels of radiation around the reactor during operation, no one is permitted to enter the reactor compartment. Heavy shielding protects the crew so well that they receive less radiation than they would from natural sources ashore.

However it is produced, propeller shafts carry the power to the propellers. They run from the reduction gears through long watertight spaces called *shaft alleys* in the very bottom of the ship. Propellers drive the ship. Aircraft carriers and many cruisers have four propellers. Most destroyers have two propellers, but many new ones have only one. Some newer ships have *variable-pitch propellers,* the blades of which can be rotated on the hub to provide more or less "bite" into the water for additional control of the ship's speed or to provide reverse thrust.

DESIGNING AND BUILDING NEW SHIPS

The Naval Sea Systems Command (NavSeaSys-Com) is responsible for the design, procurement, and construction of Navy ships. New designs, requested by the Chief of Naval Operations and approved by the Secretary of the Navy, are developed in consultation with other Navy officers.

A ship is built in a drydock or on sloping concrete building ways. The ways are sloped so that when the ship is launched, it slides into the water under its own weight. The blocks under the ship are high enough so workers can work under the hull while the ship is being built. As the hull is built, scaffolding is raised along the sides to make construction easier.

Today in some shipyards, large portions of the ship are built in subassembly bays away from the building site. As whole sections of the ship are completed, they are carried to the building site with large cranes. Some of these sections weigh more than 50 tons. This way of building enables the projects to move along much faster. The sections are welded together at the building site.

In constructing a ship, the first operation is placing the keel sections on the building blocks. After the keel is laid, it is extended in both directions, from the center outboard, and at the same time, forward and aft. Everything is done step-by-step. Early in the construction the main propulsion plant and major auxiliary machinery and shafting are installed. The whole bow section is usually assembled at a subassembly point and placed in position late in the building schedule. The last step

Side-launching the merchant cargo ship *Amazonia*.

in the prelaunching construction schedule is painting the exterior of the hull of the vessel.

LAUNCHING

A ship can be launched in any of four ways: drydock launched, side launched, end launched, or float-off launched. In drydock launching, the dock is simply flooded to the outside water level and the ship is floated out. Side launching is often done for small ships like tugs and other harbor craft. Ships are end-launched down the ways stern first; this is probably the most common way average-sized naval and merchant ships are launched. In the float-off launching method, the ship is constructed on powered pallet cars, which are rolled onto a pontoon with tracks. The pontoon is towed into deep water and ballasted down. When submerged far enough, the ship is towed off to the outfitting docks.

During regular construction, the vessel is supported by keel blocks, heavy shoring, and cribbing. Before actual launching, wooden tracks are installed below and on both sides of the ship. These tracks extend into the water. Mounted on the ground ways, and temporarily secured to the ship, are sliding ways on which the ship rides into the water. The sliding ways serve like runners on a sled. A heavy layer of grease is laid between the ways to reduce friction.

Workers proceed to wedge up the ship shoring timbers to the sliding ways. They drive scores of long wooden wedges under the ship at right angles to her, so the sliding ways are forced up under the ship and hard down on the fixed ground ways. Then the shoring and cribbing is gradually removed according to carefully timed plans, to shift the weight of the ship to the launching ways.

The ship is now ready to slide down the incline of the building ways by her own weight. Only a trigger mechanism holds her back until the right time. The signal to launch is flashed to the sponsor's stand and the trigger pit at the same time. It takes about thirty seconds for the ship to slide into the water. Chain drags and tugs are used to slow and stop the ship after it reaches the water.

The name of the ship is chosen by the Secretary of the Navy, upon recommendation of the Chief of Naval Operations (CNO). A female sponsor is selected by the Secretary of the Navy according to naval tradition.

At the time of launching, the sponsor, naval officers, officials of the shipbuilding company, and the commandant of the naval district in which the ship is being built meet on a flag-decorated platform at the bow of the ship. There may be some speeches, and a chaplain offers a prayer. For the ship's future service, he or she asks, "May this new vessel of our Navy be guarded by Thy gracious providence and care. May she bear the sword to bring peace on Earth among the nations. Let her be a terror to those who do evil and a defense to those who do well."

The band plays the national anthem, flags and pennants wave, and as the ship begins to move, the sponsor breaks on her bow a gaily wrapped bottle of champagne, wine, or water, saying, "I name you _____, in the name of the United States." She often adds, "May success always attend you."

After the christening and launching, the ship is fitted out alongside a pier. Here giant cranes move the heavy machinery into the ship. Superstructure, masts, guns, and other equipment are installed.

Living quarters, galleys, messing compartments, and other spaces are painted and fitted with furniture and equipment. The fitting-out period may take over a year for large ships.

COMMISSIONING

When the ship is ready for commissioning, the shipyard commander or another senior officer representing the CNO is ordered to place her in commission.

On that day, her officers and crew assemble in dress uniforms. Many dignitaries are usually present. The CNO representative and staff are in attendance also. As the band plays and all stand at attention, the representative orders the national ensign hoisted to designate her as a ship in the official service of the government. The commission pennant is unfurled at the mainmast.

Then the CNO representative formally turns the ship over to the prospective commanding officer. The CO reads aloud orders from the Navy Department to command the ship. The first order is "Set the watch." The officers and crew take their stations in the new ship.

After commissioning, the ship starts her trials. The weapons are calibrated and fired. Communications gear is tested. The ship goes on a "shakedown" cruise to test seaworthiness, speed, endurance, and ability to maneuver. After the ship returns to the outfitting yard, any problems are corrected. More checks and tests are made at sea of fuel consumption, speeds, propeller revolutions, and other operations. Finally the ship and her crew undergo a six- to eight-week underway training cruise, usually out of San Diego or Guantanamo Bay, Cuba. Upon successful completion of this cruise, the ship is ready to join the fleet.

SHIP DESIGNATIONS

The Navy has some 300 oceangoing ships operating under their own commanding officers. In addition to these, there are over 1,000 service craft, many without crews and with no self-propulsion.

Navy ships have both a name and a number called a *designation*. The designation is a group of letters and numbers that identify the ship. The *let-*

AD	Destroyer Tender		FF	Frigate
AE°	Ammunition Ship		FFG	Guided Missile Frigate
AFS°	Combat Stores Ship		LCAC	Landing Craft, Air Cushion
AO°	Oiler		LCC	Amphibious Command Ship
AOE	Fast Combat Support Ship		LCU	Landing Craft, Utility
AOJ	Jumboized (lengthened) Oiler		LHA	Amphibious Assault Ship (general purpose)
AOR	Replenishment Oiler		LHD	Helicopter/Dock Landing Ship
AR	Repair Ship		LKA	Amphibious Cargo Ship
ARS	Salvage Ship		LPD	Amphibious Transport Dock
AS	Submarine Tender		LPH	Amphibious Assault Ship
ASR	Submarine Rescue Ship		LSD	Dock Landing Ship
ATF	Fleet Ocean Tug		LST	Tank Landing Ship
ATS	Salvage and Rescue Ship		MCM	Mine Countermeasure Ship
BB	Battleship		MHC	Mine Hunter Ship
CG	Guided Missile Cruiser		MSO	Minesweeper Ship
CGN	Guided Missile Cruiser (nuclear propulsion)		PBR	River Patrol Boat
CV	Aircraft Carrier		PC	Patrol Combatant
CVN	Aircraft Carrier (nuclear propulsion)		PHM	Patrol Combatant Missile (Hydrofoil)
DD	Destroyer		SSN	Attack Submarine (nuclear propulsion)
DDG	Guided Missile Destroyer		SSBN	Fleet Ballistic Missile Submarine (nuclear propulsion)
DSRV	Deep Submergence Rescue Vehicle		YFU	Harbor Utility Craft
DSV	Deep Submergence Vehicle		YO	Fuel Oil Barge
			YP	Patrol Craft
			YTB	Large Harbor Tug

° A *T* preceding a designation denotes a ship owned and operated by the Military Sealift Command and crewed by civilians.

ters tell the ship type and general use; the *hull numbers* indicate the number of ships of that type built, in sequence. These designations are used in correspondence, records, and plans, and appear on ships' boats and ships' bows.

The first letter in a designator is a general classification. The designator letters are as follows:

A	Auxiliary	M	Mine warfare
B	Battleship	P	Patrol
C	Cruiser	S	Submarine
CV	Carrier	T	Military Sealift Command
D	Destroyer		
F	Frigate	Y	Yard and Service Craft
L	Amphibious		

In combatant designations, the letter *N* means nuclear propulsion and the letter *G* means that the ship carries guided missiles. Other letters serve to

further identify the vessel and her purpose. When a number of ships are built to the same design they make up a *class,* which is named for the first ship in the class.

Let's look at a couple of examples of ship designations to show how they help identify a ship: the USS *Kidd* (DDG-993) and USS *Ohio* (SSBN-726). The *Kidd* is a guided-missile destroyer, DD meaning destroyer, and G meaning guided missile. The *Ohio* is a nuclear-powered ballistic missile submarine, SS meaning submarine, B, ballistic, and N, nuclear-powered. The *Ohio* also happens to be the first of the latest class of Trident missile submarines, so that group of ships is known as the *Ohio*-class fleet ballistic missile submarines.

All Navy ships can be easily identified as to their type, mission, armament, and propulsion by their designator. On the previous page is a partial list of principal Navy ships and craft designations.

In recent years, many auxiliary-type Navy ships have been taken over by the Military Sealift Command and crewed by contract civilians. These ships are identified by a T preceding their designator, for example, the replenishment oiler USS *Neosho* (TAO-143).

Chapter 2. *Study Guide Questions*

1. List the major factors considered in the construction of naval ships.

2. Provide the nautical terms for these civilian terms:
   A. outer walls
   B. inner walls
   C. floors
   D. ceilings
   E. hallways
   F. stairs
   G. entrance hall

3. What nautical names are given to these parts of a ship?
   A. front part
   B. back part
   C. middle of ship, lengthwise
   D. lengthwise direction
   E. crosswise direction
   F. midpoint area
   G. widest part of ship
   H. main deck, forward
   I. main deck, aft
   J. main deck and above
   K. below the main deck
   L. right of centerline
   M. left of centerline
   N. in the rigging

4. A. What name is given to the girders attached to the keel that support the watertight skin of the ship?
   B. What is the watertight skin called?
   C. What additional strengthening beams run fore and aft?

5. What is another name for the deck-edge where the main deck meets with the shell or side plating?

6. A. How are all compartments in a ship identified?
   B. How are the decks of a ship supported?
7. A. How are decks numbered below the main deck?
   B. Above the main deck?
8. What is *watertight integrity*?
9. A. What name is given to all structures above the main deck?
   B. What is the highest structure above the main deck?
   C. What equipment is installed on this structure?
10. A. What main components does a steam propulsion plant have?
   B. What is the biggest difference in a nuclear-powered vessel?
11. Briefly describe how a gas turbine engine works.
12. What part of the propulsion system actually drives the ship through the water?
13. Why is there heavy shielding around the reactor compartment of a nuclear propulsion plant?
14. A. What is the main responsibility of the Naval Sea Systems Command?
   B. Who requests, and who approves, new ship designs?
15. In or on what are ships built?
16. What are the basic steps in building a ship?
17. What four ways can a ship be launched?
18. Who chooses the name of a new ship?
19. A. Who places a naval ship in commission?
   B. What is the first order of the new commanding officer after he or she reads the orders?
20. What are the purposes of the shakedown and underway training cruises?
21. A. What is a ship's *designation* composed of?
   B. What are the first-letter designators of major naval vessels?
22. A. What determines a *class* of ships?
   B. What do the letters G and N indicate in a ship's designator?
   C. What does a T before a ship's designator mean?

propulsion	bow, stern	weather deck	rpm
armament	forecastle	scuppers	propeller shaft
seaworthiness	fantail	levels (shipboard)	nuclear reactor
maneuverability	watertight integrity	list, trim	variable-pitch
endurance	amidships	collision bulkhead	propeller
habitability	port, starboard	superstructure	building ways
fuel consumption	beam, quarter	mainmast, foremast	subassembly
landlubber	keel	pigstick, gaff	sponsor
bulkhead	gunwale	jackstaff, flagstaff	christening
overhead	roll, pitch, yaw	stack	commission pennant
quarterdeck	draft	boiler	shakedown cruise
fore, aft	freeboard	turbine	hull number
athwartships	compartment	reduction gear	ship designator

Chapter 3. Damage Control and Firefighting

A ship's ability to do her job may one day depend on her crew's damage control abilities. Damage control covers firefighting, collision and grounding damage, explosion damage, battle damage, and care of the injured. The duties and responsibilities of the ship's damage control organization are outlined in the ship's battle bill and covered in detail in the *Damage Control Manual*. The objectives of the damage control organization are:

- To prevent damage by making the ship watertight and gas tight, to maintain reserve buoyancy and stability, to remove fire hazards, and to make emergency equipment ready.
- To keep the damage from spreading, while helping those who are hurt.
- To repair and restore damaged equipment, including the supply of emergency power.

THE DAMAGE CONTROL ORGANIZATION

The shipboard damage control organization consists of Damage Control Central (DCC) and repair parties stationed in and responsible for various areas of the ship. The engineer officer is the damage control officer. He or she is assisted by the damage control assistant (DCA), who is responsible for preventing and repairing damages; training the crew in damage control; and caring for machinery, drainage, and piping assigned to the damage control organization (such as firemains, foam systems, and water washdown systems). In addition to these key leaders, each department has a damage control petty officer who coordinates the training of departmental personnel in damage control.

Damage Control Central is the headquarters for all damage control activities in the ship's battle organization. It coordinates all the repair parties for hull, propulsion, electronics, weapons, and air, and the battle dressing (first aid and emergency operating) stations. DCC is the place where the reports from damage control parties go. DCC assesses the damage and decides which area is most in need of repairs. It also reports to and receives orders from the CO on what must be done to keep the ship in fighting shape.

The DCA has a battle station in the DCC. He or she uses various visual tools to help coordinate plans to contain damage. These include charts and diagrams of the entire ship, her systems, and her access routes to different areas. A casualty display board enables the DCA to visualize the damage sustained, and the corrective action necessary and in progress, based on repair party reports. The DCA also coordinates the decontamination stations; monitors teams to detect nuclear, biological, or chemical (NBC) attacks; and routes casualties to the battle dressing station. He or she lays out safe routes for these teams to travel.

REPAIR PARTIES

Repair parties are the DCA's representatives at the scene of the casualty or damage. They are the main units in the damage control organization. The number and ratings of crew members assigned to a repair party are determined by the location of the station, the size of the area to be covered by that station, and the total number of people available.

Each repair party will have an officer or chief petty officer in charge, a scene leader to supervise all on-scene activities, a phone talker, messengers, and personnel equipped with special oxygen breathing apparatus (OBA). (For further discussion of OBA, see the section on firefighting equipment.) Repair party personnel are assigned to various teams within each repair party, including: investigation teams; hose teams; dewatering, plugging, and patching teams; shoring, piping repair, structural repair, casualty power, interior communications repair, and electrical repair teams. There are also NBC monitoring teams and decontamination teams. Stretcher bearers are available for each team. Every person in the repair party should be able to perform effectively on any team.

Besides the general repair parties, there are special departmental teams to handle aviation fuel repair, aviation crash and salvage, and ordnance disposal.

Repair parties are assigned to each major part of the ship (identified as main deck repair, forward repair, after repair, and amidships repair), and to propulsion repair, ordnance repair, and electronics repair.

Repair parties must be capable of:
- Evaluating and reporting correctly on the extent of damage in their areas.
- Controlling and extinguishing all kinds of fires.

- Giving first aid and transporting the injured to battle dressing stations.
- Detecting, identifying, and measuring nuclear radiation, and carrying out decontamination procedures.
- Performing the special duties assigned to their parties, such as ordnance, propulsion, and electronics repairs; and maintaining watertight integrity, structural integrity, and ship's maneuverability.

In addition to her repair parties, each ship also has an auxiliary at-sea and in-port *fire party* organization, consisting of enough on-duty repair party personnel to handle a moderate-sized fire. A large fire requires general quarters (GQ) to be sounded and all repair parties to be fully manned to fight it.

Battle dressing stations are equipped to handle casualties. They are manned by medical department personnel. Stretcher cases may be brought directly to the station by the repair party stretcher bearers. Emergency supplies of medical equipment are placed in first aid boxes at various stations throughout the ship in addition to those stored at the battle dressing stations.

MATERIAL READINESS CONDITIONS

The success of damage control depends partly on the proper use of watertight-integrity equipment. As discussed earlier, each ship is divided into compartments to control flooding, withstand NBC attacks, protect and strengthen the structure of the ship, and control buoyancy and stability. The original watertight integrity of a ship may be reduced or destroyed by enemy action, storms, collisions, or negligence.

Navy ships have three material conditions of readiness, each representing a different degree of "tightness" and protection. These are X-RAY, YOKE, and ZEBRA.

Condition X-RAY signifies the least protection. It is set when the ship is in no danger of attack, such as when at anchor in a well-protected harbor or secured at home base during regular working hours. During this condition, any closure (door, hatch, valve, and so on) with a black X on it will be secured. X-RAY fittings are also closed for conditions YOKE and ZEBRA.

Condition YOKE provides for a bit more protection than X-RAY. YOKE is set and maintained at sea. In port, it is maintained at all times during war, and at times outside of regular working hours during peacetime. YOKE closures are marked with a black Y; they are also closed during Condition ZEBRA.

Condition Zebra is set before going to sea or when entering port during war. It is set immediately, without further orders, when general quarters stations are manned. Condition ZEBRA is also set to localize and control fire and flooding when not at GQ. When Condition ZEBRA is set, all closures marked with a red Z are secured.

Once a material condition is set, no fitting marked with that condition symbol may be opened without permission from the commanding officer, given through the DCA or OOD. It is the responsibility of all hands to maintain the material condition.

Damage Repairs

Battle-damage repair is emergency action taken to keep the ship afloat and fighting. Drills and personal qualification training are continuously done to teach everyone how to use damage control equipment. An important part of winning in any emergency is to keep calm, remain alert, and work rapidly with the tools at hand. Unless the damage is very bad, there is much that damage control teams can do to keep the ship afloat and ready for action.

Any rupture, break, or hole in the ship's outer hull plating below the waterline can let in seawater. If flooding is not controlled, the ship will sink. When the underwater hull is pierced, there are only two ways to control flooding. The first is to plug the holes. The second is to establish and maintain flood boundaries using the watertight compartmentation in the ship so flooding will not spread.

Communications

Communications between different parts of the damage control organization are of vital impor-

tance. Without adequate communications, the whole system could break down. There are three main communication systems used in the damage control organization: the general announcing system (usually called the IMC), sound-powered telephones, and messengers.

The IMC is not the primary means of transmitting damage control information, but it is a way of getting orders, information, and alarms throughout the ship. It may be used to announce the location of a bomb or shell hit, fire, or collision.

Emergency alarms include the general alarm, used to call the crew to general quarters because of impending enemy attack, and general quarters for fire, collision, and NBC attack. The *general alarm* used for attack or fire is a series of single gong tones; the *chemical alarm* is a steady tone signal; and the *collision alarm* consists of a series of three pulses, with a short pause before the next series. Battle stations are manned for all of the emergency alarms.

Sound-powered telephones are used on the ship's battle circuits. They are the principal means of communication throughout the ship. Their advantage over other systems is that they require no external source of power other than the talker's voice. Each repair party has its own circuit connecting it to Damage Control Central, to its roving patrols, and to other stations in its area.

When other methods of communication fail, *messengers* must be used to relay orders and information. Messengers must learn how to get around the ship to all the repair party stations and other areas. Messengers will often be given written messages for delivery, but they must also be able to deliver oral messages accurately.

Fire and Firefighting

Any person aboard ship who discovers a fire must give the alarm. Another person must be notified to go for help. The fire report may be spread by any means, such as the telephone or other internal communication system. Damage Control Central is the headquarters area for fighting any fire. Once the alarm has sounded, anyone nearby should act promptly to check or extinguish the fire.

Other personnel in the fire or repair party will arrive quickly on the scene with the necessary equipment to carry on the fight.

Fire is a constant threat aboard ship. All measures must be taken to prevent fires. They may start from spontaneous combustion (self-generated heat), carelessness, hits by enemy shells or missiles, explosion, or collision. A fire must be controlled quickly, since it may cause extensive damage or loss of the ship.

In order for a fire to occur, three physical requirements must be met. There must be a burnable fuel, it must be heated enough to start burning (combustion), and there must be enough oxygen to keep it burning. These requirements form what is called the *fire triangle*, whose sides consist of *fuel, heat,* and *oxygen.* Removing any side of the triangle will result in extinguishing the fire (putting it out). Firefighters must determine the best way to put a fire out—in other words, which side to remove. This is not always an easy task.

Removing the fuel is often not possible. It could be done, however, in an instance where liquid fuel was being fed by a pipeline. Closing the valves would cut the flow of the fuel, and the fire could then be allowed to burn itself out.

Oxygen can be removed in two ways. In a closed space, carbon dioxide (CO_2) can be pumped in to dilute the oxygen and starve the fire. Another method is to smother the fire with a blanket of chemicals, foam, or sand.

Removing the heat side of the triangle, or cooling the fire, is the method most often used. The usual method is to use lots of water, both solid stream and fog (spray), to cool the burning surface rapidly.

CLASSES OF FIRES

Fires have four classes according to the type of fuel or material burning and the methods required to extinguish them.

Class A fires involve solid materials such as wood, cloth, or paper. They often leave ashes. Explosives are also in this category. Water is the usual means of putting out Class A fires. Carbon dioxide may be used on small fires, but not on explosives. The flames of a large fire are usually cooled down with fog. Then, a solid stream of water is used to break up the material for further cooling.

Class B fires involve flammable liquids such as oil, gasoline, other fuels, cleaning agents, and paints. CO_2 is good for putting out small Class B fires. For larger fires, light water (a mixture of

The classes of fires and recommended extinguishing agents are listed in order of priority.

Combustible	Class	Extinguishing agent
Woodwork, bedding, clothes, combustible stores	A	Fixed water sprinkling, high-velocity fog, solid water stream, foam, dry chemical, CO_2.
Explosives, propellants	A	Magazine sprinkling, solid water stream or high-velocity fog, foam.
Paints, spirits, flammable liquid stores	B	CO_2 (fixed system), foam, installed sprinkling system, high-velocity fog, PKP, CO_2, light water.
Gasoline	B	Foam, CO_2 (fixed), water sprinkling system, PKP, light water.
Fuel oil, JP-5, diesel oil, kerosene	B	Foam, PKP, water sprinkling system, high-velocity fog, CO_2 (fixed system), light water.
Electrical and radio apparatus	C	CO_2 (portable or hose reel), high-velocity fog, fog foam or dry chemical (only if CO_2 is not available).
Magnesium alloys	D	Jettison overboard, low-velocity fog.

water and chemicals) should be used. A solid stream of water should never be used on Class B fires; it will only scatter the fuel and spread the flames.

Class C fires are those burning in electrical or electronic equipment—radios, radars, generators, electric control panels, and so on. The main extinguishing agents are CO_2 and dry chemical extinguishers. Liquids should not be used because they will damage the equipment and may be a shock hazard. If at all possible, electrical gear should be deenergized before any firefighting is undertaken, as the shock hazard is extreme. Electricity will travel on wet decks and can electrocute firefighters.

Class D fires involve combustible metals such as magnesium, sodium, and titanium. These metals are used in certain parts of aircraft, missiles, and electronic gear. A magnesium aircraft parachute flare, for instance, can burn at a temperature greater than 4,000 degrees Fahrenheit, with a brilliancy of two trillion candlepower. Only light water or low-velocity fog should be used on this type of fire. Firefighters dealing with Class D fires should wear welders' goggles with dark lenses to protect their eyes from the intense glare of the fire.

FIRE PREVENTION

A fire is certain to cause some damage. The most firefighters can do is to hold down the damage and keep it from spreading. In any event, some property will be destroyed, productive work interrupted, and additional effort and materials will be needed to clean up the mess. The objective, therefore, is to prevent fires from starting. The rules for preventing fires are pretty much the same anywhere, but special precautions must be taken in the Navy and aboard ships because of the concentration of flammable fuels and explosives.

The first rule is to keep things squared away—clean, shipshape, and in their proper places. Flammable materials must be kept away from fire-starting articles such as torches, cigarettes, and sparking equipment.

Firefighting equipment must be kept in the proper places and in good working condition. If a fire starts, the right gear must be immediately ready to prevent it from spreading.

One of the more common causes of Class A fires is lighted cigarettes or matches thrown into trash cans. Smoking in bunks is strictly forbidden by regulations, but the regulations have been broken; in homes, smoking in bed or on couches is one of the most common causes of fires. Through spontaneous combustion, piled up oily rags and papers commonly cause such fires.

Class B fires are very difficult to predict, especially if a leak of fumes occurs in voids and tanks aboard ship. Sparking from welding torches, light switches, and even flashlights can be sufficient to cause an explosion and fire in gasoline fumes. *The smoking lamp is out* whenever handling fuels or explosives aboard a ship. (The smoking lamp is the naval term used to give permission to smoke in authorized spaces.)

Paint and oils should be kept away from electric wires. Frayed or worn wires and insulation must be repaired or replaced. Dust and dirt should not be allowed to accumulate around electrical equipment. Unauthorized electrical appliances and overloading circuits with appliances and plugs are an open invitation to overheating and fires.

FIREFIGHTING EQUIPMENT

The *firemain system* aboard ship is designed to deliver seawater to fireplugs and sprinkler systems, just like a city's firemain delivers water under pressure to the fire hydrants. Two connected 50-foot lengths of fire hose, one end attached to the firemain, are placed on racks at each *fire station* throughout a ship. Additional lengths of hose are rolled and stowed in repair lockers. The Navy's all-purpose nozzle can produce a solid stream of water, high-velocity fog, or low-velocity fog.

Sprinkler systems are installed in magazines, turrets, ammunition-handling rooms, spaces where flammable materials are stored, and hangar bays aboard aircraft carriers. Some systems are automatically triggered when the temperature in the protected compartment reaches a certain temperature, but most are operated manually by control valves.

Light water used to fight Class B fires acts as a blanket that floats on top of the burning liquid and smothers the fire. It should not be used on Class C fires because it can cause short circuits at a later time.

Two types of portable extinguishers are used. Both are effective in fighting Class B and Class C fires. The CO_2 extinguisher is used mainly for putting out electrical fires but is effective on any small fire. Because CO_2 is heavier than air, it forms a smothering blanket over the fire. CO_2 is quick to use and leaves no mess, but carbon-dioxide "snow" can be blown away by wind or draft. It is not poisonous, but contact with it can cause painful skin blisters.

Dry chemical extinguishers are provided mainly for Class B fires. The chemical used is potassium bicarbonate (similar to baking soda). It is called *purple-K powder,* or PKP. PKP is not poisonous and is four times as powerful as CO_2 for extinguishing fires. The dry chemical is an excellent firefighting agent, but its effects are temporary. It has no cooling effect and provides no protection against reflash. PKP should be used sparingly in confined spaces because it will reduce visibility and make breathing difficult.

PKP can be used with light water to produce a highly effective foam. When the water drains from the foam, a vapor-tight film is formed on top of the fuel. The dry chemical beats down the fire, and the light water prevents a reflash.

PROTECTIVE FIRE CLOTHING

Any clothing that covers the skin will protect it from flash burns and other short-duration flames. If in an area or situation where fire or explosion is likely, one should keep covered as much as possible, and eyes should be protected with antiflash goggles. If clothing catches on fire, one should not run, since this will fan the flames. Lie down and roll up in a blanket, coat, or anything that will smother the flames. If nothing is available, the person should roll over slowly, beating out the flames with his or her hands. If another person's clothes catch on fire, he or she should be put down and covered up (except the head) with a blanket or coat.

The *proximity firefighting suit* (close-in suit)

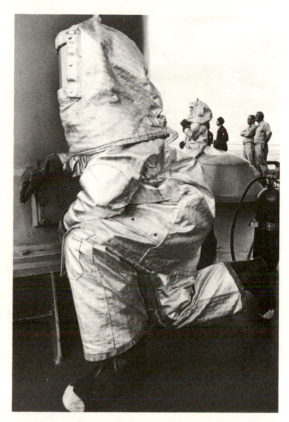

A crash-crewman in a *proximity firefighting suit* stands by, ready for action during helicopter flight quarters on a guided-missile cruiser. The suit is made of asbestos cotton, aluminized on the outside for reflective purposes. The suit resists the penetration of water or other liquids. The wearer is not expected to enter burning spaces or walk through flames but to get close enough to be effective in putting the fire out.

consists of a one-piece coverall, gloves, hood, and boots. It is made of glass fiber and asbestos, with an aluminized surface. Its hood provides a protective cover for the oxygen breathing apparatus (OBA) that is normally worn with it. It is lightweight and resists penetration of liquids. The suit allows crew members to enter overheated or steam-filled compartments and to make crash fire rescues.

The Navy's OBA is a self-contained unit de-

A damage control petty officer first class adjusts the OBA on a trainee in damage control school. The OBA is designed to protect the wearer in places lacking oxygen or containing harmful gases, vapors, smoke, or dust. It is a closed, self-contained unit in which oxygen is supplied by chemicals in a canister that purifies exhaled air.

signed to protect the wearer in a place lacking oxygen or containing harmful gases, vapors, smoke, or dust. The wearer breathes in a closed system in which oxygen is supplied by chemicals in a canister that purifies exhaled air. All Navy personnel are trained in the use of the OBA in boot camp and in fleet training schools, as well as aboard ship during repair party instruction.

Fighting a Fire

A fire may gain considerable headway before smoke is discovered, especially if it has originated in an unattended space. The first sign may be smoke coming out of a ventilation outlet or seeping around a door or hatchcover. The smoke may have traveled some distance. Therefore, the first job of a repair or fire party is to locate the fire. This is done by team members called *investigators*, normally the first people to go out to respond to any damage or fire that may have occurred.

The investigators check bulkheads, decks, and vents for heat to see if the fire is in an adjoining compartment. They may have to follow a trail of smoke. Once the fire is located, they check adjoining compartments to be sure it has not spread to them.

As soon as the extent of the fire is determined, a full report should be made to Damage Control Central.

While the firefighting is under way, the team sets up *fire boundaries* to isolate the fire and prevent it from spreading. A fire in several compartments is treated as a single unit, with boundaries being set around the entire area. Fire boundaries are set in several ways. Combustible materials in adjoining spaces are moved or cooled to prevent spread by heat transmission. Since fire can blister and ignite paint on bulkheads in adjoining compartments, fog or sprinklers are used to cool the bulkheads, decks, and overheads in adjoining spaces. Ventilation systems in the area are secured to cut off the oxygen supply to the fire and to limit the spread of smoke and gases to other compartments. Fire watches are posted in surrounding compartments.

When the fire is isolated, electrical circuits in the area should be deenergized to protect against shock. Doors should be opened carefully, checking for heat and gas pressure before removing all *door dogs* (heavy latches).

After the fire has been extinguished, the area must be overhauled to prevent reflash of the fire. All smoldering or charred materials should be saturated thoroughly and removed if possible. The compartments must be checked for explosive vapors or liquids that might remain. Dewatering (removing water used in firefighting) is then begun. At this time, a full report is made to Damage Control Central on fire and smoke damage and flooding. The final step in fighting the fire is to set a *reflash watch* to be sure that the fire does not start again from a smoldering fragment or through vapor ignition. Gases, especially from fuels, can be ignited by heat or sparks if allowed to concentrate in or near an area that has not been properly overhauled.

1. A. What does damage control cover?
   B. What are its primary objectives?
2. A. Which officer is the ship's damage control officer?
   B. Who is the principal assistant?
3. A. What is the name given to the control station for shipboard damage control?
   B. What is the name given to the on-scene groups of people who are responsible for damage control in assigned sectors of the ship?
4. A. What is the task of a repair party scene leader?
   B. What are the special teams within a repair party?
5. A. What is a *battle dressing station*?
   B. Who brings stretcher cases to the battle dressing station?
6. A. What are the three basic material conditions of readiness?
   B. What is the extent of protection for the ship in each?
7. What are the two ways to control flooding?
8. A. What are the emergency alarms used aboard ship?
   B. When are they used?
9. A. What is the principal means of internal communication throughout a ship?
   B. What is the particular advantage of this system?
   C. When internal phone and electrical systems fail, what method is used to relay messages?
10. Who must be the first person to report a fire?
11. A. What is the "fire triangle"?
    B. How can a fire be put out?
    C. What is the method most often used?

12. List the four classes of fires, fuels for each, and best method of extinguishing each.
13. Why must a stream of water *never* be used to put out fires in electrical or electronic equipment before it is completely deenergized?
14. A. Why must special precautions against fire be constantly observed aboard ship?
    B. What are some of the key rules for shipboard fire prevention?
    C. Why do these rules make sense in your own home?
15. Where are shipboard sprinkler systems used?
16. What should you do if your clothes catch on fire?
17. A. What is the name of the shipboard firefighting suit?
    B. When is this suit used with best results?
18. What is the purpose of the Navy's OBA?
19. A. What are the first steps a firefighting party must take in fighting a fire?
    B. Why do they check bulkheads and decks for heat?
20. What is the purpose of a *fire boundary*?
21. What is dewatering?

Vocabulary

damage control	sound-powered
DCA, DCC	telephones
repair party	OBA
battle dressing station	fire boundaries
low-velocity fog	dewatering
smoking lamp	reflash watch
all-purpose nozzle	fire triangle
PKP	carbon dioxide (CO_2)
light water	door dogs
asbestos suit	

4

The Nation, the Navy, and the People

Chapter 1.   Our Government and Our Navy

The Constitution of the United States is said to be the best base for government ever worked out by humans. This is because it truly states the will of the people to govern themselves. The Declaration of Independence had been written earlier to tell everyone that the American people believed that only independence could protect their basic human rights. The Founding Fathers created a constitution based on the belief "that all men are created equal, that they are endowed by their Creator with certain unalienable Rights, that among these are Life, Liberty, and the pursuit of Happiness."

These men believed that the first duty of government is to protect the people's rights. They thought that any power granted to the government should help safeguard these rights. Knowing that the people might, from time to time, be faced by enemies, either foreign or domestic, who could take away their rights, the Constitution gave the Congress the power to:

- Raise armies.
- Maintain a navy.
- Make rules for running the land and naval forces.

Today, many nations have governments that oppress their own people and threaten to conquer others by force. The U.S. government has always sought to safeguard liberty for all as outlined in the Constitution.

In this chapter we will discuss how the U.S. government operates, and how the Department of Defense and the Navy Department fit into it. All citizens should learn about our government, Constitution, and armed services. All of our citizens must take part in government and support the armed forces if our ideals and rights are to be safeguarded.

THE FEDERAL SYSTEM

In 1781, during the American Revolution, the thirteen original states agreed to govern the country under an agreement called the Articles of Confederation. This document set up a congress, but gave it no power to levy taxes, raise military forces, issue money, or regulate commerce. The Articles let each state do pretty much as it pleased. While the Articles also set up a department to handle foreign affairs and a post office, it soon became clear that a better form of government had to be worked out. Otherwise, the whole idea of a united country would fail.

In 1787 delegates from the thirteen states met in Philadelphia to hammer out a constitution for a central government that would be above the states, but at the same time, would keep certain states' rights. But many people did not want a powerful central government. These people came to be called Anti-Federalists. Those who wanted a strong central government were called Federalists. This was the beginning of our two-party political system. Both groups got together, though, for the benefit of the nation and all its citizens, and after four months of struggle and compromise, they had written the Constitution.

The Constitution went into effect in 1789 when George Washington took his oath as the first president of the United States. The federal form of government has been the national government of the United States ever since.

RIGHTS AND DUTIES

Before they would accept the new Constitution, many of the thirteen states said that certain *amendments* guaranteeing individual rights had to be added to it. Congress added these first ten amendments, called the *Bill of Rights,* to the Constitution in 1791. The Bill of Rights includes the freedoms of speech, press, religion, assembly, petition, and trial by jury, among others. Because these rights are spelled out in the Constitution, every American can call himself or herself a free person.

All Americans have the same legal rights under the Constitution. Our federal government has a policy of equal opportunity for all. Each citizen, regardless of background or race, has the same legal rights, and is due full protection under the law and the Constitution. Accepting each person as an equal is a responsibility of each citizen.

The Constitution guarantees basic human rights but these rights carry duties. Each person must use his or her freedom so that it does not hurt the freedom of others. In our democracy, our government must protect the rights of all citizens by making sure that no one unlawfully injures or takes away the rights of others.

REPRESENTATIVE DEMOCRACY

The Constitution requires the government to rule with the consent of the people. Our form of government is called a democratic *republic.* Under this form of government, the citizens choose persons to be their *representatives* by voting. These representatives make and enforce the laws. At elections, the voters decide whether to keep these representatives or to vote in new ones. Representatives must carry out the wishes of the people, and that is what is meant by "government by consent of the governed." The belief that government should be by consent of the governed is a basic belief of all free people. It is the way they protect their freedom and their rights.

In a *direct democracy,* all the voters meet and vote on all matters and laws concerning their lives. The majority rules. While this works well in a small town, it couldn't work for the whole country. The country is too large and has too many people to make direct democracy work. For this reason, Americans elect representatives who speak and vote for them in the state legislatures and the U.S. Congress. Our state and national governments, therefore, are called *representative democracies.*

POWERS OF CONSTITUTIONAL GOVERNMENT

We read above that the rights of the people are safeguarded by the Constitution, and that the people elect their representatives to form a government on their behalf. But the Constitution also limits the power of government. The wrongs done by an all-powerful government caused the American Revolution; therefore, the Founding Fathers made sure that the Constitution did not allow such a government in the United States. The Constitution permits the government to do certain things and not others. The powers denied to the government are reserved for the states and the people. This makes our government *constitutional,* in which the Constitution is the law of the land, which both the government and the citizens must obey.

To ensure that the government runs smoothly, the Constitution gives each of the three branches —legislative, executive, and judicial—separate powers. These separate powers of each branch check, or limit, the powers of the other two branches. This system of *checks and balances*

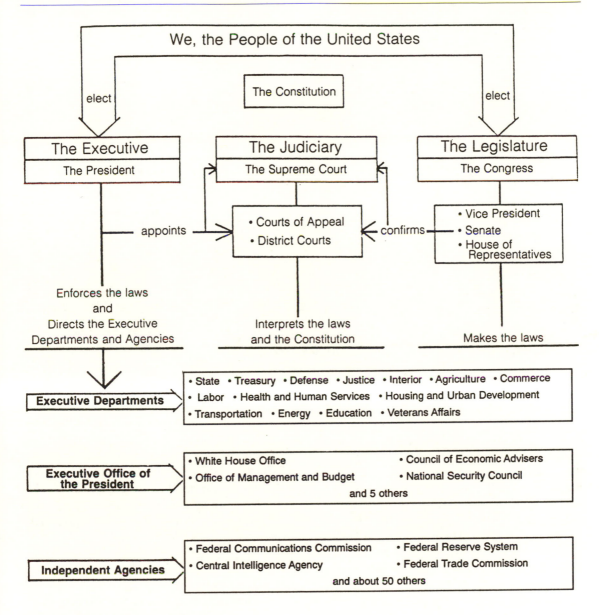

We, the People of the United States

The Constitution

elect → The Executive / The President

elect → The Legislature / The Congress

The Judiciary / The Supreme Court

appoints → • Courts of Appeal / • District Courts

confirms ← • Vice President / • Senate / • House of Representatives

Enforces the laws
and
Directs the Executive
Departments and Agencies

Interprets the laws
and the Constitution

Makes the laws

Executive Departments → • State • Treasury • Defense • Justice • Interior • Agriculture • Commerce • Labor • Health and Human Services • Housing and Urban Development • Transportation • Energy • Education • Veterans Affairs

Executive Office of the President → • White House Office • Council of Economic Advisers • Office of Management and Budget • National Security Council and 5 others

Independent Agencies → • Federal Communications Commission • Federal Reserve System • Central Intelligence Agency • Federal Trade Commission and about 50 others

Structure of the U.S. federal government.

keeps the branches from going beyond their constitutional limits of power.

The Constitution gives the *legislative branch* of government the power to make laws. Our legislative branch is Congress. The U.S. Congress is made up of two bodies, the Senate and the House of Representatives. The Senate has two senators elected from each state, a total of 100. The House has 435 members elected from the *congressional districts* of the states. The size and number of the

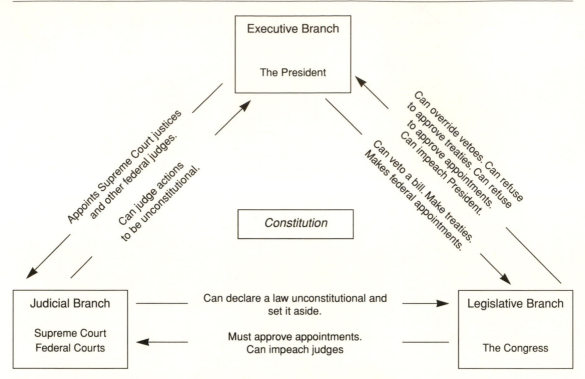

Executive Branch

The President

Appoints Supreme Court justices and other federal judges.
Can judge actions to be unconstitutional.

Constitution

Can override vetoes. Can refuse to approve treaties. Can refuse to approve appointments. Can impeach President.
Can veto a bill. Make treaties. Makes federal appointments.

Judicial Branch

Supreme Court
Federal Courts

Can declare a law unconstitutional and set it aside.

Must approve appointments.
Can impeach judges

Legislative Branch

The Congress

How the U.S. government's checks and balances work.

congressional districts are based on population. These districts change every ten years, after each national *census* is taken.

The laws must be enforced after Congress makes them. This enforcement is carried out by the *executive branch*. The president directs the executive branch of government, and must sign each bill before it can become law. The president may refuse to sign a bill, and thereby *veto* it. The veto power is a check by the president on Congress. But if two-thirds of the members of Congress pass the bill again, they override the veto and make the bill a law without the president's signature. This is a check by Congress on the president.

The Supreme Court heads the *judicial branch* of government. The Supreme Court consists of a chief justice and eight associate justices. The judicial branch sees to it that the legislative and executive branches of government obey the Constitu-

tion. The Supreme Court makes a final decision on whether any law conflicts with the Constitution. If it does, the court has the power to declare the law *unconstitutional,* and set it aside. Thus, the Supreme Court checks both the president and the Congress.

PRESIDENTIAL POWERS

The president is elected in November every four years, and takes office on 20 January of the next year, with the following oath of office: "I do solemnly swear (affirm) that I will faithfully execute the office of President of the United States, and will, to the best of my ability, preserve, protect, and defend the Constitution of the United States." Each member of the armed forces takes a similar oath. The president and all uniformed service people have the duty to defend the Constitution.

The president has the power, with agreement by the Senate, to make treaties. Also with the advice and consent of the Senate, the president appoints ambassadors, consuls, judges of the Supreme Court, members of the cabinet, and many other government officials.

The president must keep Congress advised on the nation's progress, and propose needed laws. One way this has come to be done is through the president's annual *State of the Union Address* given in January to each new Congress.

The president is the commander in chief of the armed forces of the United States in peace and in war, sharing power over the military with Congress, which makes rules, appropriates money, and declares war. The Senate confirms promotions of military officers made by the president.

In a war or other national emergency, the powers of the presidency are greatly enlarged. The president directs the armed forces on land, sea, and air and governs captured territory until Congress provides by law for its government by civilians. The president may declare an emergency prior to war and call out the military reserves, and the president may commit the armed forces to action before the declaration of war by Congress if the president decides such action is required.

THE PRESIDENT'S CABINET

The president is the head of the executive branch of the government. The vice president must know about all ongoing business, in order to take over if the president were to die or otherwise be unable to serve.

The president appoints, with the advice and consent of the Senate, the top officials in each of the various executive *departments*. These officials are called *secretaries*. Each secretary is a member of the president's *cabinet*, an important group that advises the president in all matters of government. The cabinet plays an important part in making policy, and doing the daily work of the executive branch.

There are fourteen executive departments of the federal government, each represented in the cabinet by a secretary: State, Treasury, Defense, Justice, Interior, Agriculture, Commerce, Labor,

Health and Human Services, Housing and Urban Development, Transportation, Energy, Education, and Veterans Affairs. The secretary of state is the highest-ranking cabinet officer. The secretary of defense is the cabinet officer in charge of military services.

In addition to the departmental secretaries, the president may appoint heads of various government agencies such as the National Economic Council to the cabinet as well.

NATIONAL SECURITY COUNCIL

In addition to the cabinet, the president has more than a dozen other groups and agencies that help in carrying out the many duties of the office. Among the more important of these is the National Security Council, the body that advises the president on national security. By law, the National Security Council is made up of the president, vice president, and secretaries of state and defense. Other executive officers and agency heads are called upon as needed for information and advice.

Since its formation in 1947, the National Security Council has played a very important role in meeting threats to U.S. security. The council gives advice on foreign aid and all foreign military alliances. The council makes recommendations on foreign policy. It gives advice on such things as disarmament, treaties, peaceful uses of atomic energy, assistance to other nations, and all significant military actions being taken or contemplated.

The matters taken up by the National Security Council affect all Americans. Since almost all of the council's actions affect the armed forces of the nation in one way or another, students of U.S. government and the NJROTC must be aware of it and its duties and importance.

DEPARTMENT OF DEFENSE

The Department of Defense (DoD) was created by Congress in 1949 to carry out U.S. military policies. DoD manages all matters concerning the U.S. armed forces. The department is headed by the secretary of defense (SecDef), who is a member of both the cabinet and the National Security Council. This person reports to the president on

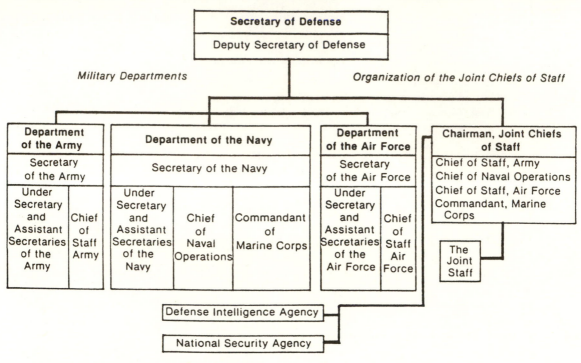

Organizational chart of the Department of Defense.

all military matters concerning the department.

Within the Department of Defense are the three service departments—Army, Navy, and Air Force. Each is headed by a civilian secretary who is not of cabinet rank.

Under this civilian secretary in each DoD department is the top uniformed officer of that service. They are the chief of staff, U.S. Army; the chief of naval operations; and the chief of staff, U.S. Air Force. These three officers together with the commandant of the Marine Corps form the *Joint Chiefs of Staff* (JCS), headed by a chairman who is selected by the president. (The U.S. Marine Corps is an independent organization under the secretary of the Navy. The commandant of the Marine Corps attends the meetings of the JCS as an equal with the other service chiefs, but only on matters that directly concern the Marine Corps.) The members of the JCS are the main military advisers to the president and the National Security Council. The JCS issues military orders to the operating forces of all three services.

The three military departments control all the equipment and personnel of the U.S. armed forces. The Army handles most military operations on land. The Air Force is responsible for land-based air and space operations. And the Navy has charge of sea-based air and naval forces. Almost all major military operations in recent years, however, have involved all three areas at once, so these have been handled by joint operating forces from all three services acting together.

DEPARTMENT OF THE NAVY

The Department of the Navy is made up of the following organizations and forces:
- The Navy Department (the executive part of the Department of the Navy), located in Washington, D.C.
- Headquarters, U.S. Marine Corps
- All operating forces, including naval aircraft, of the Navy and Marine Corps

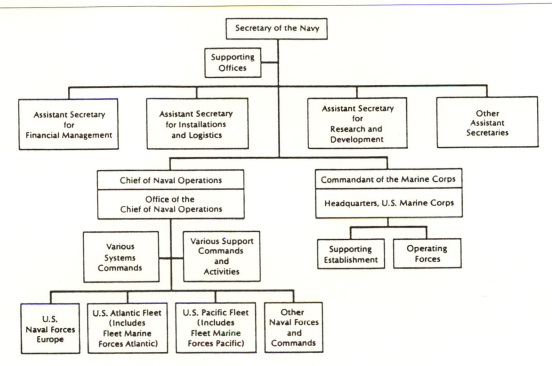

Organizational chart of the Department of the Navy.

- All shore or field activities and bases under the control of the secretary of the Navy
- The U.S. Coast Guard during wartime, or when the president directs

The chart above illustrates the basic organization of the Department of the Navy.

Secretary of the Navy

The secretary of the Navy (SecNav) is the head of the Department of the Navy, and reports to the secretary of defense. The SecNav is directly responsible for the Navy and Marine Corps. The secretary has a number of civilian assistants, the most important of whom is the undersecretary of the Navy. There are also several assistant secretaries who handle most of the day-to-day business of the department.

Chief of Naval Operations

The chief of naval operations (CNO) is the highest military officer in the Department of the Navy. The CNO is the main naval adviser to the president, the SecDef, and the SecNav, and is a member of the Joint Chiefs of Staff. The CNO manages the operating forces of the Navy and the Navy's shore establishment.

U.S. Coast Guard

The U.S. Coast Guard has a double role. By law it is a branch of the armed forces. Normally, it operates in the Department of Transportation. In war, however, it becomes part of the Navy and continues to perform its specialized duties, also taking part in some naval operations.

The Coast Guard's peacetime organization, training, and customs are like those of the Navy. Personnel receive the same pay and allowances as similar ranks and rates in the Navy.

The main jobs of the Coast Guard are law enforcement, port security, search and rescue, icebreaking and ice patrol, seizing of illegal drugs, safety, and maintenance of navigational aids. It enforces all federal laws upon the territorial seas and in U.S. waters.

The Coast Guard removes or destroys wrecks and other dangers to navigation. Its icebreakers open ice-blocked channels and ports. It maintains stations in the North Atlantic and North Pacific to provide weather services, communications, and navigation aids. Its cutters and patrol boats search and seize vessels trying to smuggle illegal drugs into U.S. ports.

In addition, the Coast Guard has many responsibilities relating to marine safety. It investigates disasters and collisions. It inspects ships and licenses officers, harbor pilots, and seamen. It enforces the rules for lights, signals, speed, steering, sailing, anchorage, and movement of vessels. It maintains aids to navigation such as lights, long-range electronic aids, radio beacons, radio direction-finder stations, buoys, and unlighted beacons.

U.S. MERCHANT MARINE

Though not a part of the Navy, the nation's merchant ships are an important part of our seapower. They make the entire world a market for our products. They bring to our ports the materials we need for our industries and carry to foreign ports the people and supplies we need there if we go to war.

The Federal Maritime Commission and the Maritime Administration, both in the Department of Commerce, are responsible for government programs concerned with the U.S. merchant marine. The commission regulates the rates and practices of ocean shipping lines. The Maritime Administration gives financial aid to companies, and directs programs of shipbuilding, ship operation, and reserve fleet maintenance. It also operates vessels carrying military goods, when privately owned or chartered vessels are not available at reasonable rates.

U.S. MARINE CORPS

The U.S. Marine Corps (USMC) has three combat divisions and three aircraft wings, along with land combat, aviation, and supporting services. The Fleet Marine Forces (FMF) are the main fighting forces of the USMC. The FMF includes all air and ground tactical units of the Ma-

rine Corps. It is organized into two commands: FMF Atlantic and FMF Pacific. The naval operating forces and the FMF are commonly referred to as the Navy-Marine Corps team, since they work together closely in any amphibious operation.

The Corps develops tactics, techniques, and equipment used in amphibious operations. The primary mission of the FMF is overseas amphibious operations. FMFs can seize and defend advance bases as part of a naval campaign. An FMF can perform nearly any military mission ashore, including land warfare.

In addition to the Fleet Marines, the Corps provides detachments (small groups) to serve on board large ships of the Navy, such as aircraft carriers. It also provides security detachments for naval stations, naval bases, and U.S. embassies in foreign countries.

The main U.S. Marine bases are at Camp Lejeune, North Carolina, and Camp Pendleton, California. Marine Corps air stations are located at Cherry Point, North Carolina, and El Toro, California, near the main bases. Marine Crops recruit depots are located at San Diego, California, and Parris Island, South Carolina. Quantico, Virginia, is the site of the Marine Corps schools where Marine officers receive basic and advanced military training.

SUMMARY

The bond between the nation, its people, its government, and its sea services is the U.S. Constitution. Based on rights of the individual, the Constitution provides the guidelines for our federal government. The Constitution gives powers to the government on the one hand, but protects the rights of its citizens on the other. Checks and balances between the executive, legislative, and judicial branches prevent any one branch from taking control.

The Constitution provides for the defense of the nation by military forces that serve under the president as commander in chief of the U.S. armed forces. The president, the department heads in the cabinet, and all commissioned officers and enlisted personnel in the uniformed services take a solemn oath to defend the Constitution of the United States.

The Department of Defense is the cabinet-level department that is most concerned with national defense. The secretary of defense, as manager of the nation's armed forces, sits on the National Security Council with the vice president and the secretary of state, to advise the president on vital matters affecting the security of the nation. The Joint Chiefs of Staff, made up of the senior military officers of each service, advise the president, the secretary of defense, and the National Security Council on military matters. They issue orders to all U.S. military operating forces.

The Department of the Navy, including the U.S. Marine Corps, and the Army and the Air Force provide the military forces to defend the nation. The Coast Guard and U.S. merchant marine perform special sea services that assist national defense as well. It can be said with pride that those who serve in the U.S. armed forces have a mission unique among U.S. citizens—to defend the Constitution and the rights of all the nation's people. There is no higher calling or more noble profession.

Chapter 1. Study Guide Questions

1. Why is the Constitution said to be the best basis for government ever composed?

2. What did the Founding Fathers believe to be the first duty of government?

3. What must all citizens do to help safeguard our nation and our rights?

4. Why didn't the Articles of Confederation work very well?

5. What are the first ten amendments to the Constitution called?

6. What are the three branches of U.S. government?

7. What is meant by "checks and balances" in U.S. government?

8. What is the basic similarity between the oaths of office taken by the president and by all members of the armed forces?

9. What is the purpose of the State of the Union Address?

10. What is the president's relationship with the U.S. armed forces?

11. A. What executive departments are represented in the president's cabinet?

B. Who is the highest-ranking cabinet officer?

12. Which federal officials are, by law, on the National Security Council?

13. What are the three departments in the Department of Defense (DoD)?

14. Who are the members of the Joint Chiefs of Staff?

15. Who is the chief civilian official of the Department of the Navy?

16. Who is the highest-ranking military officer in the Department of the Navy?

17. A. In peacetime, to which government department does the U.S. Coast Guard belong?

B. In wartime?

18. What are the main responsibilities of the Coast Guard?

19. Why is the U.S. merchant marine an important part of U.S. sea power?

20. What is the primary purpose of the Fleet Marine Force?

Vocabulary

Constitution	congressional district
government	law enforcement
Declaration of	veto
Independence	override (veto)
unalienable rights	unconstitutional
Articles of	"advice and consent"
Confederation	commander in chief
checks and balances	president's cabinet
executive branch	National Security
legislative branch	Council
judicial branch	foreign policy
federal system	disarmament
compromise	DoD, SecDef
Bill of Rights	CNO
oath of office	JCS
republic	SecNav
direct democracy	sabotage
representative	merchant marine
democracy	FMF
appropriate (money)	Marine detachment
census	

Chapter 2. Our Navy and Its People

No matter how far we go in technology, there is no substitute for the efforts of good naval personnel—the men and women who *are* the Navy. They are the ones who make it all work

The Navy is a young person's profession. The average age of all people in the Navy is about twenty years; the average age of officers is less than thirty. Most career enlisted enter the Navy at about eighteen. Most officers are commissioned at twenty-one or twenty-two. The Navy needs young, energetic people with new ideas, able and willing to adapt to a changing world.

Today's Navy is a large organization. Its job is bigger and more important than ever before. It must carry out the national policies of Congress and the president. It must support our forces and our allies. It must protect the rights of ships to move freely on the oceans. It must provide a first line of defense in protecting our country against foreign enemies.

To carry out these tasks, the Navy must be able to operate on and under the sea, in the air, and on shores all over the world. Within the Navy, there are many types of jobs.

CITIZENSHIP AND THE NAVY

Not every navy man or woman is a career navy person. In fact, most officers and enlisted personnel do not intend to make the service their career. However, while they wear the uniform of the naval

	WARRANT				COMMISSIONED									
	W-1	W-2	W-3	W-4	O-1	O-2	O-3	O-4	O-5	O-6	O-7	0-7 – 0-8	0-9 – 0-10	
NAVY	WARRANT OFFICER W1	CHIEF WARRANT OFFICER W2	CHIEF WARRANT OFFICER W3	CHIEF WARRANT OFFICER W4	ENSIGN	LIEUTENANT JUNIOR GRADE	LIEUTENANT	LIEUTENANT COMMANDER	COMMANDER	CAPTAIN	REAR ADMIRAL (LOWER HALF)	REAR ADMIRAL (UPPER HALF)	VICE ADMIRAL	ADMIRAL
MARINE CORPS	WARRANT OFFICER W1	CHIEF WARRANT OFFICER W2	CHIEF WARRANT OFFICER W3	CHIEF WARRANT OFFICER W4	SECOND LIEUTENANT	FIRST LIEUTENANT	CAPTAIN	MAJOR	LIEUTENANT COLONEL	COLONEL	BRIGADIER GENERAL	MAJOR GENERAL	LIEUTENANT GENERAL	GENERAL
ARMY	WARRANT OFFICER W1	CHIEF WARRANT OFFICER W2	CHIEF WARRANT OFFICER W3	CHIEF WARRANT OFFICER W4	SECOND LIEUTENANT	FIRST LIEUTENANT	CAPTAIN	MAJOR	LIEUTENANT COLONEL	COLONEL	BRIGADIER GENERAL	MAJOR GENERAL	LIEUTENANT GENERAL	GENERAL
AIR FORCE	WARRANT OFFICER W1	CHIEF WARRANT OFFICER W2	CHIEF WARRANT OFFICER W3	CHIEF WARRANT OFFICER W4	SECOND LIEUTENANT	LIEUTENANT	CAPTAIN	MAJOR	LIEUTENANT COLONEL	COLONEL	BRIGADIER GENERAL	MAJOR GENERAL	LIEUTENANT GENERAL	GENERAL

Chart of officer ranks in the U.S. armed services.

ENLISTED

PAY GRADE	E-1	E-2	E-3	E-4	E-5	E-6	E-7	E-8	E-9	E-9
NAVY	SEAMAN RECRUIT	SEAMAN APPRENTICE	SEAMAN	PETTY OFFICER THIRD CLASS	PETTY OFFICER SECOND CLASS	PETTY OFFICER FIRST CLASS	CHIEF PETTY OFFICER	SENIOR CHIEF PETTY OFFICER	MASTER CHIEF PETTY OFFICER	MASTER CHIEF PETTY OFFICER OF THE NAVY
MARINES	PRIVATE	PRIVATE FIRST CLASS	LANCE CORPORAL	CORPORAL	SERGEANT	STAFF SERGEANT	GUNNERY SERGEANT	1ST SGT / MSGT	SGT MAJOR / MGY SGT	SGT MAJOR OF THE MARINE CORPS
ARMY	PRIVATE	PRIVATE	PRIVATE FIRST CLASS	CORPORAL / SPECIALIST 4	SERGEANT / SPECIALIST 5	STAFF SERGEANT / SPECIALIST 6	SERGEANT FIRST CLASS / SPECIALIST 7	1ST SGT / MSGT	SERGEANT MAJOR	SERGEANT MAJOR OF THE ARMY
AIR FORCE	AIRMAN BASIC	AIRMAN	AIRMAN FIRST CLASS	SERGEANT	STAFF SERGEANT	TECHNICAL SERGEANT	MASTER SERGEANT	SENIOR MASTER SERGEANT	CHIEF MASTER SERGEANT	CHIEF MASTER SERGEANT OF THE AIR FORCE

Chart of naval enlisted rates and their counterparts in other U.S. armed forces.

service, they contribute a great deal. After they leave the Navy, many veterans continue to serve and support the active-duty Navy through belonging to the Naval Reserve, various veterans' organizations, and other civic groups.

Part of the purpose of the NJROTC program is to make cadets better citizens through knowing more about our country and its armed forces. The program also asks cadets to begin to think about their futures, their goals in life, and how they can contribute to our society. Big tasks for freshmen and sophomores in high school? Yes, indeed! But

Aerographer's Mate (AG)

Air Traffic Controller (AC)

Aircrew Survival Equipmentman (PR)

Aviation Antisubmarine Warfare Operator (AW)

Aviation Boatswain's Mate (AB)

Aviation Electrician's Mate (AE)

Aviation Electronics Technician (AT)

Aviation Fire Control Technician (AQ)

Aviation Machinist's Mate (AD)

Aviation Maintenance Administrationman (AZ)

Aviation Ordnanceman (AO)

Aviation Storekeeper (AK)

Aviation Structural Mechanic (AM)

Aviation Support Equipment Technician (AS)

Boatswain's Mate (BM)

Builder (BU)

Construction Electrician (CE)

Construction Mechanic (CM)

Cryptologic Technician (CT)

Damage Controlman (DC)

Data Systems Technician (DS)

Dental Technician (DT)

Disbursing Clerk (DK)

Electrician's Mate (EM)

Electronics Technician (ET)

Electronics Warfare Technician (EW)

Engineering Aide (EA)

Engineman (EN)

Equipment Operator (EO)

Fire Controlman (FC)

Fire Control Technician (FT)

Gas Turbine System Technician (GS)

Enlisted specialty ratings in the U.S. Navy as of January 1996.

Gunner's
Mate (GM)

Hospital
Corpsman (HM)

Hull Maintenance
Technician (HT)

Illustrator-
Draftsman (DM)

Instrumentman
(IM)

Intelligence
Specialist (IS)

Journalist (JO)

Legalman (LN)

Lithographer (LI)

Machinery
Repairman (MR)

Machinist's
Mate (MM)

Master-at-Arms
(MA)

Mess Management
Specialist (MS)

Mineman (MN)

Missile
Technician (MT)

Musician (MU)

Navy Counselor
(NC)

Operations
Specialist (OS)

Opticalman (OM)

Patternmaker
(PM)

Personnelman
(PN)

Photographer's
Mate (PH)

Postal Clerk (PC)

Quartermaster
(QM)

Radioman (RM)

Religious Program
Specialist (RP)

Ship's
Serviceman (SH)

Signalman (SM)

Sonar
Technician (ST)

Steelworker (SW)

Storekeeper (SK)

Utilitiesman (UT)

Yeoman (YN)

only by starting out on the right foot early in life can young people be successful in their lives and careers as adults.

THE NAVY AS AN OCCUPATION

The Navy is *big*—nearly 300 ships, about 4,000 small craft, 5,000 aircraft, and a force of nearly a million men and women working as officers, enlisteds, and civilian employees. The Navy is one of the top employers in the United States. It is an ideal place for a young man or woman to find an important and rewarding career. In the Navy, a young person can be someone *special.*

The men and women who do the Navy's jobs come from every part of the country and every walk of life. All have the same chance to advance and to develop their skills fully. The Navy gives equal opportunity for all, regardless of race, color, creed, national origin, or gender. This policy means that promotions are based on a person's ability and experience. In the Navy, how well a ship works as a fighting unit depends on teamwork. No prejudices can be held over from civilian life.

NAVAL RANKS AND RATES

Because the Navy is new to you, you surely have questions concerning ranks and rates. Commissioned officers have *ranks* and enlisted personnel have *rates* and *ratings.* An officer's rank refers to his or her official title: ensign, lieutenant (junior grade), lieutenant, lieutenant commander, commander, captain, rear admiral (lower half), rear admiral (upper half), vice admiral, and admiral. The rank also indicates the officer's *pay grade*—that is, the amount of pay received monthly. Pay grade is shown on a rank chart as 0-1, 0-2, and so on up to 0-10, meaning officer pay level 1, 2, and so forth. See the chart on page 72.

Enlisted personnel have similar titles and pay grades. The lowest three pay grades are in the general apprenticeship area before advancement to petty officer pay grades. The general apprentices are divided into six groups: seamen, firemen, constructionmen, airmen, hospitalmen, and dentalmen. The three pay grades are E-1, E-2, and E-3, meaning enlisted pay grades 1, 2, and 3. Another name for enlisted pay grade is *rate.* The enlisted rates are shown in the chart on page 73.

Enlisted personnel can also have petty officer rates, E-4 through E-9. These are petty officer third class, second class, first class, chief petty officer, senior chief petty officer, and master chief petty officer. The petty officer level is the pay grade or rate.

Petty officers wear special insignia to show that they are qualified in certain skills. These insignia are called *ratings.* Specialty ratings in the Navy are divided into ten groups, in which there are about seventy different rating or occupation groups. Many of these are like the various kind of *trades* in civilian life. A petty officer's rating badge, worn on the upper left sleeve, indicates both the rate and rating. The various naval ratings now available are shown on pages 74 and 75.

A person qualified to take the advancement examination for petty officer will wear the special mark of his or her rating over the apprentice stripes. This indicates that the person is *striking* for petty-officer rate in that rating specialty. Such an individual is often called a *designated striker* for the rating.

When officers move up to the next rank and pay grade, they have earned a *promotion.* When enlisted personnel move up to the next higher rate in their rating specialty, they have *advanced* in rate.

Senior specialists who supervise the operation of equipment and weapons, and the enlisteds who maintain them, are called *warrant officers.* They bridge the gap between commissioned officers and enlisted personnel. Warrant officers are former enlisteds selected for warrant status because of their ability and leadership qualities. They are like journeymen or master tradesmen in civilian life.

There are four warrant pay grades in the Navy, W-1 through W-4. Personnel in grade W-1 are called warrant officers, and receive their warrants from the secretary of the Navy. Those in the three higher grades are commissioned, and are called chief warrant officers.

Warrant officers wear collar devices or sleeve insignia to show their specialty. Warrant-officer rank insignia are shown in the chart on page 72.

Chapter 2. Study Guide Questions

1. Why is the Navy called a young person's profession?
2. What are the Navy's important jobs?
3. What is the Navy's policy concerning opportunity for all personnel?
4. List the officers' pay grades and ranks, from most junior to most senior.
5. List the pay grades and rates of enlisted personnel from junior to senior.
6. What are the six general apprentice groups?
7. What are enlisted *ratings*?
8. Where do warrant officers fit in the chain of command?

Vocabulary

career	pay grade
rank	apprentice
ensign	rate
lieutenant (junior grade)	rating
lieutenant	promotion (in rank)
lieutenant commander	advancement (in rate)
commander	warrant officer
captain	petty officer
admiral	veteran

Chapter 3. Commissioned Officers in the Navy

Command is the authority by which an individual may require subordinates to obey lawful orders. The levels from high to low through which command is exercised are known as the *chain of command*. A ship, for example, has a commanding officer, called the captain, who is a commissioned line officer of any rank. All persons serving on board that ship are under the captain's command. The next most senior officer, the executive officer, is second in command. And so on, down through the officer ranks.

Commissioned officers hold their positions of command under the authority given them by the president of the United States. A *grade* (called a rank) is a level to which officers are appointed. An officer of a given grade is *junior* to all officers of higher grade, and *senior* to all officers of lower grade and all enlisted personnel.

Officers are also divided into *line officers* and *staff corps officers*. Line officers wear a star on their sleeve and shoulders boards. A line officer is either unrestricted or restricted line. *Unrestricted line officers* are eligible for command at sea and the command of aircraft squadrons, fleets, and major shore commands. *Restricted line officers* have special duties in engineering, naval intelligence, public affairs, communications, cryptology, oceanography, or meteorology. They are not eligible for command at sea, but may assume command of certain shore facilities.

Staff corps officers are specialists in certain areas, such as supply, medicine, dentistry, law, civil engineering, and chaplains. They wear special staff corps insignia, along with their insignia of rank. They cannot command a ship or an air squadron. A doctor can become a commanding officer of a hospital or medical school. A supply officer can become commanding officer of a supply depot or supply school.

Officer Qualifications

An officer of the U.S. Navy must be capable of carrying out a wide variety of duties at sea and ashore.

An officer candidate must be between eighteen and twenty-eight years old, a U.S. citizen, physically fit, and must have a college degree.

Any physically fit college-bound man or woman who meets the qualifications can work toward a naval officer's commission. There are many programs for students desiring to seek a commission. Two programs of great interest to young NJROTC cadets considering possible careers in the Navy are the U.S. Naval Academy and the Naval Reserve Officer Training Corps (NROTC) college scholarship programs.

THE UNITED STATES NAVAL ACADEMY

Located on the Severn River near the Chesapeake Bay at Annapolis, Maryland, the Naval Academy is the undergraduate professional college of the Navy. It is one of the country's most selective institutions of higher learning. The Academy offers a fine education to outstanding young men and women who have the ability, character, and desire to assume high leadership responsibilities.

There may be as many as five midshipmen from each congressional district and for each senator in the Academy at any one time. There are also presidential, vice presidential, Regular Navy and Marine Corps, Naval and Marine Corps Reserve, NROTC, NJROTC, and honor naval schools, and secretary of the Navy appointments.

During the four years at the Academy, midshipmen receive an excellent academic and professional education. Classroom and laboratory work is combined with practical application, at the Academy and on summer cruises with the fleet. During summer indoctrination periods, midshipmen are introduced to all areas of the service: submarines, aviation, surface ships, and the Marine Corps.

Upon graduation, the new officer receives a Bachelor of Science degree and a commission as an ensign in the U.S. Naval Reserve or as a second lieutenant in the U.S. Marine Corps Reserve.

Midshipmen at Annapolis earn their college educations at no expense to their families. The government provides all tuition, room and board, and medical and dental care. Additionally, midshipmen earn a generous salary, currently about $750 per month. This covers the cost of uniforms, books, equipment, laundry, and incidentals.

THE NAVAL ACADEMY MISSION

The purpose of the Naval Academy is to prepare young men and women to become professional line officers in the Navy or Marine Corps. No one requires that an entering midshipman have firmly made up his or her mind to be a career

officer in the naval service. But a midshipman should not arrive at Annapolis planning to work toward some entirely different goal. If your primary interests lie in such fields as medicine, law, education, nursing, the ministry, or ecology, the Naval Academy is not the place for you to get your college education.

Graduates must serve as an officer in the Navy or Marine Corps for at least six years after graduation.

NAVAL ACADEMY REQUIREMENTS

Candidates for the Naval Academy should pursue studies in high school that will prepare them for a rigorous college program. The *quality* of the work is important. Three out of four candidates accepted for Annapolis come from the top 20 percent of their high school classes.

Those high school students who think they may want to try for a Naval Academy appointment (or for that matter any other academy appointment or ROTC scholarship) need to start to plan early in their high school careers to take the courses necessary to make themselves qualified. Candidates are strongly urged to include in their high school studies:

1. *Mathematics.* Four years, including trigonometry, are advised; also computer math and calculus, if offered.
2. *English.* Four years, emphasizing written composition, are recommended; speech, journalism, and debate are helpful.
3. *Sciences.* One year each of chemistry and physics is considered necessary, in addition to a year of general science or biology.
4. *Foreign language.* It is helpful, though not required, for students to have two years of a modern foreign language such as German, Spanish, French, or Russian. Two years of any given language is required of all humanities and social science majors in the Academy. A sound high school background in a foreign language is recommended if a person is planning to become proficient in that language at the Academy.

AP (advanced placement) courses offered in any of these areas are highly recommended.

Naval Academy courses include studies in a wide range of academic subjects designed to prepare midshipmen for their careers as naval officers.

The Naval Academy yard patrol (YP) squadron provides much training in the art of seamanship and shiphandling.

The course work in high school should be geared toward taking the Scholastic Aptitude Test (SAT) or the American College Testing Program (ACT) tests during the junior year. These tests must be taken no later than February of the year of admission to Annapolis. Candidates taking a test more than once will be credited with their highest scores.

High school backgrounds in athletics, school honors, extracurricular activities, and part-time work are very important considerations in selecting Academy appointees. These activities and honors show that a person can be a leader. They also indicate that the person will be able to devote the time he or she must at the Academy to military, physical, and leadership training, and keep his or her grades up at the same time.

Initial applications for the U.S. Naval Academy (or other service academies) should be made in the spring of the junior year in high school.

NAVAL ACADEMY ATHLETICS

The Naval Academy's intercollegiate athletic program is one of the largest in the nation. Academy athletics are big, nationally known, and respected. Army traditionally is Navy's top athletic opponent, and the service rivals compete in many varsity and junior varsity sports during the athletic year. Annapolis teams also face other collegiate powers in every sport—Notre Dame in football, Lehigh in wrestling, Harvard and Pennsylvania in crew, and schools such as Saint Bonaventure, Air Force Academy, and Army in basketball, to name a few. Navy football teams have participated in the Sugar, Orange, Cotton, and Holiday bowls. Each year the team competes for the Commander in Chief trophy with Army and Air Force. The Navy basketball team has been in the NCAA tournament several times in recent years.

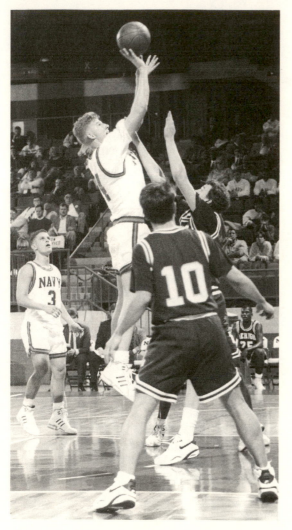

The Navy basketball program has made great strides in recent years, appearing in the NCAA tournament several times.

Some of these, in addition to the varsity sports already mentioned, are badminton, bowling, boxing, field ball, handball, ice hockey, knockabout sailing, lacrosse, rugby, softball, squash, swimming, touch football, volleyball, water polo, weightlifting, and wrestling.

THE NROTC PROGRAM

The Naval Reserve Officer Training Corps (NROTC) program develops officers from units at some sixty-five top colleges and universities. Officer candidate selection for NROTC, like the Naval Academy, is very competitive, with about 10 percent of those applying being selected for a four-year scholarship.

The NROTC is similar to NJROTC, in that NROTC midshipmen take college-level naval science courses plus other, nonmilitary courses required for graduation. There are two types of NROTC programs: the two-, three-, and four-year scholarship program, and the two- and four-year nonscholarship program, called the college program.

Applications for the NROTC *scholarship program* are accepted beginning in the spring of the junior year in high school. An academically qualified applicant is required to take a physical examination. The candidate also has an interview by a board of officers. Then the application is forwarded to a selection committee that decides on appointments. If accepted, the candidate officially takes the oath of appointment as a midshipman, United States Naval Reserve.

The Navy requires that NROTC midshipmen have a strong background in physics and mathematics and in written and spoken English. Scholarship students are permitted to select a field of study leading to a baccalaureate (bachelor's) degree in any area of study deemed of value to the Navy. Midshipmen can participate in extracurricular activities offered by the school, as long as they do not directly conflict with naval science classes and drills (normally held once per week). Either varsity or intramural athletics are encouraged.

The NROTC midshipman has the same summer cruises as a Naval Academy midshipman. The

There are also a growing number of women's varsity and junior varsity teams, including basketball, volleyball, swimming, crew, and soccer.

Perhaps even more a part of Annapolis life is the intramural sports program. Every midshipman, except for varsity athletes, must take part. There are some twenty-five intramural sports.

These NROTC midshipmen at the University of San Diego enjoy a walk between classes.

two groups are usually mixed together on cruises to ensure that both get the same professional training.

The NROTC scholarship midshipman receives full tuition at the host college or university, laboratory and administrative fees, uniforms, and $100 a month for other expenses. Room and board is not normally paid, although some schools offer free room and board as an incentive for using the NROTC scholarship to attend their institution. Midshipmen are advised to live in university dormitories for at least the first two years of college, for better study and to keep expenses low.

College program students receive uniforms and all books needed for their naval science courses. During the junior and senior years, they receive an expense allowance of $100 a month. Students apply for this program after they get into one of the colleges and universities that host NROTC programs.

Currently, graduates of the NROTC scholarship program must serve on active duty for at least four years. College program graduates must serve for three years.

MEDICAL AND PHYSICAL QUALIFICATIONS

Nominees to the Naval Academy, other service academies, and ROTCs must pass both a medical examination and a physical aptitude test. Candidates must be physically fit and sound in body and mind.

All sea service pilot programs require 20/20 vision in each eye. However, waivers may be granted to some candidates whose vision is correctable to 20/20 with glasses or contact lenses. Color blindness is disqualifying.

ADVANTAGES OF THE NAVAL ACADEMY AND NROTC

Upon graduation, Naval Academy and NROTC graduates are commissioned as Navy ensigns or Marine Corps second lieutenants. Promotion opportunities and full service benefits are enjoyed during the period of obligated service. Following obligated service, officers may choose the service for a career. Or they may choose release from active duty and a Naval Reserve or Marine Corps Reserve commission.

Many career choices are available to graduates of both the Naval Academy and NROTC. The Navy offers careers in aviation, nuclear submarines, nuclear surface ships, and conventional ships such as destroyers, cruisers, aircraft carriers, amphibious ships, and mobile replenishment ships. The Marine Corps offers careers in aviation, infantry, armor, artillery, communications, and logistics.

Career challenges will continue. Duties at sea alternate with assignments ashore, both in the United States and overseas. Chances to travel are part of the job for both officers and their families. Life is never routine. At intervals of two to three years, new and more responsible assignments provide a fresh challenge, new friends, and often, a new community. Each year, every person in the service accrues thirty days of paid leave for rest and recreation.

Beginning with completion of twenty years'

Part of the Navy BOOST school buildings at San Diego, California.

commissioned service, an officer is eligible to retire with a pension, still young enough to begin a new career. Many officers continue their careers for longer periods, as long as thirty years, at which point they receive three-quarters pay. Commissary, exchange, medical, dental, and insurance privileges continue throughout the life of the retiree.

The Boost Program

Some young men and women in NJROTC or junior enlisted ranks in the Navy may have the desire and potential to be commissioned officers, but may not have good enough high school academic backgrounds to qualify directly for the Naval Academy or NROTC program. This may be especially true for minority students in less advantaged school districts. For this type of young person, the Navy has available a program called BOOST (Broadened Opportunity for Officer Selection and Training). To be eligible for the program, candidates must be younger than twenty-one as of 1 July of the year they enter the program, with SAT scores above 390 (verbal) and 460 (math). Those interested in trying for the Naval Academy must be unmarried with no dependents.

Selected BOOST candidates not already in the Navy enlist, and are then sent to boot camp. This is immediately followed by a one-year college prep program at the Naval Training Center, San Diego, California. There they study mathematics, English, physical science, and general campus skills for six hours a day (except for Christmas vacation) from June of the entering year to June of the following year. Upon satisfactory completion of the program, graduates may apply for either a Naval Academy appointment if they are in the top 10 to 20 percent of their class, or a four-year NROTC scholarship. The Navy guarantees an NROTC scholarship to all qualified BOOST graduates who do not get an Academy appointment.

The BOOST program offers a great chance for a college scholarship, followed by a commission in the Navy or Marine Corps, for otherwise highly motivated high school graduates with diverse academic backgrounds. Full details on the program are available from your NSI or local Navy officer recruiter.

Preparatory Schools

There are a number of one-year college prep schools, both public and private, that, similar to the BOOST program, specialize in preparing qualified young men and woman with weak academic backgrounds for the service academies. One of the best-known of these is the Naval Academy Prep School (NAPS), located at Newport, Rhode Island. Prospective attendees include both civilians and Navy enlisted personnel who must build their academic skills prior to receiving an Academy appointment. Candidate requirements are similar to those of the BOOST program.

The U.S. Merchant Marine Academy

The U.S. Merchant Marine Academy was briefly introduced in the first chapter of this unit.

Qualifications for entrance to the Academy—academic, physical, and personal—are the same as those for Naval Academy or NROTC scholarships. All Merchant Marine Academy midshipmen take a program of naval science courses taught by naval instructors.

Following graduation, the new officer must

serve on active duty with the Navy for three years, or be in the Naval Reserve for eight years, or sail on board a U.S.-flag merchant ship for the next three or four years, depending upon his or her commissioning program. Today, Academy graduates serve in all parts of the maritime industry as ship's officers, steamship company executives, admiralty lawyers, marine underwriters, naval architects, and oceanographers. They also serve as career officers in the U.S. Navy and Coast Guard, and the National Oceanographic and Atmospheric Administration (NOAA).

OTHER SOURCES OF COMMISSIONS

In addition to the Naval and Merchant Marine academies and the NROTC program, there are several other ways to get a commission in the Navy. For the most part, all involve attending college as a civilian first, then applying for a commission afterward.

Officer Candidate School (OCS) is a large post-college officer commissioning program, and the only source for a commission in such specialized career fields as naval chaplain, lawyer, and dentist. Candidates for OCS must have earned a bachelor's degree in any academic area satisfactory to the Navy from an accredited college or university, and must pass an OCS qualification test. Once accepted, candidates take an intensive program of instruction in naval science at Pensacola, Florida, following which they are commissioned. The current service obligation for this program is three years of active duty.

In addition to the programs described in this chapter that are designed mostly for civilians who wish to become naval officers, there are also several programs open to both active duty and reserve naval enlisted personnel who show that they are capable of assuming the increased responsibilities that commissioned service would bring. These programs tend to change from time to time, so they will not be covered in the *Naval Science* texts. Full information on these programs is available from your local naval recruiter, or from the career counselor on board naval ships, shore stations, and reserve units.

More detailed information on all the programs covered in this chapter will be presented in Volumes 2 and 3 of the *Naval Science* series. Additional information on any of them can also be obtained from your NSI or your regional naval officer recruiter.

Chapter 3. Study Guide Questions

1. A. What is command?

     B. What are the levels of command from highest to lowest called?

2. What are the general abilities that an officer is expected to have?

3. What is the purpose of the U.S. Naval Academy?

4. What subjects does the Academy recommend that candidates take during high school?

5. What activities are recommended in high school for the person who wants to try for a Naval Academy appointment?

6. What are some of the sports that are in the Naval Academy's intercollegiate athletics program?

7. A. What is the NROTC scholarship program?

     B. Where are NROTC units located?

8. What are the academic requirements for NROTC candidates?

9. What are the financial benefits of the NROTC scholarship program?

10. How is NROTC similar to NJROTC?

11. What is the BOOST program?

12. What college programs are available to successful graduates of the BOOST program?

Vocabulary

command	candidate
qualifications	intercollegiate athletics
commission	intramurals
line officer	waiver
staff corps officer	OCS
midshipman	BOOST
nomination	NROTC
appointment	tuition

Chapter 4.   Enlistment in the Navy

As you read earlier, the Navy is a large organization. It offers jobs at many different levels of responsibility. When a person joins the U.S. Navy, he or she becomes a member of one of the most renowned military services in the world. This chapter will discuss some of the requirements for enlisting in the world's finest navy.

Navy Enlistment Opportunities

Naval ships at sea are like small towns. They have their own telephone repairmen, firemen, and cooks. They have laundries, barber shops, post offices, and medical centers. They have experts of every kind, people who can provide almost anything the ship may need. The same can be said of the Navy's shore bases in many parts of the world. That's why today's navy men and women have more choices of rating than ever before. There are some seventy different specialty ratings for enlisted personnel in the Navy.

All people want the chance to prove themselves, but sometimes it takes years to get the chance. Everyone who joins the Navy gets that chance right away. The Navy gives a person a golden opportunity to learn, train, and accept responsibility at an early age. Advancement for enlisted ratings is based on ability and performance. Every young man and woman—regardless of race, color, religion, or national origin—gets that same chance.

A high school education or its equivalent is generally needed for a person to be able to take many of the training programs in our modern Navy. A high school diploma is required for certain technical, electronics, and nuclear power programs. Ships still need sailors to perform many tasks that aren't too technical. But today's sailor also can be an operations specialist guiding a destroyer through an Atlantic fog by radar, a sonarman sounding depths from a nuclear submarine, a computer programmer at a modern supply center, an engineering technician overseeing the operation of the ship's power plant, or an aircrewman soaring high above the clouds.

Enlisted service in the Navy is an exciting opportunity for people who want to prove themselves. A high school education is normally required for one to take part in modern naval training. Here, a naval recruiter talks with students at a California school.

Today's all-volunteer Navy offers young men and women a richly rewarding life. Naval life is challenging because the jobs that naval people do require training, dedication, skill, and hard work. If a person has what it takes to be a part of the Navy's team, the challenge will make it well worth the effort.

Naval Enlisted Training

The Navy sets high standards for the new naval recruit right from the beginning of boot camp (recruit training). Each person must learn to meet those standards. Such things as being on time for formations, wearing proper uniform, and being ready for whatever task is assigned become a normal part of the day. The Navy's standards must be high because ships depend totally on their crews for operation and upkeep while at sea. And shore stations must be fully prepared to support the ships of the fleet when they come into port.

What an individual does, or how far he or she goes in the Navy, depends pretty much on that person. The new recruit can apply for schooling in a specialty area before signing up. If he or she is qualified, the Navy will guarantee to send that person to a Class "A" school for that training. Education is important throughout a naval career.

We already have learned that officers' programs require good backgrounds in mathematics, sciences, and English. These same courses are important in preparing for the many technical ratings in the Navy today, such as electronics, communications, electricity, data processing, mechanics, aviation, and construction. The Navy's training in radar, electronics, computers, and nuclear power is the best you can get anywhere. Some young people join the Navy, get superior technical training, and then, at the end of their enlistment or upon early retirement, use that training and education to get a good job in civilian life.

Three important technical areas now offer great chances for training, education, and service. These are nuclear power, electronics, and the advanced technical fields. Special naval programs offer qualified young people a chance to train for careers in these areas.

The training in all three of these programs is tough—it's not for just anyone. But smart people can make it, as long as they have the ambition. A sound preparation in high school is generally the key to success in these programs. They call for a lot of serious studying—as much as two years, in some instances—so these candidates must extend their enlistments two years beyond the regular enlistments. That extra time is used for on-the-job experience that will be helpful later. This training may be compared—although it is much more thorough—with that received in a two-year vocational technical school after high school.

Besides the training itself, another benefit of the technical training programs is that those qualifying enter the Navy at pay grade E-3, instead of E-1 like the usual enlistee. Upon graduating, these

There are many technical ratings in the aviation group. Here, an aviation machinist's mate is making some preflight adjustments on the engine of an S–3 Viking jet. This plane's job is to locate and attack enemy submarines—called anti-submarine warfare.

people also tend to advance faster than those in other less technical ratings.

THE NAVAL RECRUITER

The Navy is a large and complicated organization, with many different jobs at varying levels of responsibility. Someone has to find people to fill these jobs. That person is the naval recruiter. All larger cities have a Navy Recruiting Office staffed by a number of senior petty officers. Smaller communities are visited regularly by recruiters. The recruiters must find people who are interested in and qualified for the Navy's jobs. They explain to these young people the rewards and benefits of naval life. They are very interested in finding young men and women who want to build careers based on naval education and training programs. They are ready to provide details on these programs, and are the most up-to-date source of information on naval careers.

Usually the naval recruiters in a given area do a lot with local high school NJROTC units. The recruiters will sometimes sponsor programs or films about the Navy for the unit or the whole student body. Recruiting Office personnel should be invited to the annual NJROTC military ball. The recruiters are good people to get to know. They can answer many questions about the Navy and have booklets to give out that describe enlisted naval programs in detail.

THE PERSONAL CHALLENGE: A SUMMARY

The Navy is an exciting challenge. Young men and women willing to work hard can take advantage of the modern Navy's many opportunities. The Navy is a great place to make good—because the Navy knows that, even with the finest ships and latest equipment, good people are the most important thing in the Navy. It is *people* who defend the nation, and if need be, win its wars. The officers and enlisted personnel of today's Navy must work together as a team. Only in this way can the Navy achieve its mission.

The NJROTC, as an early but important part of the Navy's educational program, has its role to play as well. Becoming a better U.S. citizen is a task every NJROTC cadet should take seriously. Just as the seaman's role on board ship is important, so is the role of the new cadet. Seamen sail the ships, fire the guns and missiles, crew the boats, receive the communications, handle the lines, and stand the watches; without them, the Navy couldn't do its job. Junior cadets fill the ranks of the NJROTC marching unit; learn the tasks of petty officers; and acquire the skills of the color guard, drill teams, and rifle teams. They must learn to follow the orders of cadet officers, cadet petty officers, and NSIs. Only by learning to be a follower can you gain the experience and knowledge that will prepare you to lead.

Each time you advance in rate, you earn self-respect and confidence. As honest pride develops, you will feel a sense of responsibility toward your unit, school, fellow cadets and classmates, and yourself. In the Navy your rewards would include higher pay and allowances in addition to other awards. But in both the Navy and the NJROTC, the really important benefit is the chance for greater use of your abilities. By learning to serve your unit better, you will get the experience you need to serve your country and community. You have shown, by entering the NJROTC, that you want to learn about your Navy and your nation, and that you want to become a good citizen and leader as an adult. Now is the time to start getting ready.

Chapter 4. Study Guide Questions

1. How are naval ships like small towns?
2. Why is naval life challenging?
3. How much education is considered necessary in naval technical training programs?
4. What largely determines how far a person advances in rate and responsibility in the Navy?
5. Which three technical rating areas offer exceptional opportunities in the Navy today?
6. Who is the person assigned the duty of finding qualified people for enlistment in the Navy?
7. What happens each time a cadet advances in rate in the NJROTC?

Vocabulary

enlistment	guarantee
retirement	recruit, recruiter
technical training	scholarship
golden opportunity	data processing
diploma	nuclear power
sonarman	on-the-job training
computer programmer	boot camp

5

Sea Power and Maritime Geography

Chapter 1.   Sea Power: Our Forward Line of Defense

Sea power is a nation's ability to make use of the oceans. These uses may be political, economic, or military—in peace or war. The main parts of sea power are naval power, ocean science, ocean industry, and ocean commerce.

Our Navy has two missions: to control the seas for ourselves and our allies, and to deny the use of the seas to our enemies. Our naval and maritime power is made up of many things. These include combat ships and naval aircraft, auxiliary ships and craft, the U.S. Marine Crops, and the U.S. merchant marine.

Sea Power and Sea Control

Captain Alfred Thayer Mahan, U.S. Navy, was the first to use the term "sea power" in his important book *The Influence of Sea Power upon History,* first published in 1890. Mahan studied the great sea powers of the world, especially England, during the period 1660–1783. He found that the great sea powers, often called *maritime powers,* had six things in common that influenced their growth. These were:

1. Geographic position
2. Physical makeup, including natural resources, products, and climate
3. Size of territory
4. Size of population
5. Character of the people
6. Character of the government and national institutions

Mahan believed that geography was the most important factor. He pointed out that England was ideally located near the *sea lanes* of European trade. This position made it possible for England to become wealthy in peace, and to deny the sea lanes to its enemies in time of war. Because England is an island country, it did not need a large land army, as France and Spain did.

Mahan saw that *geographic position* by itself was not enough. There needed to be good harbors along a good coastline. He also believed that if a country had enough resources and good climate for crops, it was not as likely to look seaward for trade. England lacked many resources, so it had to depend on foreign trade to bring these things home.

Size of territory and size of population are closely related. The larger the country and longer the seacoast, the bigger the population needed to

The mission of the U.S. Navy is to control the seas for ourselves and our allies, and to deny the seas to any enemy in time of war. The nuclear-powered aircraft carrier USS *Dwight D. Eisenhower* (CVN-69) is shown here with the nuclear cruiser USS *California* (CGN-36) during a training exercise.

defend that country. England's population supported an army and navy large enough to protect it against larger nations. By national character, Mahan meant that people must understand how to carry on trade. He was strongly in favor of the U.S. *free enterprise system* of doing business. Also, the nation's mariners had to be willing to accept the hardships of life at sea.

Finally, the government of a seagoing nation must be interested in using the seas. Taxes must be used to develop navies and merchant fleets, and people must be in favor of spending money for these things.

Until the 1890s, the United States had been mainly interested in expanding westward across North America. The Navy was looked at mainly as a coastal defense force. Seagoing trade had decreased after the Civil War. European nations had, for the most part, stayed away from the Western Hemisphere, letting the United States grow by itself.

By 1890, however, the United States stretched across the continent. Some people in high places in government began to look beyond our natural borders. Mahan's book made many in government and the Navy decide to make the nation into a maritime power. This would increase U.S. strength and well-being. Mahan's ideas about sea power thus became a big reason why the U.S. Navy grew as it did.

Sea power has been very important in world history, and especially U.S. history. No nation has ever been completely self-sufficient. Nations have always needed the natural resources and goods of other nations. Water transportation is the only practical way to move these things between buyers

The U.S. Marine Corps is a vital part of U.S. naval power. This amphibious vehicle moves ashore from a river to attack the enemy during the Vietnam war.

The ultimate reach of sea power is the submarine-launched ballistic missile that is fired from a ballistic-missile submarine.

and sellers in different nations. In peace or war, more than 99 percent of all international trade goes by sea.

If one must use the sea, one should control it, in case an enemy tries to prevent its use. The mission of a nation's navy is to control the sea for that nation and, if necessary, prevent enemies from using the sea. Controlling the sea and denying its use to enemies is still important today. In fact, for the United States and its allies across the oceans, it is more important than ever.

In our time, control of the sea means control not only of its surface, but of its depths and the air above it. But military control is not enough, by itself. Sea power also means having merchant ships to bring home the supplies we need and to carry our products to customers overseas. We also need ships to fish, to obtain seabed oil, and to use other sea resources.

In the past, a navy could affect events ashore—reach inland—only as far as the range of its ships' guns. But today, with the development of jet aircraft and ballistic missiles, the U.S. Navy can reach across continents. Long-range missiles can now be fired from beneath the ocean by ballistic-missile submarines. Supersonic jets can go far inland with nuclear warheads. The Navy can take combat-ready Marines inland by helicopter. Today, naval forces can be used for offense and defense on land as well as at sea.

Ships are not the easy targets that shore bases are because ships can move. This mobility is the Navy's greatest safeguard against modern weapons. The oceans of the world make up nearly three-fourths of the earth's surface. The Navy is free to travel these vast ocean areas. It can go close to an enemy shore for attack, and can keep its ships far apart to limit the threat of enemy nuclear weapons.

One of the newer aspects of sea power is the development of nuclear power. Not only are nuclear weapons now available, but nuclear power can propel ships. The Navy has a growing number of submarine and surface ships that use this form of propulsion. Since nuclear-powered ships do not need to refuel for months, they have great range and mobility. Submarines can stay under the water on patrol for many months, and surface ships can roam millions of square miles of ocean for long periods of time. Such forces can block a sea or destroy an enemy's ships in its home waters. They provide a line of defense far from home.

THE U.S. NAVY FLEETS

Four major fleets carry out the Navy's basic mission of protecting national security. The Second Fleet operates from the world's largest naval base at Norfolk, Virginia. It patrols the western Atlantic, across some of the world's most important trade routes. Ships and personnel of the Second Fleet rotate with those of the Sixth Fleet, which is assigned to the Mediterranean Sea. The Sixth Fleet is a *deployed* fleet. That means that it is on duty for long periods of time away from homeports in the United States.

On the "other side" of the world, the U.S. Third Fleet operates off the West Coast of the United States and Hawaii. This fleet trains the personnel and ships that will rotate to the Seventh Fleet in the western Pacific and Indian oceans. Like the Sixth Fleet, the Seventh operates in a troubled area—Korea, Japan, Taiwan, the Philippines, and Vietnam. It was in this area that the great sea battles of World War II and the large naval operations of the Korean and Vietnam wars took place.

SEA CONTROL AND MARITIME COMMERCE

Naval power is only part of a nation's sea power. Mahan saw how much sea commerce is needed to keep a maritime nation's industry going, since many vital raw materials have to be imported. On the other side of the coin, sea routes have to be kept open so exported products can be carried to markets in foreign countries.

There was a time in U.S. life when we believed we were independent of other nations. The increasing number of people and growing needs in our nation, with our high standard of living, have changed this. Today we are very dependent on other nations to keep our economy strong, especially for oil.

The United States needs some ninety *strategic*

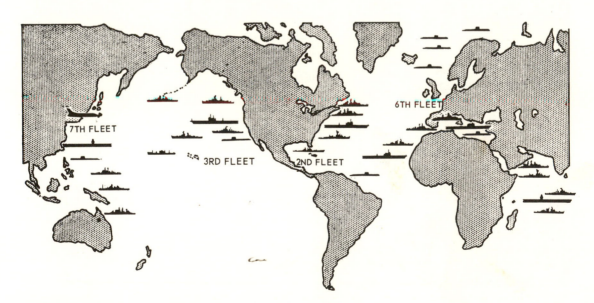

The four major fleets of the U.S. Navy shown in their areas of operation.

The United States must import more than seventy strategic materials to keep its economy supplied. The SS *Hawaiian Enterprise*, a container ship, steams past Diamond Head and Waikiki Beach, Honolulu, Hawaii.

materials to maintain its economy. Of these, we must import more than seventy from foreign lands, and about 99 percent of these materials come in by sea, in merchant shipping. Let's look at a few examples. We must import 85 percent of our manganese, used to harden steel. Ninety percent of our columbite, used in the construction of nuclear reactors, stainless steel, and rocket and missile components, must be imported. More than 99 percent of the tin we use comes from overseas, as does 86 percent of our bauxite, the ore from which aluminum is refined. And everyone is now aware of the threat facing the United States because of its energy requirements. We import nearly half of our crude oil, from which gasoline and other petroleum products are refined.

The United States, then, depends on sea commerce to keep up our way of life. No nation can live without ocean trade. Industrial nations such as the United States, Britain, Germany, and Japan are even more dependent on it than others. Many foreign nations depend on U.S. farm produce and manufactured goods to sustain their peoples.

The right of *freedom of the seas* is acknowledged by all nations. During war, however, the enemy's ocean commerce is a primary target of the warring countries. The forces of each will try their best to stop the use of the seas by the ships of its enemy. These actions may take the form of blockades, submarine warfare, the use of mines, or air and surface attacks. History has shown that when powerful nations can protect their ships and maintain their use of the sea, they will be able to win a war. Great empires have fallen when they could not do so.

Ocean Research

Researchers are increasingly trying to find new resources in the sea. Because of this, the sea has become an area of much national and international interest. More than 70 percent of the earth's surface consists of salty seawater. We know that many minerals are in the seabeds under those waters. Already, oil is being taken out by oil rigs from the seabed under coastal waters along the U.S. Gulf and California coasts, in the North Sea, off Venezuela, and elsewhere.

Only time will tell what these efforts on the floor of the seas will yield. Ocean technology may offer a whole new world to the people of this planet. The science of *aquaculture*, "farming" in the sea, may in time make it possible to cultivate plants and fish for a hungry world.

The study of all things having to do with the sea—the life in it, the air above it, and the water itself—is called *oceanography*. To explore the sea, the Navy has a fleet of surface ships and underwater research vessels. They study the wind, weather, and movement of fish. They listen to the sounds within the waters, and find ways to communicate from the ocean depths.

The knowledge gained by the Navy while it carries out its duties will contribute to our expansion into the ocean. And new Navy missions and abilities will develop, just as new uses of the sea will surely happen. Because of the increased use of the seas, the Navy will have to be able to operate anywhere in the world's oceans, at any time. Scientific knowledge of the oceans has become necessary for a nation to be a global sea power.

The seas belong to all people and all nations. The U.S. Navy uses its sea power to protect the right to explore this important "new frontier" on earth. Young people who have an interest in science should think about the great opportunities in the field of oceanography.

NATIONAL STRATEGY AND SEA POWER

Having a *national strategy* means bringing together all the powers of a nation during both peace and war to achieve national interests and goals. National strategy includes political, economic, and military strategies. Sea power is a necessary part of good national strategy, and it is a blend of peaceful and warlike powers. Governments must have power to back up their negotiations. Without it, there can be little chance of peace. Aggressive nations will take advantage of any weaknesses.

We need a strong Navy, capable of meeting any type of threat—from the most advanced to the most primitive. If the threat of force alone is not enough to deter aggression, then U.S. military forces, backed by a strong people, must be able to fight for our interests.

Our history has shown us that strength has a meaning of its own. Being right is not enough when there are countries that understand only strength. It takes *might* to preserve the *right* where nations are concerned. The power of our Navy reflects the power of the way of life it must defend, and that includes all nations that join with us in common need. If we are not a strong people with adequate naval and military forces, other countries with more strength will become the world leaders. This would end our way of life.

Chapter 1.   Study Guide Questions

1. What are the four main parts of sea power?
2. A. Who made first use of the term *sea power*?
   B. What is the title of the important book he wrote about it?
3. What are the six things that have influenced the growth of sea powers?
4. Why did Mahan think that geographic position alone was not enough to develop sea power?
5. What happened in the early 1890s to make the United States look seaward?
6. A. What are the two uses of nuclear energy for the Navy?
   B. How does nuclear propulsion affect naval operations?
7. A. Where is the home base of the Second Fleet?
   B. Where is the Sixth Fleet deployed?
8. A. Where does the Third Fleet operate?
   B. Where is the Seventh Fleet deployed?
9. Why is keeping the sea lanes open important to U.S. industry and the economy?
10. What does history show to be the outcome of sea control in time of war?
11. Why must we turn increasingly to the sea for our resources?
12. Why must sea power be an important part of national strategy?

Vocabulary

sea power	maritime
sea lanes	free enterprise system
geographic position	self-sufficient

continent
mobility
blockade
sea commerce

strategic materials
natural resources
range of guns

aspect
bauxite
aquaculture

oceanography
national strategy
international trade

Chapter 2.   Introduction to Maritime Geography

Geography is the study of where things are on the earth. It is also more than that. It is about the relationship of things in a given area—natural resources, land, climate, soils, people, governments, and economics, among other things. For naval students, an important part of geography has to do with the location of important places and the transportation routes between them, by both land and sea. Also of particular interest are the relationship of geography and politics (called geopolitics), and a field of study called military geography.

In the next two chapters, we will talk about many of these aspects of geography, especially the seas. We will call our approach to this subject *maritime geography*. During this study, it would be very helpful if you refer to a large globe or world map to find the places we will talk about.

Why Study Geography?

Geography has been considered an important subject for study since ancient times. A knowledge of geography is needed if you want to be a good citizen of your country and the world. Only by knowing your own country will you be aware of its strengths and needs. Geography helps supply such knowledge.

Citizens today need to know about more than just their own country. We are all citizens of the world, as well. An intelligent citizen must be concerned about problems in other lands. Only by understanding other people and their needs can we hope to create a peaceful world. Not all nations are blessed with great resources. We need the resources other countries can provide to maintain our standard of living.

We also must be aware of the dangers posed by possible enemies. Our nation wishes to maintain its independence and security. But it is clear that some other nations do not have such good intentions. They seek to change governments and bring nations under their control. And their objectives are not just political and social. Their actions are geared to world geography. They want to control the world from geographic strongpoints so they can spread their economic, political, and military control across the globe. All U.S. citizens should understand these *geopolitical* goals.

Understanding geography requires the use of maps. In geography, a map is the most basic tool. In this chapter you will learn where important countries and places are located. And you will learn about the oceans and seas around these places.

The World Ocean

When we speak of the *world ocean*, we mean the 71 percent of the earth's surface covered with salt water. If you were to add freshwater surfaces to those of salt water, you would find that barely one-fourth of the earth's surface is land.

Since nearly three-fourths of our world is water, it is clear that the seas are of great importance to life on earth. The science of oceanography deals with this vital aspect of all life.

But the world ocean is the political, economic, and military lifeblood of much of the world too. The oceans are the lifelines of the free world. They carry raw materials, food, and manufactured products to the whole world. They provide protein-rich seafoods. And they are becoming an important source of minerals.

The continents are large islands in this vast ocean. They divide the world ocean into six major

The world ocean. This map shows the form of the earth's crust under the world ocean.

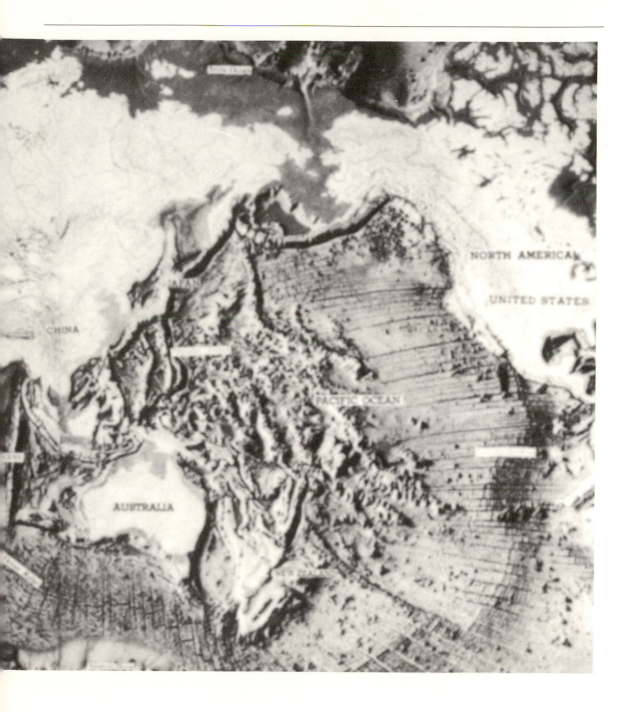

Global projection of the Northern Hemisphere, showing the Arctic Ocean and North Pole in the center of the photograph. Note that a route across the top of the globe is the shortest distance between the United States and Asia (courtesy Rand-McNally).

ocean *basins*. Still smaller, partially enclosed sub-divisions of the oceans are called *seas*. The six ocean basins, listed in order of size, are the South Pacific, North Pacific, Indian, North Atlantic, South Atlantic, and Arctic.

There are many "seas" that are really only parts of these oceans. Some of the more important, from the standpoint of location and natural resources, are the Mediterranean Sea, Caribbean Sea, North Sea, Baltic Sea, Black Sea, Red Sea,

Arabian Sea, South China Sea, Sea of Japan, Barents Sea, and Bering Sea. There are a number of important *gulfs*, or pockets of the seas that reach into the continents. Most notable of these are the Gulf of Mexico, the Persian Gulf, and the Gulf of Aden. You should be able to locate all of these on a world map or a globe.

Only in the past hundred years has mankind developed scientific instruments to map the ocean floors accurately. Detailed charts and maps of the ocean floor are now available. These show that the ocean floor is just as varied as the land surfaces. Submarine (underwater) geography shows deep sea ridges that are like mountain ranges, sea mounts like mountain peaks on land, basins and plains like valleys and surface plains on land, and great trenches even deeper than the Grand Canyon. These features fall within the study of oceanography, which is covered in unit 6.

On the edges of the oceans are the seaports and naval bases from which ships sail forth. The routes these ships travel are the strategic waterways of the world.

MILITARY GEOGRAPHY

From ancient days until World War II, military geography was largely a matter of opposing armies finding places to fortify and defend. It might also involve finding terrain that would be helpful in fighting the battle—hills, rivers, forests, and so on. At sea, the ancients looked for sheltered coves or the leeward side of islands where seas were calm. Here their oarsmen might be more effective in ramming. Narrow channels with shoals made defense easier for those familiar with the area.

In World War I military geography began to be considered. By World War II, every aspect of geography became important in military planning. Global warfare had begun. Planners had to think about fighting and supporting armies in deserts, jungles, polar regions, mountains, and islands around the world. Supply lines, routes of communications, and transport became crucial. Man-made features such as cities, roads, railroads, bridges, airfields, and harbors often decided success or failure. In the Korean and Vietnam wars

the geopolitical effects were worldwide. The same is true of the turmoil in the less developed nations of Africa, Asia, and Central America since then.

Natural resources of all kinds have become necessary for military victory. Vital metals must be shipped over long sea lanes from distant places. Soils have to grow enough food to support millions of personnel overseas, as well as the home population. Increasing amounts of water, coal, and petroleum are needed to support industry and fuel military vehicles. Raw materials, transportation, and distance have become crucial to victory in war, and to national survival.

Today, as in World War II, every aspect of world geography is taken into account by military planners. Because we depend on foreign sources for many natural resources, as well as overseas bases and alliances, the maritime aspects of military geography are very important. Sea communications routes, through geographic choke points such as straits, island groups, and canals, are more important than ever before.

Chapter 2.   Study Guide Questions

1. Why is the study of geography important?
2. Why are we all "citizens of the world"?
3. A. What is the *world ocean*?
   B. What are smaller, partially enclosed subdivisions of the oceans called?
4. Name the ocean basins in order of size.
5. How did war become truly "global" in World War II?
6. What aspects of military geography have become very important today?

Vocabulary

geography	world ocean
geopolitics	maritime
gulf	Atlantic Ocean
sea	Pacific Ocean
sea mount	Indian Ocean
ocean trench	Arctic Ocean
topography	Mediterranean Sea
geographic choke point	Caribbean Sea
shoals	North Sea
strait	Baltic Sea

Black Sea	Bering Sea	Barents Sea	Persian Gulf
Red Sea	South China Sea	Gulf of Mexico	leeward
Arabian Sea	Sea of Japan	Gulf of Aden	

Chapter 3. Maritime Geography of the World Ocean: Western Seas

The sea lanes of the Atlantic are the most traveled in the world ocean. The main shipping lanes go between the East Coast of the United States and western Europe, the two most industrialized regions of the world. The heaviest bulk cargo traffic is carried in huge tankers between the Persian Gulf-area oil fields and western Europe, traveling the long route around the Cape of Good Hope in South Africa. (The jumbo tankers are too large to go through the Suez Canal, the route taken by smaller tankers and general cargo ships en route to both U.S. and European ports from Asia.) The United States imports a large percentage of its total oil needs, and much of that comes across Atlantic sea lanes—from the Persian Gulf, Venezuela, and Nigeria.

The Atlantic also provides the water routes between Europe and South America and the Caribbean, and between Gulf and East Coast ports and Latin America.

The most important military sea lanes are those between the United States and its European NATO (North Atlantic Treaty Organization) allies, and those with the oil countries of the Middle East. The North Atlantic sea lanes are the only way aid could be delivered from North America to western Europe in time of war. The United States, on the other hand, is greatly dependent on oil from the Middle East and strategic minerals from Africa and South America. We also need European, South American, and African markets for U.S.–manufactured products and agricultural produce.

ATLANTIC OCEAN

The two Atlantic ocean basins, lying between North and South America to the west, and Europe and Africa to the east, make up the Atlantic Ocean. The total ocean has an area of about 31,660,000 square miles. Its average depth is about 10,930 feet. The deepest spot in the North Atlantic is in the Puerto Rico Trench, 28,374 feet deep. In the South Atlantic it is the South Sandwich Trench, 27,113 feet deep, about 400 miles east of South Georgia Island, off Argentina. The mid-ocean floor is dominated by an underwater mountain range known as the Mid-Atlantic Ridge. Only a few islands emerge above sea level along the ridge, most of which crests one to two miles below the surface. These islands are Iceland and the Azores in the North Atlantic, and Ascension Island and Tristan da Cunha in the South Atlantic.

Minerals. Few mineral deposits in the Atlantic Ocean's floor can be worked profitably at this time. Those that are mined are located in the shallow waters of the continental shelves (the extension of the continents out to a water depth of 600 feet). The largest mining operations in the Atlantic are for sands and gravels along the Atlantic seaboard of the United States.

The largest single offshore mining operation in the world is based on Ocean Cay in the Bahamas. *Aragonite sands,* composed mostly of calcium carbonate, are dredged up. They are used in the manufacture of cement, glass, and animal feed supplements. A cement industry also is operated in Iceland, based on shellsands. Phosphates for fertilizers are mined in a number of spots along the shores of all continents facing the Atlantic.

The most important mining operations in the Atlantic are the oil wells in the Gulf of Mexico, off the coasts of Texas, Louisiana, and Mexico. Also, there is much oil production in the North Sea between Great Britain and Norway.

Fishing. The North Atlantic has been the scene of major commercial fishing for more than a thousand years. On both sides of the ocean there are major fisheries. Cod, haddock, flounder, and ocean perch are found in the Grand Banks off Newfoundland and the northeast coast of the United States. Lobsters are a high-value harvest from the New England coast, the Caribbean, Brazil, and South Africa. Herring, sardines, and anchovies are caught in the North Sea's Dogger Bank and in the Norwegian Sea in the far north. New fishing grounds are beginning to open along the African coast and the Caribbean, especially for tuna. The Atlantic has the most heavily fished areas in the world, with an annual catch exceeding 22 million tons valued at more than $4 billion.

Ports and Naval Bases. The major U.S. Atlantic ports are Boston, New York, Baltimore, Norfolk, and Charleston. New Orleans, Houston, and Mobile are the major Gulf ports. There are many other ports of lesser importance from the standpoint of annual volume. These ports, however, are also very important to coastal shipping and the general prosperity of the nation.

The major U.S. naval bases on the East Coast are Newport, Rhode Island; New London, Connecticut; Norfolk, Virginia; King's Bay, Georgia; and Mayport (near Jacksonville), Florida. A major naval shipyard is located at Portsmouth, Virginia. The main commercial shipyards that handle major naval shipbuilding programs are located at Bath, Maine; Quincy, Massachusetts; Newport News, Virginia; and Pascagoula, Mississippi.

The major ports of Britain are Liverpool, London, and Southampton. The largest and busiest Atlantic port of western Europe is Antwerp, Belgium. Other important western European ports are Rotterdam, Holland; Bremerhaven and Hamburg, Germany; Le Havre, France; Copenhagen, Denmark; Oslo, Norway; and Lisbon, Portugal. Almost all direct support for U.S. forces in Germany comes through Antwerp or Bremerhaven. You should know the location of these ports. They all figure prominently in U.S. trade, and all are vital to the defense and economies of western Europe.

On the western side of the South Atlantic are some important South American ports. Georgetown, Guyana, sends the United States a large amount of bauxite ore for aluminum. Belém, near the mouth of the Amazon in Brazil, sends us tropical woods, quinine, and natural rubber. The great Brazilian cities of Rio de Janeiro and São Paulo-Santos send us iron ore, and receive U.S.- and European-manufactured products used in that huge country. Buenos Aires, Argentina, and Montevideo, Uruguay, send beef to the United States, and beef and wheat to Europe, while receiving manufactured products in merchant ships from U.S. and European ports.

West African ports of special trading interest to the United States include Casablanca, Morocco, for lead and cobalt; Monrovia, Liberia, for iron ore; Lagos, Nigeria, for oil; Accra, Ghana, for cocoa and gold, and Cape Town, South Africa, for gold, diamonds, platinum, and chromium, among other strategic minerals.

Strategic Geography. When we use the word "strategic" with geography, we are referring to areas on the earth's surface that are important from a military standpoint. The Atlantic side of the European coast has a number of strategic waterways. The two most important of these are the Strait of Gibraltar and the Danish straits.

The Strait of Gibraltar is the western entrance to the Mediterranean Sea. It also is the door to the Atlantic Ocean for Russian Black Sea and Mediterranean Squadron naval vessels. Under control of Britain, the Rock of Gibraltar is also vital to allied interests in southern Europe and North Africa.

Russian naval vessels from the Baltic Sea fleet must go through the Danish straits to get into the North Sea and North Atlantic. The main Russian naval bases and shipbuilding cities on the Baltic Sea are St. Petersburg and Kaliningrad. Other important eastern European ports are Riga, Latvia, and Gdynia (Ga•din'•e•a) and Gdansk (Ga•dansk'), Poland.°

Another strategic area from the standpoint of defending Allied shipping in the North Atlantic is known as the Greenland–Iceland–United

---

° The more difficult place-names in this and the following chapter are followed by syllabic pronunciation guides to assist in the correct pronunciation of the words.

The Port of New York. To the upper left is Manhattan, with the Hudson River and its wharves on the left and the East River to the right (courtesy Port of New York Authority).

Kingdom (G-I-UK) Gap. This is a wide expanse of water between Greenland, Iceland, the Faeroe Islands, and northern Scotland. It is through this seaway that Russian naval warships and sub-

marines from their northern fleet based at Murmansk, on the Barents Sea, and Archangel'sk on the White Sea, have to proceed to gain access to the Atlantic Ocean. A major objective of the

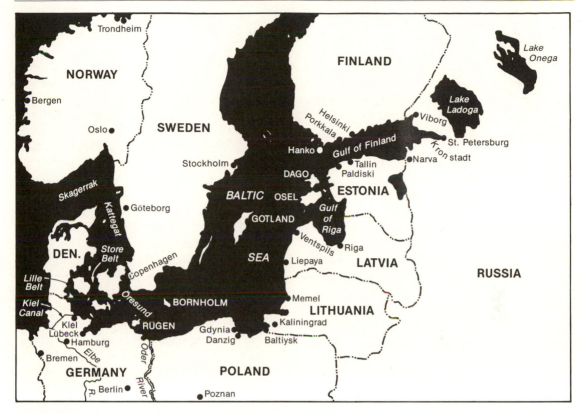

The Baltic Sea ports and bases. The strategic straits Skagerrik (Skag'•e•rak) and Kattegat (Kat'•i•gat) are the only access in and out.

United States and its NATO allies in the event of future war with any of the Russian states would be to try to keep their submarines out of the North Atlantic shipping lanes, by blocking their passage through the Strait of Gibraltar and through the G-I-UK Gap.

One of the most significant geopolitical developments in modern times—and one that has had profound and continuing effects on military strategy in northern Europe, and indeed throughout the world—was the democratization of the former Soviet satellite nations of Eastern Europe in the late 1980s, the reunification of Germany in 1990, and the demise of the Soviet Union in 1991. More on these events and their effects will be presented in subsequent *Naval Science* volumes.

CARIBBEAN SEA AND GULF OF MEXICO

The Gulf of Mexico has an area of 598,000 square miles with an average depth of 4,960 feet. From the Yucatan Peninsula of Mexico in the south, around the Gulf clockwise to the southern tip of Florida, the continental shelf extends far to sea. In the north it has been broadened even further by silt carried out to sea by the Mississippi River.

The Caribbean has an area of 1,020,000 square miles, with two deep basins separated by the underwater Nicaragua Rise. The Rise runs from the hump of Honduras and Nicaragua in Central America, northeastward past Jamaica to Haiti. This shallow rise, only 200 to 1,000 feet deep, takes up almost one-fourth of the Caribbean Sea area. To the north is the Yucatan Basin with the Cayman Trench, the deepest part of the sea at 25,216 feet. The southern and western half of the sea, extending from Costa Rica to Haiti, and then eastward to the islands of the Lesser Antilles, is as deep as 16,400 feet.

The Lesser Antilles, the small islands bordering the eastern limits of the Caribbean, are on a ridge of very active volcanoes. Mount Pelée, on Martinique, killed 30,000 people during a violent volcanic eruption in 1902. More recent volcanic action was in Guadeloupe in 1976.

Currents from the equatorial Atlantic flow into the Caribbean from the southeast along the coast of northern South America. Part of this current continues north into the Gulf of Mexico before moving eastward again between Cuba and Florida, and then up the East Coast of the United States. The prevailing winds, which to a large extent follow the currents, bring strong hurricanes into the area and up the East Coast in the late summer and fall of the year. Almost every year these huge storms cause great property damage and loss of life somewhere in the Caribbean islands, on the Gulf Coast, or along the eastern seaboard of the United States.

Minerals. The Caribbean in general has fewer mineral resources than other ocean basins. The exception to this is the Venezuelan oil fields on Lake Maracaibo (Mar•a•ki'•bo). This offshore drilling operation makes that country the world's fifth largest producer of petroleum. Venezuela is one of the top exporters of oil to the United States.

The Gulf Coast of Louisiana and Texas is also rich in oil produced from offshore rigs. Oil and natural gas fields are also being developed along the Mexican coast near Tampico. One of the worst oil-pollution catastrophes to date occurred in the Mexican field in 1979–80 when an underwater well exploded. Millions of barrels of oil escaped into the Gulf, spreading an oil slick all the way to Texas beaches.

The first offshore sulfur mine began operation off the Mississippi Delta of Louisiana in 1960. A unique system forces hot water down through two pipes bored into the sulfur bed. Melted sulfur is forced up through a third pipe by compressed air. Some of the sulfur is dried into blocks or powdered in offshore plants, and then hauled ashore in barges. Most is now pumped directly to shore in pipes and allowed to dry in natural holding basins.

Fishing. A great deal of fishing is done by the people of the many Caribbean islands. Most of this is small scale—that is, catches are brought ashore and consumed fresh. The most important commercial fishing operations are for shrimp and menhaden in the Gulf of Mexico. There is a large shrimp catch along the U.S. and Mexican Gulf coasts. This is where almost all of the shrimp consumed in the United States is caught.

Menhaden fishing is the most mechanized. Small boats pump their catch into larger carrier vessels. The fish are then brought ashore and processed into fish meal for export, mostly to less developed countries. It is a high-protein product used for fish cakes, seafood sauces, and the like.

There also are large numbers of delicious Caribbean lobsters, called *langusta,* caught around all the islands. Some are frozen into packages of expensive lobster tails. Langusta differ from Maine lobsters only in that they don't have large claws. Excellent blue crabs are also caught along the U.S. Gulf Coast, some for canning, but most for the fresh market.

Ports and Naval Bases. Houston, Texas, and New Orleans, Louisiana, are the major U.S. ports on the Gulf Coast. Other important ports are Galveston and Port Arthur, Texas; Mobile, Alabama; and Tampa, Florida. Veracruz is the most important Mexican port. Barranquilla (Bar•an•kē'•ya), Colombia, and Maracaibo and La Guaira (La Gwi'•ra) (port of Caracas), Venezuela, are important in those nations. The capital cities in the Greater and Lesser Antilles are the major ports of each of those islands. The largest and most important is Havana, Cuba. The island of Aruba, in the Netherlands Antilles, not far from Lake Maracaibo, is a major oil-refining site. Much asphalt is exported from Port of Spain, Trinidad.

The Antilles are a favorite area for luxury passenger cruise ships. To escape the winter, Americans cruise out of Port Everglades (Miami), Florida, and San Juan, Puerto Rico, on pleasure voyages to exotic Caribbean ports such as St. Thomas, Jamaica, and Barbados.

The United States has no major naval ship-operating bases on the Gulf Coast at present, but additional homeport facilities are being built at Pensacola, Florida; Mobile, Alabama; Pascagoula, Mississippi; and Ingleside, Texas. Naval stations exist at Key West, Florida, and Gulfport, Mississippi, but they are mostly shut down. There is a major naval air base complex at Pensacola, Florida, and other naval air facilities are in the Corpus Christi, Texas, area. Important naval bases in the Caribbean are at Guantanamo (Gwan•tan'•a•mo) Bay, Cuba, and Roosevelt Roads, on the eastern end of Puerto Rico.

Strategic Geography. Certainly the most important strategic spot in the Caribbean is the Panama Canal. Splitting the Central American peninsula in the Republic of Panama, the canal is the main route for most ocean traffic between the Atlantic and Pacific. The Canal Zone has been run by the United States since 1903, and the canal has been operating since 1914. The United States and Panama signed treaties in 1978 that provide for turning over operation of the canal to the Panamanian Republic on 31 December 1999, and most of the Canal Zone prior to that date.

The Panama Canal has always been vital to U.S. interests. From the naval standpoint, it has been the best way to transfer all but the largest ships of the Atlantic and Pacific fleets rapidly back and forth in the event of tension or war. The Canal Zone has long been considered an outpost from which U.S. forces could assist friendly Latin American nations. There is no question of its importance as a choke point of international trade. While the canal is probably not as important to U.S. defense as it once was, its loss to an enemy power would severely harm U.S. and Western Hemisphere security and economic interests.

Unfortunately, throughout the 1980s relations between the United States and Panama steadily deteriorated because of the involvement of its dictator, General Manuel Noriega, and his armed forces in smuggling drugs into the United States. Finally in 1989 the Panamanian Defense Forces (PDF) killed a U.S. Marine Corps lieutenant on duty there, and shortly thereafter declared that a state of war existed between the United States and Panama. In response, in late December a 12,000-

Two large bulk freighters pass through the Pedro Miguel locks of the Panama Canal. As you can see, the size of the locks limits the size of ships that can use the canal. The large aircraft carriers of the U.S. fleet, as well as most of the larger oil tankers of the world's commercial fleets, are too big to go through it.

man U.S. force invaded Panama in an action called Operation Just Cause. In a few days the PDF was defeated and Noriega was captured, eventually resulting in his being convicted of drug charges and jailed in the United States, where he is still serving time.

The successful intervention restored democracy to Panama, and, despite many protestations by neighboring Central American countries at the time, U.S. interests in the region have appeared less threatened since. Relations with the new pro-U.S. Panamanian government have since been good. All economic sanctions were lifted following the end of hostilities, and much U.S. economic and other types of assistance continue to flow to Panama to assist the country and its government.

Cuba. Cuba has been a major problem in the Caribbean for the United States for over thirty years. Under communist dictator Fidel Castro, Cuba became an ally of the former Soviet Union. Cuba has served as a base of operations for revolutionaries throughout the Caribbean and Latin America. There is a base to support submarines at Cienfuegos, in southern Cuba. A large number of gunboats are based in various small ports around the island. A number of interior airfields base fighter squadrons that fly modern fighter and attack aircraft.

For two decades prior to the demise of the Soviet Union, a constant stream of Soviet ships and aircraft supplied Soviet goods to Cuba. With the cargo came military equipment and advisers that made the Cuban armed forces one of the largest and best-equipped military forces in the Western Hemisphere. Cuban forces supported communist forces fighting in several African and Central American revolutions throughout the 1970s and '80s.

The United States broke diplomatic ties with Cuba in 1961 when Castro openly opted for communism and announced his alliance with the Soviet Union. A low-key relationship was resumed in 1977, but there have been no serious moves to re-open embassies or exchange ambassadors since.

When relations were broken, the United States made sure that the treaty granting the United

Mock-ups of two U.S. Army generals that Panamanian Defense Forces placed near a street intersection in Panama City showed their intent in the days before Operation Just Cause, December 1989.

States a naval base at Guantanamo Bay, in far southeastern Cuba, stayed in effect. "Gitmo," as naval personnel call it, is the Navy's main training base for the U.S. Atlantic Fleet. It has a fine harbor and good facilities. Except for an occasional hurricane in the fall, the weather is excellent most of the year for all types of fleet training, including aircraft operations and missile firing. The U.S. Marines maintain a force at Gitmo for defense of the base.

Cuba is only about 90 miles from Florida, and directly on major sea lanes between the United States, Central America, northern South America, and the Panama Canal. This communist presence is a constant threat to the peace and security of the area, and to the well-being of the United States. In war, Cuban air forces could directly threaten anything moving in the Caribbean sea lanes.

In the fall of 1983 the United States and its Caribbean island allies became alarmed by a huge buildup of Cuban and Soviet arms and equipment on the island of Grenada, following a takeover of the government by a communist-inspired coup there. Intelligence indicated that these arms were

Aerial view of the U.S. Naval Base at Guantanamo Bay, Cuba.

meant to support similar takeovers of nearby islands and certain Central American countries. In October, when several hundred U.S. medical students on the island were threatened with being taken hostage, the United States and its allies acted.

In a combined operation (Operation Urgent Fury) using U.S. naval ships, Marines, Army airborne forces, and support forces from the Air Force and Army and several of the allied islands, the island was attacked. After a fight of several hours, all resistance was overcome, the students were saved, and hundreds of Cuban "workers" (actually army troops in civilian clothes) and huge stores of Soviet-made arms were captured. The radical leaders of the island were removed, and a provincial government was set up until such time as a duly elected one could be formed. Thus Castro's expansionism in the area was checked, at least for a while, much to the relief of the nearby islands that had been threatened.

Following the demise of the Soviet Union in the early 1990s, all Russian aid to Cuba stopped, throwing it into a state of severe economic depression that has persisted to the present day. This has led several times in the past few years, most recently during the summer of 1994, to large-scale attempts at illegal immigration into the United States by its population. During these incidents several thousand Cuban refugees used makeshift watercraft of all imaginable description to try to make it across the Straits of Florida to land in the southern part of that state. Most of them were stopped and rescued from their often overcrowded and unseaworthy craft by U.S. Coast Guard and Navy ships and patrol boats. They were then taken to temporary camps at the Guantanamo Naval Base pending eventual return to Castro's Cuba. Such illegal immigration poses severe problems for the United States, not only because of the burden it would impose on the south Florida economy, but also because of humanitar-

During the summer of 1994 thousands of Cubans tried to cross the Straits of Florida in rickety seacraft to try to immigrate illegally into the United States. U.S. Coast Guard photo.

ian concerns for the refugees' safety at sea in their rickety craft and the large costs in manpower and operating expense to interdict and transport them back to Cuba.

Additional crises of a similar nature can almost certainly be expected in the future, as long as Cuba continues to be an economically unstable force for unrest in the area.

THE ARCTIC OCEAN

The Arctic Ocean is the smallest of the major oceans. It has an area of 4,700,000 square miles with an average depth of 3,250 feet. The deepest part of the ocean is the Abyssal Plain running across the North Pole at a depth of 15,091 feet. The Arctic Basin is divided by three major subma-

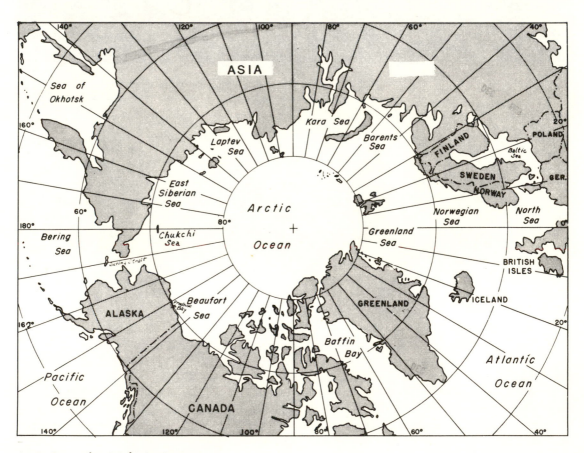

Arctic Ocean, showing the Arctic seas.

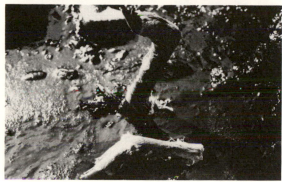

The *Exxon Valdez* oil spill was one of the worst environmental disasters in history. The tanker is shown (*top, left*) grounded atop Bligh Reef in the Gulf of Alaska.

rine ridges that separate four large undersea plains and a number of smaller plains. The continental shelf north of Alaska, Canada, and Greenland extends about 50 to 125 miles from shore. However, the continental shelf north of Asia extends from 300 to 600 miles toward the pole. That portion of the Asiatic continental shelf under the Barents Sea north of Russia and Scandinavia extends more than 1,000 miles to sea, past Spitsbergen (Spits'• bar•gan) and Franz Josef Land.

Minerals. Along the Asian side of the Arctic Ocean are five seas: Chukchi (Chak'•che), East Siberian, Laptev, Kara, and Barents. Much geologic exploration for minerals has been done there in the last few years. Large oil and natural gas deposits probably exist in the Laptev Sea north of Siberia.

The continental shelf off Alaska has also been the scene of much oil drilling. Major oil discoveries were made in the late 1960s and early 1970s in Prudhoe Bay. The 799-mile Trans-Alaska pipeline was competed in 1977 at a cost of $7.7 billion. More than 1.2 million barrels of oil now flow south daily from Prudhoe Bay to Valdez (Val•dēz'), Alaska, where tankers take it on board for delivery to West Coast refineries.

In March 1989 the largest tanker oil spill in U.S. history occurred when one of these tankers, the *Exxon Valdez,* laden with 1,260,000 barrels of crude taken on at Valdez, ran aground on a reef in the Gulf of Alaska some 25 miles south of that port. Ultimately the resulting oil slick from the 987-foot ship spread some 470 miles into the Gulf. Many formerly clean Alaskan beaches and tidal basins were covered with inches of black sludge. A two-year multimillion-dollar effort was mounted to try to clean up the worst of the spill, but the accident nevertheless killed some 10 percent of the area's bird population, along with thousands of sea otters and seals. The cause of the accident was later determined to be incompetent navigation by the tanker's captain and crew.

Large oil deposits have also been found in the continental shelf off the Beaufort Sea coast of Canada, some 400 miles east of Prudhoe Bay. Large natural gas deposits are now being tapped in the area of Melville Island in the Queen Elizabeth Islands.

Getting oil out of the Arctic is not very easy. The frigid cold, prolonged gale-force winds, and icing and freezing of lubricants and equipment make oil drilling extremely expensive and hazardous. The Arctic Ocean itself is almost always covered with constantly moving *ice floes*. Engineers have created artificial islands built from seabed sand and gravel dredged up during the brief summer melt, sometimes poured through holes cut in the 7-foot-thick ice. Much of the year the crude oil must be heated in order to flow satisfactorily through the pipelines and drilling rigs, because of the extreme cold. But the demand for oil in the world is so great that no effort is spared to solve the problems.

Fishing. Only in the Barents and Norwegian seas can commercial fishing take place. There, huge catches of cod, haddock, redfish, and halibut are made annually for the fresh-fish markets in Europe and the Russian states. Annual catches average about 2.5 million tons worth nearly a half-billion dollars. There is evidence of overfishing in these Arctic seas, so quotas have been set by the fishing nations. Some whaling is done in the area by a small Icelandic whaling fleet.

Ports and Naval Bases. Only Murmansk, in Russia, and Narvik, Norway, are important ports in the Arctic. The former we have already identified as a naval base for the Russian northern fleet. The latter is an important fishing port, and a loading place for high-grade iron ore from Swedish mines at Kiruna (Kir'•u•na) about 125 miles inland.

Strategic Geography. There are no significant commercial sea routes across the Arctic ice ocean at this time. In 1969, a specially built 150,000-ton icebreaker-tanker, the SS *Manhattan,* made a successful trip through the pack ice in the Northwest Passage. The route was from Davis Strait through Baffin Bay and Melville Sound to Prudhoe Bay and Barrow, Alaska. Though the route proved possible, the costs involved were so high that pipelines are probably a more satisfactory way to move oil south from Alaska.

Before its demise, every year since the 1950s a Soviet surface force of icebreakers, naval vessels, and merchant ships tried to transit the northern seas from the Atlantic to the Pacific. They were often successful, but it was always a great effort. The force resupplied many of the tiny settlements started by the Soviet government on the sea coasts.

In 1958, the American nuclear submarine USS *Nautilus* became the first vessel ever to reach the North Pole under the ice. Since then, U.S., Soviet, and more recently Russian nuclear submarines have made many patrols under the ice. Engineers occasionally propose having submarine tankers cross the Arctic Ocean under the ice, cutting thousands of miles off the surface routes between U.S. and Canadian Beaufort (Bo•furt) Sea oil fields and northern Europe. Since the great circle routes across the Arctic are the shortest distance between Asia and the United States for both submarines and aircraft, the region would almost certainly be a major operational area in the event of war.

MEDITERRANEAN SEA

The Mediterranean Sea is a shallow, long, land-locked sea about 1,145,000 square miles in area. Its average depth is 4,921 feet, but there are some deep basins west and south of Italy. The Hellenic Trough, south of Greece, is the deepest area, more than 16,700 feet deep. The sea lies in a broad trench between the European and African continents. It stretches about 2,500 miles from the Strait of Gibraltar on the west to Israel on the eastern shore. The word "Mediterranean" comes from the Latin words *medius,* meaning middle, and *terra,* meaning land; together they mean the sea "in the middle" of the lands (of Europe, Asia, and Africa).

The Mediterranean is divided into two basins, east and west of the Strait of Sicily. The continental shelves are very narrow around the Mediterranean, though most of the Adriatic Sea and Gulf of Gabes (Gab'•es), off Tunisia, have sea floors that are actually continental shelves. Great sediment beds extend far to sea from the mouths of the Nile River in Egypt, Rhone (Rōn) River in France, and Ebro (Ā•brō) River in Spain.

The Mediterranean basin is one of the most active volcanic areas in the world. There are at least eleven active volcanoes in the Aegean (I•jē'•an) Sea, in a belt from Athens to Rhodes. Four of these are islands, and the others are submerged. Many more underwater volcanoes are in the western Mediterranean, to the north and west of Sicily, and around the Balearic (Bal•ē•ar•ik) Islands and Corsica. The whole Mediterranean area, and especially Greece, Turkey, and Yugoslavia, often has large earthquakes. The pressures between the Eurasian and African geological plates push in on the sea from both sides. Volcanic lava from the interior of the earth wells up with huge pressure, causing volcanoes and earthquakes at the *fault line* where these plates meet.

Minerals. No handy mineral deposits have been located in the Mediterranean. Far below the sediments on the sea floor, however, drillers have found large beds of rock salt, sulfur, potash, and gypsum. All would be valuable for the chemical and fertilizer industries. At the present time these minerals can be mined only from deposits on Sicily and other islands.

Oil wells are being drilled offshore along the Adriatic coast of Italy, in the Gulf of Gabes off Tunisia, and off the Nile delta in Egypt. Although geologic studies seem to indicate that there is oil and natural gas along much of the Mediterranean coastline, there is no equipment at present that can reach the depths necessary to get it.

Fishing. The Mediterranean basin supports a fishing industry twice as valuable as that of any ocean. Catches bring high prices because most Mediterranean peoples consider fish a luxury food,

like steak. The thousands of small fishing boats bring in small catches. Hake, sole, red mullet, and many other species of fish have a recorded catch of about 1,350,000 tons each year. The total catch is probably much larger, since many local fishermen do not report an accurate number.

There is danger of large-scale pollution in the Mediterranean. This pollution threatens to destroy the balance of life in the sea. Overfishing is likewise making some kinds of fish scarce in some areas. The man-made pollution is worsened by the fact that this sea is almost totally landlocked. It loses by evaporation almost three times as much water as it gets from rainfall and runoff from land. Only the flow of water from the Atlantic keeps the sea at the same level over time. There is also a small flow from the Black Sea through the Turkish straits.

An example of humans' effect on the ecology of the eastern Mediterranean can be seen by looking at the changes that have taken place there since 1970. In that year, a high dam was completed across the Nile at Aswan (A•swan'), Egypt. This stopped the seasonal flood of fresh water and plant food into the sea via the Nile. Because of this, a fishing industry that had existed since the dawn of Western civilization has now almost ceased to exist near the mouth of the Nile.

Ports and Naval Bases. The Mediterranean was the cradle of Western civilization. For nearly seven thousand years, there has been recorded history in the eastern Mediterranean. Egypt, Crete, Phoenicia (Fi•nish'•e•a), Greece, and finally Rome led the parade of culture and trade across the sea in ancient times. The Romans called the Mediterranean *Mare Nostrum,* which means "our sea."

During the Middle Ages, Christian and Muslim cultures clashed in the Crusades. The clash ended in what can be thought of as a geographic compromise: Christians settled to the north and west in Europe, and Muslims to the south and east in Africa and Asia.

The Mediterranean Sea has always been very important to the countries around it. It is still so today. Great port cities exist in all of the countries bounding the Mediterranean coast: Barcelona and

The harbor at Naples, Italy. The twin cones of the volcano Mt. Vesuvius are in the background.

Valencia in Spain; Marseilles (Mar•say') in France; Genoa, Naples, and Venice in Italy; Piraeus (Pi•rē'•as), the port of Athens, Greece; Istanbul (Is•tam•bul'), Turkey; Beirut (Bā• rut'), Lebanon; Haifa (Hi'•fa) and Tel Aviv (Tel a•vēv'), Israel; Alexandria in Egypt; Algiers (Al•jirz'), Algeria; Odessa (O•des'•a) on the Black Sea arm in Ukraine; and a host of others.

The ports and countries around the Mediterranean are familiar places to sailors, world politicians, and tourists. There are many naval bases in the Mediterranean. The main Spanish base is at Barcelona, a favorite port of call for U.S. naval ships. The principal French base is at Toulon (Tu•lon'), near the beautiful Riviera cities of Nice (Nēis) and Cannes (Kan), also favorite places for Sixth Fleet sailors. The Italian navy's headquarters is at La Spezia (La Spet'•sē•a), and its fleet's biggest southern base is in Taranto (Tar'•an•to).

The Southern Command of NATO has its headquarters near Naples, with another important base at Izmir (Iz•mir'), Turkey. The homeport of the flagship of the U.S. Sixth Fleet is at Gaeta (Ga•at'•a), Italy, about halfway between Rome and Naples.

The Ukrainian Black Sea fleet headquarters is located at Sevastopol on the Crimean peninsula. Major shipyards for merchant and naval surface ships are located at Nikolayev (Nyik•a•la'•yaf), near Odessa, which is where Russian aircraft carriers are built.

Strategic Geography. We have talked about the Strait of Gibraltar as the doorway to the Atlantic Ocean from the Mediterranean Sea. There are two other key choke points of navigation associated with the Mediterranean area: the Turkish straits, called the Bosporus (Bos'•per•as) and the Dardanelles (Dard•n•elz'), and the Suez Canal.

In peace the Turkish straits are open to all ships by international agreement. In war, however, the straits may be closed to any nation at war with Turkey. Turkey is a member of NATO. Russian and Ukranian naval vessels freely use the straits to support and relieve the ships in the Mediterranean.

The Suez Canal is a vital waterway for the allies. On this narrow water path through the Egyptian desert, most surface cargo between Europe and Asia passes. As was proved in the Arab-Israeli wars in 1967 and 1973, the canal can be blocked quickly with mines or a few sunken ships.

Farther to the west, during the late 1970s and early 1980s the North African country of Libya, and its dictatorial ruler Muammar Qadhafi, became a growing sponsor for terrorist activity throughout the Mediterranean basin. In 1985, there were several incidents off Libya involving U.S. naval planes and Libyan aircraft and gunboats. Then, in March 1986, two Libyan missile patrol boats were sunk, and a third was damaged, after they threatened to fire at a U.S. carrier task force operating at sea off the Libyan coast.

Finally, in April 1986, after several Libyan-sponsored terrorist incidents that killed several Americans, the United States launched a retaliatory attack against Qadhafi's terrorist bases. A-6 Intruders from the carriers *Coral Sea* and *America* coordinated with Air Force F-111 bombers based in England to bomb a Libyan air base at Benina (Ben•nin'•a), and terrorist training camps near the city of Benghazi (Ben•gaz'•ē). All the targets were practically wiped out by the attacking U.S. planes, with only one Air Force bomber crew lost at sea.

The attack on Libya seems to have accomplished its objective, as not much provocative activity by Qadhafi and others like him has occurred in the area in recent years.

Chapter 3. *Study Guide Questions*

1. What are the most important military sea lanes in the Atlantic for the United States? Why?

2. A. What are the two Atlantic basins?

   B. Where is the deepest spot in the North Atlantic? The South Atlantic?

3. What are the principal mineral and mining industries of the Atlantic and its gulfs and seas?

4. Where are the major fishing areas of the Atlantic?

5. What are the major U.S. naval bases on the Atlantic coast?

6. Which two European ports handle most of the support traffic for U.S. land forces in Germany?

7. What are some important trade goods the United States receives from Africa?

8. A. What does strategic geography mean?

   B. What are the choke points of navigation leading to and from the Atlantic basins?

9. Where are the main Russian naval bases and shipyards that have access to the Atlantic?

10. Why is the Greenland-Iceland-United Kingdom Gap important to the allies?

11. What severe storms occur each fall season in the Gulf of Mexico and Caribbean Sea?

12. A. Which two minerals are the chief resources of the Gulf and Caribbean areas?

    B. Where are these minerals being mined?

13. Where are the major naval air and surface bases in the Caribbean and Gulf of Mexico?

14. A. What is the vital navigational choke point of the Caribbean area?

    B. What is the principal importance of this waterway to the United States?

15. A. What happened in Panama in late 1989?

    B. Who was Panama's ruler at the time?

16. Which Caribbean nation and government is a great worry to the United States?

17. A. What is the main purpose of the naval base at Guantanamo Bay?

    B. Why is it such a valuable base for this purpose?

18. What happened at the Caribbean island of Grenada in October 1983?

19. Where is the deepest part of the Arctic Ocean?

20. A. What valuable resource is being obtained from the continental shelf off Alaska and Canada in the Arctic Ocean?

B. What disastrous event happened in 1989 that resulted in large-scale environmental damage in the Gulf of Alaska?

21. Why would the Arctic probably become a major operational area in event of a war between the United States and any Asiatic country?

22. A. What does the word "Mediterranean" mean?

B. Which continents are by the Mediterranean Sea?

23. How has the high dam on the Nile River at Aswan, Egypt, affected the ecology of the eastern Mediterranean?

24. A. What are some famous and important ports of the Mediterranean?

B. Where are some of the important naval bases in the Mediterranean?

25. A. What are the names of the important Turkish straits?

B. Why are these straits important to the NATO allies—and to the Ukrainians?

26. Why is the Suez Canal important to western Europe?

27. A. Who sponsored much of the terrorism around the Mediterranean in the 1970s and 1980s?

B. What happened to his bases in April 1986?

Vocabulary

supplement	jumbo tanker
Lake Maracaibo	pollution
Dogger Bank	catastrophe
Suez Canal	lobster, *langusta*
Latin America	insurgent
Antwerp, Belgium	Prudhoe Bay, Alaska
prosperity	lubricant
Strait of Gibraltar	fishing quota
Skagerrik Strait	ice floe
Kattegat Strait	volcano, -ic
Yucatan Peninsula	fault line
silt	evaporation
Lesser, Greater	Dardanelles,
Antilles	Bosporus
prevailing winds	Turkish straits
continental shelf	Mediterranean
export	retaliation
import	

Chapter 4. Maritime Geography of the World Ocean: Eastern Seas

Oil—its source and the sea routes over which it travels—dominates most trade in the seas south of Asia. From the Persian Gulf and Arabian Sea, the routes go westward to the Red Sea and Suez, and eastward through the Strait of Malacca and China seas to Japan. The trade moves from eastern Africa, India, Indonesia, and western Australia to Suez. It moves from China, Japan, Indonesia, and the islands of the Pacific to the West Coast of the United States and South America. Suez to Singapore, the most important British lifeline of past years, still is the scene of trade and travel between the Orient and the West.

Because of the strategic importance of the Middle East—its warm-water ports; its oil; and its hundreds of millions of people, many trying to survive with weak governments and poor environments—U.S. naval forces operate routinely in the Indian Ocean. The United States tries to maintain friendships there despite political and economic unrest. Third World nations are trying to improve the lives of their people, and must look to the seas to do so.

The Pacific and Indian oceans are significant in the competition for markets, materials, and minds that goes on all the time in this part of the world.

THE RED SEA AND GULF OF ADEN

The Red Sea is a warm, very salty sea reaching some 1,300 miles southeast from the Egyptian port of Suez to the Strait of Bab el Mandeb. It is only from 90 to 200 miles wide, with an area of 169,000 square miles. The Axial Trough in the very middle of the narrow sea is the deepest at 9,580

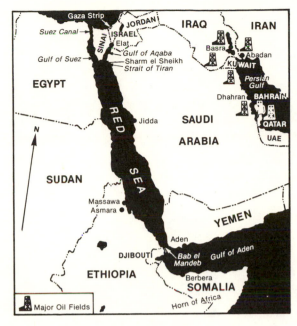

Suez, the Red Sea, the Gulf of Aden, and the Horn of Africa. The southern entrance to the Red Sea is controlled by the Strait of Bab el Mandeb. The oil fields of the Persian Gulf are at the upper right.

feet near the Saudi Arabian port of Jidda (Jid'•a).

Minerals. The Red Sea has no known oil deposits. It is a possible future source of valuable metals, however. Pools of boiling hot brine are found in the Axial Trough. These waters are rich in *dissolved metals,* including zinc and copper, in the seabed muds. Someday it may be possible to mine these minerals.

Fishing. There is not much fishing in the Red Sea. Many kinds of fish are caught, but except for sardines near the Gulf of Suez, there is no major fishery. Lights are used to attract fish to the nets, since coral reefs make bottom trawling risky and expensive.

Ports and Naval Bases. The port of Suez is important because it is the southern anchorage for ships waiting to go through the canal northward to the Mediterranean Sea. Port Said (Sa•ed') on the northern end of the canal is important for the

same reason. Mesewa (Me•saw'•a) is the only port and naval base in Ethiopia. Jidda, a seaport in Saudi Arabia, serves as a port of entry for the Moslem holy city of Mecca, about forty miles inland.

Djibouti (Ja•but'•e), the capital city and port in the nation of the same name, is the major African port on the Horn of Africa, on the Gulf of Aden. It not only serves its own country, but also is the main port for shipment of Ethiopian imports and exports. The major port of the area is Aden, capital of Yemen.

Strategic Geography. The Red Sea is a strategic waterway. Along with the Suez Canal and Gulf of Suez to its north, and the Gulf of Aden to the south, the Red Sea is the main waterway between Europe and Asia. The northern access is the Suez Canal. The choke point in the south is the Strait of Bab el Mandeb. (The Arabic word *Bab* means gate or strait.) Less than 20 miles wide, the strait separates Yemen (Yem'•an) on the Arabian peninsula from Ethiopia and the Republic of Djibouti in Africa.

THE PERSIAN GULF AND GULF OF OMAN

The Persian Gulf area is the leading oil-producing area in the world. The Gulf is bounded by Iran on the north, Kuwait and Iraq at the northwest end, Saudi Arabia on the west, and the Arab sheikdoms of Bahrain (Ba•rān') island, Qatar (Ka'•tar), United Arab Emirates (UAE), and Oman on the south and southeast. All of these countries are major oil producers. The Gulf itself has been divided for oil drilling by these nations, since much of the oil is gotten by offshore rigs.

Minerals. Though oil was known to be present in the region since ancient days, the drilling of oil wells there is a fairly recent development. The first wells in Iran were not drilled until 1935, and those in Kuwait did not start up until 1946. World War II caused a major increase in drilling in both Iran and Saudi Arabia. In the past twenty years, the wells and offshore rigs there have become very important. Today, about a third of the total oil production of the world comes from the Persian Gulf area.

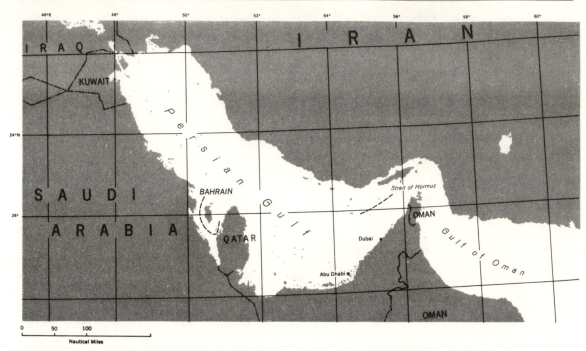

The Persian Gulf and Gulf of Oman. The Strait of Hormuz is a key point for all ships entering or leaving the Persian Gulf; it is a vital choke point.

The United States, Western Europe, and Japan have come to depend on Arab oil in large part. The United States imports about one-third of its annual oil needs from the area, Western Europe about 70 percent, and Japan more than 90 percent.

Ports and Naval Bases. The major oil-exporting ports are Ras Tannura (Tan•nū'•ra), Saudi Arabia; Abadan and Kharg (Karg) Island, Iran; Sitra, Bahrain; Das Island, UAE; and, until late 1989, two terminals near Kuwait. The oil terminals are really only oil-storage and loading places, not cities. They have man-made docks for tankers. The ships at the docks hook up to hoses from storage tanks located at the end of the oil pipelines either from refineries or direct from the crude oil fields.

Fishing. The entire Persian Gulf is shallow; half of it is less than 120 feet deep, and all but a few spots less than 200 feet. Because it is so shallow, sunlight can reach the bottom in most places, causing lots of plankton to live there. *Plankton* are

tiny animals and plants that provide food for small fish. Since there is much plankton, a large variety of fish live in the Gulf. Sardines, anchovies, mackerel, and barracuda are the main kinds caught by local fishermen. In the waters controlled by Qatar and the UAE are valuable pearl fisheries.

Strategic Geography. While oil is the big strategic resource, the political and strategic geography of the Gulf is also important. Acquiring a warmwater port on the Persian Gulf has been a major goal of Russia and the former Soviet Union for the past hundred years. A major political goal of Western nations over the same period has been to prevent this from occurring. Before the fall of the Shah of Iran in 1979, that country was an ally of the United States and the West. The United States had sold a lot of military equipment to the Shah's army and navy, and had trained thousands of Iranian military personnel. Aside from selling oil to the West and even helping to "keep a lid" on the price, the Shah also kept peace and security in the Persian Gulf and Gulf of Oman, and blocked the Soviet Union's attempt to gain a foothold in this area. The United States had helped to build two new Iranian naval bases, one at Bandar Abbas on the Strait of Hormuz, and the other at Chah Bahar (Cha Ba•har') on the Gulf of Oman.

After the fall of the Shah, however, armed uprisings of various Islamic fundamentalist factions in Iran put the country in chaos, as exemplified by the U.S. hostage situation in 1979–81, followed by a very destructive war of attrition with Iraq that did not end until 1988.

During the *Iran-Iraq war*, neutral seagoing oil tankers of several countries were attacked from time to time in the area by missile-firing aircraft of both nations, causing much concern worldwide. Loss of free transit of the Persian Gulf and the Strait of Hormuz then as now would have been a disaster to the United States, Western Europe, and Japan.

Consequently, in 1987 and 1988 U.S. and other allied warships escorted U.S. and other neutral-flag tankers through the upper Persian Gulf and the Strait of Hormuz. At least two U.S. warships were damaged during these operations by missile attacks and mines.

Iran and Iraq agreed to a U.N.-sponsored cease-fire in July 1988, ending the conflict. Peace in the area was short-lived, however, because with his forces no longer engaged in the war with Iran, Iraq's leader Saddam Hussein was then free to attempt far more serious military adventures to the south two years later.

Operations Desert Shield and Desert Storm. In August 1990, Iraqi forces under the command of Hussein staged a sudden invasion of neighboring Kuwait. After a few days the country was captured and completely subjugated. Saudi Arabia, threatened with becoming Hussein's next victim, quickly appealed to the United Nations and especially to its ally, the United States, for help. In an unprecedented show of unanimity, the United Nations passed a trade embargo against Iraq, restricting movement and sale of all goods, including oil and food products, into and out of Iraq. Simultane-ously, the United States embarked upon Operation Desert Shield, deploying the largest military and naval force assembled since the Vietnam War to Saudi Arabia.

By the end of 1990, some 450,000 U.S. military personnel and some 100 U.S. Navy ships joined forces from many other nations to form a so-called U.N. coalition. U.S. and allied ships patrolled in the Persian Gulf, Arabian Sea, and Red Sea, enforcing the U.N. trade embargo against Iraq.

The U.N. Security Council imposed a deadline of 15 January 1991 by which Hussein had to move all of his forces out of Kuwait or face military action. When he did not, on 16 January a massive air assault on every target of military significance in Iraq and Kuwait turned Operation Desert Shield into Desert Storm. Tens of thousands of air sorties (attack missions) were launched by U.S. Navy and Air Force planes and those of other coalition forces. The coalition soon achieved air superiority.

On 23 February the allied ground offensive into Kuwait and southern Iraq began. Within three days most Kuwaiti territory was recaptured, and Kuwait City was secured. On the evening of 27 February President George Bush announced a cease-fire, which became permanent on 8 April. Victory for the coalition forces was complete, thus ending the largest air and ground offensive fought since World War II. Tens of thousands of Iraqi troops were killed and many thousands more became prisoners of war.

It remains to be seen what the political outcome of this action will be in the area, and whether Hussein will be able to stay in power.

INDIAN OCEAN

The Indian Ocean is the third largest in the world. It has an area of 28,400,000 square miles with an average depth of 12,760 feet. Maximum depth is 24,442 feet in the Java Trench southwest of the Indonesian islands of Sumatra and Java on the eastern edge of the ocean.

The main feature of the Indian Ocean floor is a great midocean ridge system, which is shaped like an upside-down "Y." The Southwest Indian Ridge goes around southern Africa and joins the Mid-

The Indian Ocean basin. Stretching from Africa to Australia, and from the south Asian coast to Antarctica, the Indian Ocean has become a strategic key between East and West (courtesy Rand-McNally).

Atlantic Ridge. The Mid-Indian Ridge continues south of Australia to join with the Mid-Pacific Rise. Many volcanoes are along the submarine ridges of the Indian Ocean. Many of the islands in the ocean were formed by active and inactive volcanoes.

Two of the world's greatest river systems, the Indus River of Pakistan and Ganges-Brahmaputra (Gan•jez' Bram•a•pu'•tra) of India, have built huge *submarine fans* into the Arabian Sea and Bay of Bengal. These fans are made up of sediments carried from the Himalaya (Him•a•lā'•a) Mountains in those two countries.

Minerals. Mining in the Indian Ocean floor is becoming more important. Tin ore is mined off the shores of Thailand, Malaysia, and Sumatra in the Strait of Malacca. Deposits of sands rich in rare heavy minerals such as monazite, zircon, and magnatite are mined off Sri Lanka (Srē Lan'•ka), the Indian state of Kerala (Ker'•a•la), the east coast of South Africa, and near Perth in western Australia. A major oil field also lies off western Australia. Rich beds of manganese chunks have been found on the Indian Ocean floor. Methods are being developed to mine these valuable clusters of manganese, nickel, copper, titanium, and lead.

Fishing. The fishing industry in the Indian Ocean is small, but growing rapidly. It now exceeds four million tons annually. Tuna and shrimp are the main catches at this time, off the coast of India. Japanese, Korean, and Taiwanese vessels are now combing the ocean for these species. Most of the shrimp are canned and sold on the U.S. market. Lobsters are caught off South Africa and western Australia for the U.S. market too. The Indian Ocean catch will continue to grow in value, as fishing and canning techniques improve and the demand for fish protein increases.

Ports and Naval Bases. The United States has built a small communications station and air base on Diego Garcia in the mid-Indian Ocean to support naval communications and deployed Indian Ocean forces. An important U.S. naval communications station is in operation on North West Cape, Australia, as well.

Strategic Geography. We have already discussed two of the main sea routes in the Indian Ocean. They are the oil routes from the Persian Gulf through the Red Sea to Suez, and along the east coast of Africa and around the Cape of Good Hope. The other major sea lane is past Singapore at the tip of the Malay peninsula, through the Strait of Malacca, and across the Indian Ocean to Suez. The Strait of Malacca is a main route between Asia and Europe, and is the route Japanese oil tankers follow from the Persian Gulf to Japan. This strait is one of the key strategic choke points of navigation in the world.

Principal navies of nations around the Indian Ocean are those of South Africa, India, and Australia. Pakistan has a small but efficient navy. The French also have a naval force in the ocean, based at Réunion, to protect their Indian Ocean interests.

PACIFIC OCEAN

Covering nearly one-third of the earth's surface, the Pacific Ocean is by far the largest of the world's oceans. It covers an area of 64,000,000 square miles with an average depth of 14,050 feet. The deepest part of the ocean is the Marianas Trench, which at 36,161 feet is also the deepest part of the world ocean.

The western half of the Pacific sea floor is complex, with thousands of volcanic peaks, trenches, ridges, and submarine plateaus. Many of the volcanoes are no longer active, and are in various stages of erosion from sea and weather action. The tops of these volcanic peaks are the beautiful Pacific islands one dreams about. There are many coral reefs, which teem with colorful marine life. The most famous and largest reef is the Great Barrier Reef, which runs more than 1,250 miles along the coast of northeastern Australia.

When erosion has worn away much of a volcanic peak in the ocean, a strand of coral islands is left around the old volcanic rim. This formation is known as an *atoll.* The central *lagoon* of the atoll is what remains of the old volcanic *crater.*

The Hawaiian islands and the French Society islands, which include Tahiti and Bora Bora, are beautiful places. They are the typical South Sea islands of waving palms and white beaches. Many other South Sea islands, however, especially in the southwest Pacific, are deadly jungles with disease, stifling heat, incessant rains, and few natural resources.

Minerals. Not much mining is done in the Pacific yet, but many large mineral deposits have been located in coastal areas and on the ocean floor. Some tin is mined off the Indonesian island of Sumatra; iron ore has been mined for years off Japan; and mineral sands (titanium, zircon, and monazite) are mined off the coast of Queensland, Australia. There are small producing oil fields between Australia and Tasmania and off New

Zealand's North Island. Other oil drilling is going on off the coast of southern California and in the Cook Inlet of Alaska. Phosphates are mined along the coasts of Chile, Peru, and Baja California in Mexico.

There are vast fields of manganese chunks in much of the Pacific. An especially heavy belt extends from Baja California to Hawaii, and thence to the Palau islands and northward to Japan. It is estimated that this area, nearly 1.35 million square miles, is literally paved with manganese! A number of companies are working to find a cheap enough way to mine this vast undersea resource.

Fishing. The annual catch of fish and shellfish from the Pacific has exceeded that taken in any other ocean since 1970. More than half of all the world's catch of marine fish, shellfish, and *crustaceans* (crabs and lobsters) now comes from the Pacific each year, almost 26,000,000 tons.

Most fisheries are located within 150 miles of the coasts. The exception to this is tuna fishing, which is carried on throughout the high seas. There are large fisheries for cod, pollock, flounder, rockfish, sea bass, and red snapper all over the Asiatic continental shelf—in the eastern Bering, Okhotsk (O•katsk'), Japan, Yellow, and South China seas. Fisheries for sardines and anchovies lie off Peru, California, northern Japan, and Korea.

Pollock and salmon are fished in the Gulf of Alaska and off the coasts of Washington and Oregon states.

There are very important fisheries for shrimp, crabs, lobsters, and squid in the waters across the northern Pacific. Giant shrimp, called prawns, are caught in the Yellow and South China seas, off northern Australia, and in the Gulf of Alaska. The largest of all crabs, the Alaskan king crab, is taken in the Gulf of Alaska along the Aleutian (A•lu'•shan) Islands and in the Sea of Okhotsk. These huge crabs sometimes grow to more than three feet from claw to tail. Huge lobsters are caught around most of the islands of the Pacific.

Ports and Naval Bases. The most impressive thing about the geography of the Pacific is its size. Some examples: from the Panama Canal to Yokohama (Yō•ka•ham'•a), Japan, is 7,680 miles, or to Singapore (Sin'•ga•pōr), 10,529 miles; from San Francisco to Manila, Philippines, 6,299 miles, and to Melbourne, Australia, 6,970, to Hong Kong, 6,044, to Singapore, 7,350, and to Honolulu, Hawaii, 2,091 miles. From Yokohama to Singapore through the Taiwan (Ti'•wan') Strait is 2,880 miles. Distance, then, is certainly an important factor to consider when discussing Pacific strategy.

In addition to the ports mentioned above, there are many others of importance: Seattle and Los

A Coast Guard helicopter inspects a Russian fish factory ship that is operating in the Gulf of Alaska.

Angeles in the United States; Calleo, the port of Lima, Peru; Santiago, Chile; Wellington and Auckland, New Zealand; Sydney and Brisbane, Australia; Jakarta, Indonesia; Singapore; Bangkok, Thailand; Canton and Shanghai, China; Kobe and Osaka, Japan; Taipei (Ti•pā'), Taiwan; Haiphong (Hi•fong'), Vietnam; and Vladivostok (Vlad•a•vas' tak), Russia.

The major U.S. naval base on the West Coast is San Diego, California. Smaller operating bases are located at Seattle. There are U.S. naval shipyards at Bremerton, Washington, and Mare Island, California. Civilian shipyards with major naval ship contracts are in Seattle, San Francisco, Los Angeles, and San Diego.

U.S. naval bases in the Pacific are located at Pearl Harbor, Hawaii, and Yokosuka (Yō•ko'•ska), Japan. The U.S. Third Fleet has its headquarters at Pearl Harbor. The U.S. Seventh Fleet flagship is based in Yokosuka, where there is a large ship-repair facility with drydocks. Although most ships in the Seventh Fleet deploy from the homeports on the U.S. West Coast, some destroyers and other ships are sometimes homeported in Yokosuka and Guam.

The United States also has some small naval and air bases in the Aleutian Islands off Alaska. They guard the northern approaches to North America. These bases are located at Attu, Shemya (Shem'•ya), Adak, and Kodiak islands.

The Russian Pacific fleet has its headquarters at Vladivostok. Other naval bases are located in Nakhodka (Na•kot'•ka), Sovetskaya Gavan (Sa•vet•ski•ya Ga'•van), and Petropavlosk (Pe•tra•pav'• lofsk). A submarine-building yard is located far up the Amur River at Komsomolsk (Kam•sa• molsk).

The Chinese navy is small but growing in strength. It has bases in a number of Chinese ports including Amoy, Shanghai (Shang•hi'), Tsingtao (Chin•dau'), and Dairen (Di•ren'). The Indonesians have a naval base at Surabaja (Sur•a•bi'•a); the Taiwanese at Kaohsiung (Kau'•she•ung); the South Koreans at Pusan; and the Thais at Sattahip (Sat•ta•hip). The Japanese have a small Maritime Self Defense Force, capable of limited operations around the home islands.

Strategic Geography. The U.S. Navy has two main tasks in event of a war in the Pacific: (1) protect the long supply lines to our forces and (2) keep the sea lanes open to our allies, especially Japan, South Korea, the Philippines, Thailand, Australia, and New Zealand.

Japan is the key to U.S. foreign policy in Asia, and the principal nation to be defended in the Far East. Japan's industries and hard-working people make that country the most prosperous in the area. At the same time, the World War II peace treaty prohibits Japan from having armed forces with an offensive capability. The United States, by treaty, is obligated to defend Japan from foreign attack.

Treaties also commit U.S. forces to help our other Pacific allies in the event of aggression. We have strong mutual defense ties with Australia and New Zealand. The United States keeps an army force of 38,000 troops in South Korea. There is always some North Korean threat against this ally, including in recent years the capability to build nuclear weapons. U.S. forces were supposed to be withdrawn in the early 1980s, but this withdrawal has been delayed indefinitely by the North Korean threat.

After the Vietnam War U.S. relations with China steadily improved. Establishment of full diplomatic relations, including exchange of ambassadors, occurred in 1979. A reversal occurred in mid-1989, however. Chinese army tanks and troops brutally attacked students demonstrating for democratic reforms in Tiananmen (Tie•nan'• men) Square in Beijing (Be•jing'). Thousands of the students were killed or wounded; many were later jailed or executed as criminals. The Chinese government later tried to deny that the crackdown ever took place. The negative effects of these events on U.S.-Chinese relations have only recently begun to be resolved.

On behalf of the United Nations, the United States administers the Trust Territory of the Pacific Islands in the Central Pacific. The biggest island groups in the territory are the Marshall Islands, Caroline Islands, and Mariana Islands. These islands were taken from the Japanese during World War II. A number of major air bases were built by the Japanese and Americans during the war, but all have been either shut down or reduced to a small size.

In general, the Pacific has been calm in recent years. Smoldering difficulties remain in most Asian nations, however. The United States has to keep alert in the area by having naval forces deployed there at all times.

ANTARCTIC SEAS

The seas around Antarctica are *circumpolar*; that is, they surround the south polar continent of Antarctica. In area they total about 13.5 million square miles. More than half, about 8 million square miles, freezes over each winter, and 1.5 million square miles is frozen year-round.

The water and ice boundaries are determined by water movement. There is a rather well-defined zone in which southward-flowing warm water rises over the column of cold Antarctic waters flowing northward. The cold-water portion of the water column is called the *polar front,* and the warmer surface zone is called the *Antarctic convergence.* This convergence is the northernmost boundary of the Antarctic seas, generally about 55° south latitude.

The continental shelf of Antarctica is very narrow. Oceanic basins 13,000 to 16,500 feet deep lie beyond the steep continental slope. The northern edge of these basins is the midocean ridge system that separates the Antarctic from the Atlantic, Indian, and Pacific ocean basins.

Minerals. Modern drilling and infrared photography have found many minerals in Antarctica

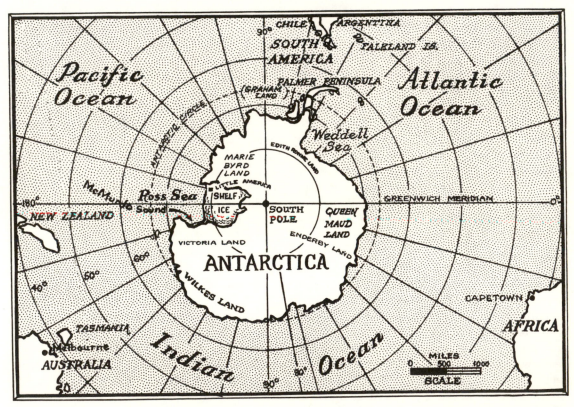

The continent of Antarctica. The continent is completely surrounded by the waters of the Atlantic, Pacific, and Indian oceans and by the Ross and Weddell seas.

Penguins climb on the ice shelf near the Antarctic peninsula, near the U.S. scientific station at Palmer.

and its surrounding seas, but these deposits are too expensive to mine.

Fishing. Whaling was a thriving business in the Antarctic for a hundred years until the early 1930s. Then modern floating factory ships and fast whalers with harpoon guns nearly wiped out the whale population. Only about one-tenth of the original whale population still exists, and a number of species are nearly extinct. The market for whale products has dropped a lot, though, so the demand for whales has decreased. Iceland and Japan still engage in some whaling, under some control by the International Whaling Commission.

There is some harvesting of krill, a name given to small shrimplike animals that abound in some Antarctic waters during certain seasons of the year. This is of only limited commercial value.

Ports and Naval Bases. The U.S. Navy has a naval research base at McMurdo Sound in Antarctica. This has been manned since the International Geophysical Year explorations in the 1960s. Australia and New Zealand have research sites in other areas of the continent.

Strategic Geography. Antarctica is out of the mainstream of the world's air and sea lanes. There is little interest in it at the present time, either for resources or for strategic reasons. Exploration and cold-weather equipment testing are now the main activities there. Also, basic research is being conducted on marine life and the weather. Studies indicate that south polar weather and currents have a great effect on many areas of both the Southern and Northern Hemispheres.

Chapter 4.   *Study Guide Questions*

1. A. What is the narrow strategic sea located at the southern approaches to the Suez Canal?

   B. What is the key strait at the southern end of this sea?

2. Why is the Persian Gulf important to the United States and its allies?

3. What happened in Iran after the Shah of Iran was deposed?

4. What is the key strait at the southern entrance to the Persian Gulf?

5. What occurred in the Middle East in late 1990 that caused U.S. and allied U.N. forces to go to war with Iraq?

6. What is the main feature of the Indian Ocean floor?

7. What have the sediments carried by the Indus and Ganges rivers built on the sea floor in the Arabian Sea and Bay of Bengal?

8. A. List the three main sea routes in the Indian Ocean.

   B. Which one is the main route between Asia and Europe?

9. Where has the United States built small but important bases in the Indian Ocean area?

10. A. Which ocean is the largest in the world?

   B. Where is the deepest spot in this ocean, and what is the depth there?

11. A. What formations are found on much of the western half of the Pacific sea floor?

   B. What often forms around the rims of volcanic islands in the Pacific?

12. A. Where is the major naval base on the West Coast of the United States?

   B. Where are major naval shipyards located?

13. Where are the major U.S. naval bases in the mid- and Western Pacific?

14. Where does the Russian Pacific fleet have its headquarters?

15. What are the two main tasks of the U.S. Navy in the event of war in the Pacific?

16. Which country is considered the key to U.S. foreign policy in the Pacific? Why?

17. What are present U.S. relations with China?

18. A. Who administers the Trust Territory of the Pacific Islands?

    B. What are its main island groups?

19. What is meant by the term "circumpolar ocean" when referring to the Antarctic seas?

20. A. What valuable Antarctic resource has now been nearly wiped out?

    B. Which two countries still engage in this industry?

21. Where does the United States have a naval research station in Antarctica?

Vocabulary

contention	krill
Singapore	prawns
unrest	circumpolar
dissolved metals	titanium
Strait of Hormuz	war of attrition
chaos	hostage
Strait of Malacca	coral reef
Marianas Trench	Strait of Magellan
crustacean	atoll
Bab el Mandeb	lagoon
Horn of Africa	crater
oil terminal	manganese
plankton	phosphates

6

Oceanography

The Navy defines oceanography as the "application of the sciences to the phenomena of the oceans, including the study of their forms and their physical, chemical, and biological features." Simply stated, oceanography is the scientific study of what happens on, in, and under the world's oceans.

Greater attention is now being given to the oceans by nearly all nations, including the United States. Some reasons for this are:

• *Social.* The coastal regions of our nation, which include estuaries, mouths of inland rivers, and the Great Lakes, are major population and job centers. More than 40 percent of the U.S. population lives and works near the nation's seacoasts. The coasts extend some 5,400 miles along the Gulf of Mexico and the Atlantic and Pacific oceans, another 2,800 miles along the shores of the Great Lakes, and over 2,000 miles along the beaches of Hawaii, Guam, Puerto Rico, and the Virgin Islands.

• *Economic.* The oceans are rich with natural resources, food, and fuel. They are the "last frontier" for many vital materials on this earth.

• *Political.* The oceans link the continents. The world ocean covers nearly 71 percent of the earth's surface. It is a field for much competition between industrialized nations. It provides the sea lines of communication over which commerce between the United States and many foreign nations takes place.

• *Strategic.* The oceans are vital to U.S. defense. The fleet ballistic-missile submarines that operate in them and their intercontinental missiles give the nation its foremost deterrent threat against aggression worldwide.

In this unit, some of the many features of oceanography are discussed. Oceanography spans the past, the present, and the future of our world and is especially important to a maritime nation such as the United States.

Chapter 1. Oceanographic History of Our Earth and Its Seas

Our study will begin with a discussion of the origin of the earth and its seas. Where did it all begin—how and why? A basic idea of how the earth began is essential in our study of the life-giving seas.

IN THE BEGINNING

Modern science has given scientists a good idea of how our earth began. This study is a part of astronomy called *cosmology,* the science concerned with the universe and its origin. We will discuss this more thoroughly in the astronomy unit of *Naval Science 3.* Scientists who study the orderly relationship of things in our universe are called *cosmologists.*

Cosmologists believe that what is now our solar system (the sun, the planets, and their moons) was originally a large cloud of gas and dust. This cosmic cloud, composed of 90 percent hydrogen, 9.7 percent helium, and 0.3 percent heavier elements such as carbon, oxygen, and iron, slowly began to whirl. As it did so, these elements bumped into each other, stuck together, and began to form solid dust particles, molecules of water, ammonia, and metallic crystals. Gradually, gravity and centrifugal forces caused this spinning cloud to take the shape of a huge disk, with the infant sun in its center.

From time to time, eddies, swirls, and collisions occurred, causing a number of smaller clusters of materials to whirl in orbits around the large cluster forming the sun; these clusters were the beginnings of the planets. At this stage, the sun began to develop tremendous internal pressure and heat; this caused *thermonuclear fusion* (a combination of two or more atoms to form a third element, with a great release of energy) to begin at its core. The hot hydrogen atoms in the sun's burning interior combined to form helium, putting out huge amounts of energy in the process. At the same time, the gravitational fields of the planets became stronger and began gathering larger amounts of dust. One of these swirling masses became our planet earth.

After millions of years of increasing pressure and temperature, metallic crystals of iron and nickel melted and sank toward the core, or center, of the earth. Because of the intense heat generated within the earth by compression, molten rock called *lava* often broke through the surface, either in large cracks in the earth's crust or in active volcanoes that expelled gases and solid materials as well. The hydrogen molecules, other gases, and water vapor that escaped from the earth gradually ascended. The sun's rays acted on the released gases and soon distributed them about the new planet to form an atmosphere. Meanwhile, the earth continued to contract into a more solid mass, developing what is now the earth's crust.

The intense heat created by the compression of the earth continued to cause thousands of volcanoes to bring molten rock and water vapor to the surface. Radiation from the sun also continued to form the earth's atmosphere by breaking up water molecules into separate atoms of hydrogen and oxygen. Being lighter, much of the hydrogen escaped into space, while the heavier oxygen atoms were retained in the atmosphere by gravity. Gradually, poisonous ammonia and methane gases in the atmosphere were dissipated by the sun, as both the sun and earth cooled. Slowly, the earth's atmosphere cooled enough to cause the water vapor in the air to condense and return to earth in the form of rain. Falling on the earth's hot surface, some water hissed into steam, joined with new water vapor brought to the surface by volcanoes, and ascended to be condensed and fall again and again as rain.

The continuous precipitation (rain and snow) probably went on for thousands, maybe millions, of years. Finally, about four billion years ago, the earth had cooled to about its present size and most of the low spots in the crust had been filled with rainwater. Lighter granite (granitic rocks) rose to higher elevations on the earth's surface, as the heavier basalt (basaltic rocks) sank further into it. These gigantic water pools were the world ocean—not in the same geographic shape we see the oceans today but, nevertheless, covering about 70 percent of the earth's surface. The cycle of evaporation and condensation continues today, though now only a small percentage of the vapor ascending into the atmosphere comes from volcanoes and other cracks leading to the molten rock surrounding the core of the earth. Most of the water vapor today comes from the ocean surface and trapped groundwater, which is heated and recycled by the sun. Over the millions of years, the oceans have overrun some coastal fringes of the early continents as the result of wind and water erosion, earthquakes, and landslides in those areas. At the same time, the buildup of polar icecaps has kept an almost constant amount of water in the seas. Ours is a continually changing geologic world, but these very gradual changes are too slow to be seen in the lifetimes of humans, except in instances of violent natural change, such as volcanic eruption or massive earthquake.

THE EARTH'S CRUST: CONTINENTAL DRIFT

The earth is made up of several "shells," somewhat like a golf ball. The *core* of the earth consists of two parts: a solid inner core of nickel and iron with a diameter of about 860 miles, and a molten outer core of these metals about 1,300 miles deep. Above this is about 1,800 miles of dense rock called the *mantle*. The uppermost layer of the mantle, several hundred miles thick, is called the *asthenosphere*; it is composed of molten rock. The rigid outer *crust*, the *lithosphere*, "rides" or "floats" on this molten part of the mantle. The crust is the earth's surface, the only part we can easily see. It consists of our continents and ocean basins. With an average depth of about 20 miles under continents, the earth's crust may be as much as 40 miles deep beneath mountains. Under the oceans, however, it is only 3 to 10 miles thick.

The lithosphere, or earth's crust, is divided into six major *plates* and about a dozen smaller ones. The major plates are the American, African, Eurasian, Indo-Australian, Antarctic, and Pacific plates. Most of the earth's volcanic eruptions and earthquakes occur on the boundaries or *margins* of these plates.

It is not known how many times the earth's plates have separated, come together, and separated again over the 4.6-billion-year geologic history of our planet. This movement of the earth's landmasses is known as *continental drift*. It was first seriously proposed about 1912. Many studies and modern oceanographic and geologic instruments have, in general, tended to confirm the theory. In the late 1960s, the theory was modified to take into account all major geological structures of the earth. The new concept is known as *plate tectonics*.

Let us trace the probable geologic history of our earth based on the continental drift theory. After millions of years of pressures and strains, some 65 million years ago Africa and South America had drifted apart, the Atlantic and Indian oceans had formed, and North America and Eu-

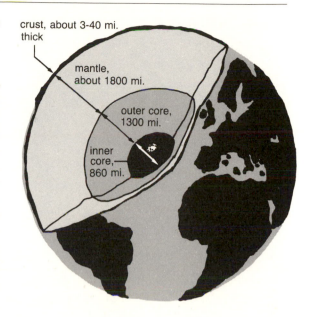

crust, about 3-40 mi. thick

mantle, about 1800 mi.

outer core, 1300 mi.

inner core, 860 mi.

Scientists divide the planet earth into the crust, mantle, outer core, and inner core. The uppermost layer of the mantle, called the asthenosphere, is composed of magma, or molten lava. The outer, rigid crust is called the lithosphere.

rope were about to split, leaving Greenland to stand between them in the Northern Hemisphere. India moved rapidly (relatively) across the Indian Ocean on its 5,500-mile, 180-million-year trip; it would collide with southern Asia and push up the world's highest mountain range, the Himalayas. Australia began to break away from Antarctica and move northward, while the latter continent moved toward the South Pole. The African plate crashed into the Eurasian plate south of Europe and pushed up the Pyrenees between Spain and France, the Alps of France and Switzerland, and the Apennines of Italy. On the other side of the globe, the Pacific plates pushed up the Andes in South America, the Sierras along the West Coast of North America, and the islands of Japan.

In time the continents gradually took their places on the globe familiar to us today. The major ocean basins and numerous seas—once a single ocean mass with one giant continent—now pro-

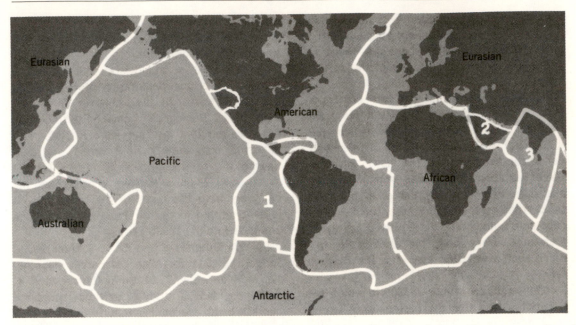

The lithosphere, or outer rigid crust of the earth, is divided into six major plates, named above. There are a number of smaller plates also, three of which are numbered above: (1) Nazca Plate, (2) Arabian Plate, and (3) Indian Plate.

vide the vital sea lines of communication and commerce between the widely separated continents. The globe we know today is the result of an evolutionary geologic process that has taken billions of years—and continues today.

THE EARTH'S CRUST TODAY

The evolutionary process just discussed created a global jigsaw puzzle of segments known as *geological plates*. The lithosphere's plates drift over the uppermost, semimolten layer of the earth's mantle like giant chunks of ice, moved by the churnings in the interior of the earth. Where these plates come together, the earth and its inhabitants experience the awesome energy of earthquakes and volcanoes. *Seismographs*, modern instruments that measure the intensity of earthquakes, have helped to locate the boundaries of the plates. Also along these boundaries, mountains rise and fall and volcanic islands push up from the sea. The energy released in the explosion of a nuclear bomb is small compared with these huge geologic forces.

Earthquakes. The great earthquake belts that lie along the plate margins are of extreme importance to sailors and people who live on seacoasts and in harbors. Volcanoes have created new islands and island chains—the Hawaiian Islands, some Aleutian and Japanese islands, and islands in the Caribbean and Mediterranean seas, among others. In the United States, the entire West Coast is in an earthquake "belt," with the best-known feature being the San Andreas Fault, which runs through the center of California and close to San Francisco. In fact, some geologists predict that all of Baja California and much of the present state of California may break away from the North American continent and drift toward Alaska, arriving there in about fifty million years!

But not all such catastrophes will happen in the distant future. In fact, many earthquakes occur daily; Tokyo for example, experiences two to three tremors daily. Fortunately, few are ever felt by people, though sensitive seismographs do record several hundred larger quakes each year. In 1902,

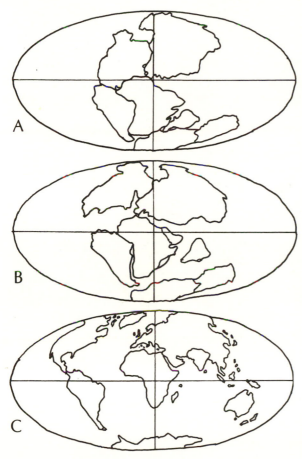

The progression of continental drift. A. The original supercontinent, Pangaea, 200 million years ago. B. 135 million years ago. Pangaea splits into Laurasia, to the north, and Gondwanaland, to the south. C. Our world today. India has collided with Eurasia, and Australia has split from Antarctica; North and South America have joined in Central America.

Mount Pelée, a volcano near St. Pierre on the Caribbean island of Martinique, erupted with an earthquake and superheated gases that killed 30,000 people within seconds. In 1906, San Francisco was almost totally destroyed by a large quake on the San Andreas Fault. Within the past ten years, devastating quakes have killed thousands of people in Italy, Iran, Yugoslavia, Turkey, Greece, Guatemala, Nicaragua, Mexico, and the former Soviet Union. Another less serious but widely reported quake disrupted the baseball World Series in October 1989 in San Francisco, causing much damage and at least 63 confirmed deaths. The largest disaster of all time from a single earthquake occurred in 1976 in Tangshan, China, when almost 700,000 people were reported to have been killed.

Tsunami. When an earthquake occurs near or under the sea, ocean waves radiate from the shock's source in ever-widening circles. There may be little movement detected on the open sea, but as these waves reach shallow waters along coastlines, the waves slow down and pile up in huge crests, sometimes more than 100 feet high. These huge waves are called *tsunami,* a Japanese word that means "surging walls of water," or seismic sea waves. These fantastic walls of water can race across the deep oceans at jet-plane speeds of 450 miles per hour but then slow to 25–30 mph in coastal waters. Tsunami are often incorrectly called tidal waves; they have no relationship to the tides at all.

The worst tsunami in the history of the world followed the eruption of the volcano Krakatoa between the islands of Java and Sumatra in Indonesia in 1883. The volcanic explosion blew off 5 cubic miles of rock and sent dust and ash as high as 50 miles into the air. The debris from Krakatoa orbited the earth for several years, sometimes falling as "brown snow" or "dirty rain" (rain or snow contaminated with dirt particles carried aloft by volcanoes or other large explosions). The resultant tsunami, as high as 120 feet, destroyed all life on many nearby islands, and 36,000 people died on Java and Sumatra alone. Another terrible tsunami killed 27,000 people and wrecked 7,000 fishing boats in Japan in 1896, and 5,000 died in the Philippines in a 1976 tsunami.

The Hawaiian Islands, Alaskan coast, and Western Pacific areas are periodically lashed by tsunami that have caused great loss of life. The last major tsunami to strike Hawaii was in 1946. Undersea landslides and volcanic eruptions resulted in a wall of water that killed 159 people and caused $25 million worth of damage.

Since these natural disasters have often oc-

Eruption of Myojin Reef Volcano, 170 miles south of Tokyo, Japan. This underwater volcano has pushed its lava above the surface of the Pacific.

curred on islands and seacoasts, the Navy has historically been called on by our government to give emergency aid to stricken areas. Ships and their helicopters have carried in medical teams, Red Cross personnel and medical supplies, construction crews, emergency housing units, food, and water after many of these disasters, especially in recent years. The U.S. Navy brought in major relief supplies for the Tokyo earthquake in 1923, the Peruvian disaster in 1970, and the San Francisco quake of 1989.

Chapter 1.   Study Guide Questions

1. What is oceanography?

2. Why does our government maintain an active program of oceanographic research?

3. How do cosmologists believe the earth was formed?

4. What is the scientific theory explaining the origin of the world ocean?

5. How much of the earth's surface is covered by water?

6. Describe the "construction" or makeup of the earth, listing and describing the major layers from the center outward.

7. What are the names of the six major *plates* of the lithosphere?

8. A. Explain the theory of continental drift.

B. When did the most recent sequence of geologic events leading to the present continental locations begin?

9. Where is the most famous earthquake belt in the United States?

10. A. What is a *tsunami*?

B. What events could cause a tsunami?

oceanography
cosmology
element
crystal
thermonuclear fusion
eddy, eddies
radioactive

evaporation
condensation
basalt
granite
continental drift
erosion
mantle (of earth)

asthenosphere
lithosphere
lava
plate tectonics
geologic plates
fault line
seismograph

tsunami
evolutionary process
earthquake
dirty rain

Chapter 2.   Landscapes Under the Sea

For many centuries people believed that the sea floor was simply a deep, smooth basin with a bottom covered with oozy mud. In fact, until the twentieth century, most knowledge of the ocean floor came from the ancient method of heaving a lead-weighted line overboard in rather shallow water and looking at the mud, weeds, and sediments that clung to the weights when retrieved. People thought that this ooze covered the bottom and "swallowed" up everything—even sunken ships and lost civilizations. It was not until echo sounders and hydrophones were invented by a U.S. Navy scientist for use in searching for submarines during World War I that oceanographers really began to understand that the ocean bottom has just as varied a geography as the land surface.

This does not mean that no progress had been made in oceanographic studies before that time. Indeed, a number of individuals had done much in the field of ocean sciences over the years. Experiments had been conducted on such things as salinity, tides, water temperatures, currents, and many aspects of navigation. But the study of the sea bottom itself was not successful until after the invention of the echo sounder in the 1920s. From that time onward, an intense effort to chart the sea floor has been under way.

RELIEF OF THE EARTH

The *relief* of the earth refers to the different elevations and form of the earth's surface, its *topography*. A *relief map*, for instance, shows the differ-ent heights of a part of the earth's surface by use of shading, colors, or numbered *contour lines* (lines along which the depth is constant).

There are two main levels in the relief of the earth: the continents, or continental terraces, including their submerged zones called the *continental shelves*; and the deep ocean floor. The *deep ocean floor* is also called the *deep sea*, the *deep ocean basin,* or the *abyss*. The deep-sea floor is described in terms of the individual features comprising it, such as abyssal plains, oceanic ridges, sea floor fractures, deep-sea trenches, islands, and seamounts. It has an average depth of about 12,000 feet (about 2 to 2½ miles), but there are regions over 7 miles deep. Though 71 percent of the earth's crust is covered by water, just two-thirds of that is truly deep oceanic basin.

Echo sounders measure the time it takes sound pulses to travel from a ship on the surface to the ocean floor and return as echoes. Echoes that bounce back quickly to the shipboard receiver outline huge mountain ranges with jagged peaks, or solitary seamounts that show the location of ancient volcanoes. Echoes that take much longer return reveal great deep trenches such as the Mariana Trench of the Western Pacific, which is over 35,800 feet deep. (In contrast, Mount Everest, the highest peak on the earth's surface, stands 29,028 feet above sea level in the Himalaya Mountains of Nepal.)

The echo sounder provides a rapid means of finding the depth of waters over which a ship is traveling. On average, sound travels 4,800 feet per second in water. An echo sent to the bottom must make a round trip—that is, from the echo box to the bottom and back to the shipboard receiver. If an echo takes two seconds to return, it has obviously traveled two times 4,800 feet, or 9,600 feet. Since it is a round trip, half that distance is the depth of the water—in this case, 4,800 feet.

THE OCEAN FLOOR

Echo soundings have determined that the ocean floor is divided into three distinct areas: the continental shelf; the deep ocean basin, or abyss; and lying between them, the continental slope.

The *continental shelf* borders on continental land areas; actually, the margins of the continents are under water. The sea, it can be said, spills over the brims of the ocean basins, covering the continental shelves with relatively shallow water. Most maritime nations of the world have agreed that, in a legal sense, the continental shelf is a part of the land out to a depth of 200 meters (about 656 feet). In that shelf area the rights of exploration and use of resources belong to the adjacent continental nation, according to international law.

The continental shelf is a gradually sloping sea bottom surrounding all continents on earth. The shelf generally drops about 7 to 10 feet every mile until approaching the 72-to-100-fathom curve (450–600 feet), and then the slope changes to a very steep slope toward the abyss. The average width of the continental shelves is about 42 miles. Off parts of North Carolina the shelf extends out to about 75 miles, in the Barents Sea off the Arctic coast of Russia it extends 800 miles, and off the coast of California it is less than a mile in width. Off parts of Peru and Japan, the plunge begins almost immediately.

The shelves are not always smooth, gradual slopes. They vary from smooth plains to irregular, rough terrain. Many sediments such as rocks, sand, mud, silt, clay, and gravel cover the shelves. Coarse sand is the most common material, consisting mainly of particles carried away from the continental landmass and deposited by rivers, currents, ice, and wind during the ice age.

Biologically, the continental shelves are sunlit areas that support most of the sea vegetation and saltwater fishes and animals of the earth. Even today, our knowledge about the ocean is mostly limited to the continental shelf regions. It is here that most fishing is done. Exploration for, and production of, oil and other minerals is today almost entirely on the continental shelves. It is here that nations are most liable to confront each other as their growing populations increase their demands for fuels, minerals, and food.

Beyond the continental shelf, no matter how deep or far from the land, the bottom drops off abruptly. This is where the continental crust of granitic rocks ends and the bottom drops off rapidly to the sediments of the ocean floor, with its base of basaltic rock. The sharp descent is called the *continental slope*. Here is where the deep sea truly begins. Oceanographers and geologists have found that the continental slopes generally drop

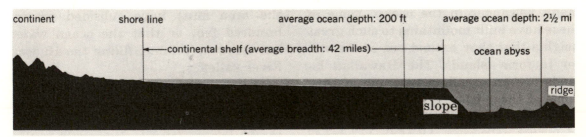

The continental shelf topography as it generally appears off the continental shores, although it varies in width and in smoothness of contour throughout the world. Submarine canyons often cut through the shelf.

from 100 to 500 feet per mile, but with increasing depth they tend to flatten out and merge into the deep ocean floor.

Humans find this area a bleak and uncomfortable world. There is no light and no plant life. The pressure, cold, and silence increase as one descends. The bottom sediments are mainly mud and clay, with small amounts of sand and gravel. There may be rocks in areas of volcanic activity. In some areas the steepness of the slope is dramatic, as along the western coast of South America, where there is an 8-mile descent from the top of the Andes Mountains to the bottom of the Peru-Chile Trench in a horizontal distance of less than 100 miles.

The continental slopes have some of the most rugged features on earth. They are scarred with spectacular features like submarine canyons, steep cliffs, and winding valleys. Some places have terraces and plateaus, while others have sheer dropoffs of several thousand feet.

Submarine canyons in the continental slope are similar to canyons found in the southwestern United States. They are often carved out of the shelf and slope by past glaciation, tidal currents, other underwater currents, and landslides. Rapidly moving underwater currents carrying debris and sediments are called *turbidity currents*. (*Turbid* means muddy.) They scour the canyon walls much like river or wind erosion does on continental surfaces.

Some submarine canyons are much larger than the Grand Canyon of Arizona. The Hudson Canyon in the western North Atlantic, for example, extends from waters with a depth of 300 feet at the canyon head, 90 miles southeast of New York harbor, to a depth of 7,000 feet some 150 miles offshore. The 50-mile-long canyon is a chasm 4,000 feet deep in places and has a number of sizable tributaries entering it. It cuts through the continental slope and joins a depression in the continental shelf that marks the entrance of the Hudson River channel off New York harbor. The Hudson Canyon is continuously scoured by silt-laden currents coming out of the Hudson River. The silt is eventually deposited on an enormous plain of mud called a *submarine fan*. Similar fans exist hundreds of miles out to sea from the mouths of other great rivers of the world, notably the Mississippi, Indus, and Ganges.

The ocean floor lies at the foot of the continental slope and is the true bottom of the ocean. The *deep ocean floor* extends seaward from the continental slope and takes up one-third of the Atlantic and Indian oceans and three-quarters of the Pacific Ocean. They are the last large areas to be explored, truly the "last frontier" on earth.

There are three ways of studying the ocean floor: seismic surveying, echo sounding, and echo ranging. In *seismic surveying*, sound waves from a small underwater explosion bend differently as they go through different layers of sediment and crust. The travel times of the refracted sound waves are recorded by a second ship some distance away. *Echo sounding* finds the depth of the bottom by timing ultrasonic pulses that are sent straight down to the ocean floor and reflected back up to the ship's receiver. This method was first used in the early 1920s, and in 1923 the survey ship USS *Guido* was fitted with an echo sounder for use in hydrographic surveys. Since that time the echo sounder has gradually been developed into a precision instrument. Today's digital equipment is accurate to within a tenth of a foot at moderate depths. Sub-bottom echo sounding has been developed in which sediment and rocks several thousand feet below the sea floor can be studied.

With *echo ranging*, short pulses are transmitted and received sideways from the ship or from a towed "fish," shaped like a torpedo. The signals are directed in a narrow beam to sweep out large areas with sound pulses to give a picture of details of the ocean floor. The echo pattern is traced on paper by a stylus (ink pen), or electronically on a video screen, like on a television screen. Echo ranging is done with a device called a *side-scan sonar*. It is a very popular device because it gives an accurate picture of features from several hundred feet to several thousand feet, depending on the water depth.

Oceanographers have determined that most of the Pacific deep ocean basin consists of hills form-

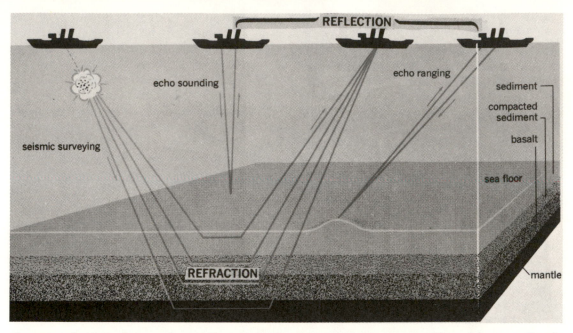

Three ways of studying the ocean floor are shown in this drawing. In *seismic surveying,* sound waves from a small surface or subsurface explosion bend differently as they go through different layers of sediment and crust; the refracted sound waves are recorded by a second ship. With *echo sounding,* ultrasonic pulses are sent down and reflected back from the ocean floor to the ship's receiver. *Echo ranging* sweeps out at an angle over large areas and gives a picture of bottom details.

ing a rough topography, while plains are widespread in the Atlantic. All these plains are connected by canyons or other channels to landward sources of sediments that are transported by turbidity currents down the slope to be deposited on the plains.

Ocean Ridges. Every deep ocean floor has impressive mountain ranges called *ridges.* The great Mid-Atlantic Ridge soars more than 6,000 feet above the nearby sea floor in some places and rises above the sea surface to form islands such as the Azores or Iceland. It extends from north of Iceland to below the tip of South Africa. It continues around Africa and joins the Mid-Indian Ocean Ridge coming down from the Arabian Peninsula. The Mid-Indian Ridge continues eastward south of Australia and New Zealand, joining the East Pacific Rise. The East Pacific Rise is the main underwater feature in the southern and southeastern

Pacific Ocean. Located about 2,000 miles seaward of the west coast of South America, it runs northward to the peninsula of Baja California. The whole 40,000-mile-long mountain chain is sometimes given a single name, the Mid-Ocean Ridge, although it is somewhat off center in the Pacific. Many underwater earthquakes occur in a *rift* running down the ridge's centerline. Large portions of the major plate margins of the earth's surface lie along the centerline of the Mid-Ocean Ridge.

Ocean Islands, Seamounts, and Guyots. All true *oceanic islands,* differing from island fragments such as New Zealand, New Guinea, or Greenland that have broken away from continental masses, are volcanic in origin. Almost all of the small islands of the Pacific are oceanic islands—the tops of former volcanic mountains.

At first, such an island has a steep peak. Gradually, surrounding reefs are built up by corals while

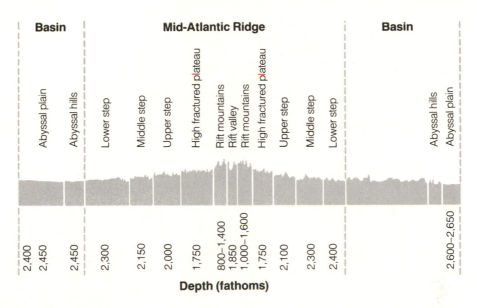

Basin			Mid-Atlantic Ridge												Basin	
Abyssal plain	Abyssal hills	Lower step	Middle step	Upper step	High fractured plateau	Rift mountains	Rift valley	Rift mountains	High fractured plateau	Upper step	Middle step	Lower step			Abyssal hills	Abyssal plain
2,400	2,450	2,450	2,300	2,150	2,000	1,750	800–1,400	1,850	1,000–1,600	1,750	2,100	2,300	2,400			2,600–2,650

Depth (fathoms)

A profile of the Mid-Atlantic Ridge.

the wind, waves, and rains erode the mountain. At the same time the mountain subsides, the coral becomes a barrier reef connecting coral islands called an *atoll*. Eventually, much of the original island wears away, leaving a lagoon surrounded by the coral reef. In some cases, coral islands continue to subside and finally disappear beneath the sea surface, leaving what is known as a *seamount*. Many strings of seamounts dot the floor of the central Pacific, the ancient remains of former islands. They are found in all oceans but are most common in the Pacific Ocean.

Scattered underwater mountains with peaked summits that never reached the surface retain the name seamounts, but those with flattened tops are called *guyots*. They have been found in the Pacific but not in the Atlantic or Indian oceans. The stacking of lava from repeated volcanic eruptions is believed to have created the seamounts and guyots. The guyots' smooth, flat tops indicate that they were leveled off by wave action. It is believed that the great weight of the guyots caused them to depress into the sea floor at the same time as the level of the ocean was rising.

The Hawaiian Islands are a volcanic island chain. Tremendous lava eruptions are regular occurrences from a number of famous volcanoes in the islands. Kilauea and Mauna Loa on the big island of Hawaii are two of the world's most active volcanoes. Mauna Loa lifts its head 13,677 feet above the blue waters of the Pacific. But this is less than half of its real height, for from its base on the sea floor to its lava-covered summit, Mauna Loa measures more than 31,000 feet. Other chains of this type include the Caroline, Gilbert, Samoan, and Society islands.

Sediments of the Deep Ocean Floor. The sediments of the ocean floor consist of three general types of materials: oozes, clays, and land-derived muds. The oozes are found in warm, shallower waters and are composed of marine shells and skeletons of minute animals. Equatorial areas and the Atlantic Ocean have concentrations of these oozes. A dark brown or reddish clay is found in the deep, cold parts of the ocean basin; it is made up of airborne, volcanic, and meteoric dusts. Most of the North Pacific floor is covered by this reddish clay. The land-derived muds are materials brought

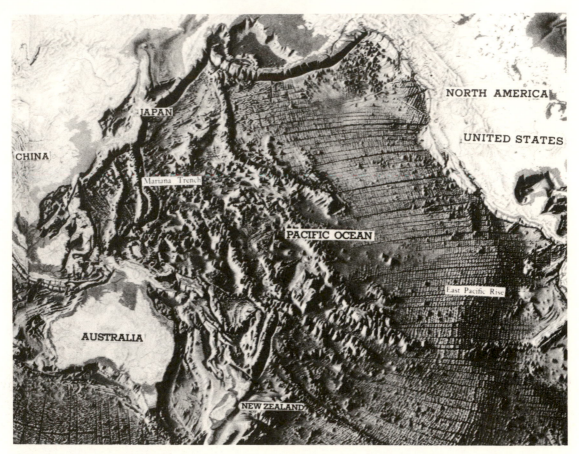

The northwestern and southwestern Pacific Ocean basins have a multitude of seamounts and guyots. Note the major system of trenches—Aleutian Trench to the north, the Mariana Trench with extensions both north and south in the western Pacific, and the Tonga Trench north of New Zealand. These trenches form the western boundaries of the Pacific Plate. The East Pacific Rise is part of the great world ocean ridge system.

down by the rivers that flow into the oceans and spread over the abyssal plains by turbidity currents.

Sediment that builds up on the ocean floor does not always remain stationary. On the continental slopes, great underwater landslides occur, especially in earthquake zones. In some areas, slow bottom currents move clay particles for hundreds of miles. Physical obstacles, such as the continental shelf, midocean ridges, submarine canyons and trenches, and seamounts cause channeling and ed-

dying of water flow. These actions result in scouring in some areas on the edge of the abyssal plains and deposits of great thickness in others.

The rate of buildup of the fine sediments on the deep seabed is very slow—about an inch every 2,500 years. Yet, in some places, the upper levels of the sea contain so much microscopic plant and animal life that the seabed beneath is blanketed with thousands of feet of sediment (ooze) from their remains. Underwater volcanic eruptions spread sediments for miles. Volcanic ash and dust

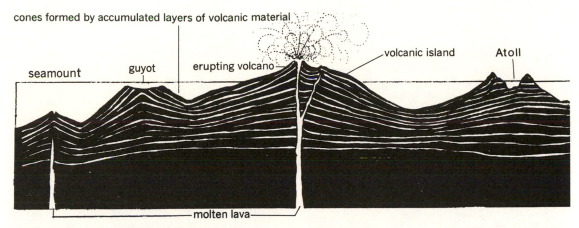

cones formed by accumulated layers of volcanic material

seamount   guyot   erupting volcano   volcanic island   Atoll

molten lava

The development of oceanic islands from submarine volcanoes. At the center, the drawing shows the volcanic island with its active volcano. At left is the seamount, an underwater volcanic peak that has become an extinct or nonactive volcano before reaching the surface. At far right, the decaying volcanic island has eroded to become an atoll with the crater now a lagoon surrounded by coral-covered island fragments of the crater's rim; and to the right of the seamount is the guyot, a destroyed island-atoll, with a flat or slightly concave top eroded away by sea action.

from eruptions on the surface may circle the globe for years before falling again to the earth's surface. Icebergs also deposit sediments in the ocean. River ice and ice formed along the shore will entrap *detritus* (loose material) that gradually sinks to the bottom as the ice melts. Seismic measurements indicate that there is a thickness of 1,000–1,200 feet of undisturbed sediments in areas of the deep oceans that have had a minimum of underwater currents.

Mineral crystals often solidify or encrust around tiny objects on the sea bottom, forming *nodules,* or lumps of metal. The most valuable of these are manganese nodules, which are also rich in copper, nickel, and cobalt. These lumps of almost pure metals have grown over millions of years and literally pave the ocean bottom over wide areas. Some of these manganese nodule beds stretch for thousands of miles across the mid-latitude oceans. They are especially abundant in very deep water in a broad band from California to Midway Island, in a triangular area southeast of Japan, in the Baltic Sea, off the U.S. East Coast, and in a band from Brazil to South Africa.

Research has been under way for years to try to develop an economical means of retrieving this wealth from the deep ocean bed, but because of the great depths involved (12,000 feet), it is a difficult task. Those who figure out how to do it will be able to gain untold wealth and much-needed resources for the world.

Coring the Seabed. Most deep seabed samples are taken by coring. *Coring* is done by dropping a weighted tube vertically into the seabed so a cylinder of sediment is trapped inside it and can be pulled to the surface.

Studying the cores and the shells of tiny animals in the ooze and sediments tells a great deal of the history of that part of the ocean. Fossils give clues about the geological age of the strata of sediments in which they are found. Animal and plant fossils indicate the temperatures of the sea when these living things existed.

The standard piston coring tube cannot go beyond 100 feet into the sediments, and 50–60 feet is the usual core length under excellent conditions. To get greater depths, hollow rotary drills are now being used in advanced oceanographic research.

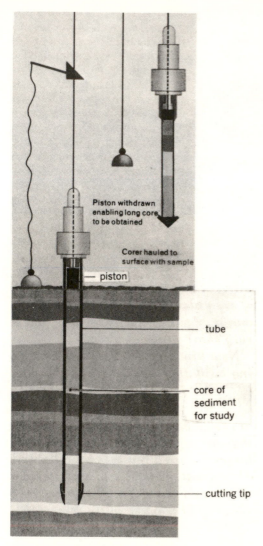

The mechanism of the piston corer. When the corer hits the bottom, the piston stops. The momentum of the tube carries it into the sediment. The piston creates a partial vacuum in the tube so that up to 60 feet of sediment core may be obtained. As the corer is drawn to the surface, the sediment sample is held in by clamps that close automatically over the end of the tube.

The rotary drills can drill in deep water and remove cores thousands of feet long (in segments). The first expedition to do this took place in 1961. The drill went 600 feet into the floor of the ocean while the drilling barge floated in 11,000 feet of water.

The *Glomar Challenger,* a drilling ship of the latest type, has brought up cores from 4,265 feet beneath the ocean floor. It can drill in 25,000 feet of water. The drilling ship is kept on station by a *dynamic positioning system.* Sonar beacons are placed on the sea floor around the site to be drilled. During operations, the sonar signals are fed to a computer, and any drift or movement away from the drill site is compensated for by activation of the ship's bow thrusters (small propellers that allow adjustment of position). The dynamic positioning system is commonly used by oil companies drilling in deep water.

Deep water drilling has told us much about the history and composition of the oceans and their sea floors, as well as about the continents of the earth. Such drilling showed that the North Atlantic began to form about 200 million years ago and the South Atlantic about 150 million years ago. Mineral and oil deposits beneath the ocean floor have also been located by deep water drilling. Cores made by the *Glomar Challenger* confirmed the theory that the earth's surface is made up of moving plates.

Chapter 2. Study Guide Questions

1. How did Navy hydrophones open a whole new area of study for oceanographers?

2. What are the two main levels in the relief of the earth?

3. What are the highest and lowest spots on earth?

4. A. How does an echo sounder determine the depth of water?

B. If it takes 5½ seconds for an echo to return to an echo sounder, how deep is the water in that spot?

5. What are the three distinct divisions or areas of the ocean floor?

6. Under international law, to what water depth does a maritime nation have the right to explore and exploit?

7. What is the *continental slope?*

8. Why are the continental shelves the most valuable part of the ocean floor today?

9. What is a submarine fan, and how does it develop?

10. What are the three ways of determining the depth and topographic features of the ocean floor?

11. What are the major segments of the Mid-Ocean Ridge?

12. Describe the geologic sequence of events in the "wearing down" process of an oceanic island.

13. What is the difference between a *seamount* and a *guyot*?

14. A. What are the three general types of sediments found on the ocean floor?

B. Why do sediment thicknesses vary widely from one part of the ocean floor to another?

15. A. How do metallic nodules form on the ocean floor?

B. What is the engineering problem that must be solved regarding the "mining" of these nodules?

16. A. What is the purpose of a coring tube?

B. How does it work?

17. What did cores from the *Glomar Challenger* prove?

Vocabulary

sediment	submarine fan
ooze	echo sounding
salinity	echo ranging
topography	ocean ridge
relief map	rift valley
contour line	oceanic island
continental shelf	atoll
continental slope	seamount
terrace	lagoon
glaciation	guyot
turbidity current	volcanic eruption
submarine canyon	manganese
detritus	nodules (metallic)
abyss	coring tube
chasm	

Chapter 3. Seawater: Its Makeup and Movements

If there is magic on this planet, it is contained in water.

—Loren Eiseley

Why is the ocean salty? What elements are in water, and in the "salts" of the sea? How do waves, currents, and tides move, and why?

People have wondered about these questions for centuries. Regarded as the founder of modern oceanography, Matthew Fontaine Maury of the U.S. Navy greatly increased our knowledge of the oceans through his studies of navigational charting and of the currents, winds, and storms from 1842 through 1861.

Since then, much has been learned about the oceans, but with each new bit of information, more questions arise. The seas are not only beautiful and interesting, they are also absolutely essential to the very existence of mankind. In addition to the untold wealth beneath their surface and within their seabeds, the seas make possible life itself on our planet.

WHAT IS WATER?

Water is one of the most abundant, widely distributed, and essential substances on the surface of the earth. It is an absolute requirement for the cells of humans, other animals, plant life, and even crystals of many minerals. Water has many forms; ice is water in a solid form, clouds (and steam) are water in a vapor form, and water in liquid form can be found in any lake, river, or ocean.

Snow is probably the purest natural source of water, and rain is next in purity, although both snowflakes and raindrops are formed with a tiny nucleus of salt or dust. Pure water is a compound of two parts hydrogen and one part oxygen. In chemical terms, this is expressed as H_2O. Only when water is between the temperatures of 32 degrees and 212 degrees Fahrenheit (0 degrees to 100 degrees Celsuis) at standard atmospheric pressure is it a liquid.

Physical Behavior of Water

In large part, the special characteristics of water make life on our earth possible. For instance, most materials expand when heated and contract when cooled. Water, however, contracts until cooled to about 4 degrees C (39.2 degrees F), but then expands rapidly as it freezes, increasing in volume about 9 percent. A milk carton filled with water and placed in the freezer will expand greatly and may split, for instance; a glass bottle will shatter as the ice expands.

If this unique expansion did not take place, ice would sink in water. As we all know, however, ice cubes float. More importantly, ice floats on the surface of the ocean, a lake, or a pond, serving as an insulating barrier and holding the heat in the water below. If this were not so, the polar seas might have frozen to the bottom long ago, and much more of the globe would probably be under an icecap.

Another quality of water is its ability to store heat. Only ammonia has a greater heat storage capacity than water. Land, on the other hand, absorbs and loses heat quickly. If the globe were all land, like the moon, it would be scorching hot every day and freezing cold every night. Not many life forms could survive under these conditions. The vast world ocean, however, acts as an enormous heat-controlling thermostat. It absorbs and loses heat more slowly than the land nearby. Also, because of the great currents in the sea, the ocean can absorb heat in one area and then transfer it to other areas where some of that heat is released.

Those who live near the seacoasts, or the Great Lakes, are well aware of this characteristic of water. In summer, the weather reports invariably show air temperatures cooler near the coast than farther inland where the sun quickly heats the ground. In the winter, because the water retains heat longer, the exact opposite will be reported: warmer near the coast, and colder farther inland.

Except under extreme pressures, such as at extreme ocean depths (or under laboratory conditions), water is not compressible. That is, a given amount of water cannot be made smaller in cubic area. On the other hand, this liquid can be stirred or mixed easily, and the molecules will readily associate with other water molecules, retaining its liquid form. This means that water can "turn over," allowing the heat from the surface to move into deeper depths, colder water to move to the surface, and water to evaporate from the surface, aided by wind and wave action. These processes of absorption and evaporation are vital to the pattern of world climate and to the transfer of heat from equatorial to polar regions.

Water affects sound and light in important ways, too. The speed of sound in water, for example, is very much greater than in air and increases with temperature, pressure, and salinity (salt content). Of these factors, temperature is by far the most important in affecting the velocity of sound. The optical properties (ability to transmit light) of seawater are of fundamental importance to life in the oceans.

There are many other fascinating facts about water. Besides being essential to all animal and plant growth, it is also widely used in science and industry as a solvent, as a blending agent, and even as a standard for certain physical properties. The reference points of a thermometer, for example, are the freezing and boiling points of water. Water is also used as a coolant, a dilutant, a cleansing medium, and in the production of heat and power.

Salts of the Sea

Chemically, seawater is a very pure substance; it is more than 95 percent water, that is, hydrogen and oxygen. About eighty elements are found in solution or suspension in the remaining 5 percent. The two basic elements in this remaining portion are sodium and chlorine, which combine to become common table salt. The most significant of the other elements in seawater in concentrations greater than one part per million, or one milligram per liter, are sulfate, magnesium, calcium, and potassium. The remaining elements, therefore, are present in extremely small amounts.

The total salt in seawater is expressed in parts

per thousand. Ocean salinity varies between 32 and 37 parts per thousand, with open ocean waters usually about 35. (That is, if a seawater droplet was divided into 1,000 tiny parts, there would be 965 parts of water and 35 parts of salt.) The enclosed basins and seas have higher salt concentrations. For example, the Mediterranean Sea has about 38.5, and some areas in the Red Sea, particularly during the summer months, have salinities as high as 41, the highest salinity values in the world ocean. Landlocked lakes that serve as basins for water running off surrounding land, like the Great Salt Lake of Utah or the Dead Sea of Israel, with salinities of 250 and 350, have the highest salt content of any bodies of water on the earth.

How did the ocean water get salty? The early world ocean probably was much less salty than today's ocean, since most of the water came from rains caused by the condensation of steam from escaping water vapors of the developing earth. But for millions of years, rain and melted snow have been running over the land, dissolving various minerals and carrying them down to the sea.

In fact, the salts of the ocean are the result of over 2 billion years of wearing away of the rocks of the earth's crust. Those materials that are soluble (can be dissolved) remain in the ocean water. Insoluble materials fall to the bottom and form sediments and clays that may eventually turn into sedimentary rocks. Though the process continues, much of the material that runs into the ocean now is from sedimentary rocks that have gone through the cycle before. For this reason, the concentration of salts in the sea is fairly stable now, having changed very little in composition for millions of years.

During all this time, the water of the oceans has been passing through repetitive cycles of evaporation and condensation. Every year about 80,000 cubic miles of seawater are drawn off by evaporation; of this huge quantity of water, about 24,000 cubic miles return to the continents as rain, sleet, and snow. Most of the rest returns directly to the ocean as rain, but 1 or 2 percent remains in the atmosphere as water vapor. Gusty surface winds carry aloft salt from ocean spray, dust, volcanic ash,

and even smokestack pollutants that become nuclei for rain or snow. The moisture in the atmosphere is attracted to these foreign bodies, and the droplets gradually grow until they become so heavy that they fall to earth as raindrops during the warm months and snowflakes during the cold months.

Thus, water evaporated from the surface of the ocean finally returns to it carrying a microscopic pollutant or mineral. This round trip of evaporation, condensation, and return travel to the sea is called the *hydrologic cycle* (water cycle). A diagram of the hydrologic cycle is shown on page 140. Plants on land also add to the amount of water vapor entering the air by the process called *transpiration*. This is a special term used to identify the evaporation process through plants and trees.

There are nearly 329 million cubic miles of seawater on our globe. The dissolved minerals carried to the ocean in the hydrologic cycle represent fantastic amounts of every known element. In only 1 cubic mile of seawater it is estimated that there are nearly 165 million tons of dissolved minerals, as shown in the following list:

Sodium chloride (common salt)	128,000,000 tons
Magnesium chloride	17,900,000 tons
Magnesium sulfate	7,800,000 tons
Calcium sulfate	5,900,000 tons
Potassium sulfate	4,000,000 tons
Calcium carbonate (lime)	578,832 tons
Magnesium bromide	350,000 tons
Bromine	300,000 tons
Strontium	60,000 tons
Boron	21,000 tons
Fluorine	6,400 tons
Barium	900 tons
Iodine	100 to 1,200 tons
Arsenic	50 to 350 tons
Rubidium	200 tons
Silver	up to 45 tons
Copper, lead, manganese, zinc	10 to 30 tons
Gold	up to 25 tons
Uranium	7 tons

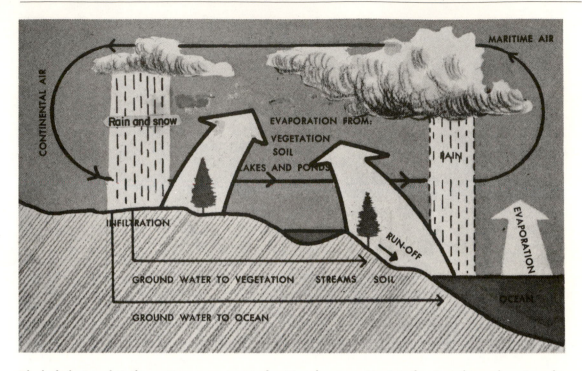

The hydrologic cycle is the continuous movement of moisture by evaporation into the atmosphere, where it condenses and falls back to the earth as precipitation, and then returns to the sea. During its journey over and under the earth's surface, the water dissolves minerals and carries them either suspended or in solution back to the ocean. This explains how the ocean became salty, for these minerals comprise the salts of the sea.

Only magnesium and bromine are presently taken from the ocean water commercially. This is because the supply of most minerals is still plentiful from land mining sites and it costs more to extract them from seawater than these minerals are now worth. Much of the magnesium used in the manufacture of lightweight alloys for airplanes and satellites now comes from the sea, however. The bromine is used in the manufacture of antiknock gasoline and other chemicals. Research is constantly under way to try to develop profitable methods of extracting dissolved minerals from the sea. This is an area of oceanography and metallurgy (the extraction of metals from ore or seawater) that must expand as continental mineral resources are used up.

WATER TEMPERATURE

Upper ocean water temperature varies from about 32 degrees F in the polar regions to a high of about 85 degrees F in the Persian Gulf. The salinity of seawater lowers its freezing point. We know that fresh water freezes at 32 degrees F (0 degrees C); seawater has a freezing point of about 28 degrees F (–2.2 degrees C). On the deep ocean bottom, however, the cold, dense water stays at a uniform temperature of about 4 degrees C (39.2 degrees F) all the time in all latitudes.

An instrument called a *bathythermograph,* commonly called an XBT, can be dropped from ships to check water temperatures at various depths. (Bathy means depth, thermo = temperature, and graph = record.) Most Navy combatants have an XBT to take readings for continuous monitoring of the ocean for antisubmarine warfare.

Ocean water samples can be taken in *Nansen bottles,* named for a Norwegian oceanographer, Fridtjof Nansen. The Nansen bottle is a metal cylinder with automatic closing valves on each end. These valves are linked by levers so they work together. The bottles are attached upside down on a long wire. During lowering, water flows straight through the bottle until it reaches the desired depth. At sampling depth, a weight called a messenger is sent down the wire, releasing the first bottle, which overturns, its valves closing to secure the sample. Another messenger weight, formerly resting on that bottle, then slides down to repeat a similar action on the next bottle below.

As the Nansen bottles capture the water at each desired depth, the mercury column in a thermometer fastened to the outside is automatically fixed. This records the exact temperature of the water when the bottle turned over. In this way, temperatures at any depth in the ocean can be measured. When brought to the surface, the water sample can also be tested for salinity, other chemical content, minute marine life, and so forth.

THE COLOR OF WATER

In shallow places, the ocean's water appears light green, while in deeper areas it seems to be blue, gray, or dark green. These are colors seen when the water does not contain silt or mud near shore or the mouths of rivers. These colors change depending on whether the day is cloudy or sunny. Actually, the water itself has no color; what we see as its color is caused by the reflection of the sky or scattering of light in the water. Some ocean bodies have been given their names because they are colored at times by plant or animal life in them, or by colored silt flowing into them. The Yellow Sea, for instance, is so named because of yellow clay silt carried into it by the rivers of northern China.

We know that the main source of energy for life is the sun. The radiant energy from the sun reaches the earth's atmosphere after traveling about eight minutes through the void of space.

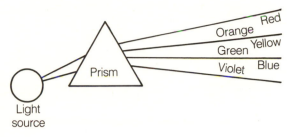

The visible spectrum of sunlight.

Sunlight consists of a range or *spectrum* of different wavelengths of energy. These include infrared, visible, ultraviolet, and X-rays. The different colors of the visible spectrum can be seen using a *prism* or in a rainbow. The atmosphere serves as a giant filter, keeping out most of the dangerous ultraviolet rays. Our own eyes act as a filter for other rays, especially the infrared (below red) light. Much infrared light is absorbed by the water vapor and carbon dioxide in the atmosphere. This atmospheric blanket acts like a big greenhouse, keeping in the warmth that helps to sustain life on earth.

Some of the visible light that strikes the surface of the ocean is reflected back, but some goes down into the water. As it descends, it changes in quality and quantity. The water acts as a filter also, gradually removing various wavelengths of light, starting at the red end of the spectrum. Therefore, the deeper one goes into the water, the greater the amount of blue light. The color of the watery world below about 90 feet (30 meters) is a dark zone of blues, violets, grays, and blacks, and nothing else. The depth to which light penetrates varies according to the position of the sun and the turbidity (suspended materials) in the water.

The oceans can be divided into three environments on the basis of light. The topmost is the *lighted zone,* which ranges in depth from a maximum of about 330 feet (100 meters) in the open, clear sea to about 3 feet (1 meter) in muddy estuaries. Next is the *twilight zone,* which is very dark violet, with only the slightest light penetration. No effective plant production takes place here; this layer ranges from about 260 to 655 feet (80 to 200 meters). Below the twilight zone is the area of total and eternal darkness called the *dark zone*. This is a very thick layer in which no plants grow and animal life consists of carnivores and detritus feeders. This area has no light at all except that which is created by an object or animal itself.

WAVES

Waves in a liquid are caused by any energy source that disturbs the water surface. The energy transmitted by ocean waves can be unbelievably great. Blocks of stone weighing more than 1,300 tons have been moved by waves.

Any disturbance, even a raindrop in a puddle, will create ripples of tiny waves. The tsunami caused by an erupting undersea volcano, a submarine landslide, or an earthquake creates huge waves that travel all the way across the ocean. But wind is the most common cause of ordinary sea waves. Sailors often call wind-driven waves "sea," or the *state of the sea*. A *swell* is a long, smooth wave coming from a distant storm center; swells may indicate an approaching storm and are quite common in advance of hurricanes.

As the wind begins to blow over a smooth ocean surface, a certain amount of wind energy is imparted by friction and pressure on the underlying sea surface, causing the formation of waves. If the wind increases, the size of the waves will increase. At about 13 knots of wind, whitecaps will begin to form. Sea waves of 12 to 15 feet are not uncommon during a strong sea. Waves of 25 to 30 feet or more occur during severe storms or hurricanes.

Waves in excess of 50 feet in height are very unusual, although some years ago the Navy tanker USS *Ramapo* reported a 114-foot wave. What may have been seen and measured by eye in that incident, however, could have been the spray associated with a large, unstable wave. One of the major difficulties in estimating wave height is the lack of reference points. There is also another factor: the perception of the observer. For example, a small frigate operating with a carrier, but out of sight of the larger ship, will frequently report larger waves than those reported by observers on the carrier.

MEASUREMENT AND MOVEMENT OF WAVES

The storm area of the sea over which wind blows to create waves may extend over more than 2,000 square miles on the open sea. The larger the wave, the more easily the wind can add more energy to its crest.

Wave height depends on three principal factors: wind speed, duration of the wind, and the length of the *fetch,* or distance the wind blows over the water. The longer the fetch, the higher and longer the wave is apt to be. There is a limit to a wave's growth, however. At the edge of the fetch—that is, where the wind effect on the waves ceases—the waves gradually change into smooth swells.

Waves are normally described by certain terms. The top of a wave is called the *crest,* while the lowest part, usually between two waves, is called the *trough.* The height of a wave is the vertical distance between the crest and the trough, while the length of the wave is the horizontal distance between two successive crests. The length of time it takes for a complete wave (successive crests or troughs) to pass a given point is called the *period* of the wave. Normally wind waves have short periods, ranging from 2 to 5 seconds. Swells far in advance of a major storm may have a period of from 12 to 15 seconds. The period of a tsunami wave ranges from 10 minutes to as much as an hour.

BREAKERS AND SURF

Waves that break, or fall over, when they hit bottom in shallow water are called *breakers.* A line of breakers along a shore is called a *surf,* or *surf line.*

There are three kinds of breakers. The kind is determined by the *gradient* or slope of the bottom. A *spilling breaker* develops where there is a mild, gradual, almost flat bottom shape. The breaker is slight and can be seen advancing as a line of foam toward the beach.

A *plunging breaker* occurs where there is a steep bottom slope, such as occurs with a coral reef a mile or so off shore. Such a gradient creates the sometimes huge surfs off Australia, South Africa, and Hawaii that are the joy of surfers. The plunging breaker creates an advancing vertical wall of water called *surf*.

A *surging breaker* occurs where there is a very steep bottom slope, generally abrupt rock formations such as along the coasts of Alaska, Chile, Norway, Maine, and much of California. These formations are very close to the continental landmass. The waves crash into the bottom rocks, and the breaker explodes in a surge of foaming, turbulent water. It is extremely dangerous to be near such a coastline in bad weather, and it is rarely safe to swim in such areas. Many people are swept into the sea by sudden surging breakers and drowned each year.

Amphibious Operations. A knowledge of sea waves, swell, and surf conditions is crucial to naval and marine amphibious operations. Surf conditions must be predicted accurately in order to determine when to land troops and vehicles from amphibious landing craft. A 4-foot surf is considered to be the "critical" height for normally safe amphibious landings on an average beach. Above that height, boats are apt to *broach*—that is, turn broadside to the beach after grounding. Broaching can cause damage to propellers and bring sand into engine intakes. At 5 feet, there is certain to be broaching and damage to some boats, and equipment and personnel could be lost. With 6 feet of surf, the risk of extensive damage and loss is too great to attempt amphibious operations except under the most urgent circumstances. However, recently developed surface effect ships/air cushion vehicles can overcome many of the hazards of heavy surf.

Underwater or oceanographic intelligence operations are often conducted by underwater demolition teams (UDTs) and special survey teams. They plot approaches to the assault beach, blow up natural and enemy underwater hazards, and plot good locations for beach tank landing ships (LSTs) and pontoon causeways (a type of floating bridge).

On the beach itself, marine reconnaissance teams take over to study the beach gradient (amount of slope), the ability of the beach to support heavy military vehicle traffic, the height of the *berm* (bank) or *berm line* (where the highest tides

The state of the surf to be expected is always an important consideration in the planning of an amphibious assault. Beaching a landing craft properly becomes a difficult proposition when the surf is heavy.

reach the beach), roads and paths away from the beach to inland areas, enemy strongpoints, the location of helicopter landing zones, and so forth.

BEACH AND COASTLINE EROSION

Coastal landforms owe their shapes to the local action of waves, tides, and currents on coastal rocks and sediments. Such wearing down and changing of the coastal outline and makeup is called *erosion*. Repeated ocean action against exposed rocky headlands, and especially sandy shores, constantly remodels beach and near-shore topography.

In some cases, the waves may lift up huge rocks bodily, break off rocky outcroppings, and throw them ashore. At other times, the steady grinding of erosive sands wears away sediments and soil, creating cliffs that may eventually crumble. In still other locations, whole sand beaches may be washed to sea, or moved and deposited elsewhere. Those who have had the misfortune of having a beach cottage undermined or washed away on the eastern seaboard or on the Gulf of Mexico during gales and hurricanes know what this means.

Waves and currents produced by waves cause most major shoreline changes. It is estimated that shorelines of the United States are being worn away at the rate of about 1 foot each year. Cape Cod, Massachusetts, may be eroded away completely in about five thousand years if the present rate of erosion by waves continues, for example.

On the other hand, waves and currents cause sediments to accumulate in other places. The great Mississippi River Delta continues to grow into the Gulf of Mexico from sediments carried down the river from interior North America. This endless struggle between construction and destruction of the surface of the earth is one reason that geology and oceanography are so interesting.

WAVE POWER

In addition to the pounding of water itself against the shore, small fragments of rocks and sand carried by the waves also scour away beaches and wear down the shoreline. Seaward of breakers, fine grains of sand and pebbles constantly move back and forth like sandpaper on a tabletop, in a ceaseless grinding action. Often, this erosion effects concentrates more in one area of the shore than in another. For example, a line of incoming ocean waves that encounters a seaward-jutting landmass or island tends to change its direction of forward motion. The waves align themselves with the bottom contours as well as conform to the general slope of the coastline. When one part of the line develops drag and changes direction or bends because of shallower water, this response is called *refraction*. Such information is very important to beach intelligence when an amphibious assault is being planned.

Engineers must also know the way water waves are bent so they can take advantage of natural phenomena when designing structures to protect shorelines and harbors. They must know where the natural energy is concentrated and where it is weaker so they can build for greatest effect and economy.

The principal structure built to protect harbors is the *breakwater*. A breakwater is a line of big rocks, sometimes strengthened by steel-reinforced concrete. It may be a single structure protecting a harbor entrance or a series of segments that actually create and protect a harbor or an anchorage. In the latter case, there will normally be two or more harbor entrances and exits for shipping. A breakwater is designed to protect ships at anchor or alongside piers in a harbor from waves, swells, or surf.

Another common structure along inhabited seacoasts is the *groin*. Usually built in a series of two or more, groins are walls of stone or wooden pilings built at right angles to a shoreline to prevent erosion by longshore currents. *Longshore currents* are part of the water movement associated with incoming ocean waves. Since water from these waves is continually moving shoreward, there must be some way for this water to return to sea. In many beach areas, this results in some of the water moving parallel to the beach in a definite flow and speed. Such currents carry scouring sediments to and from the beach out to deeper water. In the process, they may destroy the beach and make real estate along that area nearly worthless. They also sometimes create *bars* that become navigational hazards. Groins serve as dams to stop the movement of sediments by longshore currents. They may protect a given beach, but such interference with natural processes may also result in more erosion farther down the beach from waves. Careful surveys must be made before such structures are built.

Rip Currents. Rip currents are strong, seaward-moving currents that occur along some shores. They return excess water that has been pushed ashore by strong waves. They occur when a longshore current moving in one direction parallel to a beach hits another longshore current moving in the opposite direction. The result is a strong seaward movement of water that moves out to the breaker line or beyond.

Rip currents are often incorrectly called *undertow* (the seaward and downward thrust of a wave as it breaks). But these currents do not actually pull swimmers or waders *down*. They may upset a wader and will pull a swimmer *out* from shore to deep water. Some rip currents are quite fast, moving at speed of up to 2 miles an hour.

Rip currents can be very dangerous to the nonswimmer or to the swimmer who tries to fight the rip. Even a good swimmer is apt to tire quickly trying to swim against such a current. If caught in a

An aerial view of the harbor entrance for Port Everglades, Florida, port of Miami. Breakwaters of rocks protect the harbor entrance and also serve as groins to keep shifting sands from filling the channel.

rip, you must not fight the current. Rip currents are rarely more than 100 feet wide, so the best advice is to swim *parallel* to the shore or breakers until you have gotten past the current. In other words, you should try to swim across the current, getting help from the rip, and using just enough strength to avoid being pulled out to deep water beyond the breaker line. By swimming across the current, you should be able to quickly get out of the main pull of the rip and swim back to shore. You must not panic, nor struggle and overexert yourself.

OCEAN CURRENTS AND GYRES

The study of ocean currents can be quite complex. Like everything else in oceanography, new discoveries about the movements of ocean water are made each year. The effect that ocean currents have on people, the food cycle, and the weather of the world is profound. We can only introduce this

subject here and hope that some students will want to explore this fascinating area of oceanography more on their own.

The movements of the atmosphere (winds) and oceans (currents) are linked to each other. A significant factor in these movements is the rotation of the planet on its polar axis. The earth's rotation, or spin, creates an invisible force called the *Coriolis effect*, or *Coriolis force*. This force deflects free-moving particles to the right (clockwise) in the Northern Hemisphere, and to the left (counterclockwise) in the Southern Hemisphere.

Two other important factors affect global movements of wind and water. These are (1) wind acting on the water surface, and (2) the boundary effects of the continents. Because of the continents, no major ocean current runs all the way around the world.

The heating of water in the equatorial region causes surface water there to rise and then to

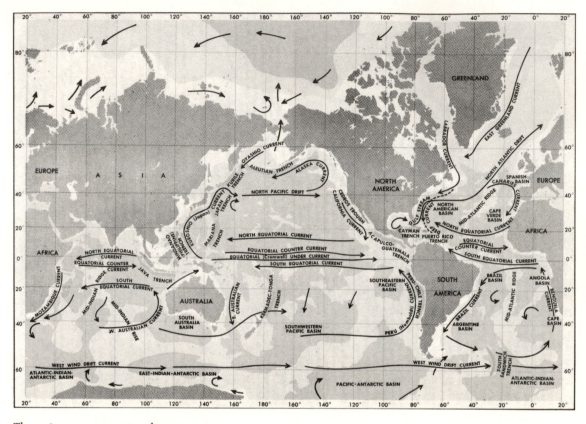

The major ocean currents and gyres.

spread out and flow "downhill" over the surface toward the poles. (The water level of the Sargasso Sea in the mid-Atlantic east of Florida is actually about 3 feet higher than the water level along the west coast of the North Atlantic basin.) As it drifts toward the poles, this water cools and sinks, pushing the water below it toward the equatorial regions. This kind of circular flow, caused by heat differences within the water, is called *convection*. The more important factor affecting global water movements, however, is surface wind, which, combined with the landmass placement, produces a different system. The resulting surface water movements—ocean currents—are a combination of these two flows.

The prevailing winds in the Northern Hemisphere blow from the northeast in the latitude belt from 0° to 30°; these are the *trade winds,* which drive the ocean surface waters to the west. The prevailing Northern Hemisphere winds in the belt from 30° to 60° blow from the southwest; these are the *prevailing westerlies,* which drive the waters back toward the east. From 60° N to the North Pole, the *polar easterlies* blow mainly from the northeast, causing general surface current movement toward the west. The combined effect of these winds is to create broad circular currents in the ocean basins in both the Northern and Southern hemispheres. The movements in the Southern Hemisphere are opposite from those in the Northern Hemisphere because of the Coriolis effect. These circular systems of currents are called *gyres.*

(Keep in mind that winds are named by the direction from which they are blowing, while currents are described in terms of the direction in which they are flowing.)

While these major currents are well defined, they continuously mingle with other currents, especially in the subpolar regions. Also, there is a constant exchange of Atlantic Ocean water with the Mediterranean Sea through the Strait of Gibraltar. This is due to the difference in salinity of these two bodies of water, which causes lighter Atlantic water to flow into the Mediterranean basin while the heavier, saltier water flows out beneath it.

The Gulf Stream. The Gulf Stream is the most important current affecting the United States and its entire Atlantic seaboard. The Gulf Stream system flows in a clockwise motion in the North Atlantic. In the center of this moving water mass is the legendary Sargasso Sea. This is a vast area of floating plants, thought to be true natives of the waters, that float near the surface by means of air bladders. This is not a thick mass of seaweed that entraps derelict ships as is so often pictured in mystery stories of the sea. On the average about 3 miles deep, this oval area is about 2,000 miles east and west by 1,000 miles north and south. The blue waters of the Sargasso Sea form one of the oceanic deserts, and the faunal species that inhabit this region are adapted to this environment.

The North Equatorial Current carries warmer waters northwestward along the West Indies on the eastern rim of the Caribbean Sea. Part of the current breaks off and enters the Gulf of Mexico. The bulk of it rushes northward to form the Gulf Stream that moves along the Florida, Georgia, and Carolina coasts, and then begins to spread out and turn eastward in the North Atlantic Drift. The water flows northward at about 3 to 4 miles an hour. The stream becomes wider and breaks off into *meanders* (different streams) in the northern latitudes. As it goes along the Grand Banks of Newfoundland, it parallels the southward-moving, cold Labrador Current. When warm moist southerly winds crossing the Gulf Stream encounter the cold sea surface of the Labrador Current, the air cools to its dewpoint and fog forms. This type of fog is particularly common during the summer months. The Labrador Current brings icebergs that have *calved,* or broken away, from the western Greenland glaciers and drifted into the North Atlantic shipping lanes. Here they meet the Gulf Stream's warm water and eventually melt away.

In wintertime, the warming effect of the Gulf Stream and North Atlantic Drift make the climate along the eastern seaboard of the United States and Canada, Iceland, Great Britain, and western Europe much warmer than other regions in the same latitude. In the late summer and early fall, the southern side of the Sargasso Sea is the spawning ground for hurricanes, severe storms with winds in excess of 75 mph. These storms, driven by winds aloft, often follow the Gulf Stream into the Caribbean and the Gulf of Mexico or up the East Coast of the United States, leaving a trail of destruction before dissipating in the high latitudes of the North Atlantic.

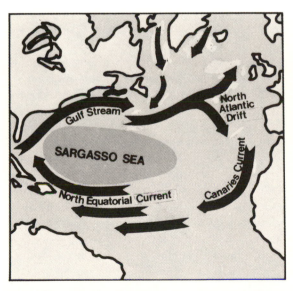

The Atlantic Ocean, showing the Gulf Stream–North Atlantic Drift and the Sargasso Sea. The North Atlantic gyre is clearly defined. The cold Labrador Current to the west of Greenland brings down icebergs that have calved from western Greenland's glaciers.

The Japan Current. The Kuroshio Current originates from the greater part of the (Pacific) North Equatorial Current. Like the Gulf Stream, which flows northwestward on the Atlantic side of the state of Florida, the Kuroshio, or Japan, Current flows northwestward from Japan's Ryukyu Islands.

During the year there are on average twenty typhoons in the Western Pacific. Typhoons are the Pacific equivalent of hurricanes. Spawned in the region of the North Equatorial Current, just north of the equator, they often roar along the track of the Kuroshio, particularly during the late summer months, when high-level hemispheric winds flow in a similar pattern. During the cooler months, the typhoon track is through the Philippines and into the South China Sea and eventually into Vietnam. As the warm Kuroshio Current spreads out north of Japan, it passes south of but close to the cold Oyashio Current coming out of the Bering Sea. The Kuroshio Current travels eastward across the North Pacific and splits into two branches. One of these is the Alaskan Current, which travels counterclockwise around the Gulf of Alaska and westward south of the Aleutian Islands. The other branch becomes the California Current, which travels southward along the west coast of the United States. The effects of the warm Kuroshio water are felt along the entire span of its journey. The interaction between surface winds, temperature, and current frequently causes heavy fogs on the Canadian and Alaskan coasts and in the Aleutians throughout the year.

Subsurface or Countercurrents. As the frictional force of the winds on the earth's surface causes the motion of the major surface currents of the world, a counterforce caused by gravity and the Coriolis effect, particularly in higher latitudes, creates an opposite motion in major segments of the deeper water layers.

At the equator, the deepest water may be moving exactly 180 degrees (opposite) from the surface flow. This amazing phenomenon was discovered in 1952 by Townsend Cromwell, a scientist working with the U.S. Fish and Wildlife Service. He was experimenting with deepsea fishing techniques.

Letting down long lines into the South Equatorial Current in the Pacific Ocean, a west-flowing current, Townsend discovered that the lines drifted eastward. This indicated the existence of a strong undercurrent. Later research showed that this undercurrent, or *countercurrent,* went 3,500 miles to the Galapagos Islands off Ecuador, carrying 30 million tons of water eastward every second.

In 1955, oceanographer Henry Stommel theorized that a countercurrent flowed beneath the Gulf Stream. In 1957, the combined United Kingdom–United States International Geophysical Year (IGY) investigation proved that Stommel's theory was correct.

The oceanographers had used in their tests a floating underwater device called the *Swallow buoy.* Invented by Dr. John Swallow, this equipment can be made to free-float while remaining at any chosen depth. It carries a simple "beeper" or "pinger" that sends out electronic signals that can be picked up by a receiver aboard ship. Using Swallow buoys at different depths, oceanographers found that the Gulf Stream surface current moves about 100 miles a day northeastward, while at depths from 1,350 to 1,500 fathoms, countercurrents move in the opposite direction about 1½ to 15 miles per day. Just above the ocean floor at 1,750 fathoms, the countercurrent was found to move 2½ miles a day in the opposite direction.

The different directions of motion and speed of the surface and the countercurrents create a turbulence between the two layers of water, resulting in considerable vertical mixing. This mixing is particularly strong at the equator, where the two currents travel in nearly opposite directions. As a result, there is an upward transfer of rich nutrients, which is responsible for large numbers of fish in these regions. These distinct layers of water also influence the transmission of underwater sounds, an important consideration in antisubmarine warfare.

TIDES

The earth's nearest neighbor in space, the moon, is the main cause of the rise and fall of ocean tides. Anyone who has lived by or visited an ocean shore has seen the ebb and flow of the tide twice daily. The ancient Greeks first recognized the relationship between the tides and the moon's monthly movement around the earth. It was not until Sir Isaac Newton worked out his theory of gravity in 1687, however, that this relationship could be explained.

Science has determined that everything in the universe exerts a gravitational force or pull on everything else. The pull of gravity is very small for small objects, but for a planet, moon, or star, the force is enormous, tending to pull every other object into its own center of gravity. The mass (amount of material) of the body and the distance it is from the other object or body determine the gravitational effect. It is gravity that holds the planets in their orbits around the sun and keeps the moon and earth "tied" together as companions in space.

The pull of the moon's gravity causes the oceans on the moon's side of the earth to bulge out toward it. The gravitational pull, however, is not the same everywhere. The points of the earth closer to the moon are pulled more strongly, and those farther away are pulled less. This effect, in addition to an outward force on the far side of earth caused by the rotation of the earth–moon system about their common center of gravity, causes the water on the far side of earth to bulge outward as well, though not as much as on the near side.

The sun also causes tides, but this effect is only about two-fifths as strong as that caused by the moon. The reason the sun's tides are smaller is simply that the sun is 390 times farther away. The variations in position of the sun and moon in relation to the earth produce the high and low ranges of tides.

At times of the new and full moons, the tides are highest and lowest because the forces of the moon and sun are working together. The result is *spring tides*. (The term has nothing to do with the spring season.) Halfway between the new and full moons, when we see the half moon during the first and third quarters, the tidal forces of the moon and sun are opposed. At this time the difference between high and low tides is much less. These are called *neap tides*.

The *ebb* of a tide is the fall of the tide; that is, the moving of the tide away from the shore. The *flood* of the tide is the rise of the tide, or the flowing of the tide toward the shore to its highest point. The ebb and flood of tides vary widely around the world. They are affected not only by basic gravitational forces but by the location of the continents and midocean ridges, the shape of the shoreline, the frictional drag between the watermass and the seabed, and the Coriolis force created by the earth's spin. Each tidal system is restricted to its own ocean basin by the continents.

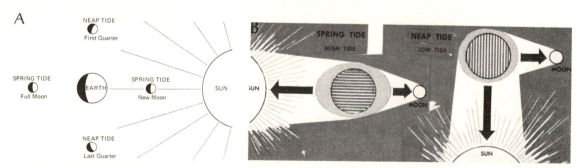

A. The positions of the sun and moon in relation to the earth shown where they exert maximum and minimum influence on the earth's tides. B. When the sun and moon are in line with one another, their combined gravitational pull results in the greatest tidal range, known as spring tides. When the moon and sun are at right angles in relation to the earth, their gravitational pull tends to reduce tidal range, called neap tides.

High tides occur twice a day in most parts of the world because as mentioned earlier, when it is high tide on the side of the earth nearest the moon, there is also a lower high tide on the opposite side of the earth. Knowing that the earth turns on its axis once in twenty-four hours, we might presume that these high tides would be exactly twelve hours apart. However, the earth and moon are not in a fixed position relative to each other. The moon revolves about the earth once in about twenty-seven days, in the same direction as the earth rotates. Because of this motion, it takes twenty-four hours and fifty minutes for a given location on the earth to again be directly opposite the moon. Therefore, there are twelve hours and twenty-five minutes between high tides.

Because these facts are known precisely, *tide tables* for each harbor on earth can be accurately predicted for many years in advance. The National Ocean Service (NOS), a division of the National Oceanic and Atmospheric Administration (NOAA), publishes *Tide and Current Tables* to assist mariners sailing in most parts of the world. Times of high and low tides figured from these tide tables normally are published daily in the *plan of the day* aboard ship and at naval bases and are used every day by a ship's navigator and officer of the deck. This information is important in port because responsible officers and the deck department can use it as a guide when providing for slack in mooring lines. The navigator must be aware of tidal changes in harbors and channels because variations in water depths may be extreme. If tidal currents are strong, boat officers and coxswains must take such information into account when planning boat runs and schedules.

HEIGHT AND SPEED OF TIDAL CURRENTS

The tides in midocean are measurable only with scientific instruments and may have a height of only a few feet. On the shorelines, however, the effect of tides is usually easy to see. In Boston, the range is about 12 feet, in Norfolk less than 6, and in the Mediterranean only a few feet. In some areas of the world, however, tidal effects are quite extreme; this is especially so in the northern latitudes. The highest tides in the world are experienced in the Bay of Fundy, between Nova Scotia and the Canadian mainland, where the spring tide often exceeds 50 feet. Another very high tide occurs at the island of Mont-St.-Michel, France, on the English Channel. This island is surrounded by 10 miles of sands at low tide, but when the 41-foot tide rises, it moves shoreward at a rate of 210 feet per minute and completely surrounds the island. Very high tides are also experienced in Alaska, Northern Europe, and the northeastern coast of Asia.

The harbor at Inchon, Korea, for instance, must enclose its piers with *graving basins* or *docks*. This is a system of locks that hold in the 40-foot tidal waters during low tide, thereby keeping ships alongside the piers afloat. Were it not for the graving dock, the ships would hit bottom and be damaged severely.

In areas where a high tide is common, a *tidal bore* or *tidal surge* is often a twice-daily event where the tide sweeps up a river whose mouth opens directly on the sea. The world's highest tidal bores sweep up the Amazon River in Brazil and the Hangchow (Tsientang) River in China. These bores rise from 15 to 25 feet and speed up the rivers at 10 to 16 miles per hour. The Amazon tidal bore affects the river more than 300 miles inland. Many rivers in Scotland, England, Norway, and Alaska have tidal bores. The River Severn in England has a 3-foot bore that travels 21 miles inland. The Petitcodiac River in Nova Scotia, Canada, has a bore wave 5 feet high that travels 50 miles inland.

Dangerous *tidal currents* occur in places where there are big inlets with narrow entrances. This occurs with some fiords in Greenland, Norway, Alaska, and Chile. Currents rushing past at 8 or 10 knots make it much too dangerous for boats and ships to attempt passage during much of the day. Tidal currents surge at speeds up to 10 knots through channels in the Great Barrier Reef northeast of Australia. And the meeting of tidal currents and winds of the Atlantic Ocean and the North Sea in the Pentland Firth between northern Scotland and the Orkney Islands creates a bore sometimes 10 feet high.

The battleship *Wisconsin* experienced a head-on collision with the Pentland Firth bore in 1947. White water hit the bridge in a smothering spray. The 54,000-ton ship rose and fell on the crest like a fishing cork in a river disturbed by a passing motorboat, and made several more pitches before settling down. The experience of sailors aboard the smaller escorting destroyers was even more dramatic. Many sailors have lost their lives in the Pentland Firth bore (called the Swelkie by local Scots) since the days of the Vikings. The firth is said to be haunted by the ghosts of the drowned, who howl and call out with the strong northwest winds to sailors passing by on dark winter nights.

TIDAL ENERGY

Tidal energy is one of the oldest forms of energy used by man. A tidal mill built in the Deben estuary in Great Britain was mentioned in records as early as 1170 and is still in operation. Engineering ingenuity has resulted in a large number of schemes that make the tides a reliable source of energy.

Tidal energy requires large capital investments, but once built, tidal power installations may last much longer (with small maintenance costs) than thermal or nuclear power stations. Favorable tidal conditions for such power plants exist in at least twenty locations in France, and in Brazil, Argentina, Australia, India, Korea, Canada, China, Russia, and some other countries. The French built the world's first highly successful tidal plant near St. Malo at the mouth of the Rance River estuary. A dam containing turbines spans the estuary. As the tides rise and fall, they spin turbines that drive banks of generators. The idea is rather simple: dam in a basin, which fills with the incoming tide; then, at low tide, release the water through sluice gates so it can spin turbines and generate electricity.

The Dutch have worked for centuries reclaiming land from the sea with dikes and pumps. Their biggest project was the enclosure of the Zuyder Zee. Their most recent project was the Delta Estuary Plan across estuaries of the Rhine, Meuse, and Scheldt rivers, completed in 1978. One part of this system generates electricity by tidal flow. At the same time, the project creates freshwater lakes for recreation, reduces and protects the amount of shoreline directly exposed to the storm waves of the North Sea, reclaims land from the sea, and creates a coastal highway system that connects many previously isolated islands in southern Holland.

Chapter 3.   Study Guide Questions

1. Who is the founder of modern U.S. Navy oceanography?

2. What is unique about the cooling and freezing of water?

3. How does the ability of water to store heat make life possible on earth?

4. A. What are the four main elements in seawater?

   B. What is the percentage of salt in open ocean water?

5. A. What are the saltiest bodies of water in the world ocean?

   B. In landlock lakes?

6. How did the ocean water get salty?

7. Describe the *hydrologic cycle.*

8. What two minerals are extracted from seawater on a commercial basis?

9. A. What is the freezing point of seawater?

   B. What is the constant temperature of water in the deep sea?

10. What determines the color of water (as seen by the human eye)?

11. What is the most common cause of ocean waves?

12. Upon what three things does wave height depend?

13. What are the parts of a wave?

14. What are the three kinds of *breakers,* and what determines each?

15. A. Why are surf and swell so important to amphibious operations?

   B. What is meant by "critical" height of surf?

16. What types of oceanographic and beach intelligence operations are conducted by Navy and Marine Corps personnel prior to an amphibious landing?

17. A. What water actions reshape coastal landforms?

B. What is such action called?

18. What is the main type of structure built to protect harbors from the sea called?

19. A. What is a *longshore current*?

B. What type of structure is built to prevent erosion from these currents?

20. A. What is a *rip current*, and how may it affect swimmers?

B. How should a swimmer move to get out of a rip current?

21. A. What force, caused by the earth's rotation, affects the major currents of the world ocean?

B. In what direction does this force deflect major currents north and south of the equator?

22. What is a *gyre*?

23. What very important current affecting the United States originates on the southern border of the Sargasso Sea?

24. A. Which currents bring icebergs into the North Atlantic shipping lanes?

B. How does the Gulf Stream affect icebergs?

25. A. What important current in the North Pacific has many similarities with the Gulf Stream in the North Atlantic?

B. What severe storms originate in the same general area as does this current?

26. A. How do deeper water layers often move in relation to the major surface currents?

B. What are these subsurface currents called?

C. How is movement of a subsurface current followed?

27. A. What is the main cause of the ocean tides?

B. How does the sun affect the tides?

28. When are tides highest and lowest, and what are these tides called?

29. How often do tides occur?

30. A. How do naval personnel find out about the tidal situation in their port of call?

B. Which persons aboard ship are particularly concerned about the tides? Why?

31. Where do the world's highest tides occur?

32. What is a *graving dock* or *graving basin*?

33. A. What is a *tidal bore*?

B. Where do the highest tidal bores occur?

34. A. In what type of natural geographic formation do dangerous tidal currents occur?

B. Where do some of these currents/bores occur in the world?

35. What is the general theory of operation of a tidal power plant?

Vocabulary

thermostat	wave length
absorption	wave height
suspension	wave period
demolition	breakers
broach (boat)	rip current
berm line	Coriolis effect
delta gradient	gyre
breakwater	Gulf Stream
longshore current	hurricane
seashore groin	typhoon
soluble	calving (glacier)
hydrologic cycle	Sargasso Sea
transpiration	Kuroshio Current
bathythermograph	countercurrent
Nansen bottle	Swallow buoy
spectrum	tides, spring and neap
prism	ebb and flood (tides)
ultraviolet	tidal bore
infrared	beachhead
lighted zone	graving basin
sea swell	fiord
crest (wave)	estuary
fetch (wave)	Pentland Firth
trough (wave)	turbine
surf, surf line	sluice

Chapter 4.   Life in the Seas

So far in this unit we have talked about some physical, geological, and chemical aspects of oceanography. There is a fourth major scientific area: biology. *Marine biology* deals with the living, or organic, content of the sea—its plants and animals.

There are many separate areas of study within modern marine biology, and we cannot explore them all in this text. One important field is biological oceanography, or marine *ecology*. This field is concerned with marine organisms and their environment. It is directly related to (1) human use of the sea for food and employment, and (2) the effect of marine life on naval operations. This latter includes how marine organisms affect ships, installations, and equipment; the ability of people to live and work on and under the sea; the effectiveness of sonar equipment; and many other important things.

PLANKTON, START OF THE LIFE CYCLE

Plankton, both plant and animal, are those billions of tiny floating organisms that wander with the ocean currents or drift in the uppermost layers of the sea. The plankton provides the "ocean pasture" for the smallest animals and fish. Materials in suspension in the sea, including decayed plant and animal life, provide the nutrients plankton need.

Phytoplankton are microscopic marine plants that start the food chain, an ecological system in which almost every form of life becomes the food for another, usually higher, form of life. Next are the *zooplankton,* tiny animals and larvae of larger sea life. Finally there is a whole range of larger fish and sea animals, which extends from fishes and crabs to the giant blue whale, the world's largest mammal.

To show how small plankton are—and to see if enough could be gathered for a meal—explorer Thor Heyerdahl dragged a plankton net behind his balsawood raft, *Kon-Tiki,* for many hours across the southern Pacific in 1947. He managed to gather a small amount of edible plankton, which he made into a sort of fish paste. He found it to be very salty. Studies have now proved that this material is almost pure protein. In fact, the sea is believed to contain a large percentage of the world's total protein supply.

Upwelling and El Niño. *Upwelling* is the movement of deeper layers of water toward the surface. This happens when prevailing winds along a shore cause movement of upper water layers away from the coast. The Coriolis force is also a factor in this process. The resultant vertical circulation from great depths brings decayed materials high in nitrogen and phosphates to the surface. Upwelling occurs near the steepest gradient of the continental slope.

The most remarkable upwelling occurs along the Peruvian coast between the shoreline and the northward-flowing Humboldt Current. The nutrients and minerals nourish plankton, which, in turn, attract great numbers of fishes, large and small, to the area. Great flocks of seabirds feed on these fish, and the islands on which the birds nest are covered with tons of their droppings, called *guano.* Over 330,000 tons of guano are "mined" annually for high-grade fertilizer. At the same time, fishermen catch up to 100,000 tons of anchovies and sardines and the larger fish that feed on them.

Every now and then, for reasons not yet fully understood but probably related to reduced trade winds, the Humboldt Current meanders from its normal course or actually disappears, allowing warmer currents to come along the coast. This stops upwelling, and without the life supporting nutrients, fish begin to die. Additionally, up to 25 million birds may die in such famines. The hydrogen sulfide from the decaying bodies of both fish and birds is so thick that ships' hulls are turned black. This occurrence is locally called the *Callao Painter,* named after the nearby port of Callao, Peru. The phenomenon that causes upwelling to stop is called *El Niño.* For marine life, it is one of the most destructive oceanographic conditions in the world.

The Red Tide and Black Sea. In the Red Sea, atmospheric and sea conditions similar to El Niño occasionally occur. There, when the upwelling of cool water stops, the surface layers become heated and bring about a population explosion (or bloom) of tiny red-colored phytoplankton called *dinoflagellata.* They become so numerous that the water takes on a reddish hue, giving it the name *Red Tide,* and consequently giving the Red Sea its name. The Red Tide clogs the gills of millions of fish, causing them to suffocate and die. The dead fish are washed ashore and the resulting stench carries for miles. A similar event occurs, more rarely, along the east coast of Florida. Some years ago, many resorts and bathing beaches had to close down until the Red Tide passed and the dead fish were cleared away.

The Black Sea, between the Russian states and Turkey, is really a very large saltwater lake. Its only opening to the oceans is through the Turkish straits (Bosporus and Dardanelles) to the Aegean Sea. The straits are very shallow, so there is little exchange of water between the two seas and no chance for upwelling or the introduction of dissolved oxygen in the Black Sea. As a result, the Black Sea is stagnant. The residue of marine life in the surface layers sinks to the bottom and remains there to decay.

The decay of animal and vegetable matter uses up whatever oxygen is available and creates hydrogen sulfide gas. Over thousands of years, this gas and lack of oxygen have completely destroyed bottom life in the Black Sea. The hydrogen sulfide layer begins about 200 feet below the surface and continues to the bottom. There is no life in this "black zone," which has given its name to the sea.

For navies, the Black Sea poses a special problem. Hydrogen sulfide gas, when mixed with water, has a corrosive effect on metals. Recall the *Callao Painter* turning the sides of ships black. A submarine operating for extended periods in the hydrogen sulfide zone would run a serious risk of ruining her hull fittings, thereby endangering the boat and her crew.

The Black Sea is considered international waters, but special rules apply. In peacetime, merchant ships of all nations may go to the ports of Bulgaria, Romania, the Russian states, and Turkey through the Turkish straits. Only light surface warships of non-Black Sea nations may pass through the straits in peacetime under provisions of the Montreaux Convention of 1936. U.S. submarines do not operate in the Black Sea and therefore do not have the problem that Russian submarines do.

THE FOOD CYCLE IN THE SEA

Life in the ocean may answer many of the questions about the origin of life and its historical past, as well as help solve the problems of improving human life in the future. The life cycle in the sea is of great importance to everyone. Oceanographers are the scientists who are working to find the answers to some of these questions.

The life cycle is the chain of natural events in which organic plants and animals take in foods and chemicals, release wastes during their lifetimes, and then die and decompose. Bacterial, current, wave, and solar (sun) energy rotate this material from the bottom of the sea, bringing it back into the sunlight where the process of photosynthesis regenerates new life.

In the sea, as on land, sunlight supports the life cycle. (See illustration of the life cycle.) It does so through the process of *photosynthesis,* the manufacture of food in a green plant. In the sea, the floating chlorophyll-bearing (green-colored) plants called phytoplankton are the basic food producers of the sea. They provide the proteins, starches, and sugars necessary to support the sea's smallest life. Phytoplankton are the food for the zooplankton, tiny animals of many shapes, which are either freefloating or self-propelled. The zooplankton—which also include the eggs and larvae of some larger fishes—are the food for small flesh-eaters (carnivores) of the ocean. In turn, the small carnivores are eaten by larger ones. Death and decay complete the cycle. The organic material of both plants and animals decays as the result of bacterial action, thereby releasing again the nutrient raw materials—carbon, phosphorus, and nitrogen—needed to start the process of photosynthesis over again. Since the organic material sinks, most of the decay occurs in deep water. Upwelling currents eventually return the nutrients to the lighted zone in the upper 15–20 fathoms of water where this life cycle can begin again.

Though phytoplankton can live only in the

The life and food cycle in the ocean. Beginning with the phytoplankton, which live on the nutrients and decayed matter from the bottom of the sea that upwell into the lighted zone, the cycle moves on around to where dead animals drop to the bottom of the sea, providing the decayed matter upon which phytoplankton live, to begin the cycle again.

lighted zone, usually in the upper 90 feet, zooplankton and larger animal life have been found in all parts of the ocean, including at the bottom of the deepest part in the 35,800-foot-deep Mariana Trench. Animals that live in these great depths are generally small, ferocious carnivores. They have very soft, scaleless bodies with a wide variety of shapes. Often snakelike with narrow fins and very pliant bones, most are black in color because of the dark environment. Many have developed long, needle-sharp teeth and huge mouths. Others are blind, having no need for eyes in the pitch-black world of the abyss. Still others have large bulging eyes, and many have luminescent spots and devices that glow in the dark. This natural luminescence (light) is believed to attract prey, their mates, or both. Much has yet to be learned about these strange deepsea animals.

LIFE AT THE EDGE OF THE SEA

At the shoreline, creatures of the sea live under very difficult conditions. They are subject to the extremes of drying, flooding, baking, and freezing if they are exposed when the tide rises and falls. Waves and currents may also wash them up on the beach to die. And, of course, there are many predators that can get them when they are exposed. Many sea animals that live on the edge of the sea are small, flat, or streamlined, and many have suction-type devices that hold them tightly to rocks. Starfish have hundreds of such suction cups on their five arms. Barnacles attach to underwater surfaces and excrete a chemical that acts as a cement to keep them in place the rest of their lives.

Other marine life is found in tidal pools and hollows of rocks and coral where they are sheltered from predators and yet have life-sustaining water around them even when the tide is out. In this category are some corals, sponges, sea anemones, sea cucumbers, and sea urchins. Others live on the beaches and burrow into the sand for protection when the tide is out. Able to remain in the air from one high tide to the next, this type includes some crabs, clams, sandworms, and sand dollars, among many others.

LIFE IN THE SHALLOW SEA

Most sea animals live in the relatively shallow water seaward of the low tide level above the continental shelf. Over much of the continental shelf, marine plant life (phytoplankton) is able to float, or in some instances to attach itself to the bottom and remain within range of sunlight. The plants vary in size from microscopic single cells such as algae and diatoms to huge seaweed plants called *kelp,* which may be 150 feet in length. Algae are the most common of all plants. They are a number of different colors; some float, and others attach themselves to rocks. There are also some grasslike plants. In general, however, the sea does not have the wide variety of plants found on land, nor the advanced members of the plant family like trees or flowering shrubs. Much of the sea and the sea floor, in fact, is barren.

Where plants exist, however, there will normally be an abundance of animal life. The smallest animals of the zooplankton group are the one-celled *protozoans.* Jellyfishes are the largest form of zooplankton. These are rather beautiful, transparent creatures composed of many white, blue-green, and blue cells, but they often have stingers by the thousands on their lacy tentacles that can cause extreme pain, convulsions, and, if one panics, even death. Others in the group of tiny animals that live off phytoplankton are the larvae, or young forms, of oysters, snails, and sea worms. More developed animals are the crabs, shrimps, lobsters, clams, oysters, squid, mussels, octopi, and scallops. These animals eat the smaller species of zooplankton and graze upon phytoplankton. Starfish and sea urchins dine on shellfish such as oysters and clams.

Jawless fish. A sea lamprey attacking a lake trout in the Great Lakes. Lampreys attach themselves to living fish, using their rasping tongues to make open sores from which they feed on blood and tissues (courtesy Great Lakes Fishery Commission).

MARINE ANIMALS

There are two major divisions of marine animals: those that do not have jaws, and those that do.

Only two types of jawless fish exist—the hagfish and the lampreys. Their mouths are circular and are used to attach to their prey. The hagfish feeds on dead or dying animals, but lampreys attach themselves to living fish, using their rasping tongues to make open sores from which they feed on blood and tissue. The sea lampreys in the Great Lakes have caused great damage to the lake trout and whiting fisheries, but in the oceans they are insignificant. The lampreys entered the Great Lakes via the St. Lawrence Seaway, illustrating how human endeavors can in some instances upset an ecological system.

There are four groups of marine animals that have jaws: fish, reptiles, birds, and mammals. Fish range throughout the seas, but most live in the shallow, warmer seas. Within this group are five subgroups: (1) bottom-living fishes of both shallow and deep seas, which have large heads and whip tails; (2) large carnivorous fishes with tough, leathery skins and sharp cutting teeth, such as the sharks and rays; this group has the largest fish—the whale shark, basking shark, and manta ray; (3) sturgeons, which have bony plates on the skin and

are commercially valuable for their eggs, called caviar; (4) the largest group, which includes most commercial fishes, such as cod, herring, turbot, salmon, tuna, mackerel, flounder, bass, and many others; and (5) lungfish, three of which are freshwater types, and one called the *coelacanth.* This oddity, once thought to have died out some 50 million years ago, was found in the Indian Ocean in 1938; an occasional specimen has been caught from time to time since.

The reptile group has only a small number of species that live in the sea today—a far cry from the Age of Reptiles, when they were the dominant form of life in the world ocean. Reptiles are cold-blooded; that is, they cannot regulate their temperatures as mammals do, so they usually inhabit warm tropical seas. There are four groups of living marine reptiles: turtles, marine iguanas, sea snakes, and a few ocean crocodiles.

Sea turtles grow to a huge size; the rare leatherback sometimes exceeds 6 feet in length and weighs over half a ton. Turtles swim with flippers. They come ashore to lay their eggs in holes dug in the sand. There, they are at the mercy of many different kinds of predators. Few of the young make it back to the sea before being eaten by seabirds.

Marine iguanas live only in the Galapagos Islands of Ecuador, off the west coast of South America. They are the only marine lizards. They live in large herds on the rocks near shore and feed on seaweed.

Sea snakes are poisonous, some related to cobras and kraits. They have paddlelike flat tails so they can swim. They inhabit sheltered coastal waters, especially near river mouths, and some live in brackish water upstream. There are nearly fifty species of these poisonous snakes living in the tropical Pacific and Indian oceans. They range from East African waters throughout southern and Southeast Asia, Oceania, Australia, and in the warm Japan Current all the way north to Japan and Korea; a few species exist along the Pacific coast of Central and South America. Although sea snakes are poisonous, they do not disturb swimmers and are said not to bite unless forcibly restrained. They feed on fish, mostly at night. This makes them dangerous to fishermen who may net them when they are attracted by schools of fish and the lights of fishing boats. Oriental fishermen are said to throw them from their nets with bare hands. There are a number of deaths caused by sea snakes each year.

The seabird group includes a number of different species. The waders live and feed along the shallows, in estuaries of rivers affected by tides, in ponds, and in mangrove swamps. Birds of the open sea, such as the albatross and petrel, live most of the time in the open ocean, coming ashore only to breed. The emperor penguin lays its eggs on sea ice in Antarctica; it is the only bird that never comes ashore. There are many other varieties of penguins, all of them in the Southern Hemisphere. Seabirds feed mainly on fish. As penguins cannot fly, they catch fish by diving and swimming. Pelicans and gannets catch them by diving. Gulls and terns spot and then pounce on their prey from the air.

The mammal group has a rather limited number of marine species, but they are some of the world's most interesting animals. They include the polar bear and sea otter, which are similar in most characteristics to land animals but are adapted to the sea. The polar bear has extra-long legs, which

A mother Adelie penguin and just hatched chick at Mammoth Penguin Rookery on Mt. Bird, Ross Island, Antarctica. Penguins cannot fly but are rapid swimmers.

makes it a powerful swimmer, and a thicker coat, which insulates it against the icy waters and winds of the Arctic. There are only about 2,500 polar bears living in the wild today because of overhunting.

The sea otter has webbed feet and is well adapted to life in the sea. It inhabits only the coastal regions of California and Alaska, where it feeds in the giant kelp beds on abalone and sea urchins. The sea otter spends most of its entire life at sea, sleeping, eating, and even giving birth to its young among the kelp. It was almost exterminated for its valuable pelt by the early 1900s, but strict hunting regulations have allowed it to make a good natural recovery.

Other marine mammals, however, have changed a great deal from the form they once had on land. There are three groups: the sea cows, the seals, and the whales. The sea cows include the manatees of Florida and the jungle rivers of South America. The sea cow eats lily pads. It is cigar-shaped with front flippers and a flat tail but no hind flippers.

There are three groups of seals: the earless, or true, seals; the eared seals, or sea lions; and the walrus. They are all fish-eaters and have streamlined bodies and limbs modified to be flippers. They are fast, expert swimmers and can easily catch their prey in the water. They have a layer of thick blubber beneath the skin to protect them from the cold. The fur seals of Alaska have luxuriant pelts much prized for coats. After many years of overhunting, they are now carefully protected and "harvested" for their pelts, a valuable natural resource. The California sea lion is the most common performer in zoos. The walrus has long ivory tusks and is found only in Arctic waters.

Whales, dolphins, and porpoises are all air-breathing mammals that bear their young alive, nurse them, and maintain a constant body temperature. They spend their lives entirely in water and have breathing devices that are called blow-holes. Movement is accomplished by horizontally flattened tail *flukes*. There are two subgroups of whales: the baleen, or whalebone, whale and the toothed whale.

Instead of teeth, the *baleen whales* have a fine mesh sieve with up to 800 or more plates of baleen or whalebone that hang like a curtain from the upper jaw. When feeding, the whale opens its jaws. When the jaw closes, the baleen allows the water to flow out but keeps any collected marine life in. The principal foods of the baleen whale are plankton and krill (a shrimplike animal that grows up to 2–3 inches in length and is found in great numbers in Antarctic waters). Baleen whales range in size from the minke (just over 30 feet) to the blue whale, which often grows to 90 or 100 feet in length and weighs 100 tons. The giant blue whale, the largest mammal that has lived on earth, weighs 2 to 3 tons at birth, doubles its weight in its first week of life, and seven months later weighs about 24 tons! The largest blue whale on record was 108 feet long. From a world population of about 40,000 in 1930, there are now only about 3,000 left. Some conservationists fear it is close to extinction, having arrived dangerously close to the point where the death rate exceeds the reproductive rate.

Giant 1½-ton elephant seals bask in the sun on an Antarctic beach. Ungainly on land, they are fast swimmers in the water, able to catch fish to eat.

A blue whale comes up for air in the Queen Charlotte Strait off the Pacific coast of Canada. This species is the largest mammal on earth.

Unlike baleen whales, *toothed whales* do have teeth after birth, which number from just a few in some species to as many as 250, although some may be concealed beneath the gum. The narwhal has a single long, tusklike tooth in the upper jaw. Toothed whales have one blowhole, in contrast to the baleen, which have two. This group includes the animals commonly called dolphins or porpoises, as well as sperm whales. The sizes in this class range from the porpoise, which is about 5 feet long, to the sperm whale, which is up to 68–70 feet long. They eat fish primarily, but the sperm whale also likes giant squid found at great depths. Records of sperm whales being entangled with submarine cables at depths to 3,700 feet indicate that some of the squid on which they feed are browsing on the bottom.

LIFE IN THE OPEN OCEAN

Beyond the shallow waters of the continental shelf, there is much less sea life because there is little plant life. Food is quite scarce. The animals of the region come to the surface to feed on the limited zooplankton and smaller fish, but in general, food is hard to find.

We talked earlier of the Sargasso Sea in the central Atlantic. Here there is a great deal of floating *sargassum weed*, which gives the area its name. This weed floats near the surface in clumps, plainly visible to sailors traversing the area. With the exception of this weed, the water of the Sargasso Sea is about the purest and clearest salt water in the world. In fact, as sea life goes, there is little life other than the tiny shrimp, fish, and crabs that live among the tangle of sargassum. Limited phytoplankton live in the area because there is almost no upwelling of nutrients from the deep sea bottom.

On the edges of the currents of the sea live many of the great game fishes of the world, such as marlin, sailfish, tuna, and sharks. Especially good fishing grounds for these fish are on the fringes of the Gulf Stream along the eastern seaboard and on the Mexican coasts in both the Atlantic and Pacific. Tuna species are found throughout the world ocean as they follow the plankton communities

and migrate to central ocean spawning grounds.

There are places on a continental or island shelf where the ocean floor rises much closer to the surface in high underwater plateaus. These areas have an abundance of marine vegetation for fish to feed on. These plateaus are called *banks.* They are the best fishing grounds in the world: the Grand Banks off Newfoundland, Georges Bank off Massachusetts, the Dogger Bank in the North Sea, and in the Pacific near Japan and Alaska.

THE FISHING INDUSTRY

About a million vessels of all sizes and about 4 million people are engaged in some phase of the marine fishing industry. Each year the oceans yield over 70 million tons of fish for a hungry world population. About 45 percent, or 31.5 million tons, comes from the Pacific; 40 percent, or 28 million tons, from the Atlantic; and the rest from the other world seas.

The amount of seafood eaten annually in different parts of the world is related to eating habits that people have developed over centuries and the local standard of living. In the United States, for instance, each person eats only about 13 pounds of fish and other seafoods annually; this amount is increasing because of improved refrigeration and canning of the catch and a gradual change of eating habits in the interior of the country. In Japan, the average person consumes over 80 pounds. Coastal peoples, especially in underdeveloped countries, may eat more than that, usually in the form of fish-meal cakes purchased from major commercial fishing nations.

The history of the fishing industry is one of the never-ending stories of world commerce and the never-ending search for food. Since the beginning of the twentieth century, many improvements in fishing vessels, nets, and preservation methods have been made. Progress made in fishing methods since 1930 alone has been greater than that made in the previous three thousand years. Three main types of new vessels have been developed: the giant *purse seiner,* a vessel that uses sonar equipment to locate and entrap schools of fish; the oceanic *long-liners,* which can fish for tuna throughout the tropical oceans; and the *factory trawlers*. The trawler fleets of the world have greatly increased, especially under Eastern European flags, and they fish the continental shelves throughout the world. Trawlers generally stay at sea for several months and bring in a catch of up to 250 tons of fish that have been automatically cleaned and stored in ice.

The large purse seiners were designed by Americans to pursue tuna on the high seas. They are based in California but cruise the world. Their large nets can catch a whole school of tuna at one set. Many of the larger ships can carry 1,500 tons of frozen fish in their holds.

The long-liners originated in Japan and South Korea. These vessels lay out from one to three floating long-lines, each more than 20 miles long and bearing baited hooks every few feet. They seek mainly to catch marlin, sailfish, and tuna.

The Japanese and Russians have developed huge fish factory ships that process and can the catch at sea. They serve as "mother ships" to a fleet of trawlers. They deliver their products directly to foreign markets at prices that cannot be matched by fishermen with less sophisticated equipment.

AQUACULTURE

The oceans are a good source of food now, but their potential is even greater. The seas alone could provide enough protein for the entire world population of about 4 billion people. At the present time, however, only about 1 percent of the protein in the human diet comes from the sea. A change in people's eating habits, careful conservation and harvesting practices, and cultivation of selected kinds of marine plant and animal life could increase food production from the sea. We must be very careful, however, not to deplete the breeding stock of fish, or to overfish given areas, lest the disaster of extinction that has occurred with some land animals be repeated.

A term used today to identify marine "farming" is aquaculture, *aqua* meaning water. *Aquaculture* means the protected cultivation or raising of marine plants and animals for food. Attesting to the success of aquaculture and its future potential is the fact that 13 percent of Japan's total ocean produce now comes from carefully cultivated "mari-farms." (The Japanese government spends much more than the United States on aquaculture research and subsidy.)

Along the Pacific coast of Asia, people have been supplementing their diets with a variety of seaweeds for ages. It is mixed in rice dishes and used as greens and seasoning. It is highly nutritious and excellent tasting. Some giant algae have been used for centuries as fertilizer for farm crops and as cattle food. Giant kelp plants of the Pacific are processed for iodine, medicines, and a variety of other products that are used in cosmetics, textiles, ink, paper, paints, drugs, and food preservatives.

Sea farming has existed for many centuries. The ancient Romans in the Mediterranean and the Chinese and Japanese have raised oysters for more than 2,000 years. Oyster bed cultivation remains one of their main commercial marine projects. Today most of the world's oysters come from such beds.

An adult oyster can produce as many as 100 million eggs at one laying! But only a few oysters per million eggs survive in their natural environment. Each egg develops into a zooplankton larva and floats about for two to three weeks before settling down on a rock or other surface. People have traditionally cultivated oysters by providing old oyster shells for the larvae to settle on; these old shells are called the *clutch*. Predators, such as starfish, are cleared out, and the area is fenced off. In a few years the oysters are ready to be harvested.

This method has been improved on, however, because it was too slow. Previously, only the food that fell to the bottom could be taken by the growing oysters. Now most oyster beds have been replaced by *suspension cultures* in which the clutch is hung from ropes attached to floating frame rafts, or to stakes driven into the bottom. This way, the oysters can take their food from plankton floating by in all depths, and they are safe from their bottom-dwelling enemies. Using this method, it is possible to harvest 6,400 tons of oyster meat per square kilometer in about two years. French oyster farms near Bordeaux produce 500 million oysters annually for the European market. The Japanese have increased productivity of oysters from 600 pounds per acre under natural conditions to 32 tons per acre under culture.

Even more productive is aquafarming the common mussel. Mussel cultivation near Virgo, Spain, on the Atlantic Ocean, nets an unbelievable 27,000 tons of mussel meat from each square kilometer of floating farms!

Fish farming has had a high record of success for centuries in Southeast Asia, the Philippines, Indonesia, and China. The raising of milkfish in shallow fish ponds filled with brackish water has reaped 206 tons per square kilometer using commercial fertilizers and an amazing 508 tons using human sewage as the nutrient fertilizer. In the open ocean, 7 tons is the natural production. The United Nations has figured that, in Southeast Asia alone, there are at least 5,500 square kilometers of shallow sea that could be turned over to milkfish production. Such production could supply most of the annual protein requirements of Asia.

Over a thousand years ago the Chinese developed a complex ecological fish farming system that they still use today. They place six different kinds of carp into a single deep pond, knowing that each species occupies a different habitat (water depth) and consumes different food. The grass carp consumes the surface vegetation. There are two midwater dwellers, one that eats zooplankton, the other phytoplankton. Finally, there are three bottom feeders that eat mollusks, worms, and the feces of the grass carp. This is an extremely efficient ecological system that even serves to eliminate "pollution." The system is ancient, but it is naturally organic—and it works.

Woods Hole Oceanographic Institute has worked out a similar system involving algae, oysters, seaweed, abalone, sand worms, and flounder, after which clean water is returned to the sea. The main crop is oysters, with abalone and flounder as secondary crops. It is a natural sewage treatment plant. The sewage is used to grow plankton algae, which in turn provide food for oysters. The waste from the oysters is consumed by seaweeds, which

is then fed to abalone. The remainder that falls to the bottom of the tank is eaten by sand worms, which are then circulated to a neighboring tank to serve as food for flounder. The system is designed to produce 1 million pounds of seafood meat annually from a 1-acre production facility of fish and shellfish holding tanks, and a 50-acre algae farm using sewage from a community of 11,000 people.

In Southeast Asia, in addition to the milkfish farming described above, the people also grow mullet, shrimp, and crabs in ponds constructed by clearing mangrove swamps and diking them with mud. These are extremely productive. The small fry are first fed in a nursery pond, while algae, bacteria, worms, and other plankton are raised naturally in production ponds with the addition of fertilizer. When the fry get to fingerling size, they are transferred to the production ponds. There they literally gorge themselves, growing to mature size in just a few months. The average yield of such ponds is about 500 pounds per acre.

Woods Hole has estimated that if only one-tenth of the 1 billion acres of available coastal wetlands (100 million acres) were converted to aquacultural development, the potential yield would equal the maximum considered naturally possible from the oceans—100 million tons each year.

The green turtle, much prized for its meat and eggs, almost became extinct because of overhunting. Experimenting in the Cayman Islands of the Caribbean, one of the places the turtles naturally breed and lay their eggs, private enterprise has created a huge turtle farm. This has proved so successful that similar farms have since been built in other places where the turtle was nearing its end. The Cayman Island facility is a 10-acre farm with about 160 concrete pens and tanks, a huge artificial breeding pond, a nesting beach, processing facilities, laboratories, and offices. About 160,000 turtle eggs, some from the farm and some collected from nesting beaches, are hatched each year. In nature, only about two hatchlings in a thousand survive. Most are eaten by seabirds in the short distance between their nest in the beach sand and the deeper water. On the farm there is a survival rate of about 95 percent.

Raising green turtles has been so successful that many are now placed in the sea, where their survival rate is good. They have an amazing internal "navigational system" that will bring them back to the place of their birth when they are mature and ready to lay their eggs. It is hoped that this conservation program will successfully restock the beaches with their natural turtle population.

Freshwater commercial fish farming in the United States has become more and more popular and successful since World War II. The varieties most commonly raised in ponds or basins are trout, walleyed pike, perch, and catfish. Most freshwater fish now seen in the frozen fish counters of supermarkets are raised in these fish farms. Most of the pike are raised in Canada, Upper Michigan, and Wisconsin. Trout are raised throughout the country, but mostly in the mountain areas and northern part of the country. Catfish and perch are raised in the South and Southwest. Freshwater fish farming has become a very prosperous business and is capable of considerable expansion.

Sea Noises

An interesting biological phenomenon in the oceans is the "deep scattering layers." Discovered in World War II, these layers have become increasingly important to mariners and oceanographers. Scientists experimenting with sonic submarine detection gear recorded echoes from layers some distance above the ocean floor. During daylight hours there are usually three distinct layers that remain at depths from 700 to 2,400 feet. At night they rise almost to the surface and diffuse, or they may merge into a broad band as much as 500 feet thick.

After some years of research, oceanographers deduced that there seemed to be a close parallel between the layers and the daily vertical migrations of certain marine animals. Today, this theory has generally been accepted, though there is still much to be learned about the phenomenon. It is believed that huge concentrations of tiny planktonic animals rise toward the surface to feed on phytoplankton, and then, at daybreak, seek the dark depths for protection from sunlight and predators. It appears that the layers are composed of a wide variety of zooplankton, including tiny fish, shrimplike animals, lantern fish, fish with bladders or gas-filled bubbles, and tiny jellyfish with gas-filled floats. Biologists consider the layers to be important in explaining the distribution of life within the sea.

These deep scattering layers create horizontal sound-reflecting bands at various depths over broad stretches of the world's oceans. Until the phenomenon was identified, it caused confusion to operators of echo-sounding devices and sonar equipment. In addition, many marine animals have sound-emitters that create a wide assortment of noises beneath the sea. A person on the surface does not hear the noises because of the frequencies and sound level at which they are transmitted, but they can become a constant clangor over hydrophones. Such noises must be contended with in naval operations, in particular antisubmarine operations. Hydrophone reception can be seriously hampered, as some noises are very similar to the sound transmitted by naval surface and underwater vessels. Such noises can also be psychologically stressful to sonar operators. Therefore, the Navy began a program to record and identify biological and mechanical sounds so sonar operators could be trained to distinguish between them. The Navy also started a continuing research program to design equipment that could filter out as much of this biological noise as possible.

The problem of identification is complicated by the fact that the recorded sound differs according to the number of animals making noises. One croaker fish makes a drumming noise, but a dense shoal of croakers sounds like a pneumatic drill tearing up a pavement, completely drowning out the noise of any ship's propeller. The tiny snapping shrimp makes a sharp snap with its claw, but a large number of them sound like radio static.

In recording marine animal noises, scientists identified the sounds by comparing them with more familiar land animals. They learned, for example, that porpoises and whales whistle, click, bark, and moan; barnacles slurp; black mussels crackle; toadfish croak, growl, and whistle; weakfish and perch produce a rapid, raspy croak; the northern puffer squeaks and coughs; and the sea robin makes a sound like fingernails being scraped over a drum.

The animals also use different means to make their sounds. Crustaceans make percussion noises with their claws. Fish usually make noises with their swim-bladder, the size and species of fish determining in which way it is vibrated. Some fish also make grinding noises with their teeth or fins. It is still not known why these animals make these noises, but they probably are related to breeding, spawning, and defensive actions, among other purposes. Through their study of these noises, biologists hope to learn more about the behavior of these animals. Such information could be used to help improve commercial fishing practices.

BIOLUMINESCENCE

Luminescence means "light created or emitted at low temperatures, not as a result of burning heat." In nature, there are at least four sources of such light: (1) mineral phosphorus (phosphorescence); (2) radioactive minerals that respond to or reflect certain wavelengths of light; (3) cool gases that can be activated by electricity (fluorescent light); and (4) *bioluminescence*—that is, light created by insects (fireflies), certain fishes of the abyss, and microscopic marine *dinoflagellata*, a single-celled phytoplankton. It is this latter source of natural light that we shall talk about here.

The luminescence of the sea at night is one of those common, yet curious, sights of the sea. It is a bluish-green, often sparkling, glow seen in waters disturbed by bow waves, wakes, and cresting waves. In some areas of the world this luminescence is very bright, to the extent that agitation of the sea by a passing vessel can briefly produce enough light on topside to read. When these organisms are stimulated by waves, their rhythmic reaction looks like a swirling movement of light, like a pinwheel. In calm conditions, the orbital movement of the seawater creates horizontal streaks where the dinoflagellata tend to concentrate. Oceanographers are constantly expanding

their study of such natural bioluminescence in the sea.

For the Navy, this luminosity of seawater is more than just an interesting natural wonder. Observed from the air or from the bridge of a large ship, the luminous wake of a ship or periscope traveling at even moderate speed can be detected for some distance, clearly revealing the vessel's position and, roughly, its course and speed. During World War II amphibious landings and other naval movements were, on several occasions, given away by bioluminescence in the warm waters of the Pacific. Naval oceanographers generally know where heavy luminescence regularly occurs and can forecast periods of this phenomenon in areas where naval operations are planned.

BIOLOGICAL ASPECTS OF FISHING

The sea contains over 30,000 species of fish and other species of sea life. Of this large number, only about 300 kinds of fish and shellfish are used for food in the United States. Actually, 60 percent of the annual catch is composed of only nine species. There are cod, tuna, salmon, herring, sardines,

Japanese fishermen take aboard a load of fresh-caught Alaskan king crabs in the Bering Sea north of the Aleutian Islands. The U.S. Coast Guard Bering Sea Patrol enforces the North Pacific fishing treaties within 200 miles of the Alaskan coast.

pollack, haddock, ocean perch, and shrimp. Also, there is a very large market for oysters, lobsters, and crabs. Such emphasis places a heavy burden on these species. Growing future demands will have to be met with a careful combination of conservation, greater use of other species, aquaculture of the popular species, and discovery of additional sources of natural supply in the oceans. Oceanography will play an important role in finding solutions to these problems, as well as other ways of increasing food harvest from the seas.

Biological research has already developed a number of methods to increase stocks of commercial fishes. Fish can be artificially reared in hatcheries and fish farms; eggs and larvae can be protected from natural predators and other adverse conditions; and fertilization can increase the growth of natural food supplies. Based on studies of natural upwellings, a plan for a nuclear-powered reactor that would pump warmer water under pressure into deep areas to induce upwelling of nutrients has been designed. Desirable species have even been transplanted from one environment to another with success. The planting of coho salmon for recreational and limited commercial fishing in Lake Michigan is an example.

To maximize harvest, we must also explore more thoroughly the open oceans to find additional places where commercial species are living. Some, like the roving tuna family, move from place to place following their food supplies. Many of these tuna routes have been charted in recent years, leading to the development of new ocean-going fishing ships to seek them out. There certainly are many other places that await discovery.

In order to catch fish in the open seas, we must learn more about the behavior and characteristics of various types of fish. Scientists have to learn their schooling, breeding, and shoaling habits, and how they react to the presence of fishing gear. The form, size, color, and other features of the gear and the region in which it is used help determine its effectiveness. More sophisticated capturing methods that are being tried include strong underwater lights to attract fish; the use of electronic pulses to frighten, block, or fence fish; and the use of a wall or stream of air bubbles to guide fish into traps and nets. All have worked with varying degrees of success.

FOULING AND DETERIORATION

Of the many important problems with which marine biology is concerned, none has greater economic significance to the Navy and commercial maritime interests than the control of marine fouling and deterioration. The effects of marine growth on ships' hulls, their saltwater intakes, valves, and piping are costly. Important also is the damage by marine organisms to the wood, plastics, metal, and concrete of shore installations. For the U.S. Navy alone, the protection and maintenance of ships, waterfront structures, and offshore equipment against biological deterioration and fouling costs about $100 million annually. More importantly, such uncontrolled fouling and deterioration can reduce the combat readiness of naval ships and shore facilities.

Constant scientific research has developed chemical agents that have successfully protected hull surfaces for as long as twenty-four months. The problem is far from solved, however. New naval equipment constantly requires the development of better antifouling agents.

Biological fouling impairs sonar gear by weakening sound transmissions. In some areas of the world, such fouling can make sonar gear unfit for ASW operations in just a few months. The problem is complicated by the need to develop an antifouling agent that will not itself degrade the acoustic qualities of the equipment.

The growing use of underwater optical instruments, such as fixed television and camera lenses, has created further problems. Such lenses can be fouled in a very short time. Some kind of transparent protective coating must be developed before planned submerged television monitoring stations can be installed.

Large, stationary structures built on the continental shelf for both military and commercial projects have additional fouling problems. Offshore oil-drilling platforms, lighthouses, radar stations, and oceanographic research stations are generally intended to be permanent structures. Fouling and deterioration by bacteria, fungi, and marine animals are serious threats to such platforms.

Submarine cables containing telephone and electric power, and underwater pipelines, have been attacked by shrimplike animals called *gribbles*; they have gnawed through wooden pilings and rubber and plastic insulation. The famous *teredo,* or "shipworm," can destroy wooden pilings, burrow into rocks and cement, weaken stone seawalls, and destroy insulation on cables. They have even drilled through solid lead sheathing of submarine power cables laid as deep as 7,200 feet!

DANGEROUS MARINE LIFE

People generally think of danger at sea as attack by fearsome animals. Actually, animal life in the sea is more apt to be helpful than harmful. Nevertheless, there are two categories of marine species that can be very dangerous to humans: poisonous or venomous, and carnivorous.

Carnivorous Animals. Sharks are the leading carnivores of most marine ecosystems; of the 300 species identified, the larger species are the top predators in their environment. Although infrequent, shark attack remains a significant physical and psychological problem for naval personnel.

The danger of being attacked by a shark or barracuda is exaggerated in the minds of most people. The amount of hazard depends both on the locality and on the condition of the individual in the water. Sharks are unpredictable and curious and will investigate any object in the water. They are likely to attack the dead or the wounded. They have an exceptional ability to detect a disabled or wounded animal at long range. Blood in the water attracts and excites them through their sense of smell.

The largest of all fish in the ocean is the tropical whale shark, which may reach 70 feet and weigh several tons. Basking and white sharks, found in temperate and tropical waters, reach more than 40 feet in length, while the tiger shark averages about 18 feet but may reach as much as 30 feet in length.

Sharks are found in all oceans from 45° N to

Sharks are a real threat to swimmers. The danger of shark attack is greatest in tropical and subtropical areas, but sharks have been recorded along all coasts of the United States. The white shark, above, is the most dangerous of all.

45° S latitude. The danger of shark attack appears to be greatest in tropical and subtropical areas between latitudes of 30° N and 30° S. The most dangerous areas are Australia, South Africa, Cuba, and the Pacific coast of Panama; however, fatal attacks have occurred on all coasts of the United States.

The sharks considered most dangerous to people are the great white shark, most dangerous of all; the tiger shark, probably the most common of tropical sharks; the sand shark, most dangerous in East Indian waters; and the hammerhead shark, found throughout the oceans in both tropical and temperate zones.

When sharks are present, persons should not dangle arms or legs in the water. Injured swimmers should be removed from the water quickly. Any flow of blood should be stopped as quickly as possible. Dark clothing and equipment is safest for swimmers. All movements should be slow and purposeful to avoid attracting sharks; if sharks appear, swimmers should remain perfectly still. Some sharks have departed when struck on the snout, but this should be used only as a last resort because it could aggravate them.

Barracuda are extremely dangerous. They may reach 6 to 8 feet long. They have knifelike canine teeth and, being swift swimmers, strike rapidly and ferociously. They are feared more than sharks in some areas of the West Indies. Found off the Florida coasts and in the Indian and Pacific oceans, they are attracted by almost any bright or colored object in the water and attack quickly. Because of the poor visibility, they can be especially dangerous in murky coastal waters, where they will attack at the slightest movement.

Killer whales are found throughout the oceans, from the Arctic to the Antarctic. They are nearly fearless. They reach a length of 15 to 30 feet. In packs, they often attack much larger whales. They are very swift swimmers, seeking out seals, walruses, and penguins as prey. Despite their name, attacks against people are rare and are thought to be the result of confusion with their natural prey. The only defense against the killer whale is a hasty retreat from the water.

Moray eels have narrow, powerful jaws with knifelike teeth. They may reach a length of 10 feet. They can inflict severe cuts or may hold a bulldog-like grip until death. They dwell mostly in crevices and holes under rocks and coral in tropical and subtropical seas. Morays seldom attack unless provoked, so it is very wise not to poke around in places where they may be lurking. They are common along the California coast.

The *giant devil ray* or *manta ray* may reach a spread of 20 feet and a weight of 3,500 pounds. They have a wide range in the topical seas. They are very curious and may investigate air bubbles of divers, getting entangled in the air hose. They have a very coarse skin, which will produce severe abrasion on contact. Otherwise, they are not apt to attack man.

Stinging Animals. Poisonous marine invertebrates that inflict injury by stinging are divided into four main groups:
1. Corals, sea anemones, jellyfishes, and hydroids.
2. Mollusks, including octopi and certain shellfish.
3. Bloodworms and bristleworms.
4. Sea urchins.

Corals and *sea anemones* have stinging cells that are used to capture food or as a defense against enemies. These cells inject a paralyzing drug into the victims, causing illnesses common among skin divers, sponge fishermen, and other marine workers. This group includes the elk horn coral of the West Indies and rosy sea anemones of the Atlantic.

Coral cuts and stings are very painful, slow to heal, and apt to become ulcerated. The wounds should be promptly cleaned and any particles removed. Bed rest, elevation of the limb, and packing with a mustard pack will help. When you are walking on a coral reef, heavy shoes, gloves, and wet suits are recommended.

The *hydroids* include poisonous invertebrates like the *Portuguese man-of-war,* often mistakenly called a jellyfish. The *fire coral,* a false coral that is sometimes called stinging coral, is found among true corals in the warm waters of the tropical Pacific, Caribbean Sea, and Indian Ocean. The Portuguese man-of-war floats on the surface of all tropical oceans and the Mediterranean Sea. Its tentacles trail many feet into the water and can give paralyzing stings.

Most *jellyfishes* look like big, white mushrooms. They swim by water jet propulsion at many depths in the oceans. The *sea wasp* of the tropical seas, and especially those of the Australian, Philippine, and Indian Ocean areas, are extremely dangerous. Oftentimes they are seen in huge numbers in the South China Sea.

Swimmers who brush against the Portuguese man-of-war and jellyfishes may be stung by their threadlike tentacles. Sting symptoms may vary from a mild prickly sensation to a throbbing pain that can render the victim unconscious. Pain may be localized or radiate to the armpit or abdomen. There may be redness and swelling, blistering, or small skin hemorrhage. There are no specific antidotes, but washing with diluted ammonia or alcohol and swabbing with mineral oil or baking soda may help.

The sea wasp jellyfish is very venomous. It can cause death in three to eight minutes. Symptoms are almost immediate shock, muscular cramps, loss of sensation, nausea, constriction of the throat, paralysis, convulsions, and, finally, death.

There are two members of the *mollusk* group

with a venomous sting or bite: (1) those with spirally twisted single shells, such as snails, and (2) those with no shell, such as the octopus and squid.

Those with cone-shaped shells are potentially dangerous. They have a head with one or two pairs of tentacles, and a flattened fleshy foot. *Cone shells* are favorites of shell collectors. There are some 400 species, and most have a fully developed venom apparatus. They are found in tropical waters of the Pacific and Indian oceans, and the Red Sea. They are common on the beaches of the Pacific islands.

The venom apparatus of the cone shell lies near the shell opening. The round teeth at the end of a tubelike appendage are thrust into the victim, and the venom is forced under pressure into the wound. The sting usually produces numbness and tingling, which quickly spread, becoming especially noticeable about the lips and mouth. Paralysis and coma may follow, with death as the result of heart failure.

Cone shell wounds must be quickly cleaned and suction applied to remove poison. Antibiotics may be desirable. The patient should be kept warm; stimulants may be required. Hospitalization is recommended.

The *octopus* has eight arms or tentacles, the *squid* and *cuttlefish* ten, around a muscular central body mass. They have powerful, parrotlike beaks and well-developed venom apparatus. They can move rapidly in the water by water jet propulsion.

Fortunately, these perilous-looking animals are timid. Octopi hide in holes in the coral and among rocks of the continental shelves. They are curious but very cautious. The danger of the octopus is its bite, and a small one can cause as much venom damage as a large one. The fear of being entangled by eight choking arms is unfounded. Bites usually occur when captured specimens are being handled. Bleeding from a bite is profuse, indicating that clotting is retarded by the venom. A burning sensation, nausea, and swelling are likely. The victim usually recovers, but at least one death has been reported from the bite of a small, unknown variety.

Bloodworms and *bristleworms* have tufted, silky bristles in a row along each side. These bristles can penetrate the skin in the same manner as cactus spines. Their strong jaws can also inflict a painful bite. The bristles and bite of a bloodworm result in a pale area that becomes hot, swollen, and numb or itchy. Bristleworm irritation may last several days. Bristles are best removed with a forceps, or by placing adhesive tape over the bristles and pulling them out. Scraping will break them off and may cause infection. The wound should be rubbed with alcohol to soothe discomfort. Bloodworms are handled mostly by fishermen, for these worms are the saltwater equivalent of the angleworms often used for pier fishing.

Sea urchins occur in large numbers in coastal waters. They have a round body covered with needle-sharp spines, many of which are poisonous. They are a real danger to swimmers, waders, and divers. The spines, poisonous or not, can inflict deep puncture wounds. Those with poison are long, slender, sharp, and hollow, permitting easy entrance deep into the flesh. They are extremely brittle and are likely to break off. The tip of the spine has tiny pincers and a sense bristle that releases the venom. This apparatus will continue to inject poison into the victim for several hours after parting from the sea urchin.

Penetration of the skin produces an immediate burning sensation. Redness, swelling, and generalized aching are likely to follow, and deaths from muscular paralysis have been reported.

Vertebrate marine animals that have venomous stings include a number of fishes and sea snakes. Sea snakes were discussed earlier in this chapter. The fishes fall into a number of species: (1) the stingrays, (2) catfish, (3) weeverfish, and (4) scorpionfish.

Stingrays are a much-feared flat fish found in warm coastal waters. They may grow to weigh several hundred pounds. They are a serious menace to waders. They lie on the bottom, largely concealed by sand and mud. Stepping on one will result in the ray driving a venomous barbed tail into the foot or leg with great force. The spines may be driven clean through a foot or well into the leg bone of the victim. The stingray wound causes im-

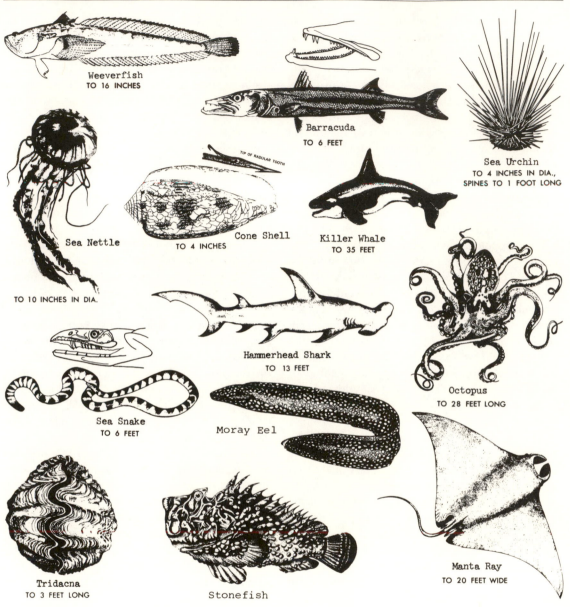

Weeverfish
TO 16 INCHES

Barracuda
TO 6 FEET

Sea Urchin
TO 4 INCHES IN DIA.,
SPINES TO 1 FOOT LONG

Sea Nettle

Cone Shell
TO 4 INCHES

TIP OF RADULAR TOOTH

Killer Whale
TO 35 FEET

TO 10 INCHES IN DIA.

Hammerhead Shark
TO 13 FEET

Octopus
TO 28 FEET LONG

Sea Snake
TO 6 FEET

Moray Eel

Tridacna
TO 3 FEET LONG

Stonefish

Manta Ray
TO 20 FEET WIDE

Some of the dangerous animals of the seas.

mediate shooting pain. The wound area will swell and become gray, and later red. Severe stings by large specimens can be deadly.

Catfish of about a thousand species exist in the world. Some marine catfishes are venomous. Venom glands are located in the sheath of the dorsal and pectoral spines. Some species have curved barbs on the ends of the spines, which make venom absorption more certain. Some freshwater catfishes are excellent eating, but marine catfishes are not often eaten. They usually live in rivers, open reef areas, estuaries, and large sandy bays. They are common all along the eastern seaboard, the Gulf of Mexico, India, the Philippines, and Indonesia.

A wound from a catfish spine results in instant stinging and throbbing. The pain may radiate or localize, numbing an arm or leg. Oriental catfish can inflict a violently painful wound that may fester for forty-eight hours and then result in gangrene and death. There are no known antidotes for catfish and other poisonous fish stings.

Weeverfish are very venomous animals of the temperate zone. They are aggressive, small marine fishes less than 18 inches in length. They inhabit sandy or muddy bays. They bury themselves in the mud with only their heads exposed. With little provocation, they will dart out with poisonous fins erect and strike with unerring accuracy, driving the spines into the victim.

There is instant stabbing pain after being struck. Within thirty minutes, the pain becomes so severe that the victim may scream and thrash about wildly, then lose consciousness and die. The venom attacks both the nervous and blood systems. Immediate first aid and treatment by a doctor may save the patient's life. Recovery time takes several months, depending on the condition of the patient and the amount of venom received. There is no antivenom.

The Great Weever is found along western Africa, in the Mediterranean Sea, and around the British Isles and Norway. The Lesser Weever inhabits the North Sea, southward along the European coast, and the Mediterranean.

The *scorpionfish family* comprises the most poisonous of all fishes. There are three main groups: (1) zebrafish, (2) scorpionfish, and (3) stonefish. The sting of any of these fish will produce serious results. The deadliness of some of the stonefishes may be ranked with that of the cobra.

The *zebrafish* is a beautiful, shallow-water fish of tropical and temperate seas. They live around coral reefs, spreading their fanlike, lacy fins much like peacocks. They are usually found in pairs. Beneath the beauty are hidden as many as eighteen long, straight, needle-sharp fin-spines. Each spine is equipped with lethal venom. These fish are a real menace to anyone exploring tropical coral areas.

The *scorpionfish* inhabits shallow water bays and reefs in the Pacific Ocean. These fishes conceal themselves in crevices among debris, under rocks, or in seaweed. They have nearly perfect protective coloration that makes them almost invisible. When alerted or removed from the water they erect poisonous spines like zebrafish do.

Stonefish of the Pacific Ocean are found in tidepools and shoal areas. They are hard to see because they usually lie motionless and partly buried in the mud or sand. They are not afraid of any intrusion in their area, making them a danger to anyone with bare feet. The fish is a mud-brown color and warty like a toad. It has thirteen dorsal, three bottom, and two pelvic spines, all short and heavy with enlarged venom glands.

Symptoms produced by all of the scorpionfish family may vary in degree, but the pain is immediate, sharp, and radiates quickly. Pain may cause a victim to thrash about in a wild manner, scream, or lose consciousness. The immediate wound area may be pale, surrounded by a zone of redness, swelling, and heat. Paralysis of an entire arm or leg may result. Death is the usual result of an encounter. A sting should be treated like a snake bite. In some cases the victim may recover after months of treatment, but with general health impaired.

Persons swimming where scorpionfish live must be alert to the danger and absolutely avoid touching them. Since the species are generally fearless, one should not aggravate them as they will attack. A direct encounter with any of the scorpionfish is an invitation to disaster.

UNDERWATER RESEARCH

In order to see firsthand what goes on in the sea, oceanographers for years have been seeking ways to enter the depths. The lack of air, tremendous underwater pressure, utter darkness, and the cold have all combined to prevent researchers

The research submarine (bathyscaphe) *Sea Cliff*. This is a free-moving underwater research vessel used to take photos, collect samples with mechanical arms, and stay at great depths for extended periods.

from descending into the deep ocean and remaining there for an extended time. Only in recent years have people succeeded in exploring the sea in meaningful ways. New individual diving gear and methods and almost fantastic undersea research vessels have been developed and successfully operated. It is a whole new scientific frontier.

The traditional rubber-canvas suit with metal hard hat and lead-filled shoes has been used successfully in depths up to 600 feet. Movement underwater is slow, and the diver is tied to a lifeline

and air hose to the surface. More recently, the self-contained underwater breathing apparatus (SCUBA) has been developed. A qualified scuba diver can carry his or her own compressed air tanks and swim freely, if extremely careful, into water up to 200 feet deep. A diver usually uses a wet suit, flippers, and mask, especially for deeper descents and for extended underwater periods.

Individual diving gear should supply the diver with sufficient air when underwater and protect him or her from water pressure while permitting

The Navy's floating instrument platform, called FLIP, is towed out to sea in a horizontal position, and then "flipped" into a vertical position by flooding one end, as shown here. The FLIP consists of a 350-foot cylindrical tube with many instruments to take ocean measurements of temperature, salinity, and currents. The crew's quarters remain above water, and all equipment and furniture inside are on swivels so they remain horizontal regardless of the ship's position.

movement. Underwater diving and towing vehicles have been developed for faster and deeper underwater operations by scuba divers. Even with new improvements and vehicles, however, deep diving operations are still difficult and hazardous.

Scuba diving has also become a popular sport worldwide. Many amateur divers try out their gear, especially in warmer waters where coral reefs and abundant sea life make a rainbow of colors. Much of the Virgin Islands National Park is an underwater fantasyland of coral reefs and tropical sea life set aside for such sportsmen and women. Scuba diving is not for the novice, however. Divers must have had a complete training course in the use of the equipment, must be good swimmers, and must be in good health.

For much deeper exploration, oceanographer Auguste Piccard developed the *bathyscaphe* in 1948. The name comes from two Greek words, *bathy* meaning deep, and *scaph* meaning boat. The bathyscaphe is a free-moving underwater research vessel with some characteristics of a submarine. The U.S. Navy bathyscaphe *Trieste* successfully descended 35,800 feet to the bottom of the Challenger Deep in the Mariana Trench, about 200 miles southwest of Guam, in 1960.

When under the sea, scientists in bathyscaphes can look through ports at an underwater world

A Navy trainer attaches a special harness to Tuffy, an Atlantic bottlenose dolphin. Instruments attached to the harness measure Tuffy's heartbeat, respiration, and temperature during tests off the Naval Missile Center at Point Mugu, California. The dolphin was trained to work with the Navy's Sealab underwater habitat program.

lighted by powerful waterproofed lights. They can take photos, collect samples with mechanical arms, and stay down at great depths for long periods of time.

Since the journey of *Trieste,* the Navy, in cooperation with Woods Hole Oceanographic Institute in Massachusetts and Scripps Institute of Oceanography of California, has constructed a number of newer-model bathyscaphes and other underwater research platforms. Of various sizes, these are capable of operating at different depths.

One very interesting vessel is the FLIP ship (floating instrument platform). This research platform can flip from a horizontal position to a vertical one. The bow, carrying a marine laboratory, remains 50 feet in the air, while the stern, containing various measuring and sounding instruments, is plunged 300 feet below the surface. All of the furniture and equipment in the laboratory section is mounted on gimbals, so it stays right-side-up and level during the flip operation.

Another Navy project has been the development of a deep submergence rescue vessel (DSRV) to be used in case of submarine accidents.

The Navy has also conducted extensive underwater living experiments. These have included *underwater habitats*—living and research quarters—where underwater scientists called *aquanauts* have learned to live for long periods at great depths.

In recent years increasing use has been made of remote-controlled self-propelled exploration vehicles fitted with TV cameras, lights, and a variety of other sensors and grappeling devices. Many are capable of operation at great depths, and have produced amazing video shots of sunken ships such as the famous passenger ship *Titanic* and the German battleship *Bismarck*.

THE THREAT OF POLLUTION

Human beings are consumers of vast quantities of raw materials and fuels. A tremendous amount of waste material results from this use—individual, societal, industrial, and accidental. A large part of this waste finds its way into the sea. Fortunately, only a small percentage of this consists of pollutants. *Pollutants* are substances that damage marine processes or cause loss or the restricted use of an ocean resource. Some pollutants interfere with the life processes of marine organisms and reduce biological productivity of the oceans. Others, including oil and litter, are dangerous to people, interfere with recreational activities, or detract from the beauty of the seascape.

It is impossible to completely stop pollution of the oceans. It may be possible to stop pollution of some inland lakes and rivers and to significantly reduce it in others. But the mere fact that people use raw materials makes it impossible to eliminate waste materials. The real issue is what level of pollutants society is willing to accept. This depends directly on the amount of money, research, and effort people are willing to put into reduction and control of individual and industrial waste.

Governments are now taking a firm stand, enacting and enforcing good pollution laws. Individuals, however, must now be educated about the problem. We have the resources and capability to solve the problem, but it is going to be difficult and expensive.

Six main groups of pollutants presently affect

One of the worst accidents resulting in widespread sea and beach pollution was the breakup of the American tanker *Torrey Canyon* aground on Land's End, England. The 61,263-ton ship spilled more than 120,000 tons of oil on the sea and beaches of southwestern England.

the marine environment and cause international concern: (1) petroleum; (2) heavy metals; (3) radioactive materials; (4) chemical and synthetic fuels, solvents, and pesticides; (5) litter; and (6) domestic sewage.

Petroleum. The worldwide "energy crunch" came into focus in the 1970s and will continue for the foreseeable future. Since the early 1970s, millions of tons of crude oil, gasoline, and other petroleum fuels have crossed the oceans in thou-

sands of tankers. Each year, it is estimated that in excess of 6.1 million tons of this oil enters the oceans, much of it washed out of fuel tanks and when pumping bilges, but some as the result of ship collisions and groundings. Additionally, there have been terrible spills from undersea oil rigs in the North Sea, the Gulf of Mexico, the California coast, and elsewhere. During Operation Desert Storm in early 1991 crude oil was intentionally dumped into the Persian Gulf by Iraqi forces in

Kuwait. These catastrophes dumped thousands of tons of oil per day into the water, creating oil slicks that covered thousands of square miles.

Oil slicks on the high seas can kill plankton in the surface zone but in general will dissipate over a period of time, often gathering in tarlike balls that eventually sink to the bottom. While such "oil litter" can do no good, it probably does not do much permanent harm either. On the other hand, when such an oil slick reaches shore or collects in harbors, coves, or bays, the results are disastrous for the seabirds, mollusks, and other shallow-water life. Also, an oil spill will devastate the economy of a beach resort area.

The Navy's major pollution problem in harbors, ports, channels, and U.S. waters is the discharge of oils and oily wastes. The Navy has an active program to eliminate all such pollution and works closely with the Environmental Protection Agency and the Coast Guard in this effort.

As a result of the Navy program, special piping systems have been installed in ships so they can offload oily wastes from bilges and fuel oil overflows to barges or pierside facilities and vehicles. Improved motors and fuels have been developed that reduce such oily wastes. And special equipment such as oil skimmers, collection and containment booms, offloading barges, oil disposal rafts, and oil/water separators are being used to clean up accidental spills. More recently, certain forms of bacteria have been developed that will consume floating oil slicks when they are spread on them.

Heavy Metals. The sea's main heavy metal pollutants are mercury and, to a lesser extent, barium. These metals are discharged in the effluent from chemical plants, cement works, and other manufacturing processes, doubling their natural accumulation in the sea. As a result, increased traces of mercury have been found in shellfish and other fish species throughout the world, including the Arctic Ocean and the Great Lakes. Sea life, especially shellfish, absorb the mercury; fish, oysters, and clams retain the mercury, which continues to build up, never being cast off. In certain coastal areas near where the pollution enters the water,

deadly concentrations occur in the fish. This has occurred in Minimata Bay, Kyushu Island, Japan. Many people have become severely crippled and mentally ill from eating mercury-poisoned seafood caught in the bay.

Radioactive Materials. Since World War II, many countries have begun to develop nuclear power stations and fuel-processing plants to help solve their energy shortages. In theory such plants can be made safe from leaks so they will not contaminate nearby land and water environments. The fact is that the cost for so doing is very high, and accidents have occurred. Ever-increasing amounts of radioactive pollutants have found their way into the water.

Radioactivity in coastal fish and on some beaches in western Great Britain has increased from 3 to 7 percent of the safe limit since the completion of a nuclear reprocessing plant there. There is widespread construction of nuclear power facilities throughout Western Europe. However, there has been a slowdown on such projects in the United States since the Three-Mile Island (Pennsylvania) accident in 1978 and other nuclear plant incidents, such as the accidental reactor explosion at Chernobyl in the Soviet Union in 1986. In the long run, it is probable that more nuclear plants will be built worldwide to satisfy growing energy needs.

Recently much concern has arisen over radioactive waste products and reactor parts dumped into the seas over the years. In some cases old sunken sealed drums of radioactive wastes have corroded and leaked, causing contamination of local fish populations. Most countries with nuclear capabilities have agreed to dispose of future wastes in land dumps as the result of international accords dealing with this issue.

Chemical and Synthetic Compounds. Chlorine, fluorine, bromine, and iodine are proving very dangerous to marine life. These compounds fall into two main groups: (1) pesticides, such as DDT and other chemical weed and insect killers; and (2) the biphenols, such as aerosol propellants, solvents, refrigerants, and cleaning agents.

DDT is known to cause reproductive problems in some marine birds. The brown pelican, for instance, is an endangered species in some areas now. When the pelicans eat fish that have absorbed DDT from field and river runoff into coastal bays, their eggs have flimsy shells that break in the nest.

Most of the adult fish in the Great Lakes have absorbed pesticide and herbicide runoff from the intensely cultivated farmlands along the rivers that drain into the lakes. Pesticides often kill the eggs and small fry, so they have greatly reduced the natural reproduction of game fish in streams, rivers, and ponds, especially in the Upper Middle West and Great Lakes states. As a result, these states now have to restock their waters annually from fish hatcheries in order to retain acceptable sport and commercial fish populations.

Litter. Marine litter is solid waste of society and ships at sea. It is trucked, barged, and dumped into rivers and into the oceans at a rate of more than 6½ million tons each year. The ocean floor and coastal areas are littered with this debris; much of it consists of packing materials—plastic, aluminum, wood, and glass—all of which may take centuries, at best, to be broken down by the salts of the sea. In recent years various types of medical refuse have become of particular concern. Much of this litter is not *biodegradable*; that is, it will never break down. Beaches the world over are cluttered with this trash, some of which floats to the farthest corners of the earth. It is unsightly, poses a hazard to swimmers and small craft navigation, clogs harbors, and may destroy the natural habitat of shorebirds and animals.

On the sea bottom, however, some of this trash actually helps create habitats for plant and animal life. Derelict ships, car bodies and tires, and cement blocks, among other things, have been used to make artificial reefs that are eventually covered by marine growth. The vegetation brings fish, and a flourishing cycle of sea life is created where previously there may have been none. This beneficial result of litter, however, is unique and differs greatly from its usual effect on the environment.

Domestic Sewage. The organic pollutants from sewage are especially troublesome in enclosed water areas. They contain high levels of nutrients that promote rapid plankton growth, in both fresh and salt water. This great increase in plankton population uses up the available oxygen, upsetting the natural *ecosystem.* Some 8,000 tons of sewage sludge is dumped daily from barges into the Atlantic Ocean off New York City. Many coastal areas, especially along the shores of the Mediterranean, have been contaminated by unprocessed sewage flow. Coastal wetlands have become "dead" areas, choked with algae and filled with disease-bearing bacteria. Estuaries and salt marshes are the natural spawning grounds of many species of fish, shellfish, and crustaceans, and the nesting areas for water birds.

When such areas are destroyed, either by raw sewage, or by draining, filling, or reclamation projects, a devastating blow is struck to the natural reproductive capacity of marine wildlife.

The U.S. Navy has had an active environmental protection program since 1968. This program has brought about such shoreside improvements as the construction of sewers, sewage and wastewater treatment plants, air pollution control equipment on boiler plants and in industrial processes, and solid waste recycling facilities.

To help prevent pollution of inland waterways and harbors, Navy ships are equipped with two types of sewage systems: (1) marine sanitation devices (MSDs), which enable sewage to be treated before it is discharged from the ship; and/or (2) collection, holding, and transfer systems (CHTs), which collect and hold sewage until it can be transferred ashore in port or pumped overboard in unrestricted waters beyond the territorial limits (at least 3 miles from shore). Many commercial ships and most U.S. pleasure craft are fitted with similar equipment.

Besides the foregoing types of substance pollution, in recent years various kinds of biological pollutants have also caused concern. These include both animal and plant organisms that find their way into bilge and ballast water of ships visiting foreign ports, which is then discharged into coastal and inland waters of the United States. Once released into our waterways these organisms can grow and spread without bound owing to the lack of any effective control mechanisms that may be present in their native environments. Two such instances of great concern in recent years have been the introduction of the Zebra mollusk into the Great Lakes and various rivers such as the upper Mississippi and Susquehanna by ships arriving from Europe, and a type of sprawling marine weed called hydrilla that chokes out native vegetation in the Chesapeake Bay.

What Is the Answer?

One thing is very clear. If ocean pollution continues at its present pace, instead of the sea becoming the aquaculture garden of the future, it could become a biological desert. This would have grave consequences for a world that is going to become increasingly dependent on the sea for food and mineral resources. Instead of becoming a living and recreation area for millions, it could become a polluted, stagnant pool. Wastes that are disposed of in the sea must be treated before dumping so they will not pollute. We must learn to recycle wastes. We must pass effective and practical laws and then enforce them. Life on earth is dependent on the sea and will continue to be increasingly so.

There is still much hope. People are gradually learning about the importance of our relationship with the sea and the ecological balance that exists between the sea, the land, and all plant and animal life. All nations together must develop an international policy that will protect the common heritage of mankind.

Chapter 4. Study Guide Questions

1. What is marine biology?
2. In what areas does marine biology have a direct impact upon naval matters?
3. What are the two basic families of plankton in the seas?

4. A. What is *upwelling*?
    B. What is the effect of El Niño?
5. What oceanographic phenomenon has given the Red Sea its name?
6. Why has the Black Sea been so named?
7. Describe the steps in the food cycle.
    A. In what area of the sea do phytoplankton live?
    B. Zooplankton and larger life?
8. What are some of the unique characteristics of marine animals that live in the deep sea (abyss)?
9. What are some special characteristics of sea animals living at the edge of the sea?
10. A. What are the smallest animals of the zooplankton group?
    B. The largest?
11. How has the St. Lawrence Seaway affected the ecological environment of the Great Lakes?
12. What are the four groups of marine animals with jaws?
13. A. What are the four groups of living marine reptiles?
    B. Where are the most dangerous of these animals found?
14. What part of the world is the penguin's native habitat?
15. A. What are the three groups of seals?
    B. Which are protected by hunting laws?
16. A. What are the two main groups of whales?
    B. What is the main difference between the two groups?
17. A. Why is the Sargasso Sea so named?
    B. Why is this area almost a "desert" in the sea?
18. What are three things that can help increase food production from the sea?
19. To date, what types of ocean fish or shellfish have proved to be most successful in aquafarming?
20. A. How do the *deep scattering layers* affect naval operations?
    B. What causes these layers?
    C. Because of biological noises in the sea, what special training did the Navy begin for sonarmen?

21. A. What does *bioluminescence* mean?

B. What causes it?

C. How can this phenomenon affect naval operations?

22. What are the principal food fishes used in the United States?

23. What is the most serious effect of marine fouling and deterioration for the Navy?

24. What are the two categories of marine species that can be dangerous to people?

25. What are the four groups of stinging marine animals that can injure humans?

26. What are the four species of poisonous fish that are particularly dangerous to people?

27. A. What does *scuba* mean?

B. Before divers use scuba gear, what qualifications should they have?

28. What is the purpose of a bathyscaphe?

29. What are the six main groups of sea pollutants?

30. A. What are the main causes of petroleum pollution in the sea?

B. Where is the most damage caused by an oil spill?

31. What is the particular danger of heavy metal pollution?

32. How does pollution by synthetic compounds affect natural reproduction of seabirds and animals?

33. How do radioactive pollutants affect marine life and humans?

34. A. How does domestic sewage upset the natural ecosystem in enclosed water areas?

B. What must be done to sewage before it can safely be returned to rivers, lakes, or the ocean?

Vocabulary

marine biology
zooplankton
larva, -ae
nutrients
decomposition
upwelling
protein
guano
hydrogen sulfide
Callao Painter
El Niño
Red Tide (dinoflagellata)
Montreaux Convention
food cycle
chlorophyll
carnivore
predator
kelp
algae
diatoms
protozoan
tentacle
octopus
lamprey
brackish water
flukes
baleen (whale)
extinction
endangered species
purse seiner
stingray
aquaculture

marifarm
oyster bed "clutch"
habitat
deep scattering layer
acoustics
bioluminescence
marine fouling
teredo
venom
repellent
mollusks
sea anemone
ulcerated
hydroid
jellyfish
sea urchin
vertebrate
dorsal, pectoral spines
scorpionfish
SCUBA
bathyscaphe
aquanaut
pollution
pesticide, herbicide
radioactivity
biphenols
biodegradable
ecosystem
litter
heavy metals
bilge
ballast water

7

Naval History Through 1860: The Early Years

Chapter 1.   Sea Power and Western Civilization

The ability to use the sea is a nation's *sea power*. If a nation can use the sea to meet its needs, it then has control of the sea. *Sea control* means (1) being able to defend one's own sea lanes, and (2) the ability to deny an enemy the use of the sea in time of war.

In many wars throughout history, a single major naval victory has made winning possible. Defeat of the enemy's fleet kept it from resupplying its land forces. The victor was then able to attack the enemy's homeland, ending the war on land.

Let us now take a look at a few of the most important historic victories at sea. These victories have had a great effect on the world as we know it today. They prove what a vital role navies have played in the history of our world.

EARLY SEAFARERS AND NAVIES

Early people looked with fear upon the seas. They saw them as barriers. Eventually, however, they learned to use the waters—not only to eat the fish living in them, but for an easier way to travel. They were now able to carry things they had grown and made to other places, for barter. Before long, the countries that carried on the most *trade* became the richest and most powerful. The earliest seafarers began our sea heritage in the eastern Mediterranean Sea. In the eastern and central Mediterranean, travel by sea was faster, cheaper, and safer than crossing the deserts on land.

The first people known to use sea power were the sailors and traders of ancient Crete, a large rocky island south of Greece. About four thousand years ago (2500–1200 B.C.), the Cretans dominated their neighbors on the shores of the Aegean Sea, now Greece and Turkey. This was natural, because of Crete's geography. The island was too rugged for farming, and it sits right on the major sea routes of the eastern Mediterranean. Crete was in just the right place to attack its commercial rivals, and *had* to engage in trade to survive.

The Phoenicians were the next to gain from their mastery of the sea. They often are called the real pioneers in the use of maritime power. From about 2000 to 300 B.C., Phoenician ships not only covered the Mediterranean, but their adventurous traders also carried tin from Britain, amber from the Baltic Sea, and slaves and ivory from western Africa. The Phoenicians established great ports at Tyre and Sidon, in what is now Lebanon.

These port cities were at the end of the Asian caravan routes, which brought in the wealth of the Orient. Phoenician ships carried this wealth to the

An artist's conception of the type of galley used in the Mediterranean *circa* 500 B.C.

coastal trading cities around the Mediterranean and to northern Europe. The Phoenicians also started colonies and trading stations, which grew into new centers of civilization. The Phoenician alphabet became the written language of traders. Later, it became the basis for our own alphabet. The greatest of the Phoenician colonies grew to be the empire of Carthage, later the main opponent of Rome.

Next came the Greeks. The ancient Greeks gave us the best stories of early sea power. Famous Greek authors—Herodotus, Thucydides, and Homer—wrote detailed histories of early sea power at work. The Trojan War was fought to secure control of the Hellespont, now called the Dardanelles (Turkish straits), in order to take control of Aegean–Black Sea trade. By 500 B.C., the Greek city-states had a high level of civilization,

and their trading ships and naval vessels sailed the entire Mediterranean. Many prosperous Greek colonies developed in Asia Minor (Turkey), Sicily, Italy, France, and Spain. They took over sea control from the Phoenician colonies.

Early trading ships were clumsy sailing craft. Loaded with the wealth of the bazaars, they were easy prey for armed robbers in smaller, swifter craft. So merchants began to crew vessels with hired marines (soldiers of the sea) to protect their ships and to patrol the seaways. Navies thus came into being, using special ships called galleys, which could be propelled by oars as well as sails, and crewed by trained fighting men.

Galley tactics in fighting were simple: overtake, ram or grapple, board, and capture in hand-to-hand combat. At other times, galleys patrolled and guarded the sea routes over which most ships trav-

Route of the Persian fleet and army against the Greeks in 480 B.C.

eled. This task has been the main job of navies since the beginning: defend sea routes for one's own use, and disrupt them for the enemy. These main sea routes are often called a nation's *sea lines of communication.*

Greece vs. Persia. By 492 B.C., Greek expansion had run into the mighty forces of Persia (now Iran) moving westward into the eastern Mediterranean. The Greeks held off two Persian invasions in the next twelve years, but then were forced to withdraw from their northern lands in Thrace and Macedonia. In 480 B.C., Persian King Xerxes planned a huge invasion to conquer the Greeks once and for all. Knowing that sea power was necessary for a victory, Xerxes built a navy of 1,300 galleys. This fleet followed his 180,000-man army

down the coast, guarding his flank and carrying his supplies.

Themistocles, the Greek commander, realized that the only way the Persians could be stopped was to break the sea lines of communication supporting Xerxes' army from Asia Minor. He convinced the Greeks to build a naval force of 380 *triremes,* a type of fast war galley.

Greek strategy was to hold the Persian army at the narrow pass of Thermopylae, while the Greek fleet struck the invader's fleet in a series of hit-and-run attacks in the narrow straits among the Greek islands. But a traitor showed the Persian army a secret mountain path, and they surrounded and destroyed the Greek defenders at Thermopylae. Xerxes' army now moved south to plunder the

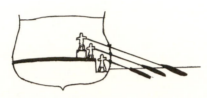

An ancient Greek trireme, of the types that defeated the Persians at Salamis. There were three rows of oars and rowers, one above the other on each side of the ship. Often the rowers were slaves.

abandoned city of Athens. The Greeks took up new positions at the Isthmus of Corinth, while their fleet moved south to the waters around the island of Salamis, near Athens, to protect their eastern flank.

Bad weather and Greek hit-and-run attacks had by this time reduced the Persian fleet to 800 vessels. There were 300 surviving Greek triremes. Splitting his force, Xerxes sent 200 galleys to block the retreat of the Greek fleet around Salamis. The remaining 600 galleys moved directly against the Greek fleet in the narrow strait between Salamis and the shore. But crammed as they were in the narrow strait, the Persians lost their advantage of numbers, since only the front ships had contact with the Greek fleet. So the better-armed Greek sailors and marines were able to outfight the Persian soldiers at every turn. About half of the Persian fleet was sunk with great loss of life, compared to a Greek loss of forty ships. Xerxes watched the disaster from a throne set up on a hill overlooking the battle. Soon realizing that his sea communica-

tions were no longer secure, he ordered his army to begin a long retreat.

Following this battle, there was a short period of peace and prosperity, known as the Golden Age of Athens. Theater, sculpture, writing, and philosophy flourished. The concept of democracy in government was born. Thus the foundations of Western civilization were established, and the turning point was the sea battle of Salamis in 480 B.C.

During the next 150 years, Greek civilization moved steadily eastward, conquering most of what was the Persian Empire. Under Alexander the Great of Macedonia, Greek culture secured the entire eastern Mediterranean, founded the great port of Alexandria in Egypt, drove Persia from the seas, and ended the reign of the Phoenicians. Macedonia became the world's greatest sea power, and conquered most of the civilized Western and Middle Eastern world.

Rome vs. Carthage. The Greeks controlled the eastern Mediterranean for two centuries. In the western Mediterranean, the Greek colonies and the rising power of Carthage kept each other in check. But on the Italian peninsula, a new power was rising: Rome. In 275 B.C. the Romans conquered Italy, including the Greek colonies in the south. In the process, they absorbed Greek culture, continuing the advance of Western civilization. In the way of Rome, however, was a strong rival. This rival was Carthage, the former Phoenician colony in North Africa (in what is now Tunisia). In 265 B.C., the first of the *Punic wars* between the two powers began, in Sicily. (*Punic* is a Latin variation of the word Phoenician or *Punicus.*)

At the beginning of the Punic wars, Rome saw the need for sea power and a strong navy. It was the Carthaginian navy that protected Carthage from Roman attack, and it was this fleet that harassed Roman sea commerce and plundered the Roman coast.

The Romans studied Greek tactics and improved on them. During the Punic wars, Roman seamanship and tactics beat the Carthaginians, driving them from the sea. The first Punic war gave Rome the island of Sicily as a province; the second conflict gave Spain to Rome. The third began with an amphibious invasion of North Africa. By the time it was over, Carthage had been burned, and Carthaginian power was destroyed forever. The Roman Empire was free to spread throughout the Mediterranean. The Roman navy cleared the Mediterranean of pirates, moved and supported Rome's armies, and defeated any hostile fleet.

In the first century B.C., rebellious Romans and their Egyptian allies, under the command of Mark Antony and Queen Cleopatra, tried to overthrow the Roman Empire during the confusion following the assassination of Julius Caesar. The rebellion was crushed, however, in 31 B.C. at a great sea battle near Actium (Greece). The Roman Admiral Agrippa destroyed the enemy fleet with blazing arrows and pots of flaming charcoal. In an earlier battle at Naulochus, Agrippa had defeated Pompey, Caesar's other rival to power, and secured the western Mediterranean. The Battle of Actium put the whole eastern Mediterranean in the Roman Empire.

For more than five centuries after Actium, trade vessels could move freely from the Black Sea to Gibraltar with little fear. The Mediterranean had become the Roman *Mare Nostrum* (Our Sea) with all coasts, ports, and naval bases controlled by Rome. On land and sea the *Pax Romana* (Roman Peace) was established, the longest period of peace in world history. Roman law, government, art, language, and religion were firmly established in Europe, the Middle East, and North Africa. Western civilization today can be traced to Rome and to the earlier Greek contributions.

THE MIDDLE AGES

Eventually, Rome's greatness began to decline, for too many reasons to discuss here. As Rome declined, the empire broke up into two parts. The Eastern or Byzantine Empire had its capital at Constantinople (after 1930, called Istanbul), and the Western Empire kept its capital at Rome. Barbarian invaders from northern and central Europe conquered Rome and deposed the last emperor in A.D. 476.

Thereafter, for the next thousand years, Europe was in constant turmoil, and there was an ever-present threat of Muslim/Arab expansion into the Mediterranean from northern Africa. The period of Western European history from the fall of Rome until about the eleventh century is often called the Dark Ages, because of numerous invasions of barbaric tribes, incursions of North African Moors, religious bigotry, and a general lack of education among the masses of people. Only in the region around Constantinople was there a general advance of culture during this period. In the late eleventh century, the Crusades, religious-military expeditions to retake the Holy Lands from the Muslims, began gradually to bring about a reawakening of culture and education in Western Europe, flourishing in the thirteenth through sixteenth centuries. This time is referred to as the Renaissance (the Rebirth) in Western European history.

In the eastern Mediterranean, however, the Byzantine Empire centered in Turkey defeated the advancing Muslims at Constantinople in A.D. 717. The Byzantines thereafter prospered and blocked further westward Muslim overland expansion. The Muslims became largely content with piracy on the Mediterranean and with strengthening their control over their huge North African and Middle Eastern territories. Muslim fleets dominated the Mediterranean at this time. By the eleventh century, though, Christendom was ready to contest Muslim control. The Muslims were expelled from Sardinia and Sicily, and pushed into southern Spain. The First Crusade, initiated by Pope Urban II in 1095, recaptured Jerusalem and nearly swept the Arabs from the Mediterranean.

Over the next three hundred years, the religious fervor that had brought on the Crusades turned more to commercial expansion by the Italian states. Their merchant fleets took advantage of the Muslim retreat. Venice profited most from the increased trade, and became the biggest center of commerce between the Orient and Europe. Venice profited from both sides of the Arab–Christian Crusades, hiring out ships to Crusaders, and then giving the Arabs commercial favors. Venice acquired Crete and Cyprus in the course of these events. By 1400 Venice was at the height of its power, with a fleet of three thousand ships.

The north German port cities were on the opposite end of much of the Venetian trade. They formed the Hanseatic League, or the Hanse, which dominated the northern and western European economy. The Baltic and North seas became in the north what the Mediterranean had been for centuries in the south.

But by now, the Islamic cause had been taken over by the aggressive Ottoman Turks. They swept across the Dardanelles into southeastern Europe, and captured Constantinople in 1453. The fall of the Byzantine Empire removed the barriers to Muslim advances into Europe. The Turks swept to the very gates of Vienna, Austria. Muslim fleets sought domination of the Mediterranean and control of the profitable east–west trade.

The Battle of Lepanto. For some time the divided Christian states could not get themselves organized to oppose the Turks. But after the Turkish conquest of Cyprus in 1570, fear of the Turks finally drew the Christian Mediterranean powers together. Spain and the Italian states agreed to combine their fleets for a showdown with the Turks. The winner would determine the course of Western civilization.

The Christian fleet, commanded by Don John of Austria, was composed of some 200 galleys, mostly Venetian and Spanish. The Ottoman fleet, commanded by Ali Pasha, numbered about 250 galleys. The Turks still relied mainly on the bow and arrow. Many Christian soldiers, however, were armed with the *arquebus,* an early type of musket. The encounter took place in the Gulf of Lepanto (near Patras, Greece) in 1571. This was just a few miles south of where Agrippa had defeated Antony in the Battle of Actium, sixteen centuries earlier. In the terrible battle that took place, the Christian navies defeated their Turkish opponents. Some 30,000 died. All but sixty of their ships were captured or destroyed. Christian losses were 7,700

The Battle of Lepanto ended in the defeat of the Ottoman Turks by a Christian fleet of Spanish and Venetian ships. The battle ended Muslim attempts to move farther into Europe or control the Mediterranean Sea.

men and twelve ships. Nearly 15,000 Christians captured earlier by the Turks and used as slaves to row the galleys were freed by the victory.

The Battle of Lepanto demonstrated that, while naval triumphs often make victory possible, the final decision is usually made on land. After Lepanto, the Christian countries again began bickering among themselves, rather than following up their victory with operations ashore. The Turks never again seriously challenged control of the Mediterranean, but Muslim pirates continued to harass merchantmen on these waters for the next 250 years.

Lepanto was the end of the age of the galley. By the time of Lepanto, the Mediterranean had begun to decline as the center of world maritime interest. It had served for two thousand years as the cradle of Western European civilization and commerce. Its period of greatest influence was the age of the galley. But the Turkish hold on the Middle East had caused seafaring nations to seek new routes to the Orient. The Age of Discovery had dawned. Columbus claimed the New World for Spain in 1492. Portuguese, Spanish, English, Italian, French, Dutch, and Swedish seafarers were sailing across the Atlantic to new markets, new wealth, and new conflicts.

THE AGE OF DISCOVERY

The Age of Discovery was an age of sea power. Brave men in ships explored the world and founded colonies while seeking fortunes for king and country. The hardships were great, but the lure of gold and adventure was even greater. As before, the nations with sea power became rich and powerful. They profited by what ships brought them, and the world profited by what they sent out in ships. Inevitably, there were rivalries and wars between opposing great powers.

The Portuguese were the first to seek a new sea route to the Indies and the Orient. Prince Henry the Navigator hired explorers to try to find a route to the East by sailing around Africa. Bartholomeu Dias rounded the Cape of Good Hope at the southern tip of Africa in 1488. This proved that a sea route to the Orient did exist. Vasco da Gama sailed from Portugal to India in 1498, opening a Portuguese trade route to the Indies and China, and establishing colonial trading sites. Portugal's leadership was short-lived, though, for it was soon overwhelmed by neighboring Spain.

Contributing about $5,000 in royal jewels, Queen Isabella financed Christopher Columbus on his first voyage. It certainly was the most profitable investment in history. Columbus went on to discover America and thus helped put Spain into a position of European leadership. Through sea power, Spain established a huge empire. Millions upon millions in gold, silver, and jewels poured into the royal treasury. Treasure-laden ships sailed in groups escorted by warships to protect them against pirates and privateers of rival nations. This was an early example of a *convoy,* a method used through World War II to protect merchant shipping in time of war.

At the time, national wealth was thought to be measured by the amount of treasure in the royal vaults. The total wealth of the world was limited. Thus, to become richer and more powerful, a nation had to make some other nation poorer through capture of its trade and colonies. This *mercantile theory* kept the world in almost continuous conflict well into the 1800s.

The flow of new wealth into Europe, however, created new political and economic problems. Precious metals from Spanish America upset the value of European money. Raw materials from the colonies competed with European agricultural produce. This drove people from the farms to the cities. A new commercial class of people, the middle class, came into being. They supported themselves by providing services and manufactured goods. This undermined the power of the old landowning aristocracy. The Age of Discovery, therefore, was the start of a gradual shift of wealth, and thus power, from the nobility to the middle class.

England Challenges Spain. Pope Pius V in 1570 called upon King Philip II of Spain to drive the Muslims from Europe and the Mediterranean.

At the same time, the pope called upon Philip to crusade against the "heretic and usurper," Queen Elizabeth I in Protestant England. Having proved himself and his great fleet at Lepanto, Philip accepted this task.

Elizabeth, on the other hand, wanted to protect her throne against the Catholic Mary Queen of Scots. She began to strengthen England's defenses against the attack she knew would soon come from Spain. After securing England's flank by an alliance with the king of France, she secretly released her fortune-seeking seamen to raid Philip's treasure ships from the New World, a practice called "privateering." And she began rebuilding her navy.

The privateering of the English "seadogs"—Sir Francis Drake, Martin Frobisher, and Sir John Hawkins—was extremely successful, and pleased the queen. In 1578, Sir Francis Drake, the most famous of the English raiders, sailed his *Golden Hind* into the Pacific through the Strait of Magellan and raided Spanish cities and shipping along the west coast of South America. He returned to England in 1581 via the Cape of Good Hope, laden with gold, silver, and jewels worth half a million pounds sterling (equal to many millions of today's dollars). Queen Elizabeth accepted the treasure and knighted Drake on the quarterdeck of his ship.

Hawkins became the treasurer of the Queen's Fleet. He disliked boarding tactics, preferring instead that the English ships be fast floating gun platforms. Since he controlled shipbuilding funds, he made sure that such ships were built. Advances in naval guns matched the new ship designs. Especially useful was the *culverin,* a long cannon that could throw a 17-pound cannonball 1¼ miles— more than a quarter-mile farther than heavier conventional cannon. In 1587 Drake sailed boldly into the Spanish port of Cadiz and destroyed eighteen cargo ships with his culverins. The heavier guns of the surprised Spanish galleons in the harbor were no match for the longer-range English batteries.

Elizabeth had a big advantage in her superb seamen. The widespread privateering had created a group of men who had great knowledge of ships and the sea. With these seadogs in command of the world's best sailors, England prepared to meet Spain in a great contest for supremacy on the seas.

In 1588 Philip sent forth what he believed to be an unbeatable naval armada. Its purpose was to stop the successful raids on his ships and ports, and to bring England back into the Catholic church. The Spanish Armada was a fleet of 124 galleons with 1,100 guns. It was crewed by 8,000 sailors and carried 19,000 soldiers, all under the command of the Duke of Medina Sidonia.

To oppose it, the English had reinforced the queen's 34 men-of-war with 163 armed merchantmen, 16,000 men, and 2,000 guns. The English fleet was under the overall command of Charles Howard, Lord Admiral of England. The fleet was in four squadrons commanded by Drake, Hawkins, Frobisher, and Howard himself.

So the scene was set. The Armada had fewer guns, but had superior total firepower. The English had small ships and long-range culverins. The English had an advantage in maneuverability, clear decks, and range. King Philip's orders were to "grapple and board and engage hand to hand." But the English intended to fight with guns alone, for they carried fewer soldiers. The sailors and marines doubled as antiboarding defenders and cannoneers.

Defeat of the Spanish Armada. During the first battle in the English Channel, each side used more than 100,000 rounds of shot. Spanish fire had little effect, because of the distance kept by the English ships. The English pounded the Spanish ships, causing many casualties on the packed decks, but little damage to ships.

Ignoring a chance to attack the English off Plymouth, the Spaniards sailed on up the channel. The English picked away at them with little effect. But by the time Medina Sidonia sought rest and resupply in the neutral French port of Calais, he found that he had fired all of his heavy shot. During the night, Howard sent eight fireships into the Spanish ships anchored at Calais, forcing the Spaniards out in confusion during darkness. The next day the English and their Dutch allies attacked without fear of the now silent big Spanish guns, facing only the small border-repellers and muskets.

However, the English supply system also

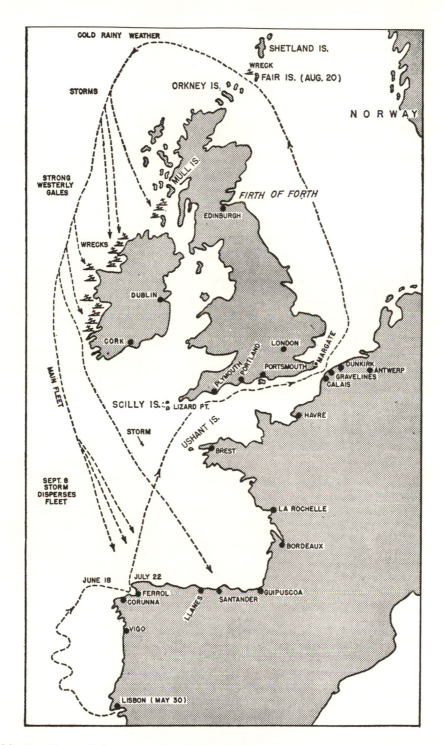

The sortie of the Spanish Armada began in Lisbon. The British defeated the Armada in the English Channel near Calais. The Spanish fled around Scotland to return home, an half of the 124 galleons and more than 13,000 men were lost in storms off the rocky coast of Ireland.

proved to be inadequate. After Howard had sunk two Spanish ships, driven three onto the rocks, and littered the enemy decks with casualties, he too ran out of ammunition. But the Spanish were already on the run. With the wind against them and the English behind them, the Spaniards fled northward into the North Sea, intending to round Britain and Ireland on the way home.

If the English ammunition had held out, they would have probably crushed the Spanish Armada then and there. As it was, hunger and thirst, storms, and poor navigation completed the task started by the English. Some thirty-five or forty Spanish ships sank at sea, and at least twenty were wrecked on the rocky shores of Scotland and Ireland. In October, Philip received back about half of the great naval force he had confidently sent to conquer England.

The failure of the Armada marked the beginning of Spain's decline. The defeat of the Armada was a signal to seafaring nations, especially England, France, and Holland, to strike out for colonies and commerce around the world. The fact that these efforts often involved taking over territories and trade routes claimed by the king of Spain made little difference to the mariners. They did not attempt to conquer Spanish colonies in Central and South America. But the Spanish Main in Colombia and Panama, and the islands in the Caribbean, were often *plundered* by pirates and privateers. Asia, Africa, and North America east of the Mississippi River were considered wide open for colonization and trade.

ENGLAND BUILDS ITS EMPIRE

England's efforts at colonization in the seventeenth century, unlike those of its rivals, were paid for by private groups who received charters (licenses) for that purpose from the Crown. The first successful one in North America, at Jamestown, Virginia (1607), nearly failed because most of the settlers were "gentlemen" who thought they were too good to work. Later colonies in Massachusetts, Pennsylvania, and Maryland were begun by groups seeking religious freedom. The last colony on the East Coast to be started was Georgia (1732), whose settlers volunteered as a way to get out of debtors' prisons.

With the English, French, and Dutch all eagerly seeking colonies, conflict was sure to occur. Between 1665 and 1674, the English and Dutch fought three fierce naval wars. The English were the winners, and one of their gains was the Dutch colony of Nieuw Amsterdam, which the English soon renamed New York. Between 1689 and 1763, the English fought a series of wars with the French, now their only serious rival at sea. During the Seven Years' War (1756–63), known in America as the French and Indian War, the two powers fought what amounted to a world war, with land and sea battles occurring in almost every part of the globe. England's ultimate victory gained it many new possessions, the main one in North America being Canada.

Whatever may have been happening among the superpowers, throughout this period of nearly two centuries the colonies existing in a thin strip of cultivated land on the East Coast of North America did so only because of the sea. It was across the Atlantic Ocean that all of the settlers had come, bringing with them the bare necessities of their ways of life from the Old World to the New. And it was across this same ocean that additional colonists, livestock, and hardware came, to sustain and expand what the hardy first folk had begun. The sea provided them with an industry, particularly in New England, where they soon discovered some of the richest fishing grounds in the world. Virginians used the sea to send large quantities of tobacco to the Old World, which had taken an almost instant liking to the stuff. Within and among the colonies, the inland rivers and coastal waters became highways whereby the products in inland regions could be traded for imported goods and sent on their way to the larger coastal communities and then overseas, primarily to England.

Born of the sea, kept going by the sea, enriched by the sea, England's American colonies by 1760 had reached more than 1.5 million people, and fifteen years later had added another million. American seamen and American-built ships made up about one-third of the entire English merchant marine.

With the Treaty of Paris in 1763, the war in North America between France and England ended. England was supreme, and its navy and merchant fleets controlled the world's seas.

Chapter 1.   *Study Guide Questions*

1. What is meant by a nation's sea power?
2. A. How did navies start?
   B. What was their purpose?
3. What were the two main types of commercial and war ships used in ancient times?
4. Why did ancient Crete develop into the first sea power in the Mediterranean?
5. How did the Phoenicians contribute to Western culture?
6. Which great Middle Eastern empire was the main enemy of ancient Greece?
7. What were King Xerxes' invasion plans against Greece?
8. What was the Greek plan of battle at the Battle of Salamis?
9. A. Who followed the Greeks as the leader in Western culture?
   B. Which country was their principal enemy during their rise to power?
   C. What were the wars between these countries called?
10. What two sea battles won the Mediterranean for Rome after Caesar's death?
11. What is the period of Western European history from the fall of Rome until about the eleventh century often called?
12. A. Which of the Italian states became a great commercial and naval power during the Crusades?
    B. How did it do this?

C. What organization of ports dominated the trade of northern Europe at the same time?
13. What happened in 1571 to end the threat of control of the Mediterranean by the Moors?
14. What happened between the fall of Constantinople and the Battle of Lepanto that caused the Mediterranean to decline as the center of world maritime interest?
15. Which country led the way to the Age of Discovery with early explorations around Africa?
16. What great economic changes occurred in Europe as a result of the discovery of the Americas and sea routes to the Orient?
17. Which country rose to oppose Spain as the leading sea power in the sixteenth century?
18. Who were the famous English squadron leaders who defeated the Spanish Armada in 1588?
19. A. Which country challenged the English first?
    B. What was the outcome of these wars in America?
20. What was the main result of the French and Indian War in America?

Vocabulary

center of commerce	amphibious invasion
sea lines of communication	trade
	bazaar
prosperity, prosperous	rebellion
grapple	piracy
invasion	depose
plunder	fervor
flank	privateers
galley	convoy
Mare Nostrum	mercantile theory
harass	broadside
assassination	encounter
seaboard	maneuver
homesteader	colonization

Chapter 2.   The American Revolution

Let us consider the events that led to the birth of our nation and our navy. You will see that our destiny is bound up with naval and maritime power.

SETTING THE STAGE

The Seven Year's War was fought from 1756 to 1763. During this war, Britain captured French and Spanish colonial possessions around the world, mainly because of its superior naval strength. Chief among these were Canada and Florida in North America, and India in Asia.

England's prime minister during these years, William Pitt, planned the naval strategies that made it possible for England to win half the world by the end of the war. The English prime ministers who followed Pitt, however, allowed the Royal Navy to decline in the years after the war. On the other hand, France began to rebuild its navy immediately.

While England and France were busy fighting each other, the American colonies grew and prospered. Thus, once the war was over, British officials saw that raising money in the colonies would help pay off the debts built up during the long war. So England began taxing its imports to the colonies in 1763, with a decree called the Revenue Act. Then by the Stamp Act of 1765 it tried to reassert Parliament's powers in the colonies. The colonists soon became upset with the unfair way they thought that Britain was treating them.

In 1767 Parliament passed the Townshend Act, which taxed paper, lead, and tea. All over the colonies people protested. Anti-British feelings were especially high in Boston. There, on the evening of 5 March 1770, a crowd of angry protesters led by a mixed-blooded African American named Crispus Attucks gathered and began to jeer British soldiers. One thing soon led to another, and in the scuffle that followed, the soldiers shot and killed Attucks and several other people—considered the first casualties of the American Revolution. This incident was played up in the press so much that it quickly came to be called the "Boston Massacre." It made many colonists want to seek revenge.

Three years later, irate Bostonians dressed up as warlike Indians so they would not be recognized, boarded a merchant ship, and dumped some British tea into the harbor rather than pay the taxes due on it. Parliament soon responded to this "Boston Tea Party" with the Coercive Acts, which closed the port of Boston, abolished the right of the people of Massachusetts to select their own council, and cut down on other liberties.

These were the events that led to the American Revolution, which began at Lexington and Concord in April 1775. "The die is cast," wrote King George III. "The colonies must either triumph or submit." There was no longer room for a peaceful settlement.

BRITISH SEA POWER

The Royal Navy, in 1775 still the mightiest in the world, soon found out that it would not be easy to fight the Americans. For one thing, the British had been getting much of their shipbuilding materials such as tar, pitch, turpentine, and timber for masts and hulls from the colonies, and now, of course, the colonies would not supply these materials to England. The British also soon found that many officers in the British army and navy believed the Americans should be treated like English citizens, and refused to fight against them.

Another force that had earlier been on England's side was now turned against it—the *privateers,* the armed American merchant ships that had helped the British win the French and Indian War. Now these *privateersmen,* with the blessing of the Continental Congress, set out to capture British ships and goods.

The 1,800-mile-long American East Coast now presented a big problem for the British. How could they defend their merchant ships from privateers in English waters, patrol the American coastline to keep ships from supplying the colonies with arms and other goods, and at the same time supply British land troops with the weapons and other things they needed?

THE BIRTH OF THE AMERICAN NAVY

In July 1775 the Continental Congress petitioned King George III to restore liberty to the colonies in a final attempt to avoid war with England. Despite the difficulties facing the British, the king refused to accept the petition, and the colonists knew that they must prepare for war.

George Washington, who had been a British colonial officer in the French and Indian War, had taken command of the Continental Army surrounding Boston on 3 July 1775. Washington knew he could not wage war without a navy. "Whatever efforts are made by land armies, the navy must have the casting vote in the present conflict," he said.

Just one month before Washington had taken command, a group of Maine backwoodsmen under Jeremiah O'Brien won the first real sea fight of the Revolution. The patriots captured a small British merchant sloop, and then they used her to capture the British armed cutter *Margaretta* and all of the supplies that ship was taking to British troops in New England.

This action was similar to most of the naval warfare done by the colonies throughout the war. Every colony except New Hampshire put some ships into commission, and Virginia and South Carolina had squadrons of some size. Nearly all of these ships were small. They operated all along the Atlantic seaboard, in river mouths, bays, and coves. They carried on coastal commerce, and attacked British supply boats and parties whenever the opportunities and odds were favorable. But most important they kept open the coastal lines of communication on which so much of the life in the colonies depended.

Partly because of this "coastal cavalry" force, Congress was reluctant to establish a Continental navy. Many representatives thought that no warships built and manned by colonists would be able to stand up to the powerful ships of the Royal Navy. But the colonies needed supplies to wage war, and capturing them from British ships was a very good way to get them. When Congress

Sketch of a U.S. frigate of the late eighteenth and early nineteenth centuries.

learned that two unescorted transport ships loaded with supplies for the British army in Quebec had sailed from England, it decided that the time had come to launch the Continental Navy.

On 13 October 1775 Congress took the step that the U.S. Navy regards as its official birth. It approved a plan for buying, fitting out, and arming two vessels, the *Andrew Doria* and the *Cabot*, to intercept the British supply ships. Two larger ships, the *Alfred* and the *Columbus*, soon were added. These ships were not only to attack British transports; they were also to protect and defend the colonies.

Congress quickly enlarged the navy even more. New men-of-war were built, and merchant vessels were converted into fighting ships for the navy to use. Privateers also helped the navy. They would capture some 2,200 British vessels by war's end. Afterwards, many privateer captains would become famous in the new U.S. Navy.

George Washington himself commissioned seven ships to capture some of the supplies that were streaming in to the British troops in Boston. In November 1775 his "navy" took muskets, shot, and a huge mortar, which Washington's poorly armed forces needed desperately, from the British ships.

John Adams drafted regulations for naval personnel, and Congress adopted them on 28 November 1775. These regulations were based on British naval rules, but they were more humane than the British. For example, punishment in the American navy was not so severe as it was in other navies of the time.

On 10 November 1775 Congress established a Marine Corps of two battalions. These men would help man the new navy. The Marine Corps still celebrates this date as its birthday.

In the early days of the Revolution, men were eager to join the navy, but as the war went on, recruiting crews for the navy's ships became more and more difficult. Reports of stricter punishments and low pay kept many men away. Others believed they could do better for themselves as privateers. The navy's ships needed crews, though, so the navy had to take on inexperienced landsmen and criminals, who were given a "choice" between serving their sentences in jail or joining a ship's crew. The navy also attempted to force men to serve by taking them on board against their will. This practice was called *impressment*. Finding men to serve in the Continental Navy was a problem throughout the war, and ships were often unable to go to sea because they lacked crews.

FIRST NAVAL OPERATIONS

The first Continental naval squadron was composed of six small schooners, brigs, and sloops donated by several states and assembled at Philadelphia. They were placed under the command of Esek Hopkins, a Rhode Islander. On 22 December 1775, the first American naval flag was broken out from one of them, the *Alfred*, by the senior lieutenant on the list of the Continental Navy's officers, one John Paul Jones. More would be heard of him later.

In February 1776 Congress directed Hopkins to take his squadron to the Virginia Capes to neutralize any loyalist craft he might find there. But in keeping with his independent New England spirit, once at sea, Hopkins decided to go after bigger game. He sailed straight for New Providence (later Nassau) in the Bahamas, where the British were reported to have a large supply of naval stores, ordnance, and powder.

On 3 March 1776 his seamen and marines landed. Two forts there surrendered without a fight, and Hopkins's men got eighty-seven artillery pieces and a load of powder, very much needed by the Continental forces. On their way home, the squadron captured several British ships loaded with more British arms, which they took to Washington's troops as well. The expedition was not without casualties, however. Just after midnight on 5 April, the squadron happened upon the 20-gun British corvette *Glasgow* off New England. After damaging many of the squadron's ships, the *Glasgow* escaped, even though she was outnumbered six to one.

This incident showed in many ways what kind of navy the Continental Congress had gathered. For the most part, the squadron captains were privateersmen, who did not know or appreciate how to cooperate with each other, teach their men gunnery, or maintain squadron discipline. One of the captains, Tom Hazard of the sloop *Providence*, was dismissed for cowardice, and his ship was given to Lieutenant Jones.

A few weeks later when Hopkins took the squadron south to Providence, Rhode Island, troubles began to multiply. Several of the ships began to break down; an epidemic of smallpox sent a hundred men ashore; and General Washington wanted returned another hundred men he had loaned to the squadron. There was no money to pay those who were left. It was nearly impossible to recruit men for such duty when the crews of the coastal privateersmen got better shares of the prizes they captured, plus quick payoffs for their efforts.

Thus, the Nassau expedition turned out to be the last time American ships would put to sea as a squadron during the war. Later, various officers who had been in the squadron set out by themselves in their ships and took on many British ships in hard-fought actions.

One such officer was Lieutenant John Paul Jones. With his sloop the *Providence*, in a single month, August 1776, Jones captured sixteen

Action on the gunnery deck of an American frigate during the Revolutionary War.

enemy vessels and destroyed many others. Later, as captain of a makeshift frigate, the *Alfred,* Jones cruised off the New England coast and raided enemy shipping and fishing in that area. One of the ships he captured carried British winter uniforms, and soon 10,000 American soldiers were wearing them. John Paul Jones was a courageous naval leader whose fame would soon grow along with his importance to the American cause.

The Battle of Lake Champlain. In the fall of 1775, the American patriots attacked Quebec in Canada, but they were unsuccessful. Their leader, General Benedict Arnold, was injured, and another American general, Richard Montgomery, was killed. Still the American forces stood their ground through the winter and continued to bombard the city. In the spring, when the ice melted on the St. Lawrence River, British reinforcements arrived by ship, and the patriots were forced to retreat toward the colonies. The British, under Generals Sir Guy Carleton and John Burgoyne, pursued them.

When he reached Lake Champlain in June 1776, General Arnold assembled a rag-tag flotilla of sixteen craft. General Carleton had no choice.

He had to construct his own naval force there because he did not want to leave the lake in American hands. It was early October by the time Carleton was ready to continue his advance against the Americans.

Strength was not on Arnold's side, but he outwitted the British general. At Valcour Island he hid his flotilla until the enemy's fleet sailed past before a strong north wind. Then the Americans showed themselves, and Carleton's ships had to turn and attack against the wind. Over the next two days Arnold and many of his men were able to inflict much damage on the superior British fleet though they lost most of their ships in the process. Afterward they ran their few surviving craft ashore, set fire to them, and escaped into the woods. By this time, winter was coming, and Carleton had to return to winter quarters in Canada.

This action could not be considered a "victory" in the usual sense because Arnold lost all his ships. However, the colonists were able to stop the southerly British advance, and in this way gained time to regather and train their forces until the following spring.

Meanwhile, the Second Continental Congress had signed the Declaration of Independence on 4 July 1776, making the colonists' rebellion a revolution. The patriots were more determined than ever to be free from British rule.

WASHINGTON SAVES THE CAPITAL

While these events were taking place on Lake Champlain, farther east things were not going well. The British general Sir William Howe held the city of Boston. The Americans placed cannon on Dorchester Heights overlooking the city in March 1776, but the colonial militia did not have enough gunpowder to engage Howe's troops and enter the city. Also the American navy was not large enough to stop the British from evacuating by sea; so Howe's troops and 1,000 loyalists escaped in ships to Halifax, Nova Scotia, to await reinforcements.

After the reinforcements arrived, General Howe sailed south from Nova Scotia with the main British army to join British Generals Sir Henry

John Paul Jones

John Paul, as he was first named, was born at Arbigland, Scotland, in 1747. He went to sea as a teenager, and had his first command by the age of twenty-one. In 1773, while captain of the British merchantman *Betsey,* he was involved in an incident that would change his destiny. During a mutiny, he had to kill the ringleader. Afterward he was warned that he would be accused of murdering the sailor, a charge he did not want to have to fight. So he left England and came to America, where in 1775 he got a commission in the American Continental Navy.

After turning down two commands, he accepted command of the sloops *Providence* and then *Alfred,* and had two successful cruises in them in 1776. Then in June 1777 he received command of the new sloop-of-war *Ranger,* which he was to take to France, where he was promised command of a new and bigger ship. He arrived in France in December, and spent most of 1778 cruising in the English Channel and awaiting a chance at a larger command. He left no doubt about the type of ship he wanted: "I wish to have no connection with any ship that does not sail fast; for I intend to go in harm's way." Finally in February 1779 he settled for an old East Indiaman, *Le Duc de Duras,* which he renamed the *Bonhomme Richard* in honor of Benjamin Franklin, then a special commissioner to France for the American colonies.

It was in the *Richard* that Jones would gain everlasting fame. After a short shakedown cruise in June, Jones took the *Bonhomme Richard* to sea on 14 August 1779, on a war cruise around the British Isles, in company with four other ships of French origin. In September the squadron rounded the north cape of Scotland and headed for the Firth of Forth, where Jones had come up with a daring plan to hold the Scottish city of Leith for a 200,000-pound ransom. Bad weather intervened, however, and 23 September found the *Richard* in company with the frigate *Alliance* just off Flamborough Head on the northeast coast of England. There, at 1500 hours, Jones spotted a British convoy of 41 sail, escorted by the British warships *Countess of Scarborough* and *Serapis,* under Captain Richard Pearson.

Slowly the *Richard* closed with the *Serapis,* and as the moon came out, the two ships began to do battle. The *Richard* had the worst of it; the *Serapis* began to make matchwood of the *Richard*'s hull. Jones was able to make the *Richard* fast alongside the *Serapis,* when for no apparent reason the *Alliance* fired three broadsides into the *Richard.* Captain Pearson of the British ship asked if Jones was ready to strike. Jones replied with the immortal words "I have not yet begun to fight!"

Jones kept up a steady fire at the base of the enemy mainmast with his only three remaining deck guns while his crew fought hand to hand with the British. Finally, as his mainmast was about to fall at 2230, Pearson surrendered to Jones to end the epic battle. After the *Richard* sank, Jones sailed his squadron and prizes to Holland.

When Jones arrived in Holland, the people idolized him. He returned to America to a hero's welcome in 1781. He was to have taken command of a new frigate, the *America,* then building in Portsmouth, but by the time she was launched, Congress had given her to France, and the war ended shortly thereafter. After the war Jones returned to France, and following a brief stint in the Russian Navy under Catherine the Great, he died in Paris in July 1792, a forgotten man.

It was not until the start of the twentieth century, a hundred years later, that the U.S. Navy and the general American public began to give Jones the honor he deserved. John Paul Jones was recognized then, as now, as a complete naval officer, not just a war hero. As the inscription on his tomb in the basement of the Naval Academy chapel reads, "He gave to our Navy its earliest traditions of heroism and victory."

Clinton and Charles Cornwallis at New York on 5 July, the day after the Declaration of Independence was signed. Five hundred British ships anchored off Staten Island. The Americans did not have a single warship, and the few small craft they had could not guard the entire shoreline to keep the enemy out of New York. Altogether, the British landed more than 30,000 well-equipped and well-trained troops. Washington's opposing troops numbered only about 20,000, many of them untrained militiamen.

By late fall, General Howe's superior forces had driven the patriots from Long Island and then from White Plains, New York. General Washington's army fled again and again before the advancing British. By December 1776 the American forces were reduced to only about 3,500 men because of casualties and desertion, and also because most of the men whose enlistments had run out went home to take care of their families for the winter.

Washington and his remaining troops were cold, hungry, and tired. They badly needed a victory. As his men crossed the Delaware River to escape the enemy yet again in late December, Washington developed a bold plan. He ordered the men to take all boats from the New Jersey side of the river to the Pennsylvania side. Then, on Christmas night, in a raging sleet storm, the nearly frozen American soldiers quietly rowed through the ice floes on the river back to the New Jersey shore. Their surprise attack on the enemy troops at Trenton was a huge success. One week later, Washington surprised the British again, this time at Princeton, and his men won another complete victory.

The British then returned to New York for the winter, while Washington and his troops wintered in Morristown, New Jersey. They had saved the colonial capital at Philadelphia from the enemy, but, more important, the tide was turning. The patriots would be ready to fight again with the coming of spring.

THE CRUCIAL YEAR, 1777

British forces poured across the Atlantic into America during the winter, spring, and early summer of 1777. The British prepared to use the same three-pronged plan of attack that had failed the year before because of the delays caused by the naval operations on Lake Champlain. General Burgoyne would move south from Montreal with 8,000 men, to the Hudson Valley. An army of pro-British Tories and the Indians would advance eastward from Lake Ontario. The main army, commanded by Howe, would march north from New York City. The three forces were to meet in Albany, New York, after destroying all patriot forces in their paths, thus splitting the colonies in half.

Burgoyne moved south and recaptured Fort Ticonderoga in early July, but in late August, patriot militia beat the Tories and Indians near Fort Stanwix. The plan probably still would have worked if Howe had proceeded according to plan. But Howe decided to take Philadelphia en route to meeting Burgoyne at Albany.

On 25 August 1777, Howe landed 15,000 men on the shores of the Chesapeake Bay about 50 miles south of Philadelphia. Howe's use of water transport had kept Washington guessing about his intentions for two months. When he finally received word that Howe's armada of 260 ships had entered the Chesapeake, Washington quickly moved most of his army south of Philadelphia to Brandywine Creek. But the Americans were no match for the superior British forces, and after a two-day battle on 10 and 11 September, the British marched in triumph into Philadelphia, as the Continental Congress fled. Howe then quartered his army comfortably in Philadelphia for the winter, while Washington's men faced terrible cold and hunger at Valley Forge, northwest of the city. But as events were to turn out, although Howe had taken Philadelphia, by not following the British plan he contributed to the eventual defeat of the British in the colonies.

The Turning Point: The Battle of Saratoga. Burgoyne was now by himself in northern New York, and he was in trouble. His supply line was stretched through the wilderness, and his men were running short of food. Militiamen from New York and New England constantly harassed his troops. In August 1777, Burgoyne sent 800 men to

Bennington, Vermont, to find food, but 2,000 Americans, called the Green Mountain Boys, fought and captured them, as well as a second force Burgoyne sent after them.

Almost in desperation, on 19 September, Burgoyne marched his men European-style through an open field to try to break through the American lines near Saratoga, New York. The bright red uniforms of his men all in line made easy targets for American sharpshooters, who were firing from behind trees. When the British retreated, the Americans followed, only to be driven back by British bayonets. The two forces took turns advancing and retreating. By dusk, when the Americans retired, Burgoyne had lost 600 men, who could not be replaced. In the meantime, Major General Horatio Gates was gathering a growing force of Americans.

On 7 October, Burgoyne led his trapped Redcoats in a final attempt to break through American lines. Once more, Daniel Morgan's riflemen mowed them down. The British retreated when General Benedict Arnold led a charge. Burgoyne had lost 1,200 men and was surrounded by a total of 15,000 American militiamen and regulars under Gates. Burgoyne finally surrendered on 17 October 1777.

Saratoga marked the turning point of the war in two ways. First, after Burgoyne's defeat the British government was less willing to carry on the war. Lord North, England's prime minister, offered to repeal the British tax laws that had caused the war if the patriots would stop fighting and remain under British rule. But by now the leaders of the Revolution were dedicated to winning freedom for a new nation.

Even more important, the American victory at Saratoga now brought the French into the war on the American side. Benjamin Franklin had gone to France and had been trying for some time to convince the French that joining the American cause was the best way for France to take world leadership away from England. After Saratoga, the French finally were convinced that the Americans had some chance of winning the war, and they signed a treaty of friendship with the former colonies on 6 February 1778. In June, France declared war on England, and began actively helping the patriots to win their freedom.

The naval battle on Lake Champlain had set the stage for Saratoga. Saratoga helped bring France, and later, Spain, into the war on the American side. And these allies made American victory and independence possible.

THE WAR AT SEA

American naval efforts in American waters during the war were mostly just a nuisance to Britain. By 1780, only a few of the forty converted merchantmen and thirteen frigates built for the Continental Navy remained in American hands. Though these vessels captured many British ships, they did not affect the outcome of the war. The small naval forces of the coastal states were also largely ineffective, as British ships were able to sail freely up and down the coast throughout most of the war years.

American privateers were the biggest problem for the British in the offshore waters of the Atlantic. They hurt British trade in the West Indies, delayed troop transports that were bringing reinforcements, and captured arms and supplies that the colonial forces badly needed in the early years of the war. However, privateering also took away men, ships, and weapons that the Continental Navy could have used. Despite the damage they caused, the privateers did not greatly harm the British war effort. Washington had been right when he said that naval power would decide the outcome of the war, but in the end, it was French, not American, naval power that made the difference.

The American naval record in more distant waters, however, was impressive. The tiny Continental Navy and American naval heroes such as Joshua Barney, John Barry, Nicolas Biddle, Lambert Wickes, and Gustavus Conyngham won glory overseas during the war, but the greatest officer of the Continental Navy was John Paul Jones, who took the war to European waters with inspiring results.

Jones received command of the new 18-gun *Ranger* in June 1777 and sailed to France. In the spring of 1778, Jones took the *Ranger* around

The *Bonhomme Richard*, commanded by Captain John Paul Jones, engages HMS *Serapis*, a powerful British frigate under command of Captain Richard Pearson, on 23 September 1779.

Britain and Ireland and captured HMS *Drake* and several merchant ships.

One year later, Jones was given command of an old 40-gun East Indiaman, which he renamed the *Bonhomme Richard* in honor of Benjamin Franklin, who had written *Poor Richard's Almanac.* In August 1779, Jones sailed in command of a small squadron that included the American frigate *Alliance,* which carried 36 guns, and three smaller French vessels. The captain of the *Alliance* was an erratic Frenchman named Pierre Landais.

On 23 September 1779, Jones's squadron was trailing a large English convoy off the northeast coast of England, when its two escorts approached at dusk. The British warships were the 50-gun HMS *Serapis,* under Captain Richard Pearson, and the 20-gun *Countess of Scarborough.* Jones immediately ordered an attack, but the small French ships turned away. Later, though, the French frigate *Pallas* took the *Countess* after a sharp fight.

The *Richard* and the *Serapis* both began to fire broadsides as soon as they came into range. Early in the exchange, however, two of Jones's 18-pounder cannons exploded on the lower gun deck, killing all the crewmen there and blowing a huge hole in the deck above. Jones saw that his only hope was to lay the *Richard* alongside and take the *Serapis* by boarding. He ordered grapples heaved, and then he seized one of the forestays from the British vessel and tied it to the *Richard*'s mizzenmast himself. For the rest of the battle, the two ships swung together stern to bow and bow to stern, their guns firing directly into each other.

After two hours of fighting, the crew of the *Richard* had cleared the topside weather decks of the *Serapis,* but the *Richard* was full of holes. At this point the *Alliance* reappeared. A glad shout went up from the Americans, but it was quickly drowned out when the *Alliance* fired a broadside that ripped into the *Richard* instead of the *Serapis.* The *Alliance* fired two more broadsides into the

Richard, and then withdrew. Landais later told a friend that he had hoped to become the victor by sinking the *Richard* and capturing the *Serapis* himself. Jones later brought charges against the captain, who was dismissed from the French navy.

The *Richard* slowly began to sink. About 2130 hours an American seaman dropped a grenade through an open hatch of the *Serapis*. The grenade hit powder cartridges in the British vessel, and the explosions killed many of her gunners.

Jones's crew now came to topside to fight hand to hand. The fighting continued for an hour, until at 2230 Captain Pearson tore down his flag with his own hands. He had been shaken by the explosions and the ferocity of the hand-to-hand fighting, and was afraid his tottering mainmast would collapse.

The battered *Richard* went down two days later, and Jones raised the American flag on board the *Serapis*. Then, avoiding the British ships that were trying to find him, he sailed his squadron and prizes to Holland.

THE CLOSING CAMPAIGNS

With France its enemy, Britain could no longer concentrate all its efforts in the colonies. The British were now determined to stand on the defensive in the north, mount an offensive in the south, and take the war to the West Indies.

Sir Henry Clinton, who was put in command of the British forces in the colonies, abandoned Philadelphia and moved his army through New Jersey to reinforce New York City. Meanwhile the French Vice Admiral Comte d'Estaing was on his way to America with a French fleet of twelve ships. Had he arrived sooner, he could have caught General Howe, who was transporting Clinton's artillery and supplies on the Delaware River. But d'Estaing arrived too late, and Howe completed his transit of the Delaware on 28 June 1778. Howe delivered Clinton's supplies the next day, and then he stationed frigates in the New York harbor to warn of the approach of the French naval forces.

When d'Estaing arrived off New York on 11 July, General Washington offered to launch a land attack at the same time d'Estaing attacked by sea.

But d'Estaing's ships could not get into the shallow harbor, and d'Estaing sailed away to the Caribbean.

During the winter of 1778, d'Estaing's fleet captured Grenada in the West Indies, and then held the island against attack by a British fleet commanded by Admiral Byron. Lord Howe was ordered home to explain why he had failed to link up with Burgoyne in the summer of 1777. In December 1778, the British captured Savannah, Georgia, in a combined naval and land attack.

D'Estaing returned to the colonies in September 1779 to help the Americans try to recapture the city. On 9 October, French ships and troops, together with American troops, launched their attack, but the British held them off. D'Estaing returned to France with his fleet.

In Morristown, Washington's troops were suffering through their most difficult winter. Confident that Washington's troops were not a threat to New York City, Clinton mounted a major offensive in the south in February 1780. His large fleet set sail for Charleston, South Carolina, and surrounded the American forces there. The city had held off the British for three years, but Clinton's new force was overwhelming, and the city's defenses broke down. The British cut off American supply lines and escape routes and bombarded the city for one month. Finally, on 12 May, the entire garrison of 5,000 men surrendered to the British. The last Continental naval squadron was captured in the Charleston harbor at about this time, so the Continental Navy was never again an effective fighting force.

In August 1780, Clinton received word that a French fleet bringing 5,500 soldiers had arrived in Newport, Rhode Island. He left General Lord Charles Cornwallis, who had come with him, in command in the south, and hurried back to New York. General Cornwallis defeated General Gates's forces at Camden, South Carolina, and took the city in mid-August. Then Cornwallis moved into North Carolina, and Washington could do nothing to stop him.

In October, General Nathanael Greene's troops defeated a Tory force at King's Mountain, South

Carolina, and in January 1781, General Morgan destroyed a British force under General Tarleton at Cowpens. Cornwallis followed Morgan and Greene through North Carolina. He won a battle at Guilford Courthouse, but he lost so many men that he had to retreat. He retreated to Wilmington, North Carolina, and asked the Royal Navy to send help to him there. When help did not arrive, Cornwallis disobeyed Clinton's orders and led his troops into Virginia, where he would soon be trapped.

The Battle of Yorktown. Cornwallis successfully raided some areas in Virginia and then followed Clinton's orders to entrench his army at Yorktown, on the Chesapeake Bay, late in the summer. The Marquis de Lafayette immediately sent word of Cornwallis's move to General Washington. Lafayette and General "Mad Anthony" Wayne commanded some 5,000 ragged militia in the area, and these troops kept Cornwallis under observation.

In the meantime, General Comte de Rochambeau, who had brought his troops to Newport a year earlier to aid Washington, learned in May 1781 that reinforcements were not coming. In spite of this, he and Washington agreed to battle Clinton's superior troops in New York. Washington wrote to the French minister to ask him to urge Admiral de Grasse to come north from the Caribbean to join the New York operation.

On 14 August 1781, the letter on which everything hinged arrived at Washington's headquarters. De Grasse reported that he would arrive in the Chesapeake with more than 25 warships and 3,000 troops in September. Four days later, Washington ordered 4,500 Americans and General Rochambeau's French army of 5,500 to march from New York to Yorktown. He left enough men behind to protect West Point and to keep Clinton busy in New York. The French Admiral de Barras led the Newport fleet south. Washington hoped to bring his land and sea forces together to battle the British at Yorktown.

On 5 September, the American and French troops passed through Philadelphia, and General Washington learned that de Grasse was in the Chesapeake. On the evening of 14 September, Washington and Rochambeau greeted Lafayette and Wayne at Williamsburg, Virginia, and then set up siege lines around Yorktown. The next morning the land forces learned that off the Virginia Capes de Grasse had driven the British fleet back to New York on 5 September, and that de Barras had arrived with artillery and supplies on 10 September. Cornwallis was now surrounded.

Twenty thousand French and American troops attacked Yorktown on 9 October. For eight days the combined land forces attacked the British with artillery, while the French fleets bombarded the city. American forces also stormed two key defensive positions and kept the British from fleeing across the York River to Gloucester. The British fleet that had retreated to New York returned to the Chesapeake with Clinton and 6,000 British troops one week too late to help Cornwallis. He had surrendered his entire army of 7,600 men to General Washington on 19 October 1781.

The British loss at Yorktown marked the end of the fighting in the colonies. The war shifted to the West Indies, the Mediterranean, and India. England, tired of war, now faced the powerful combined forces of France, Spain, and Holland in Europe.

In February 1782, Lord North resigned, and the new pacifist cabinet in Parliament decided not to launch any more offensive attacks in North America. England sent a representative to Paris to discuss peace with the Americans there. The American delegation, headed by Benjamin Franklin, John Jay, and John Adams, insisted on American independence. England still held New York, Charleston, and Savannah in the colonies, but the pressure in Europe was working to the Americans' advantage.

The treaty that the Americans and the British drew up gave the colonies their full independence—they would not be under British rule or protection in any way. The colonies received a territory that extended west to the Mississippi, north to the Great Lakes, and south to Florida. The U.S. Congress declared the war over on 11 April 1783, but it was not until 3 September that the American and British representatives signed the Peace of Paris.

The small Continental Navy was generally ineffective throughout the war in the face of what was then the most powerful navy on earth. But it was plain that sea power had played a major role in America's gaining its independence. Much of the artillery and other supplies used by the Continental Army came from prizes captured at sea, and were delivered by sea routes of supply. Though no one won the battle off the Virginia Capes in 1781, the French fleet prevented the British from helping Cornwallis, leading directly to his surrender. To many Americans, it was obvious that to keep its freedom America needed a navy of its own.

Chapter 2.   Study Guide Questions

1. As a result of the Seven Years' War, whose worldwide colonial possessions did Britain obtain?

2. A. Why did the British Parliament begin to lay burdensome taxes on the American colonies?

B. What happened in 1773 as a result of the Townshend tax acts?

3. What did the British response to the Boston Tea Party lead to in April 1775?

4. What naval stores did the colonies supply to the British navy?

5. When was the Marine Corps established?

6. What were the problems of recruiting a crew in the early Continental Navy?

7. How did the American invasion of Canada in 1775 turn out?

8. A. Who was the American commander at the first Battle of Lake Champlain in 1776?

B. What was the important outcome of the battle?

9. A. What was the overall British plan to defeat the Americans in 1777?

B. What happened?

C. Why was the Battle of Saratoga vital to the American cause?

D. What were the names of the opposing generals in this battle?

10. Who was the great American diplomat who brought about the French alliance early in 1778?

11. Who was the greatest American naval hero of the Revolutionary War?

12. A. Where did John Paul Jones have his famous battle with HMS *Serapis*?

B. What was the name of the ship commanded by Jones?

C. What was Jones's strategy in the fight?

13. What was Jones's famous reply when the British captain asked if he had struck his colors?

14. A. What crucial naval battle made the Battle of Yorktown possible?

B. Who were the American and French commanders at Yorktown?

15. A. After Yorktown, where did the British concentrate their war effort?

B. When did the war officially end?

Vocabulary

assert	ammunition
protester	artillery
abolish	delegation
impressment	diplomat
desertion	surround
reinforcements	surrender
evacuation	skirmish
rebellion	garrison
militia	

Chapter 3.   The United States Builds a Navy

When the Treaty of Paris ended the Revolutionary War in 1783, the new nation was badly in debt. The U.S. government did not have authority to raise money through taxation, so there were no funds for keeping ships seaworthy and building new ones. In 1783 the Continental Navy passed into history when the government sold the *Alliance*, the only ship left in that navy.

After the war, the officers and men who had

served in the Continental Navy returned to their peacetime jobs of merchant shipping and ship-building. They soon found, however, that the British were going to make these enterprises diffi-cult. In fact, the British government issued Orders in Council that sought to keep Americans out of the West Indies trade, limit U.S. exports to Eng-land, and make it illegal for British subjects to buy U.S.-built ships.

U.S. merchants had to find new markets for their trade. Some looked to China, but China was far away, and getting there was expensive and time-consuming. Americans trading in the Mediterranean Sea and outside the Strait of Gibraltar missed the protection the British flag had always provided them. Pirates from the Barbary states of Morocco, Algiers, Tunis, and Tripoli had been capturing ships and kidnapping crews for ransom in these waters for two hundred years. Britain, France, and Holland paid these states trib-ute money so they could sail in their waters in safety. The United States had not yet made such an agreement, and the Barbary pirates seized three U.S. ships in 1784 and 1785. The United States bought a treaty of impunity from Morocco in 1786, but Algiers would not be bought off. British merchants were happy to see U.S. compe-tition held back in this area of the world.

A NEW AMERICAN GOVERNMENT

In 1789 the Articles of Confederation were re-placed by the U.S. Constitution. The Constitution authorized Congress "to provide and maintain a navy," but the new country's other needs came first. Also, a war had started between Portugal and Algiers, and thereafter U.S. merchantmen joined Portuguese and Spanish convoys in the Mediter-ranean for protection, which made building a U.S. Navy less urgent.

The first act of the new U.S. government did help U.S. merchants, however. The government taxed incoming foreign shipping, which gave U.S. shipping an advantage. At the same time, British West Indian planters began welcoming U.S. ships, despite the Orders in Council that prohibited such trade. British officials in London knew how much

the planters needed U.S. goods, and so they did lit-tle to stop the U.S. smugglers.

U.S. shipping and shipbuilding grew rapidly until 1793. That year, soon after Portugal and Al-giers declared a truce, a pirate fleet captured ten U.S. ships in the Mediterranean. In addition, the Napoleonic wars had broken out in Europe, and France had declared war on Britain. So, just as U.S. trade was beginning to flourish, British war-ships began seizing neutral vessels trading with France, and French privateers began capturing neutral vessels trading with British possessions such as the West Indies.

The time had arrived for the United States se-riously to consider building a navy.

THE NAVY ACT OF 1794

Not everyone in the United States wanted their country to build a navy. Many Americans who lived inland did not want to be taxed for a navy that would mostly benefit those who lived on the At-lantic coastline. For this reason, the Navy Act that Congress eventually passed, on 27 March 1794, provided for only six frigates. The bill also stated that naval shipbuilding would stop if the United States made peace with Algiers. In 1796 this hap-pened, but President Washington convinced Con-gress to allow three of the frigates to be com-pleted. The *United States* and the *Constitution*, both of which had 44 guns, and the *Constellation*, which carried 38 guns, were launched in 1797.

The British saw early in their war with France that they would need trade goods carried in U.S. ships, and so they stopped seizing them. The British and the Americans worked out their other maritime differences in Jay's Treaty, which the two countries signed in 1797.

The French were outraged by this agreement, and increased their raids on U.S. ships. In one year French privateers in the West Indies and along the U.S. Atlantic coast seized 316 U.S. merchant ships. In the fall of 1797 President John Adams sent three representatives to Paris to work out a settle-ment. The French wanted these men to pay a huge bribe to begin the talks, but they refused. Americans everywhere responded to the French insult with the slogan "Millions for defense, but not one cent for tribute!"

The French XYZ affair, as this came to be called, put the U.S. Congress in the mood to finish building the six frigates authorized in 1794. The *President,* with 44 guns, and two 36-gun ships, the *Congress* and the *Chesapeake,* were soon launched, along with some smaller vessels. On 30 April 1798, Congress established the Navy Department. The following month, it allowed U.S. vessels to seize armed French ships that were found cruising in U.S. coastal waters. The United States had started an undeclared naval war, the Quasi-War with France.

QUASI-WAR WITH FRANCE, 1798–1800

As commander in chief, President Adams made sure that U.S. sailors were well paid and well fed. Therefore, the Navy had plenty of recruits from the merchant marine. Many of the fifty ships that eventually made up the wartime navy also came from the merchant marine.

Adams had men and ships; now he needed a leader. He chose a merchant shipper from Maryland, Benjamin Stoddert, to be his first secretary of the navy. Stoddert wasted no time in ordering his warships to patrol the Atlantic coast. The first American prize was the *Croyable.* Captured in July 1798, this privateer was renamed the *Retaliation* and put in service in the U.S. Navy.

That same month, Congress extended its authorization and allowed U.S. ships to capture armed French ships on the high seas. Stoddert was then able to send a series of expeditions to the West Indies, where most of the French privateers were based. The first mission, led by Commodore John Barry, captured only two privateers because most of the French ships were able to escape into shallow water where the U.S. vessels could not follow. In the second expedition, which arrived in the fall of 1798, Lieutenant William Bainbridge was defeated in the *Retaliation,* which was returned to French hands.

After the U.S. Navy cleared U.S. coastal waters, Stoddert sent twenty-one ships in four squadrons to the West Indies. There, U.S. vessels were allowed to use British bases, and had the support of the Royal Navy. U.S. officers and sailors learned many useful things as they served with what was then the finest navy in the world.

Commodore Thomas Truxtun was one of the Americans who worked hard to profit from the lessons learned from the Royal Navy. In his ship the *Constellation,* Truxtun fought the two most famous battles of the Quasi-War.

In February 1799, the *Constellation* was alone on patrol in the Caribbean Sea when she spied the *Insurgente,* the fastest frigate in the French Navy. The French ship tried to escape, and the *Constellation* pursued her. A sudden gale wind toppled the *Insurgente*'s main topmast, however, allowing Truxtun to bring the *Constellation* close alongside the enemy vessel. He fired all of the guns on his ship's *leeward* side down into the hull of the *Insurgente.* The French frigate returned the fire from her windward side, but because of the high angle of the guns there, she only slightly damaged the U.S. vessel's rigging. After the *Constellation* fired on the *Insurgente* twice more, the French captain hauled down his colors.

One year later, Truxtun fought his second battle in the *Constellation.* Cruising off Guadaloupe, he sighted the French frigate *Vengeance* and gave chase. The *Vengeance* was loaded with passengers and money, and she tried to avoid battle by sailing away. After pursuing the French vessel for an entire day, Truxtun finally overtook her at dusk and began firing. At one point during the five-hour battle that followed, the French captain tried to surrender, but the Americans could not see or hear his hail in the darkness amid the roar of the battle. After the battle both ships were in shambles. The *Vengeance* slipped away to Curaçao and ran aground to avoid sinking. The *Constellation* limped to Jamaica.

Finally, in October 1800, after more than two years of undeclared war, a convention of peace was concluded between France and the United States. One of the provisions in the treaty was a very unpopular clause canceling U.S. claims against the

French for attacking U.S. merchant ships. Partly because of all the uproar the treaty caused, Thomas Jefferson was able to defeat John Adams in the presidential election of 1800.

During the war, the U.S. fleet had grown rapidly. U.S. exports had risen to more than $200 million, and the income from imports was more than $22 million. The Navy had spent only $6 million to protect this commerce from the French. It was clear that the Navy benefited New England shipping, but it also benefited the economy of the entire nation.

THE WAR WITH TRIPOLI AND THE BARBARY PIRATES, 1801–5

In his election campaign, Jefferson had promised to reduce government spending. The Navy cost the country $2½ million every year; so making the Navy smaller was one way for Jefferson to make good on his promise. He began to sell off smaller naval ships.

Then the Barbary pirates started to cause more trouble. When the frigate *George Washington* arrived in Algiers with a tribute payment in September 1800, the Dey ordered Captain William Bainbridge to take passengers and the tribute payment to the sultan in Constantinople. When Bainbridge refused, the Dey turned the guns of the fortress on the frigate, and forced Bainbridge to carry out his orders. After this incident, other Barbary states increased their tribute demands.

Jefferson refused to meet the Barbary demands. In May 1801, when the United States did not meet the tribute demands of the Bashaw of Tripoli, he declared war on the United States.

That summer, the twelve-gun schooner USS *Enterprise* blockaded the port of Tripoli for eighteen days and then left for Malta. On the way, the U.S. vessel met and defeated a Tripolitan cruiser, the *Tripoli,* by outmaneuvering and outfighting her.

Other U.S. warships convoyed U.S. merchantmen through the Mediterranean. However, by the end of summer, most of the enlistments of the crews were running out, so the squadron had to return home.

A more powerful squadron was prepared for the next year. This squadron arrived in the spring of 1802 under the command of Richard Morris. The Americans were able only to capture one Tripolitan cruiser and destroy another. Morris's blockade of Tripoli was not effective, and Tripoli refused to lower its price for peace. Embarrassed by these failures, President Jefferson ordered Morris replaced by Commodore Edward Preble.

The officers serving Preble at first did not like their commander because he was very strict. After seeing their leader in action, however, the officers were soon proud to be called "Preble's Boys." For his part, Preble was at first worried because his officers were all younger than thirty. "They have given me nothing but a pack of boys!" he said. But the officers' aggressive spirit and quick minds soon won Preble's respect.

When Preble arrived in Gibraltar in September 1803, he found that Morocco had broken its treaty with the United States by capturing a U.S. vessel. He quickly sent the *Philadelphia* under Captain Bainbridge and a schooner to blockade Tripoli. Then he assembled a powerful force in the Moroccan port of Tangier. The emperor of Morocco was impressed by Preble's display of strength, and after that he kept his treaty with the United States.

THE *Philadelphia* INCIDENT

While she was blockading Tripoli, the *Philadelphia* had run aground and been captured. Her 307 crewmen were then held for ransom. Unfortunately, the Tripolitans were able to free the U.S. vessel from the reef she was on, and they anchored her near the guns of the castle.

Commodore Preble's squadron arrived off Tripoli in December. Preble saw that the *Philadelphia* was too closely guarded to be recaptured, but he wanted to destroy her so that Tripoli could not use her.

Lieutenant Stephen Decatur, Jr., volunteered to lead a crew into the harbor to burn the *Philadelphia*. On 16 February 1804, Decatur and his men

The burning of the captured frigate *Philadelphia*.

When news of the exploit reached the United States, Decatur was hailed as a hero and given a captain's commission. At twenty-five he was the youngest man to reach that rank in the short history of the U.S. Navy.

ATTACK ON TRIPOLI

During the summer of 1804, Preble tried to convince the Bashaw of Tripoli to release the crewmen of the *Philadelphia*, but he refused. Preble decided he would have to use force. He borrowed six gunboats and two mortar boats from the king of Naples. The fort of Tripoli and the flotilla of Tripolitan gunboats were still a superior force, but this did not stop Preble. He ordered the six gunboats to attack Tripoli on 3 August, and nine Tripolitan gunboats came out beyond the reef to do battle. The Tripolitans were ready to board and fight hand to hand, but the Americans surprised them by leaping into the lead Tripolitan vessels and fighting wildly.

Stephen Decatur and his men captured the first enemy gunboat while the squadron kept the others away. During the battle, Decatur broke off the blade of his cutlass and would have been killed if a seaman named Reuben James had not thrust his own head under a sword meant for Decatur.

As Decatur was towing his prize out of the harbor, he learned that his younger brother James had been shot as he stepped on board to take control of another enemy gunboat that had surrendered. That gunboat was trying to escape when Stephen Decatur overtook her, boarded her, and killed her captain in a hand-to-hand fight.

When Preble called an end to the battle, the *Constitution* covered the U.S. vessels as the Tripolitans fled. The Americans had captured three enemy gunboats. Following this attack, the Bashaw of Tripoli offered to return the U.S. crewmen for $150,000 in ransom money and to demand no more tribute. Preble rejected the offer and ordered his forces to bombard Tripoli again. The Americans continued the bombardment during the next few weeks, but the enemy gunboats never again engaged the U.S. vessels.

President Jefferson and the U.S. public were

slipped into the harbor in a captured Tripolitan ketch renamed the *Intrepid*. Decatur disguised himself in Maltese dress and stood next to his vessel's Sicilian pilot. Some of the seventy volunteers, also in disguise, stayed on deck, but most hid below.

As the *Intrepid* came near her target, a Tripolitan guard warned the vessel to stay away. The pilot told the guard that the *Intrepid* had lost her anchors in a storm, and asked to be allowed to tie up. The guard agreed, but then, just as the *Intrepid* was passing her lines, the guard became suspicious and shouted "Americanos!"

Decatur immediately ordered "Board!" and led his men over the side. The few guards on duty in the *Philadelphia* put up little fight. Several were killed, and the rest jumped overboard. Decatur's men set fire to the ship, and the *Philadelphia* was soon engulfed in flames. The Americans re-boarded the *Intrepid* and pulled away just in time, for the *Philadelphia* burned quickly. The Tripolitan fort and warships opened fire, but the *Intrepid* returned safely to the squadron.

Stephen Decatur

Stephen Decatur was born in Newport, Rhode Island, in 1779. He received a commission as midshipman in the U.S. Navy in 1798, with the help of a close family friend, Captain John Barry. Barry then saw to it that Decatur was assigned to his frigate, the *United States*. During the undeclared war with France in the next two years, Decatur took part in several cruises in the *United States*. As a young officer, Decatur advanced quickly. He became a lieutenant in 1799, a first lieutenant in 1801, and received his first command, the brig *Argus*, in 1803. He distinguished himself as an able and courageous officer with great promise.

In December 1803 Decatur received command of the schooner *Enterprise,* part of Commodore Edward Preble's squadron then blockading the port of Tripoli in the Mediterranean. In October 1803 the U.S. frigate *Philadelphia* had been captured by the Tripolitans after having run aground in the harbor. In January Preble assigned Decatur the task of leading a boarding party to sneak into the harbor and burn the *Philadelphia,* so the Tripolitans could not use her. This was no small task, since the ship was fully armed, well guarded, and anchored under more than 100 shore guns, not to mention several patrolling gunboats.

Despite these hazards, on the night of 16 February 1804 Decatur successfully carried out his mission. After a short hand-to-hand scuffle, the guards on board the *Philadelphia* were subdued, the ship was burned, and Decatur and his men escaped with no serious casualties. Decatur had been the second man to board and the last to leave the ship. Decatur received much praise both in the United States and elsewhere for this feat. The British sea hero Lord Horatio Nelson called it "the most bold and daring act of the age." As a result, President Jefferson promoted Decatur to captain, thus making him at age twenty-five the youngest to achieve this rank in U.S. naval history.

Following the conclusion of a peace treaty with Tripoli in 1805, Decatur returned home and was welcomed as a hero. In 1810 he received command of the frigate *United States*. Two years later, in June 1812, Congress declared war on England. In October, Decatur in the *United States* encountered the British frigate *Macedonian* while cruising between the Azores and the Canary Islands. After a ferocious battle marked by great long-range marksmanship by the U.S. vessel, the *Macedonian* struck her colors, having lost all her masts and 104 of her 301-man crew. The *United States* suffered only 12 casualties and minor damage. Once again Decatur was hailed as a hero.

Following the Treaty of Ghent, which ended the war in 1815, Decatur returned to the Mediterranean to subdue the Barbary states once more. They had taken advantage of the war to resume harassing merchant traffic. Only two weeks after arriving in the area, Decatur was able to force a peace treaty with Algiers, and then to exact payments from Tunis and Tripoli for U.S. vessels they had allowed to be captured during the war.

Once more Decatur returned to a grateful United States, and throughout 1815–16 he was honored by a series of banquets, speeches, and toasts. It was during one of these events in Norfolk in April 1816 that he gave his famous toast: "Our country. In her dealings with foreign nations, may she always be in the right, but our country, right or wrong." Although later this statement was often criticized as being blindly patriotic, for many years thereafter it was almost a motto for the young U.S. Navy.

For the next several years Decatur went on to distinguish himself both professionally and socially in several high posts in Washington. Then in the spring of 1820, when he was forty-one, a tragic thing happened. Years earlier Decatur had taken part in a court-martial of Captain James Barron, of the frigate *Chesapeake,* that had found the captain guilty of dereliction of duty in surrendering some alleged British deserters when challenged by the British ship *Leopard* in June 1807. Between 1813 and 1820 Barron had been requesting reinstatement in the Navy, but Decatur had opposed him. Finally Barron challenged Decatur to a duel, which the honor-conscious Decatur promptly accepted. They met at Bladensburg, Maryland, on 22 March 1820. Firing from a distance of eight paces, Barron was only wounded, but Decatur was shot in the abdomen. He died from his wounds later that night.

News of Decatur's death shocked the nation. During his brief career, he had distinguished himself by his daring, personal honor, exceptional leadership abilities, and love of country. In that time, with the young United States struggling to establish itself as a new nation, these qualities caused him to be greatly admired as a military hero and patriot. Later generations, however, questioned some of his more extreme values, and his death by dueling caused many to call for an end to the practice. Nevertheless, his combat record was unequaled in his time, and he did much to earn the respect of the nation he loved.

spurred to action by Preble's aggressive attacks. They hoped that a final victory would end the war with Tripoli and make all the Barbary states stop demanding tribute. Jefferson sent the most powerful U.S. naval force ever assembled to the Mediterranean, and he ordered Captain Samuel Barron to replace Preble. The United States gave Preble a hero's welcome when he returned to Washington.

The U.S. naval forces kept Tripoli blockaded through the early part of 1805, and plans were made for a better blockade and more attacks on the city in the summer when more gunboats were to arrive from America.

In the meantime, however, William Eaton, a bold U.S. naval agent to the Barbary states, devised a scheme to topple the Bashaw from his Tripolitan throne. He convinced the Bashaw's dethroned older brother, Hamet, to join his ragtag hired army of about 400 men. In return, Eaton agreed to restore Hamet to the throne.

Eaton's army, which included a few U.S. Marines, marched 600 miles across the Libyan desert in early March 1805. Along the way, 700 men joined to help Hamet's cause. This force captured the Tripolitan city of Derna with the help of two brigs and a schooner from the naval squadron. (The phrase "to the shores of Tripoli" in the Marine Hymn refers to this operation.) Eaton held the city for several weeks, and then came word that the war was over. In return for stopping U.S. support for his brother and $60,000 in ransom, the Bashaw agreed to a treaty that released the captive crew members and stopped all tribute payments by the United States. Eaton did not want to break his promise to Hamet, but the United States was anxious to end the war.

Some Americans were pleased by the treaty with Tripoli. They believed the ransom was reasonable and should be paid to free the captives, who had already suffered for a year and a half. They also welcomed the end of tribute paying. The Americans who did not like the treaty thought that more attacks on Tripoli would have made Tripoli and other Barbary states eager to accept treaties that were more favorable to the United States. As

it turned out, the Americans who opposed the treaty were correct.

TRIPOLI'S HISTORY LESSON

Between 1803 and 1805, the only vessels built for the U.S. Navy were small gunboats. President Jefferson did not favor building large seagoing ships because he believed the Navy should protect the U.S. coastline, not carry out attacks on the high seas.

Other nations immediately saw this "gunboat policy" as a weakness. The Dey of Algiers began capturing U.S. ships again, and making slaves of their crews and passengers. The British began impressing U.S. seamen to serve in the Royal Navy in England's war with France.

Impressment and other British actions against the United States led to the War of 1812. During that war the forces of the United States were too busy to take steps against Algiers. But on 2 March 1815, less than two weeks after the peace treaty ending the War of 1812 went into effect, Congress declared war on the Barbary states.

In the Algerine War, as it was called, the Dey's fleet was quickly defeated by a powerful U.S. naval squadron commanded by Commodore Decatur. U.S. victory and the end of our troubles with the Barbary states finally came in 1816.

The lesson offered by the war with Tripoli has two parts. First, giving in to demands for tribute and ransom usually only leads to more demands. Second, a weak navy invites aggressive actions by enemies. Refusing to give in to demands and maintaining a strong navy help to keep a nation out of war.

Chapter 3. Study Guide Questions

1. What were the immediate effects of independence on U.S. maritime trade and shipbuilding?

2. A. What was the "system" operated by pirates of the North African Barbary states?

   B. Which states were involved in this system?

3. What occurred in the United States in 1789 that enabled Congress to authorize construction of a navy?

4. What were the names of the first three U.S. frigates?

5. When was the Navy Department established by Congress?

6. Who was the U.S. naval officer who fought the two most famous battles of the Quasi-War with France?

7. A. What was the outcome of the war?

B. Why was John Adams defeated in the next election?

8. What was the affair involving Captain William Bainbridge and the frigate *George Washington* with the Dey of Algiers in 1800?

9. A. How did the term "Preble's Boys" come into being?

B. How did Preble make the emperor of Morocco an "offer he couldn't refuse"?

10. A. What was the *Philadelphia* incident?

B. Who was the hero of the exploit?

11. What was the main offensive naval action taken against the Barbary pirates by Commodore Preble?

12. A. How did William Eaton finally get the war to end?

B. How did the Marines figure in this action?

C. What line in the Marine Hymn refers to this operation?

13. A. Why was American public opinion divided on the Tripolitan treaty?

B. Why were the opponents of the treaty correct?

14. What was President Jefferson's "gunboat policy," and how did it affect U.S. national interests?

15. What are the lessons of the war with Tripoli concerning naval power?

Vocabulary

enterprise	windward
ransom	outmaneuver
tribute money	seamanship
expedition	concession
leeward	

Chapter 4. The War of 1812

As we saw in the previous chapter, Commodore Edward Preble left his mark on the U.S. Navy. This was the result of his leadership, discipline, and devotion to duty. Under Preble, the officers of the U.S. Mediterranean Squadron had become a fighting team, with pride in the service and a desire to make it their life's work.

The war with Tripoli developed many naval leaders. They had beaten great odds, far from home. They had learned how to succeed when things went wrong. They had become diplomats in their dealings with friendly countries in southern Europe. They had learned much from being with British officers in the Royal Navy's squadrons fighting the French.

Carefully planned naval attacks against Tripoli cost only thirty killed and thirty-four wounded under Preble's command. The lessons of careful planning, too, were well learned by the new band of officers. The ideals Preble started took time to spread through the fleet. But when the nation again went to war against Britain in the War of 1812, his influence was felt. By 1812, "Preble's Boys" held most of the Navy's better commands.

So, despite Jefferson's weak naval policies, the U.S. Navy had two advantages that would make U.S. naval operations in the War of 1812 among the greatest in the nation's history. The first advantage was that it had a corps of skilled officers. Second, the *Constitution*-class frigates were the finest ships of their type in the world, and were the result of U.S. genius.

EFFECT OF EUROPEAN WAR ON THE UNITED STATES

One of the best things Jefferson did as president was to purchase the Louisiana Territory from Napoleon, in 1803. Napoleon made the deal to get

$15 million to finance his war in Europe. At the same time, he hoped to help the United States become a thorn in the side of Britain.

After the sale of Louisiana, Napoleon unleashed his war in central Europe. This was to affect the United States directly, in spite of Jefferson's hope to stay out of European problems. For about two years, the U.S. merchant marine made great profits as the world's leading neutral carrier. But in 1805 that changed. At the Battle of Trafalgar in that year, the British fleet under Admiral Lord Nelson smashed the combined French and Spanish fleets, making Britain the ruler of the seas. At the Battle of Austerlitz in Austria, Napoleon crushed the combined Austrian and Russian armies and made France master of the continent. England and France then struck at each other's sea lines of communication. This action had to involve the United States.

Again, U.S. merchant ships were subjected to harassment and capture as prizes on the high seas. British Orders in Council closed French ports to foreign shipping, and French decrees ordered French privateers to seize any ships trading in English ports.

Despite the dangers, U.S. shippers made great profits. However, when the Royal Navy started impressing seamen from neutral U.S. ships, U.S. anger turned against Britain.

For four centuries European navies had used *impressment* as a standard way of adding sailors to ships' crews. The "press gang" method was simple: they went into taverns and waterfront inns, knocked drunks and sleeping men on the head, and hauled them into a ship. Upon waking up, the men would be out at sea and forced to serve as part of the crew.

According to British naval custom, each ship captain was responsible for keeping his ship fully manned. If he couldn't, he would lose command. If unable to find enough men ashore, he could stop any British merchantman and take the men he needed to fill his crew. Problems arose when the British began seizing seamen who were U.S. citizens, claiming they were deserters from the Royal Navy. This was done more and more as the

Napoleonic wars created a need for replacements for casualties and good crewmen for new warships. Records show that between the years 1808 and 1811, 6,000 U.S. citizens were impressed into the Royal Navy. Many were killed in combat or died of disease, leaving angry and fatherless families at home.

Britain claimed that U.S. ships lured British seamen away with higher pay and a better life. This was probably true, for conditions in British ships were very bad. It was common for a Royal Navy man to desert when a British ship visited a U.S. port. The British insisted they could not give up impressment of crew members. The United States was making money while England made war. Without its navy, England would lose the war against Napoleon.

THE *Chesapeake* AFFAIR

Bad as it was to have civilians taken from merchant ships, it was even worse when a U.S. man-of-war was overtaken and boarded. This happened in 1807, when the U.S. frigate *Chesapeake* of thirty-six guns with a new crew was set upon by HMS *Leopard,* a large fifty-gun frigate, off Cape Henry, Virginia. When hailed and told to stop and submit to search, Captain James Barron refused. The British then fired three broadsides into the *Chesapeake,* killing three and wounding eighteen men. Barron hauled down his flag and gave up four seamen, one of whom was soon hanged as a British deserter.

The nation was outraged, and there were many demands for a declaration of war against England. Jefferson, ever the pacifist, was opposed to a foreign war. He had allowed the Navy to become very weak, and the Army was even weaker. Figuring that the warring nations in Europe depended on American raw materials and food, Jefferson tried to stop the drift toward war by having Congress pass an *embargo* (stoppage) on exports. He thought this would force the European powers to respect U.S. rights.

All this did, though, was cause a disaster for U.S. shipping companies in New England, and farmers in the South and West. Soon smuggling was taking place everywhere, further draining tax income from the government. And neither France nor Britain stopped impressing U.S. sailors and taking U.S. merchant ships on the high seas. By 1812, the French had taken 558 U.S. ships, and England had taken 917. The embargo cost the nation dearly. With only a fraction of the money lost, a strong Navy could have been built. Such a force could have forced respect for Americans on the high seas, and might well have prevented the War of 1812. As Alfred Thayer Mahan later pointed out, a "true defense consists of imposing upon the enemy a wholesome fear of yourself."

FINAL MOVES TOWARD WAR

James Madison became president in 1809. The next year congressional elections brought into office young "War Hawks" from the South and West. These men called for an end to pacifism, and urged an invasion of Canada as punishment for the outrages at sea. They also wanted to expand U.S. territory. Madison did not want war, so he urged Congress to make a last try to halt the harassment at sea. Congress passed a bill stating that the United States would cease importing from any nation that did not do away with restrictions on U.S. trade.

Napoleon quickly repealed all French decrees against U.S. shipping, hoping to bring the United States into the war against Britain if the United States boycotted British goods. He was correct. Britain did not repeal the Orders in Council, so Madison enforced the law against importing British goods. The angry British saw that the United States was teaming up with France against them. Britain and the United States were moving toward war. Britain kept up the impressment of sailors on the high seas and harassment of U.S. ships, and "Freedom of the seas!" became the War Hawks' slogan.

Matters reached the boiling point in April 1811, when the British frigate *Guerrière* of thirty-eight guns stopped a U.S. merchantman off New York and impressed one of the ship's seamen, a native of Maine. Commodore John Rodgers was sent to sea in the forty-four-gun *President* to protect U.S.

shipping. On the evening of 16 May off the Virginia Capes, the *President* came upon a ship that refused to identify herself. It is unclear who fired first, but the *President* soon silenced the stranger by pouring broadsides into her. The ship drifted away in the night, but the next morning Rodgers saw her a short distance away in great distress. The British sloop of war HMS *Little Belt,* twenty guns, which the ship turned out to be, managed to limp into Halifax, Nova Scotia, with thirty-two dead and wounded crewmen. Rodgers was hailed as a hero for having got revenge for the *Chesapeake.*

Also in 1811, the British incited Tecumseh, a Shawnee Indian chief, to unite the tribes in the old Northwest Territory against white settlers. The usual horrors of Indian warfare took place in the Indiana and Ohio territories. In November 1811, General William Henry Harrison led a well-trained U.S. frontier army against the Indians at Tippecanoe Creek in Indiana. He won an important victory, and Tecumseh fled to Canada to join British forces.

New England senators and congressmen did not want to go to war, for in spite of the harassment at sea, their voters back home would be rich if only one ship in three made it to port. But the War Hawks, under the strong leadership of Henry Clay, speaker of the House, and Senator John C. Calhoun, finally persuaded Madison to ask Congress to declare war. On 18 June 1812, the United States declared war on Britain, for impressment, interference with neutral trade, and British plots with the Indians in the Northwest.

THE WAR OF 1812 BEGINS

The U.S. Navy in 1812 had only sixteen ships, seven of them frigates. Many were in need of repairs, and all were short of crew. Wood for shipbuilding and stores had been used up. Several hundred useless little gunboats built by Jefferson lay rotting in rivers and harbors along the East Coast. The same congressmen who voted the nation into war had, only seven months before, voted down a plan to build a dozen large ships of the line and twenty frigates.

Britain, on the other hand, had more than 600

Seamen and gunners of the USS *Constitution* cheer at the start of action with the British frigate *Guerrière*. British shot bounced off the hull of the U.S. ship, giving her the name "Old Ironsides."

men-of-war, among them some 250 ships of the line and frigates. Most of this fleet was in European waters blockading France. The only Royal Navy squadron off the U.S. coast consisted of the *Africa,* sixty-four guns, seven frigates, and some smaller vessels. But a hundred more ships were within easy sailing distance off Newfoundland and in the West Indies.

The U.S. strategy was clear—to protect the nation's sea trade and to harass the British navy and commerce. But how could that be done against such odds? Decatur and Bainbridge recommended that not more than two frigates patrol together. Rodgers and Paul Hamilton, Madison's secretary of the navy, argued for squadrons built around one or more heavy frigates. The politicians won, and several squadrons under the command of Rodgers were sent out. They ended up chasing around the Atlantic looking for convoys, but taking few prizes. Changing to tactics suggested by "Preble's Boys" soon got far better results. The Navy began sending out one or two ships at a time as commerce raiders. They also set upon warships at times, but only when the odds were good.

U.S. land forces, in the meantime, launched a poorly planned invasion of Canada. The effort came to nothing. The Americans were not well organized and met with stiff British and Canadian opposition. The Canadians took a U.S. fort at Mackinac Island in Lake Huron, giving Britain control of the upper Great Lakes. Then they chased the Americans out of Detroit, built a fleet on Lake Erie, and helped Tecumseh and his Indian allies continue fighting in the Northwest Territory.

Constitution vs. Guerrière. Some victories were needed to improve U.S. morale, and the Navy proved equal to the task. The *Constitution,* under the command of Isaac Hull, one of "Preble's Boys," gave the country what it craved.

First, using great seamanship, Hull escaped from a whole British squadron off New Jersey. Becalmed, he had his men row ahead of the ship with the anchor. when the anchor was dropped, the ship heaved in on the anchor windlass, pulling ahead in a process called *kedging.* Then Hull wet his sails so they would hold the wind better, and caught a slight breeze. On sailing into a little squall, he quickly let his sails loose, making it appear as though a severe storm was blowing. Seeing this, the British quickly trimmed their sails for heavy weather. With that, Hull drew his sails tight again, and sailed merrily away from them.

The British were to see more of Hull and the *Constitution.* Of all British ships, Americans hated the *Guerrière* most, because of her impressment of sailors. British Captain James Dacres, a prideful though able officer, had earlier sent an insulting challenge by merchantman into New York, to any U.S. frigate. On 19 August 1812 he got his wish, when the *Constitution* sighted him off the coast of Nova Scotia. As the trim U.S. ship gave chase, Dacres prepared for what he thought would be an easy victory.

The *Guerrière* opened fire first, and Hull calmly told his gunnery officers to wait. By 1800 hours, Hull had brought the *Constitution* to within a hundred yards of his opponent. With both ships running before the wind, he ordered his first broadside fired. Exchanges of broadside after broadside followed. Dacres saw his shot rip through the rigging or bounce harmlessly off the

The *Constitution* defeats the British frigate *Guerrière,* pounding her to a hulk that would sink the next day.

heavy oaken hull of the American, earning for her the nickname "Old Ironsides." The U.S. captain first aimed his fire at the enemy ship's waterline, making gaping holes that let water pour inside. Next he aimed at the masts. Within twenty minutes the *Guerrière's* mizzenmast had been knocked off and fell in a tangle of debris. It was soon followed by the foremast and mainmast. The battle was over, and Dacres surrendered. The *Guerrière* sank the next day.

Although at the time Americans called this one of the greatest battles of the war, it was really not very important. Though surprised and dismayed, the British could easily afford to lose one frigate in battle. But for Americans, this was a great boost to morale. On the day Hull returned to Boston, word had been received of bad U.S. defeats in the land battles to the west. Detroit had fallen almost without a fight, and the Indians had captured Fort Dearborn (Chicago) and massacred everyone in it. The victory of the *Constitution* was indeed cause for joy.

OTHER HIGH SEAS BATTLES

In October 1812, another famous battle took place far across the Atlantic. The frigate *United States,* forty-four guns, under command of Stephen Decatur, met the British frigate *Macedonian,* thirty-eight guns. In two hours, Decatur wore the enemy down and captured the ship, a valuable prize.

In December, the *Constitution,* now under command of Captain William Bainbridge, met the British frigate *Java,* thirty-eight guns, off the coast of Brazil. Both had good officers and crews. The *Java* was the faster ship and tried to outmaneuver the more powerful Yankee. The U.S. ship lost her wheel early in the fight, but Bainbridge used men

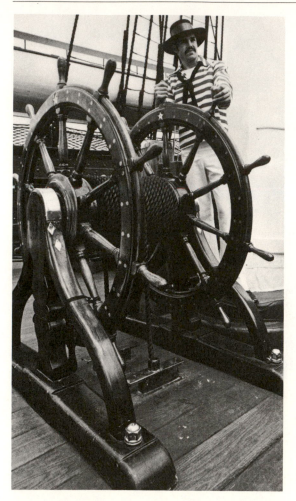

Modern-day member of the crew of the USS *Constitution*, now in Boston Harbor. The ship is a popular historical attraction and she is kept in sailing trim. She is the oldest U.S. ship still in commission.

to turn the rudder using block-and-tackles. Though wounded, he remained in command. After three hours of gunfire, the two ships came together and the British foremast was shot away. Half an hour later, with all masts now gone, the *Java* surrendered, after suffering 124 casualties.

Off British Guiana in February 1813, Captain James Lawrence in the sloop-of-war *Hornet* met the brig HMS *Peacock*. The two ships exchanged broadsides. Lawrence's fire badly damaged the Britisher. In only eleven minutes, the *Peacock* struck her colors, and then hoisted them upside down in a sign of distress, for she had six feet of water in her hull. A few minutes later her mainmast came crashing down. The ship sank a short time later, despite attempts by both the British and the Americans to save her.

The opening months of the war at sea had given the Americans much success. Not only had three British frigates and several smaller men-of-war been beaten and captured, but Lloyd's of London (the major insuring agent of merchant ships) reported that nearly 500 merchant ships had been bagged by Yankee privateers and commerce-raiders.

The British could not say this long string of U.S. victories was just luck. They were quick to point out that the victor in most of the battles was more heavily armed. True as this might have been, damage to British vessels was much greater than the difference in armament could account for. The fact was that after Admiral Horatio Nelson's victory at Trafalgar in 1805, most British captains had not done much gunnery practice. The British had never bothered much about marksmanship; they depended more on seamanship to get them close, where broadsides could not miss. The Americans, on the other hand, never forgot their marksmanship tradition. Though they also fought in close, they had the advantage of being able to make hits at longer range.

Chesapeake vs. Shannon. Despite these victories, the U.S. Navy also suffered tragic losses. Probably the most important came on 1 June 1813 at the hands of HMS *Shannon*, thirty-eight guns, off Boston Harbor. Captain Broke of the *Shannon* learned that the USS *Chesapeake*, thirty-six guns, now under command of Captain James Lawrence, was in the harbor being refitted.

While the two ships were well matched on the face of it, Broke probably had one of the best-trained crews in the Royal Navy. He had commanded the *Shannon* for seven years, and had trained his men well in gunnery, contrary to general Royal Navy practice. He had the guns fitted with sights and had arcs marked off in the deck be-

James Lawrence

James Lawrence was born in Burlington, New Jersey, in 1781. He entered the U.S. Navy in September 1799 and served in the frigates *Ganges* and *Adams.* In the war with Tripoli, 1801–05, he was first lieutenant and later commander of the schooner *Enterprise,* first lieutenant of the *John Adams,* and commander of *Gunboat #6.* He earned a reputation for outstanding gallantry as second in command of the two most daring operations of the war, Commodore David Porter's gunboat attack on Tripoli, on 2 June 1803, and Decatur's burning of the captured frigate *Philadelphia,* on 16 February 1804.

Following the war with Tripoli, Lawrence served as first lieutenant in the frigate *Constitution,* and then commanded the *Vixon, Wasp, Argus,* and *Hornet.* He was promoted to the rank of master commandant in December 1811 and sailed for Europe in the *Hornet,* returning the following May with the last dispatches from England before the War of 1812 broke out on 19 June 1812. Three days later he took the *Hornet* to sea in the squadron of Commodore John Rodgers, and captured three of the seven prizes taken by the squadron over the next several weeks. After returning to Boston from this cruise, he set sail in October for the coast of South America in company with Commodore Bainbridge in the *Constitution.* Following a blockading action and the capture of the brig *Resolu-*tion off Brazil in February 1813, he fought the British brig *Peacock* off the coast of British Guiana. The *Peacock* surrendered after fifteen minutes of intense fighting, and sank shortly thereafter, with the *Hornet* relatively undamaged.

Upon his return to the United States in late March, Lawrence was hailed as a hero for his victory over the *Peacock,* and was promoted to captain in March 1813.

On 20 May he took command of the frigate *Chesapeake* in Boston Harbor. On 1 June 1813 he sailed out of the harbor to accept the challenge of the British frigate *Shannon,* despite having a green crew and a ship that was not yet fully outfitted. During a furious exchange of broadsides at pistol range, the *Chesapeake* fouled her mizzen rigging with the *Shannon's* forechains. Unable to answer her helm, she was helpless before a raking fire. Lawrence was badly wounded, but spent his remaining strength urging his men to "Fight her 'till she sinks," and "Don't give up the ship!" He died four days later, and was interred with honors by a respectful enemy at Halifax. His body was returned to Salem, Massachusetts, in August. After public services of great homage, he was brought to New York for final burial in Trinity Church yard on 16 September 1813.

James Lawrence will always be remembered in naval circles for his fighting spirit and leadership in the face of superior odds.

hind each gun so they could fire an entire broadside at the same point on the target. Such preparations were bound to pay off in battle.

The U.S. ship had an inexperienced crew and new officers. In the face of such a challenge, Lawrence would have done better to remain in port and wait for a better time. The *Chesapeake* was mainly needed for merchant raiding—not for taking on British warships. But Lawrence felt he had to fight.

The two ships outdid each other in gallantry, each declining early raking (lengthwise) fire at some distance. As they came alongside at a distance of barely 40 yards, both fired a broadside.

Marines in the rigging kept up small-arms fire. The *Shannon,* hulled at and below the surface, began to take water. Of 150 men on the *Chesapeake*'s weather deck, fewer than 50 remained standing. A round shot had taken her sailing master's head, and Captain Lawrence was left clinging to a binnacle with a wounded leg.

Forging ahead and pretty much out of control with her headsails shot away and helmsman killed, the *Chesapeake* swung her bow to the wind and began backing down. She took another bad raking fire which she could not return, since her guns no longer bore. The two ships came together, and both captains called boarders away. Lawrence then fell, mortally wounded. Carried below, he cried out the immortal words, "Don't give up the ship!"

The U.S. bugler failed to sound Lawrence's boarding order, and in a moment, with Captain Broke personally leading the boarding party, the British swarmed over the ship. In the fierce but short hand-to-hand combat that followed, Broke was disabled for life with a cutlass blow to the head. But the U.S. flag was already being hauled down by British hands. The bloody battle had lasted only fifteen minutes, but more than 200 men were dead or wounded on both sides. The *Chesapeake* was sailed into Halifax by a prize crew, followed by the *Shannon,* pumps going to keep her afloat. Lawrence died on the way.

BRITISH SEAPOWER PREVAILS

The early victories at sea had given the Americans new pride and foreign respect. By 1813, however, the British had driven the French from the sea, and they began to increase the number of ships patrolling the U.S. coast. The U.S. frigates were bottled up in port after their return from victorious cruises. Many could not get to sea again during the war. The *Constellation* was moored at Norfolk for the entire war, while the *United States* and the captured *Macedonian* were blockaded in New London, Connecticut.

A few warships managed to get through the tightening blockade, but the task of fighting the British fell more and more to the privateers. Mixing patriotism with greed, some 515 privateers were commissioned, most from Massachusetts, New York, and Maryland. They were credited with capturing 1,345 vessels, many off the coasts of Spain and Portugal where they were carrying supplies to the Duke of Wellington's army in Spain. Because of their successes, the British were forced to start a convoy system to protect merchant shipping.

In spite of all their efforts and damage to British commerce, the privateers could not take the place of a powerful navy. They did nothing to weaken the British blockade of the U.S. coast. In fact, about half of the prizes they captured ended up in British hands as they tried to make port.

U.S. trade sank to very low levels. Exports, which had been valued at $108.3 million in 1807, had fallen to only $7 million in 1814. Coastal shipping was almost completely stopped. A Boston newspaper printed a gloomy picture of conditions: "Our harbors blockaded; our shipping destroyed or rotting at the docks; silence and stillness in our cities; the grass growing upon the public wharves."

The Jeffersonians had claimed that no enemy would be able to detach enough ships to blockade the entire coast, so it was not necessary to have a seagoing navy to protect shipping. The United States and its merchant marine paid a stiff price for that mistake.

THE BATTLE OF LAKE ERIE

With the war at sea beginning to go well for them in the Atlantic, the British and Canadians began moving around the lower Great Lakes to try to safeguard their lines of communication to the upper lakes. On Lake Ontario, both sides began building fleets. Neither fleet ever came into battle, though, for fear the other was superior. On Lake Erie, however, twenty-seven-year-old Oliver Hazard Perry showed what brilliant naval leadership and cooperation with the army could do.

When the British found out that Perry had been assigned to Lake Erie, they scoffed. They figured him too young for such a responsibility. Besides, most of his ships were still trees in the forest. Ammunition and artillery would have to be carried hundreds of miles through the wilderness

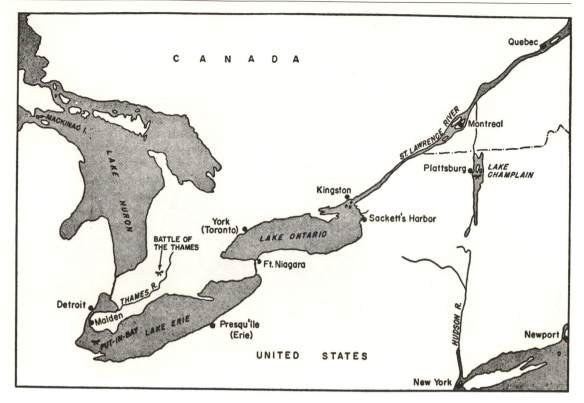

Campaigns of the eastern Great Lakes in the War of 1812. Principal actions were fought on Lake Erie and Lake Champlain.

to get to his little base at Presque Isle (now Erie, Pennsylvania).

Perry's task was to bring some schooners and a captured British brig over from Buffalo, and to build two new brigs. He named one brig the *Niagara*. The other he named the *Lawrence* for his good friend, the late captain of the *Chesapeake*, and chose it for his flagship.

Perry's men worked day and night to build the brigs, and by July they had them done. The British fleet of six vessels, under the command of Commander Robert Barclay, a Trafalgar veteran, had been in control of Lake Erie for over a year. Now he became alarmed and sent his ships to blockade Perry's vessels. Catching the British off guard, Perry floated his new unarmed brigs over the Presque Isle bar, and quickly installed his guns—

two long twelve-pounders and eighteen thirty-two-pound carronades—on each. Now, with a fleet of nine ships, Perry had the most warships on the lake. But the side that would control it had to be determined in battle.

Barclay retired to his main base at Fort Malden, Canada, to finish building his new brig, the *Detroit*. Perry's control of Lake Erie began to interrupt Barclay's supply line, so he quickly finished the *Detroit*, arming her with seventeen long guns and two carronades from the fort.

While Barclay was fitting out the *Detroit*, Perry received a hundred and fifty seamen and junior officers from the *Constitution* to help man his fleet. General Harrison, heading the American army at Sandusky, Ohio, sent a hundred Kentucky sharpshooters to man the rigging. The number of sailors

Battle of Lake Erie, during the War of 1812. Oliver Hazard Perry is rowed from his damaged flagship, the *Lawrence*, to take command of the *Niagara*, from which he won a decisive victory.

was barely enough to get his ships under way. Though Barclay's squadron carried sixty-seven guns to Perry's fifty-four, the Americans' carronades gave them greater weight of broadside if they could get close enough to use them.

Perry moved his fleet to the eastern end of the lake in August, patrolling the area and using Put-in-Bay as an anchorage. Barclay moved out of Malden and arrived in sight of the U.S. anchorage at dawn on 10 September. Perry, in the *Lawrence*, sailed forth to meet Barclay, in the *Detroit*. The winds were light and southerly, so they sailed slowly. In the U.S. line were the *Lawrence, Caledonia,* and *Niagara.* For the British, it was the *Detroit* and the *Queen Charlotte.*

Perry took some punishment from the *Detroit's* long guns before opening up with his carronades and rifle fire at pistol-shot range, nearly clearing Barclay's decks. If Lieutenant Elliot in command of the *Niagara* had done the same to the *Queen Charlotte,* the battle would have been won. However, Elliot chose to remain out of the *Charlotte's* range. So for the next several hours, Perry was forced to fight the whole British squadron by himself. While damaging the British, the *Lawrence* was badly damaged herself, suffering many casualties. At 1430, Perry himself fired the last workable gun. Leaving the national ensign still flying, and taking along his twelve-year-old midshipman brother, James, he had himself rowed a half-mile through a hail of fire to the *Niagara.*

Perry ordered Elliot into his rowboat to bring up the straggling small gunboats, and took command of the *Niagara.* With his fresh new flagship, Perry steered across the British line, firing double-shotted broadsides. The *Detroit,* trying to avoid raking fire from Perry, put the *Queen Charlotte* in such a position that the *Niagara* was able to rake both ships at the same time. At 1500, Barclay struck, surrendering his entire squadron.

After making repairs, Perry's squadron ferried Harrison's army across the lake. The Kentuckians pursued the retreating British and Indians, and defeated them in the Battle of the Thames. Tecumseh was killed in this battle, ending Indian support of the British cause. Detroit was thus recaptured, and the United States held the Northwest Territory, which now makes up the states of Ohio, Indiana, Illinois, Michigan, Wisconsin, and part of Minnesota.

BRITAIN ON THE OFFENSIVE

Perry's victory gave the Americans complete control of Lake Erie. But British victories in Europe began to have an effect on the United States. Napoleon's defeat in Russia in the winter of 1812 was followed by a series of defeats in 1813, and the break-up of his alliances. In April 1814, Napoleon gave up his throne and was sent into exile. Britain was now able to release major troop and naval forces to fight the war against the United States.

With no sea forces to oppose them, the British were able to put ashore landing parties any place they wanted to disrupt trade and prevent U.S. vessels from getting to sea. Many such operations took place in the Chesapeake Bay. These were climaxed by amphibious assaults on Washington, D.C., and Baltimore in the late summer of 1814.

A little flotilla of Jeffersonian gunboats tried to slow down the attack on Washington, but they were brushed aside and finally burned to prevent their being captured. On 24 and 25 August, the militiamen defending Washington were driven off, and the capital fell to the British.

Because of the U.S. burning of Toronto the previous year, the British burned the Capitol, the White House, the Treasury, and the War Office. President Madison and Congress barely got out of town as the British entered. Dolley Madison managed to cut a portrait of George Washington out of its frame, role it up with the original draft of the Constitution, and escape in a coach. Before they set the building on fire, some British officers entered the White House and ate the meal that had just been prepared for the Madisons. The Washington Navy Yard and its stores, along with the

frigate *Colombia,* were burned by the retreating Americans to prevent capture by the enemy.

The British next turned their attention to Baltimore. They regarded this city as a "nest of pirates" because it was the home of 126 privateers. A British army of nearly 5,000 men stopped before the city's defenses and waited for a fleet of frigates and bomb vessels to silence Fort McHenry at the entrance of the harbor.

The night-long bombardment on 14 September failed to bring down the U.S. flag waving defiantly over the fort. Francis Scott Key, a U.S. civilian held in one of the British vessels, was inspired by the stirring sight, and that night wrote the words of "The Star-Spangled Banner" that later would become our National Anthem. The fleet bombardment failed because a line of sunken hulks blocked the channel, preventing the ships from sailing past the fort. A few days later, the British army got back on board the ships and sailed away.

The Battle of Lake Champlain. With the war over in Europe, the British were anxious to conclude the war with the United States as well. In August 1814, President Madison accepted a British proposal to begin peace negotiations in Ghent, Belgium. Madison sent John Quincy Adams to head the U.S. delegation at the talks.

At the same time the talks began, however, the British began rebuilding their forces in Canada and planning to capture New Orleans. Their plan was to win victories that would force the Americans into giving up U.S. land at the peace talks. A British army of 12,000 men including four brigades of Wellington's veterans launched an invasion south of Montreal, along the same route traveled by General Burgoyne in the Revolutionary War. To face this large force, the Americans could muster only 1,500 men. They took up a stand at Plattsburgh on the shores of Lake Champlain. A small U.S. naval squadron on the lake, under the command of Master Commandant Thomas Macdonough, assisted in the American defense.

Sir George Prevost, the governor general of Canada, halted his invasion force before Plattsburgh, insisting that as long as the Yankees were

Oliver Hazard Perry

Oliver Hazard Perry was born the son of a U.S. naval officer in 1785. He was commissioned as a midshipman at the age of fourteen and served on board his father's frigate, the *General Greene.* He would remain in the service from then until his premature death at age thirty-five.

Perry rose rapidly in the young U.S. Navy. He was commissioned a lieutenant at seventeen and took command of a schooner, the *Nautilus,* at twenty. He was chosen to direct the building of a large number of President Thomas Jefferson's coastal gunboats at twenty-two and was placed in charge of them when war broke out against England in 1812. But he was eager for more important action.

In February 1813 he was ordered to proceed to Lake Erie to assist in defending the lake against any British thrust down from Canada. It was there that he would fight one of the most decisive naval battles in U.S. history.

When Perry reached Presque Isle in Lake Erie on 27 March, he faced a very difficult task indeed. Not only would he have to get together a squadron from scratch, but all the nonwood materials for it would have to be hauled from Pittsburgh, 130 miles away, or from Philadelphia, even farther. Nevertheless he set to work, scrounging men, iron, and cannon wherever he could get them. By August he had built and outfitted two brigs, the *Lawrence* and the *Niagara,* and had managed to acquire seven other smaller craft. He named the *Lawrence* after his friend Captain James Lawrence, killed in a battle with the British frigate *Shannon* that July. He flew a battle flag on which were sewn Lawrence's last words, "Don't Give Up the Ship," which today hangs in Bancroft Hall at the Naval Academy.

In September the British, who had a similar force at the north end of the lake, sailed south to do battle with Perry. They met off Put-in-Bay on 10 September. After three hours of fierce fighting, the *Lawrence* was nearly sunk, and only a handful of her crew of 142 plus Perry were still fit for duty. At that point Perry transferred by small boat to his second brig, the *Niagara,* which had held back from the fight because of her cowardly captain. Perry took the *Niagara* into the midst of the British line, raking the vessels to left and right with furious fire. Soon the badly wounded British commander struck his colors. The rest of his ships quickly did the same, marking the first time in history a full British squadron was surrendered. Thus the British thrust southward was halted, and the Northwest Territory was saved for the United States. To the secretary of the navy, Perry reported, "It has pleased the almighty to give the arms of the United States a signal victory over our enemies on this Lake." To the army commander of the area he wrote, "We have met the enemy and they are ours."

Following the war not much of great significance happened to Perry, until 1819 he was ordered to proceed to Venezuela to negotiate a treaty with its leader Simón Bolívar. But on arriving there, he found only torrid summer heat and clouds of mosquitoes carrying yellow fever, from which he died on 19 August 1819.

Perry was long remembered in naval circles for his kindly attitude toward friends and enemies alike. He expected the best from his men, and he got it, by appealing to their pride and standing with them in the heat of battle. His only fault was a tendency to gloss over poor performance to protect the feelings and record of subordinates, which often gave him trouble during his career. But he will always be remembered for his "signal victory" on Lake Erie.

on the lake, his flank and supply lines were endangered. The British built a naval flotilla made up of the frigate *Confiance,* thirty-seven guns, one brig, two sloops, and twelve gunboats to take control of the lake from Macdonough. Completely outgunned by this force, Macdonough, who had been with Decatur at the burning of the *Philadelphia,* worked quickly to enlarge his little force. He built the twenty-six-gun corvette *Saratoga* and the twenty-gun brig *Eagle,* two sailing vessels, and ten oar-propelled gunboats carrying one or two cannon, in a little more than a month. Five days later he took them into battle.

Macdonough took a page from the history book, from the First Battle of Lake Champlain at Valcour Island. He anchored his ships in Plattsburgh Bay, a deep inlet on the western side of the lake, to await the British attack. He placed his ships close enough to shore that his line could not be got around. Then he ran out spring lines from the sterns to the anchor cables so the ships could be swung and the guns brought to bear from both sides.

The British flotilla, under the command of Captain George Downie, sailed south on 11 September. When he saw it rounding the point, Macdonough called his officers and men to prayer—and then to quarters. Early British shots fell short, but one hit a coop that housed a pet gamecock. Unharmed, the rooster flew to a gun where it crowed and flapped its wings defiantly. Macdonough's crew thought this was a good omen. The commodore then fired the first U.S. shot, and it hit the British flagship.

The British sailed into the bay in line abreast, coming under heavy U.S. fire. Downie tried to pass down the U.S. line, but inside the bay the wind fell off. He was forced to anchor his flagship only 300 yards from the *Saratoga.* A *Confiance* broadside ripped through the *Saratoga,* killing or wounding forty men, but Macdonough bravely returned fire. Fifteen minutes later, a cannon blown off its mounting fell on Captain Downie, killing him instantly. The death of their commander had a serious effect on British morale.

Macdonough himself had several narrow escapes. Once a broken spar fell down on him, knocking him unconscious for awhile. A bit later a round shot tore off the head of a man on a gun crew, and drove it into Macdonough's face with such force that he was knocked down.

Fighting spread up and down the line. The two British sloops and a small U.S. vessel were knocked out of action. The *Saratoga* and the *Confiance* suffered the most, however. Both were taking on water, and the *Saratoga* was set afire twice by hot shots. The *Saratoga* was hulled 55 times and her enemy 105 times. Within two hours, every starboard gun on the *Saratoga* had been disabled. But, heaving in on his spring lines, Macdonough pulled his ship around so that her undamaged port battery faced the *Confiance.* The British tried to accomplish the same feat, but failed, and the enemy was soon forced to surrender. One by one the British ships surrendered. Both sides had suffered many casualties, the Americans more than a hundred dead and wounded, and the British twice that many.

During the sea battle, Governor General Prevost had attacked the U.S. lines at Plattsburgh, and had been driven back. With the British fleet lost, Prevost called off the invasion and retreated back into Canada.

The Battle of Lake Champlain had a great effect on the peace negotiations in Ghent. The Duke of Wellington, who had been offered command of the British forces in the United States, said that unless Britain could get "a naval superiority on the Lakes," peace should be made at once, and without demands for territory.

On Christmas Eve, 1814, a peace treaty was signed. It made no mention of impressment, or of neutral shipping rights at sea, the main reasons given by Madison for declaring war in the first place. These issues were no longer important since the British had repealed the Orders in Council and the war in Europe was over.

The Battle of New Orleans. News traveled slowly in the early nineteenth century. Thus, even though the peace treaty had been signed, the fighting went on. The British continued their preparations for the invasion at New Orleans. The expedition had arrived off the mouth of the Mississippi River on 8 December 1814. They could not proceed to attack the city until they dealt with a handful of gunboats and sailing vessels, however. Forty-two British launches, armed with carronades and carrying 1,000 troops, captured all of the little U.S. flotilla in a short bloody battle. The British lost

Thomas Macdonough's victory at the Battle of Lake Champlain, September 1814. The U.S. victory caused the British to retreat into Canada and sign the Treaty of Ghent, which ended the War of 1812.

over 100 men killed and wounded, and valuable time, but finished off the gunboat navy. Meanwhile, U.S. General Andrew Jackson put the time gained to good use in preparing his defense of the city.

On 23 December, the British landed eight miles below New Orleans and began skirmishing with Jackson's riflemen. The Americans' accurate aim and longer range gave them confidence. By the end of the first week of January, more than 8,000 British veterans under Major General Sir Edward Pakenham were ashore and ready to attack. Upstream Jackson's force had grown to more than 4,000 men, including Jean Lafitte's pirates and a naval battery manned by seamen gunners from the schooner *Louisiana*.

On 8 January 1815, Pakenham foolishly marched his veterans in a frontal assault against Jackson's strong position between the Mississippi and a swamp where he had dug in to prevent encirclement. Jackson's earthworks and cotton bales

were too strong. When the smoke of battle cleared, over 2,000 British troops lay dead or wounded, and the rest were in flight. U.S. losses were 71 dead.

The peace treaty finally arrived in the United States on 11 February and Congress ratified it six days later. It opened the way to the peaceful settlement of all disputes between Britain and the United States, such as those involving the Canadian–U.S. border and fishing rights. And, it ended any question about the ability of the United States to defend itself as a nation.

Summary

The War of 1812 had been a limited war from the British standpoint, while they fought Napoleon in Europe. From the U.S. point of view, the war was a struggle to end British-backed Indian attacks in the territories to the north and west, to acquire Canada, and to defend the nation's rights at sea.

On the Atlantic coast, the war became a matter

of blockade and reprisal. The British were on the defensive in 1812, being unwilling to give more resources to the North American war. In 1813, the British slowly gained the upper hand in the Atlantic despite some great U.S. naval victories and privateer successes. They remained on the defensive in Canada. By 1814, with Wellington's veterans in the fight, the British took the offensive and suffered defeats that can be blamed in part on their internal political problems as well as on good U.S. leadership and defenses.

At sea there were twenty-five major battles between British and U.S. warships. Of these, the Americans won thirteen and the British twelve. In all but two instances the victory went to the vessel with heavier firepower. British superiority at sea, however, allowed them to blockade and make landings wherever they wished. The Jeffersonian gunboat defensive policy proved to be a very bad idea, as was made especially clear by the burning of Washington.

The U.S. campaign for Canada was doomed to failure because of poor preparation, lack of forces, and poor leadership. The militia system of making up an army proved to be no good. If it had not been for the naval victories on Lake Erie and Lake Champlain, it is unlikely that the United States would have been able to obtain a favorable treaty at Ghent. Perry's victory on Lake Erie also set up the British defeat at the Battle of the Thames, which destroyed the Indian revolt in the Northwest Territory.

The Treaty of Ghent was not a surrender of one side to the other, so there was no booty won or territory lost. By and large, the treaty was welcome in both countries, as both had much more to gain from trade together than from war.

U.S. seamen and the U.S. Navy won new respect for themselves and for the nation throughout the world. U.S. diplomats were again treated with respect—one of the many benefits of sea power. The victories of the young U.S. Navy united the nation and started a great tradition. The United States at last stood as an equal among the powers of the world, respected as never before. Sea power had played a decisive role in gaining that reputation.

Chapter 4.   Study Guide Questions

1. What lessons had Preble's junior officers learned from him during the war with Tripoli?

2. What two great battles occurred in Europe in 1805 that greatly affected U.S. shipping?

3. Why did the British insist that they could not give up impressment?

4. A. What was the *Chesapeake* affair?

B. Why could Jefferson do little about it at the time?

5. What were the final moves leading to war with Britain?

6. A. What was the U.S. strategy in the face of British naval superiority?

B. Which naval strategy proved to be the most effective?

7. What ill-advised and ineffective U.S. land operation was attempted in 1812?

8. A. What great naval battle fought in August 1812 helped sagging U.S. spirits?

B. Who was the naval officer who provided this encouragement?

C. What famous nickname was the USS *Constitution* given in battle?

9. A. What caused the "difference" in capabilities of the *Chesapeake* and the *Shannon*?

B. What famous battle cry was made by Captain James Lawrence in the battle between these two ships?

10. What was the result of the British blockade against U.S. ports as the war progressed?

11. A. Who was the U.S. naval hero of the Battle of Lake Erie?

B. What was the result of the battle?

12. Where did the United States suffer the greatest insult because of British naval superiority?

13. What famous song was written on board a British ship during the British attack on Fort McHenry? Who wrote it?

14. Why did the British plan offensive operations in the United States at the same time they started peace negotiations?

15. A. Who was the U.S. naval hero of the Second Battle of Lake Champlain in 1814?

    B. What was the great significance of the U.S. victory?

16. A. What is the name of the peace treaty that ended the War of 1812?

    B. When and where was it signed?

17. A. Why was the Battle of New Orleans fought after the peace treaty was signed?

    B. Who was the U.S. general who won the battle?

18. A. What very important benefits did the United States receive as a result of its naval victories at sea?

    B. Why are the lessons of the War of 1812 important today?

Vocabulary

ratify
embargo
smuggling
boycott
commerce-raider
becalmed
squall
waterline
block-and-tackle
heavy weather

massacre
mainmast
raking fire
gallantry
binnacle
retaliation
omen
commodore
marksmanship

Chapter 5. The United States Advances as Sea Power Prospers, 1815–1860

The nation and the Navy emerged from the War of 1812 stronger and more confident than ever. Within a few months of the Battle of New Orleans, the Navy had grown and hundreds of merchantmen plied the world trade routes. A large naval squadron sailed to the Mediterranean in the war with Algiers to wind up the unfinished business with the Barbary states. After so doing, the United States kept up its Mediterranean Squadron regularly until the Civil War.

Many changes were to come in the business of seafaring. The Navy now enjoyed prestige and popularity because of its successes in the war. For the first time, the Navy was able to build up after the end of a war, with public support. Piracy demanded the attention of the Navy, especially in the Caribbean and Mediterranean. The desire to stop the slave trade added other patrol duties. Commercial trade grew rapidly. Whaling became a major industry in New England ports. And some of the most "romantic" days in the history of sailing were about to unfold. American clipper ships would become the queens of the sea.

The age of technology began to have an effect on life at sea. The science of oceanography came into being. Better instruments, mapping, and clocks improved navigation methods and helped American firms compete for world trade. Steam propulsion came into the world of sea power. With it came the screw propeller, iron hull, armor, and heavy ordnance with the first rifled barrels. No major wars, and consequently no major sea battles, were fought in the period 1815–60. For the first time, wars in Europe did not directly affect American progress. Americans went their way, across the seas and across the continent.

PIRACY AND PROTECTION

The chief task of the U.S. Navy between 1815 and 1860 was promoting and protecting U.S. overseas commerce. American trade increased fivefold during the period. American traders were everywhere on the globe. Often the traders sailed into areas of rebellion and turmoil—the type of situation in which piracy flourishes.

After taking care of Algeria, along with Morocco, Tunis, and Tripoli, in naval operations during 1815 and 1816, the United States signed treaties with the Barbary states that stopped the need to pay tribute. In large shows of force, American naval squadrons cruised the home waters of the Barbary states, and this is what "changed the attitudes" of their rulers. American squadrons continued being present, however, operating from a base in Port Mahon, Minorca, to make sure that the deys did not revert to their old ways. The squadron also fought piracy in the eastern Mediterranean in the 1820s, during the long Greek War of Independence from Turkey.

When revolts against Spain began in South and Central America in the early nineteenth century, piracy increased in the West Indies. Some of the new South American countries issued letters of marque to their ships, commissioning them as privateers. However, many of these ships began piracy against all shipping. This affected American shipping, for at this time New Orleans was developing into the second-largest port of the nation. This was a result of the westward migration and agricultural expansion in the Mississippi Valley.

Jean Lafitte was the most notorious American pirate. He established his base on an island at the mouth of the Mississippi River. He and his men had been given pardons for their assistance to General Jackson at New Orleans, but they returned to piracy after the war. The Navy was given the job of wiping out the pirates. At the same time, they had to deal with the Latin American governments and colonies from which most of the pirates came.

Between 1815 and 1822, nearly 3,000 merchant ships were attacked by pirates in the West Indies. Merchants, shipowners, and insurance companies demanded an end to these attacks. In 1819, Congress authorized President James Monroe to launch a campaign against the pirates. He sent Oliver Hazard Perry to Venezuela to talk with President Simón Bolívar about stopping the letters of marque. Bolívar agreed, but the piracy did not stop. The new governments had no power to stop the marauders already on the seas. Perry contracted yellow fever during his mission, and died the same year at the age of thirty-four.

So piracy continued to flourish. By 1822 the damage to American trade in the Caribbean became so great that the United States decided to put an end to the pirates once and for all. A West Indies Naval Squadron, under the command of

Commodore James Biddle, was sent to the area. Biddle captured or destroyed thirty pirate vessels in less than a year, but his large ships could not pursue the smaller pirate vessels into the coves and close to shore where many lurked. Spanish officials in Cuba and Puerto Rico refused Biddle permission to pursue pirates who beached their vessels and escaped ashore. Yellow fever and malaria caused many deaths in the American crews.

In 1822, David Porter took command of the West Indies Squadron. Porter learned from Biddle's operations. He gathered a squadron of smaller vessels, gunboats, and the first steam-powered paddle wheeler to be used in naval operations. He then followed the pirates into the coves and inlets for the next two years. His larger ships escorted merchantmen at sea. By mid-1826, a new commodore, Lewis Warrington, had succeeded in driving Lafitte and other pirates out of the Caribbean. For the first time in three centuries, the ships of all nations could sail those waters without fear of being plundered.

WHALING

Colonial Americans had begun whaling in the early 1700s. Sailing out of New Bedford, Nantucket, and other New England seaports, whalers flourished until the Civil War. After the War of 1812, the whaling industry grew rapidly. Between 1830 and 1860, many great fortunes were made by the owners of whaling vessels. By 1846 the Americans had over 700 whaling ships, about three-quarters of the total world's whaling fleet.

Life aboard the whaling ships was unbelievably primitive and dirty. Many crewmen died from disease and injuries, but the lure of profits from a share of a successful voyage pushed men on. Many sea stories of the era have been passed down from writers of the day and have become a part of American history and adventure. Probably the most famous of these stories is *Moby Dick*, by Herman Melville.

The era of American whaling ended with a series of important developments. The principal products made from whales were whale oil for

A whaleboat with a harpooner in the bow is rowed toward a whale, with the whale ship standing by on the horizon. The whaling industry was profitable, but was a dangerous life in severe living conditions.

lighting, whalebone, spermaceti for candles, and ambergris for perfume. In 1859, oil was discovered in Pennsylvania, starting the petroleum industry. Petroleum could be distilled into kerosene and used for lighting and heating. Later, lighting by natural gas dealt the final blow to whalers. The flexible whalebone used for hoopskirts, corset stays, buggy whips, and umbrella ribs was replaced by other materials as dress styles and needs changed. During the Civil War, Confederate raiders attacked and destroyed many Northern whaling fleets, and the trade never revived. Weather and the Arctic ice claimed most of the surviving American whaling fleet in the 1870s.

THE MERCHANT MARINE

The American colonists had designed and built ships since the earliest days of settlement. By the mid-1600s, British investors were buying fishing vessels to harvest the huge schools of cod, haddock, and pollock along the New England coast and on the Grand Banks of Newfoundland. Favor-

able tax rules encouraged the industry, which soon became the largest in early New England. The cod was so important to Massachusetts that a huge wooden carving of the fish was made and hung in the State House in Boston in 1798. It is still there today.

The weather, tricky currents, shoals, and tides along the east coast of North America made it necessary for colonial shipbuilders to develop special ships for the fishing industry. In the northeast they needed sturdy vessels that could withstand storms. In the Chesapeake Bay and South, they needed fast craft with large cargo space to haul the catches of oystermen, crabbers, and fishermen. New England lobstermen developed boats to handle fish traps. They gradually came up with the design for the *topsail schooner*, a sleek sailboat that combined speed, seaworthiness, easy handling, and ample cargo space.

By 1776, more than five hundred schooners were fishing for cod off Newfoundland. Hundreds of smaller boats fished for herring, mackerel, and other sea animals. The large number of fishermen skilled in sailing and navigating in the rugged seas off North America were the group from which the future navy and merchant seamen came.

The merchant seamen became involved in the profitable trade with Europe and coastal trade among the colonies and, later, the states. The demands of the fishing industry, and of transatlantic and Caribbean trade, were met by the world's best frigates, developed for the Navy in 1794. The finest of these was the USS *Constitution*—"Old Ironsides"—a ship that combined firepower with speed and maneuverability.

By the end of the eighteenth century, American merchant ships had begun the trade to Hawaii, China, and the Orient. They explored the Pacific coast up to the Columbia River and helped establish the later claim of the United States to Oregon.

Soon after the War of 1812, when American trade began its rapid expansion, a new idea in transatlantic trade began to take form. It was a regular, scheduled service for passengers, mail, and freight between New York and Liverpool, England. In 1816 a group of merchants formed a company called the Black Ball Line. The name was derived from a big black ball painted on the ship's foresail, and the company or house flag, which was a red square with a black disc on it. The first run of these Black Ball *packet ships* began in 1818.

Sailing to Europe was called the "downhill" run because the prevailing winds blow west to east. This trip took about 24 days. The return trip was called the "uphill" run and took 38 to 43 days. This return trip took longer because the ships had to go against both the winds and the Gulf Stream. En route to Europe, both of these natural factors were favorable for sailing ships.

By 1838 several competing lines were operating between Europe and the United States. Also, a service connecting New York, Charleston, New Orleans, and the Mexican port of Veracruz had begun. Most of the freight carried to Europe was raw materials, especially cotton, tobacco, indigo, and naval stores from the South. From Europe, the ships brought back English cutlery, hardware, fine clothing, books, wines, luxury goods, and manufactured products.

The packet ships were the most amazing vessels of their day. Captained by expert mariners, crewed by the toughest men ever to put to sea, these packets had luxury features for rich passengers. Quarters were cramped but finely finished. Some even carried farm animals so that there were fresh meat, eggs, and milk at meals.

As the numbers of well-to-do passengers declined, and ships became bigger, the packets began carrying immigrants. Often the living conditions were terrible. Immigrants were packed in like sardines, without sanitary facilities and with poor food. Sometimes, up to 10 percent of the immigrants died in the "'tween deck spaces," as they were called. Nevertheless, the packets brought hardy peasant immigrants to the United States at a time when they were badly needed for the country's development. This was probably the most lasting effect of the packets.

The packet ships gave America world leadership in the building and operation of sailing ships. Even the English could not contest the American position. By 1824, the packets were carrying most of the passengers and freight that crossed the North Atlantic. America held onto its transatlantic supremacy until the middle of the nineteenth century, when steamships began replacing sails.

The British had developed a profitable type of *triangular,* or three-cornered, *trade* between Britain, North America, and the British West Indies during the years immediately following the War of 1812. British ships carried manufactured products to America. There they loaded up with lumber, salt fish, flour, and livestock and sailed to the Indies. Offloading these trade goods, they reloaded with raw materials for British factories and sailed back to England. American ships were prohibited by British law to trade in the Indies, so this part of the British transatlantic trade prospered, even with growing American competition in other areas.

THE SLAVE TRADE

Another, much less praiseworthy and more infamous triangular trade developed during the colonial years: the slave trade. This persisted until the mid-nineteenth century, despite laws to the contrary. Much of the wealth and prosperity of New England in the eighteenth and early nineteenth centuries was founded on the slave trade. The rich businessmen and shipowners and their families never saw the loads of human misery for which they were responsible.

This triangular slave trade most often originated in Bristol, Rhode Island, from which the slave ship sailed, loaded with rum made in New England's distilleries from West Indies molasses. The ship sailed to West Africa, where the rum was exchanged for slaves, and the slaves were taken to the West Indies and sold. Then another cargo of molasses would be carried back to New England. The equatorial route across the Atlantic Ocean from Africa was called the Middle Passage. Over fifteen million black Africans were transported to slavery in the Americas over this route.

Slave trade began in 1619 when a Dutch ship brought the first slaves to Virginia. In 1806 the British Parliament passed a law forbidding slave trading by English ships. In 1808 the U.S. Congress passed a law prohibiting American vessels from trading in slaves, but this law was not enforced.

At the height of the triangular slave trade in the last half of the eighteenth century, American slavers sold their cargoes to the British in Jamaica and Barbados, where they received the highest prices. Some slaves were sold in Cuba. From these places, fast ships carried them to southern and Caribbean ports. In later years, when this trade was made illegal, smuggling slaves became a major business. This was one of the main sources of income for Lafitte's pirates. During the peak years as many as 20,000 blacks were landed in the United States annually.

Following the War of 1812, the British made treaties with most European nations that allowed Royal Navy ships to search and capture any of their vessels involved in the slave trade. The United States refused to sign such a treaty, partly because of their recent sad experience with British impressment of sailors. But it was also a result of political pressures in Congress by Southern planters and New England slavers, who were becoming wealthy through the illegal trade. The result was that other nations' slavers would often hoist the U.S. flag when the Royal Navy was in the area on antislavery patrol.

In 1819 the U.S. Navy was authorized to conduct antislave patrols off the African coast in the Gulf of Guinea. It was here that the slave trading posts or "factories" were set up in what now are the countries of Liberia, the Ivory Coast, Ghana, and Togo. In 1820 a federal law was passed that defined the carrying of slaves as an act of piracy, making it punishable by death. At the same time, the Navy was assigned the task of helping resettle freed blacks in a new country they named Liberia, in recognition of the liberty of the freed slaves. These people named their capital Monrovia after President James Monroe, who helped them start their new country.

The antislave patrols were not very successful. Involvement in the Liberian venture and the unpopularity of the patrol in Congress were the main reasons. The campaign against piracy in the Caribbean, which was going on at the same time, was given more support than antislave operations. In 1824 the United States withdrew its patrol because of a dispute with the British over rights of visit and search at sea. As soon as the patrol had gone, the slavers again took cover under the American flag, much to the frustration of the Royal Navy.

Not until the Webster-Ashburton Treaty with Britain in 1842 did the United States send a formal African Squadron to cooperate with the British in stopping the slave trade. This effort too was only half-hearted.

Between 1845 and 1850 the U.S. Navy captured only ten slavers, carrying about a thousand captives. The Royal Navy took 423 prizes with 27,000 blacks in the same period. Clearly, the American naval squadron made only a small dent in the slave traffic. Both Americans and British returned the captives to Africa, where they were freed. But American ships and capital, as well as foreign ships illegally flying the Stars and Stripes, continued the slave trade until the start of the Civil War in 1861.

American naval officers considered the slave trade a terrible business and wanted to stamp it out. They were handicapped by lack of support in Congress, which was heavily influenced by the Southern proslavery politicians. Also, American juries often failed to convict captured slavers, making the Navy's task seem futile. Immediately before the outbreak of the Civil War, however, an American squadron under command of Flag Officer William Inman was given adequate logistic and political support. In a short time his vigilant ships captured 25 slavers and freed 4,800 blacks. When the Civil War began, Inman's squadron was withdrawn, but that conflict itself ended the African slave trade.

THE MEXICAN WAR

Americans began moving into Texas in the 1820s when that territory was still a part of Mexico. By 1835 nearly 30,000 Americans had moved into the area, and many problems had started with the Mexican government. After a year of skirmishing, Texans declared their independence and organized the Republic of Texas with its "Lone Star" flag. In February 1836, Mexican forces under General Santa Anna entered Texas and overran a small Texan garrison at the Alamo near San Antonio, killing all the defenders. Rallying under the cry, "Remember the Alamo!" Sam Houston and 800 Texans routed the Mexican army and captured Santa Anna at the Battle of San Jacinto about six weeks later. In April 1836 Santa Anna recognized Texan independence.

Texas remained a "hot spot" during the next ten years, however. American settlers poured into Texas, and the new government claimed the Rio Grande as its southern border. In 1845 Texas was admitted to the Union and U.S. troops under General Zachary Taylor moved to garrison the Rio Grande boundary. In April 1846 a Mexican force crossed the river and attacked elements of Taylor's command, inflicting a dozen casualties and capturing some soldiers. Taylor responded by invading Mexico and capturing the border town of Matamoros. A few days later, President James K. Polk called on Congress to declare war on Mexico. Both houses of Congress voted by a large majority for war on 13 May 1846.

A four-ship naval squadron in the Pacific, under command of Commodore John Sloat, was operating off the coast of California when war was declared. Sloat's forces went ashore at Monterey, the capital of Mexican California, occupied the city without a fight, and raised the American flag. A day later, on 8 July 1847, another naval force under command of Commander John Montgomery, took possession of Yerba Buena (later San Francisco). The naval forces then joined land forces that had fought their way across the New Mexico–Arizona territory into California, defeating poorly organized Mexican forces en route. The little American army proceeded to capture Los Angeles, San Diego, Santa Barbara, and other California settlements. The Mexican defense force signed the Treaty of Cahuenga in early 1847, giving California to the United States.

The United States had now brought the entire Southwest under the protection of the American flag and for all practical purposes had won the war. The Mexican government, however, did not recognize the American victories, so President Polk planned to carry the war into the heart of Mexico. Zachary Taylor's army, though greatly outnumbered, spent the next few months defeating Mexican forces in a number of battles in northeastern Mexico. This was not enough to conclude the war, so Polk ordered General Winfield Scott to assemble an army of 14,000 men to take the capital, Mexico City.

Since Mexico had no navy, there were no sea battles. But sea forces had to carry out the operations leading to a successful end to the war. Scott's army was loaded in army transports and sailed to join with the Navy's Home Squadron, which was blockading Mexico's east coast. The transports and the Home Squadron met at Veracruz in March.

In the largest U.S. amphibious operation carried out before World War II, over one hundred ships landed the American force without losing a man. Included in the landing were 1,200 sailors and marines. As the ground forces surrounded Veracruz, the Navy took up bombardment positions off the major Mexican fort. A naval battery was sent ashore to aid the army in its bombardment of the city. The fort and the city were pounded into submission in less than two weeks.

With the port in American hands and supply lines clear, Scott and his army swept into Mexico. A series of stiff engagements were fought before the army and marines captured Mexico City on 14 September 1847. It is this military operation that is remembered in the beginning phrase of the Marine Hymn, "From the Halls of Montezuma."

The Treaty of Guadalupe Hidalgo ended the Mexican War in February 1848. By its terms, Mexico recognized the U.S. annexation of the New Mexico–Arizona Territory and California, and set the Rio Grande as the U.S.–Mexican border. The United States had now reached its second seacoast. This realized the American "manifest destiny," the dream of a country stretching from coast to coast, and was the most important result of the Mexican War. As always, such a great victory meant both immense benefits and increased re-

The landing of 12,000 American troops under General Winfield Scott at Veracruz during the Mexican War in 1847. The landing was made without casualties while U.S. ships fired on shore batteries in the fort and city.

sponsibilities for the American people. A navy would now have to be maintained in the Pacific to defend the nation's new shores and to protect the many merchant ships that were soon to ply the trade routes to the Orient.

THE CLIPPER SHIPS

Just as the Mexican War was about to start in 1845, the most colorful and dramatic era of sailing ships began. The square-rigger clipper ship *Rainbow* slid down the ways in New York that year. The era of the clipper ships was beginning.

The Navy had sailed the frigate *Congress* to the East Indies as early as 1819. Other naval and commercial vessels made trips in succeeding years. In 1829 the Navy sloop *Vincennes* had crossed the Pacific and then returned home via the Indian and

Atlantic oceans. It thus became the first American warship to circle the globe. Such voyages by naval vessels were intended to impress foreign nations with American naval strength and thus reduce the threat of raids on merchant ships. In 1835 the Navy established a regular East India Squadron to protect American ships and interests in the Pacific.

As early as 1784 American ships had been taking part in the China trade. By 1825 American trade with China was second only to that of England. In 1840 this rich commerce stopped during the Opium War between China and Britain. Trade was reopened in 1842 when Commodore Lawrence Kearny sailed into Canton, China, with the USS *Constellation* and USS *Boston* of the East India Squadron. Kearny used a combination of courtesy, firmness, fairness, and show of force to

Clipper ships were the "Queens of the Seas" from about 1845 to 1855.

lay the foundation for a successful trading treaty that was signed by China and the United States a year later.

The trade with China always involved a race against time. In the early days it took as much as a year and a half for a round trip between New England and China. The Chinese trade offered tea, silk, porcelain, ivory, and other luxuries. Profit was so great that one successful trip would pay for a ship. But time was important, especially for tea, which could spoil on a long trip. Therefore, Yankee shipbuilders sought to build a ship that would cut the sailing time to China. The clipper ship was their answer. The clippers were the most beautiful ships ever to sail the seven seas; in their time, they were also the fastest. By the 1850s, American "China clippers" were sailing from New York to Hong Kong in about ninety days. In 1845, the *Rainbow*, mentioned earlier, was the fastest ship in the world, having made the trip home to New York from Canton in eighty-eight days.

At the same time the China trade began to make great fortunes in New England, the Mexican War ended, opening up the Pacific Coast to American shipping. Later that year, gold was discovered in California. Now the clipper-ship builders had another great demand: to bring supplies and passengers to San Francisco. The beautiful ships were used to haul thousands of gold seekers between East Coast ports and California. Often, the clip-

pers raced one another, and large bets were placed on the outcome. In 1851 the record trip time, never bettered, between New York and San Francisco was clocked at eighty-nine days and two hours by the *Flying Cloud.* By the mid-1850s the whole East Coast was excited about the clipper races. The people loved the excitement and were thrilled by the beauty of the clippers.

The clippers had their greatest year in 1853; 145 of them sailed for San Francisco's Golden Gate. In all, 161 clippers were launched between 1850 and 1855. Then the shipbuilding boom collapsed. Clippers were expensive to build and keep up. Their rapid decline was caused partly by the completion of a railroad across the Isthmus of Panama in 1855. This made the long, dangerous trip around South America unnecessary. Over the much shorter distance, larger and slower carriers could haul bulk cargoes and more passengers much more cheaply. With profits down, the fast clippers could not carry enough cargo to make further construction of this type of ship worthwhile.

Other things happening in America and the world at this same time also affected merchant shipping. Steamships began to overtake sail as the preferred means of sea transport. Then, in 1858, the first transcontinental stagecoach made the trip from St. Louis to San Francisco. This brought a complete change of attitude in America.

In the early years of the nation's independence, young, energetic Americans and businessmen had turned toward the sea for adventure and fortune. Now the great expanse of the American West beckoned. Farms, cattle, mining, lumbering, land speculation, and railroads captured America's imagination. And in the late 1850s the turmoil of the Civil War was about to break loose, turning the people's attention to internal affairs. As the clipper ships moved off the American historical stage, all other aspects of American life began to change.

OPENING THE DOOR TO JAPAN

With the reopening of the China trade in 1842, the next objective of American sailors was Japan. After a brief relationship with Portuguese traders and missionaries in the late sixteenth and early seventeenth centuries, Japan had driven all foreigners out of the country. Except for Chinese traders, and a few Dutch envoys isolated on an island in Nagasaki harbor, no foreigners were allowed in Japan during the 215 years after 1637. In fact, a Japanese law in 1825 decreed that any foreign ship that attempted to anchor in a Japanese harbor was to be destroyed. Any sailors coming ashore were to be arrested or killed. Any Japanese who left to visit a foreign country was to be killed upon his return. Such isolation, of course, kept Japan in a feudal age, with no technological, scientific, or social advances.

Westerners could not understand the Japanese. When the American East India Squadron tried to open the trade door in 1846, Commodore James Biddle was treated in an insulting manner. When pushed by a Japanese guard, he chose not to make an issue of the matter. He was not aware that this caused him to "lose face"—a major mistake in the Orient. The Japanese would not even consider talking with such a "weak" individual, so Biddle's trade proposals were rejected and his ships were towed out to sea.

Two years later, when the Navy sloop *Preble* called at Nagasaki to pick up fifteen shipwrecked American whalers, the commanding officer found the Japanese still bragging about their "victory" over Biddle. Commander James Glynn decided quick action was the only answer to such behavior. He threatened to bombard Nagasaki if the whalers weren't released within two days. The whalers were safely turned over, and the *Preble* sailed away without further problems.

But the lure of the Japanese market, the need for a coaling station for ships crossing the Pacific to China, and demands for protection of shipwrecked sailors caused America to want an open door to Japan. President Millard Fillmore chose Commodore Matthew Calbraith Perry to head a naval squadron to Japan. Perry, the younger brother of Oliver Hazard Perry, the hero of Lake Erie, was the perfect man for the job. He had more diplomatic experience than any other naval

The second landing of Commodore Perry and his officers to meet the Imperial Commissioners at Yokohama, Japan, in February 1854. The Treaty of Kanagawa was signed in March, opening several Japanese ports to American shipping. Other parts of the treaty led to a trade agreement opening Japan to trade with the United States and other nations.

officer. He had forty-four years of naval service and had taken part in most important naval actions since 1808. Perry's mission was to carry a letter from the president to the emperor of Japan and to conclude a treaty that would satisfy all three main American interests.

Perry's seven ships sailed in November 1852 from the United States and met in Hong Kong the following spring. Leaving three ships in Okinawa, he entered Japanese waters with his steam frigates and anchored at the entrance to Tokyo Bay on 8 July 1853. The Japanese had never seen steamships, and they could not fail to be impressed with the fact that Perry had all guns loaded and readied for action.

Having arrived, Perry put into practice all the things he had learned from previous attempts to trade and negotiate with the Japanese. He ordered away the Japanese guard boats and refused to deal with anyone whose rank was lower than his own. He made it clear that he would entrust President Fillmore's letter only to a member of the imperial family. For a week the commodore refused to allow himself to be seen, while the Japanese fretted and debated about what was to be done.

Finally, on 14 July the Japanese sent the Prince of Izu, one of the imperial counselors, to act on the emperor's behalf. They set up a fine pavilion on the shore to receive Perry. Perry moved his squadron closer to shore, where the Japanese could easily see that this mission of peace was well supported by the equipment for war. Perry realized the importance of ceremony and "face" in the conduct of affairs with the Japanese.

A thirteen-gun salute echoed over the anchorage as Perry stepped into his barge. One hundred Marines in well-starched dress uniforms, a company of seamen, and two Navy bands preceded the barge in fifteen gunboats, to serve as a guard of honor. Perry was flanked by two huge black seamen who served as bodyguards, the first blacks the Japanese had ever seen. In front of them marched two young midshipmen carrying the president's letter in a beautiful rosewood box. After the letter was delivered to the prince, Perry announced that the squadron would depart for China in a few days, but would return in the spring with more ships for a reply to the president's letter.

He returned in February with a much larger squadron. The Japanese had been convinced by the first visit that America was a nation worthy to carry on trade with Japan. When the Americans returned, more ceremonies took place, and there were exchanges of gifts. The Americans were given silks and carvings and other oriental handicrafts. The Japanese received firearms, tools, clocks, stoves, a telegraph, and even a quarter-sized locomotive complete with tender, coach, and circular track. The track was quickly laid and the Japanese envoys were treated to rides on the little cars, with their robes flying in the breeze as the train went around at 20 miles per hour.

After more than a month of detailed talks, the Japanese and Americans signed the Treaty of Kanagawa in March 1854. It provided for the opening of the ports of Shimoda and Hakodate to American shipping, the protection of shipwrecked American seamen, start-up of an American consulate at Shimoda, and granting of most-favored-nation (reduction or elimination of trade barriers such as tariffs, and other favorable trade provisions) status to the United States. This latter provision enabled a trade agreement to be signed two years later. That completed the opening of Japan to commerce with foreign nations.

The Perry mission was regarded as the most important "peacetime battle" of the nineteenth century for the U.S. Navy. Perry was showered with honors upon his return to America. Washington Irving, the great American author, wrote of his exploit: "You have gained yourself a lasting name, and have won it without shedding a drop of blood or inflicting misery on a human being." Truly a new era was about to dawn for America as a trading nation in the Pacific, and the U.S. Navy had helped make it possible.

Chapter 5. Study Guide Questions

1. What tasks were of immediate concern to the new Navy after the War of 1812?
2. A. Who was Jean Lafitte?
   B. Where was his base of operation?

3. What diseases caused many deaths in American crews during operations to clear the Caribbean of pirates?

4. A. What area was the center of the whaling industry in the 1800s?

B. By 1860, what caused the industry to lose its former importance?

5. A. Why did American shipbuilders have to develop special fishing boats for the American coast?

B. What ship design did they create?

6. What was the importance of the American Black Ball Line?

7. What was the infamous *triangular trade* that developed during the colonial period and continued illegally from 1820 through 1860? Describe the route and cargoes carried.

8. Why were the American antislavery patrols not very successful?

9. What action caused the United States to declare war on Mexico in 1846?

10. What were the Navy's contributions to the war in California?

11. What was the Navy's part in the land offensive against Mexico?

12. By what treaty did Mexico recognize U.S. annexation of the Southwestern territories?

13. A. What was the "manifest destiny" of the United States?

B. What responsibility did the Navy now have to take on?

14. A. What type of ship designed by Americans became the fastest ship on the seas in the mid-1800s?

B. What were the products carried in this trade?

15. A. In 1849 what caused the great demand for fast transportation to the West Coast of the United States?

B. What happened to cause the era of the clipper ships to end?

16. What was the next step in Far Eastern commerce after the China trade reopened in 1842?

17. A. Whom did President Fillmore choose to lead the American naval squadron to Japan?

B. How did he go about ensuring the success of his mission?

18. What was the outcome of Perry's mission to Japan?

Vocabulary

show of force
marauder
harpoon
schooner
triangular trade
skirmish

gun salute
envoy
most-favored-nation
   trade status
packet ships

8

Introduction to Navigation and Time

Chapter 1.   Introduction to Navigation

Navigation is the art and science by which mariners find their ship's or aircraft's position and guide it safely from one point to another. Most of you would know how to guide yourself, or a ship, by following the compass needle. The problem is trying to find your location in the first place. This is the navigator's first job: to locate the ship exactly on the earth. The navigator can then recommend a course to be steered in order to arrive safely at the destination.

To find out where we are now, we must locate ourselves in relation to something else. For instance: your desk is 20 feet from the back door, and directly in front of the teacher's desk. Or your house is on the corner of Elm Street and Western Avenue. Using a road map, we can say that the town of Jefferson is on Highway 26, 15 miles south of Watertown.

We have now used a tool that is important in locating places: a *map*. In this unit, we will talk about maps of the earth—particularly, maps that show on a flat surface the locations of places important to the maritime nations of the world.

The type of map used to navigate on the water is called a *chart*. The charts we will talk about may be defined as "a picture of the navigable waters of the earth." Charts are what the navigator uses when plotting courses and finding positions of his ship. The navigator cannot refer to a highway, a crossroads, or towns. There has to be a way of locating the ship on the ocean. This chapter will talk about how this is done.

THE TERRESTRIAL SPHERE

To discuss navigation and navigation charts, we must first understand the earth. In navigation, the earth is called the *terrestrial sphere* or *globe*. (This term comes from the Latin word *terra*, which means earth.) A sphere or globe is spherical. Actually, the earth is a little flattened at the poles instead of being perfectly spherical. But this can be disregarded in most cases in navigation.

There are several reference points for locating objects on the earth. The *North Pole* and *South Pole* are located at the ends of the axis on which the earth rotates. The imaginary lines running through the poles and around the earth are called *meridians*. They divide the surface of the earth into sections—much as you might cut an orange for easy peeling.

The imaginary line that runs around the center of the earth, cutting every meridian in half, and dividing the earth into top and bottom halves, is called the *equator*. The word "equator" implies

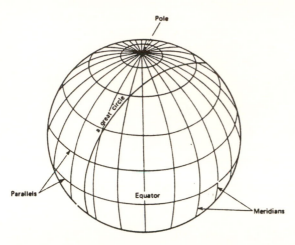

The terrestrial sphere with meridians of longitude and parallels of latitude. Any line that cuts the globe into equal parts is a great circle. An random great circle is shown cutting the meridians. The other great circles in this drawing are the meridians and the equator.

"equal parts." It is exactly halfway between the North and South poles. The top half of the globe is called the Northern Hemisphere (northern "half-sphere"), and the lower half is the Southern Hemisphere.

Great Circles

Meridians and the equator are called *great circles* because they each divide the globe into two halves. Any circle drawn around the earth so as to divide the world into equal parts, or hemispheres, is called a great circle.

The great circle is very important, so it must be clearly understood. A great circle is any circle whose *plane* passes through the center of the earth. Remember that the plane must go through the *center* of the sphere, cutting the whole sphere into two halves.

Look at the globe. You will note that *all* meridians—that is, lines going through the North and South poles—are great circles. Of all the lines going around the globe from east to west, however, only the equator is a great circle. These other lines

are called *parallels,* since they go around the globe parallel to, and north and south of, the equator. They are all smaller circles than that made by the equator. Of the parallels, only the equator cuts the globe into two hemispheres.

You can also see that a great circle does not *have* to be a meridian or the equatorial parallel. A great circle is *any* circle whose plane passes through the earth's center, no matter what direction.

What is the significance of the great circle in navigation? Just this: the shortest distance between two points on the earth (or any sphere) lies along the path of a great circle passing through those two points. The great circle is an *arc* on the earth's rounded surface. It has to be an arc, because a *straight line* between two points would go under the earth's surface!

Circular Measurement

You already have learned in your math classes that a circle's *circumference* (the distance around) contains 360 degrees (°). Regardless of the size of the circle, whether it's the size of a ping-pong ball or of the globe, the circumference has 360°. Each degree contains 60 minutes ('), and each minute contains 60 seconds ("). Measurement along a meridian is expressed in terms of degrees, minutes, and seconds of *arc* (the curve of the circle).

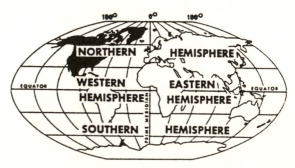

Equal-area projection of the globe shows the four hemispheres, as divided by the equator, the prime meridian, and the International Date Line.

MERIDIANS

For every degree around the equator, there is a meridian. There are 360 of them, 60 minutes or 3,600 seconds of arc apart. The starting point for numbering these meridians is the meridian on which the Royal Observatory at Greenwich, England, is located. The Greenwich meridian, therefore, is numbered 0, or 0°, and is called the *prime meridian.*

Halfway around the globe from the prime meridian is the 180th meridian. The 180th meridian is the other half of the 0 meridian; together they make a great circle that cuts the globe into the *eastern* and *western hemispheres.* The 180th meridian is called the International Date Line, which we will discuss in detail in the next chapter. Every meridian runs vertically, north and south, through the poles, but is numbered from 0° to 180°, depending on how far east or west it is from the prime meridian.

PARALLELS

We mentioned earlier that the equator is a line bisecting the earth on a horizontal plane. Since the northern and southern hemispheres are equal halves of the globe, there must be 90° in the arc from the equator to a pole. However, parallels drawn around the earth get smaller and smaller as you get closer to the poles. But remember, no matter how small a circle it is, it still contains 360°. What this means, then, is that the *distance* represented by a degree of longitude measured along the parallel circles becomes ever smaller as you get nearer the poles.

The starting point for numbering the parallels is the equator, the 0° parallel. Parallels are numbered from 0° to 90° north and south of the equator. Every parallel runs east and west, but is numbered north or south from the equator to the poles.

LATITUDE AND LONGITUDE

We now have drawn a network of meridians and parallels all the way around the globe. Every spot on the earth may be located at the intersection of a meridian and a parallel. The navigator describes every location on the earth in terms of its latitude or longitude. *Latitude* is the distance of arc north (N) or south (S) of the equator. It is expressed in degrees, minutes, and seconds, measured along the meridian of the place. *Longitude* is the distance in degrees, minutes, and seconds of arc east (E) or west (W) of the prime meridian, measured along the parallel of latitude. Let's state it again: latitude is always measured north or south from 0° through 90°; and longitude is always measured east or west from 0° through 180°.

For example, the position of Washington, D.C., is 38°58'N latitude, 77°01"W longitude. This is spoken as thirty-eight degrees, fifty-eight minutes north; seventy-seven degrees, one minute west. Every spot on earth can be located precisely by this method. You should become very familiar with locating places on the globe this way.

NAUTICAL MEASUREMENTS

Distance. In talking earlier about degrees of arc, we were actually talking about *nautical distance,* or distances at sea. The *nautical mile* is used to measure nautical distance. It is about equal to 1 minute of arc measured along the equator, or any other great circle. That is about $1\frac{1}{7}$ statute or land miles. A nautical mile is about 6,076 feet; for most problems in the Navy, we consider this to be 2,000 yards. A land mile is 5,280 feet, or 1,760 yards.

Since meridians of longitude are great circles, they may be used as distance scales. Distance is measured along the meridian, using *dividers.* One minute of latitude along any meridian equals one nautical mile. (Distances are not measured on parallels of latitude, because one minute equals one nautical mile only along the equator.)

Speed. The word *knot* is a seagoing speed term meaning nautical miles per hour. It is incorrect to say "knots per hour," except when referring to increases or decreases in speed. The term comes from old sailing days, when ships determined their speed through the water by running out a line knotted at fractions of one nautical mile. The line was attached to a flat piece of wood called a *chip log.* The amount of line (numbers of knots) run out in two or three minutes gave an estimate of the ship's speed, from which the number of nautical miles covered per hour could be figured.

Direction. *True nautical direction* is measured from true north (North Pole) as located on a globe. This used to be given in olden days by points on the *compass rose,* such as north, north by east, north north east, and so on. Modern navigators use a system of circular measurement using 360° of arc, which is more accurate and convenient. A *compass card* shows the readings of degrees of arc. Note that the true bearings of the so-called *cardinal points* are: north, 000°; east, 090°; south, 180°; and west, 270°.

A direction is always expressed in three figures, regardless of whether three digits are necessary. In other words, it is not 45° (forty-five degrees), but 045° (spoken "zero four five degrees").

The direction in which a ship is facing is called its *heading.* The direction that a ship is steered through the water is called its *course.* Because they are directions, headings and courses are always expressed in three digits.

Most larger naval ships and aircraft are fitted with an instrument called a *gyrocompass* that always points toward true north. It is used as the basis for all true direction and course measurements. However, a gyrocompass is expensive and needs a power supply to operate. Therefore, most smaller vessels, boats, and many ground vehicles use a relatively inexpensive *magnetic compass* as a directional reference, similar to those you may have used as a Boy or Girl Scout or in a science class. Directions referenced to the magnetic compass are called *magnetic* or *compass* directions.

Magnetic compasses point to the earth's northernmost magnetic pole, located in Northern Canada. Because it is at a distance from the true North Pole, there is usually an angle between magnetic and true north at all locations on earth. This angle is called the *variation angle.* If the magnetic compass points east of true north, the variation angle is labeled east. If the magnetic compass points west of true north, the variation angle is labeled west. See the figure below.

One type of direction can be converted into the other very simply. To convert from magnetic to true, just add or subtract the variation at your location to the magnetic bearing. Westerly variations are subtracted, and easterly variations are added. For example, if your ship were heading 090° magnetic in a region where the variation was 10° East, the true heading would be 090° + 10°, or 100°

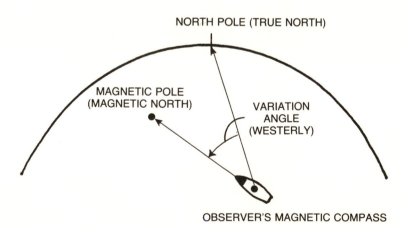

The relationship between true and magnetic north. The variation angle is westerly in this case, because at the observer's location the magnetic compass needle points to the west of true north.

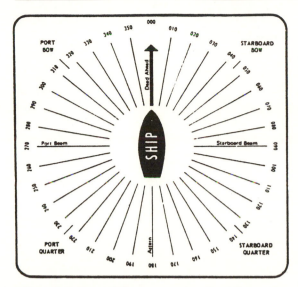

Relative bearing card showing numerical and describing relative bearings from a ship.

the letters M or R. For example 030°M means 30° to the right of magnetic north, spoken "030 degrees magnetic," while 030°R means 30° off the starboard bow, spoken "030 degrees relative." Objects seen by lookouts are reported in terms of relative bearing by degrees. Note the following relative bearings: dead ahead, or bow, 000°R, starboard beam, 090°R; dead astern, 180°R; and port beam, 270°R.

Sometimes a three-digit true bearing is followed by the letter *T* to emphasize that it is a true bearing, as for example 030°T, spoken "030 degrees true."

To go from a relative to a true bearing just add the ship's true course to the relative bearing of the object sighted. If the sum is less than 360°, that sum is the true bearing of the object. If the sum is more than 360°, subtract 360° from the sum, and that difference will be the true bearing of the object. See the figure on page 238.

The *reciprocal* of a bearing is its opposite, 180° away, on the other side of the compass card. For example, the reciprocal or opposite bearing of 000°, dead ahead, is 180° or dead astern, and vice versa. When you obtain a bearing on some object, the bearing from that object to you is the reciprocal.

To find the reciprocal of any bearing expressed in degrees less than 180°, simply add 180° to that bearing. If the bearing is greater than 180°, subtract 180° to get the reciprocal. For example, the reciprocal bearing of 030° is 210° (030° + 180° = 210°); the reciprocal of 275° is 095° (275° − 180° = 095°).

In the Navy it is common to say someone is "180 out" if he or she is completely wrong about something. This implies that the opposite (or reciprocal) of what that person is saying or doing is correct.

CHARTS

A *chart* is a picture representing part of the navigable waters of the earth. A chart has reference lines on it to show water areas and nearby land outlines to help a ship's navigator find his way at sea. Navigation charts give a great deal of infor-

true. If you wanted to proceed on course 270° true in the same region, you would steer 270° − 10° or 260° magnetic. The size and direction of the variation can easily be obtained from the nautical chart of the area in which you are operating.

It is important to be able to make these kinds of conversions because nautical charts and land maps are drawn up based on true directions, but small ships, boats, and land vehicles are most often fitted with magnetic compasses, necessitating navigation using magnetic courses and bearings described below.

A *bearing* is the direction of an object from an observer, measured clockwise in one of three standard ways. A *true bearing* is the direction of an object measured clockwise from true north. A *magnetic bearing* is the direction of an object measured clockwise from magnetic north, and a *relative bearing* is the direction of an object measured clockwise from the ship's head (bow).

Bearings are given in three digits, as with nautical direction. When recording a bearing, it is assumed to be a true bearing unless it is followed by

TRUE NORTH

TRUE BEARING OF LIGHTHOUSE·135°

HEADING OF SHIP·045°

RELATIVE BEARING OF LIGHTHOUSE·090°

MERIDIAN OF SHIP

LIGHTHOUSE

A comparison of true and relative bearings, showing how to figure each.

mation to the navigator. This is called *hydrographic* information. It includes a graphic (pictorial) display of water features such as depth, overhead obstructions, and navigational aids such as buoys, lights, and anchorages.

The globe is a spherical object, or three-dimensional (length, width, and height). But it is not practical to work navigation problems or chart courses on a round surface. Therefore, it is necessary to convert the round surface of the globe to one that is flat and two-dimensional (length and width)—in short, a flat piece of paper on which a chart is drawn.

Cartographers (map and chart makers) have used math to work out chart *projection* techniques. These techniques make it possible to create charts with a minimum of distortion from the actual spherical globe.

Mercator Projection. The best-known map or chart projection is called the *Mercator projection*. It is the one your teachers generally use to locate geographical places when they pull down maps on

rollers in front of the room. It is the projection used for road maps on land.

The Mercator projection was developed by a Dutch cartographer, Gerardus Mercator, in the 1500s. It is the most useful of all chart projections for navigation. In making the projection, one must first project the spherical globe onto a cylinder-shaped piece of paper, wrapped around the globe at the equator. Then, one must lay out the cylindrical paper flat, after cutting it at a convenient meridian. A Mercator projection of the world, for instance, is usually cut near the International Date Line so the continental land areas are shown almost unbroken.

It is obvious that *distortion* occurs the farther the area on the chart is from the equator. However, this distortion is made uniform in both latitude and longitude, so the finished chart is usable for navigation even at high latitudes. The space between parallels increases with latitude, but the distance represented by 1° of latitude is always the same, one nautical mile. Because of the distortion at high latitudes, the island of Greenland appears much larger than the United States on a Mercator projection. Actually the reverse is true.

The meridians on a Mercator chart appear as straight lines, north and south, parallel to and equidistant from one another. They represent the imaginary curved meridian lines that come together at the poles on a globe.

Scale of Charts. The *scale of a chart* refers to a measurement of distance. It is a comparison of the actual distance or size of a landmass with that shown on the chart. The scale of a chart or map is normally printed near the *legend* in the form of a ratio, such as 1:5,000 (meaning that the feature shown is actually 5,000 times larger than its size on the chart). Said in another way, an inch or centimeter or other measurement on the chart represents 5,000 identical units on the real earth's surface. The smaller the ratio, the smaller the scale of the chart. A chart with a scale of 1:5,000 is on a much larger scale than one whose scale is 1:4,500,000, for example. Small scales are used to depict large areas on a chart, and large scales are used to depict small areas.

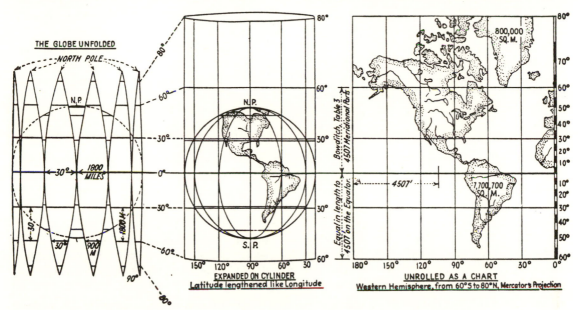

Development of the Mercator projection. A Mercator chart is made by projecting the spherical globe onto a cylinder-shaped paper tangent at the equator. The globe is cut much like an orange peeling might be sliced. This means that the distortion increases toward the poles.

Another way of expressing scale, called the *numerical scale,* is in inches, miles, or kilometers to the nautical mile. This is shown near the legend as a straight line (linear scale) with both compared measurements shown, one on either side of the line. By using a pair of dividers, set to the linear scale desired, you can find distances by "walking" the dividers on the chart and using simple arithmetic. For example, if an inch on the chart represents 50 miles, five inches would represent 250 miles.

Remember, the larger the scale, the smaller the area shown on a given chart or map. Large-scale charts show areas in greater detail. Features that appear on a large-scale chart may not show up at all on a small-scale chart of the same area.

Types of Charts. Charts used in the Navy are prepared by the Defense Mapping Agency Hydrographic Center (DMAHC), the National Ocean Service of the National Oceanic and At-

mospheric Administration (NOAA), and the British Admiralty. All charts used by the Navy, whatever the source, are issued by the depots of the Defense Mapping Agency.

Navigational charts, as listed in the previous section, are those with the necessary information for safe navigation. They have standard symbols, figures, and abbreviations that tell the depth of water, type of bottom, location of navigational aids, and so forth.

Harbor charts are large-scale charts that show harbors and their approaches in detail. Coastal charts are intermediate-scale charts used to navigate a vessel whose position may be determined by landmarks and lights, buoys, or soundings offshore. For navigating inside outlying reefs or shoals, or well offshore in large bays of sizable inland waterways, a coastal or harbor chart may be used.

General ocean sailing charts are small-scale charts showing the approaches to large areas of the coast. These charts show offshore soundings, principal lights and outer buoys, and any natural landmarks visible at a distance.

Scattered all over any navigational chart are many tiny figures, each representing the depth of water in that particular place. Depths may be given in feet, fathoms (six feet to one fathom), or meters. A notation under the title of the chart is the key; for example, "Soundings in feet at mean low water." Most charts also contain dotted lines called fathom curves, marking the limits of areas of certain depths. Most new charts will give water depth, heights of lights, and land contours in meters as well as in feet.

Aids to navigation are indicated on a chart by standard symbols. We will not go into detail on navigational aids in this text, saving that for *Naval Science 2.*

All unclassified DMAHC and National Ocean Service charts are available for purchase at nautical supply stores in most coastal cities and towns throughout the United States.

Chapter 1. Study Guide Questions

1. What is navigation?
2. A. What is a map?
   B. What is a chart?
3. What is the terrestrial sphere?
4. What are the imaginary lines that run through the poles around the earth?
5. What name is given to the imaginary line that runs around the center of the earth, cutting every meridian in half?
6. What is a great circle?
7. What are the lines going around the earth parallel to the equator called?
8. A. What is the circumference of a circle?
   B. How many degrees does it have?
9. A. Into what equal parts may degrees be divided?
   B. What is a *degree of arc*?
10. A. Where is the reference place for the 0° meridian?
    B. What is the meridian exactly opposite the 0° meridian on the other side of the world called?

C. What two hemispheres does this great circle line create?

11. In an atlas or other reference book locate the following places in terms of latitude and longitude, in degrees and minutes:
    A. Washington, D.C.
    B. Chicago, Illinois
    C. San Diego, California
    D. Honolulu, Hawaii
    E. Colón, Panama
    F. Gibraltar
    G. Port Said, Egypt
    H. Tokyo, Japan
    I. Sydney, Australia
12. How are distances measured at sea? Compare a land or statute mile with a nautical mile.
13. How is nautical direction or course measured?
14. What are the true bearings of the cardinal points, N, E, S, W?
15. How are these bearings or courses spoken?
    A. 135°T
    B. 060°M
    C. 090°R
16. Define a true bearing, a magnetic bearing, and a relative bearing.
17. If a ship is on course 050°T, and a lookout sights an object on the starboard beam at 090°R, what is the true bearing of the object?
18. If a lookout sights a merchant ship at 285°R, forward of the port beam, and the ship's course is 135°T, what is the true bearing of the contact?
19. Find the reciprocals of these bearings:
    A. 048°T
    B. 195°T
    C. 256°T
    D. 101°T
20. What does hydrographic information on a chart consist of?
21. A. Which projection is used for almost all navigation charts?
    B. Where is the greatest distortion on this kind of projection? Why?
22. What is the shortest distance between two points on a globe?

23. A. What is the scale of a chart?

B. Where is it normally shown on a map or chart, and in what form?

24. Why is it correct to say, "The larger the scale ratio, the smaller the area shown by the chart"?

25. If a chart has a linear scale of 1 inch equals 3 miles, and the entrance to a harbor is shown as ½-inch wide, how wide is that entrance?

26. What tool is used to determine distance on a chart with a linear scale?

27. A. What are soundings?

B. How are they shown on a chart?

C. What are the three measures with which depths may be indicated?

28. A. How many feet are in a fathom?

B. If water depth on a chart indicates a 15-fathom curve, how deep is the water in that area in feet?

Vocabulary

navigation	knot (nautical speed)
mariner	relative bearing
map	true bearing
chart	reciprocal
navigable waters	hydrography
meridian	cartographer
great circle	chart projection
hemisphere	distortion
parallels	chart scale
equator; equatorial	map legend
latitude	ratio
longitude	sounding
nautical mile	fathom
degree, minute, second (arc)	

Chapter 2. Time and Navigation

You probably have not given much thought to the study of time. The navigator of a ship, however, needs to know the exact time in order to determine the ship's position at sea.

If you have ever taken a long plane trip across the country, or to Hawaii or Europe, you have felt the effects of time-zone changes. It often takes a day or two to get one's body adjusted to the new time schedule—when to get up, when to eat, when to go to bed. This condition is called *jet lag*. This occurs because time is based on the relationship of the earth and the sun. This relationship is different for different longitudes at any given time.

In this chapter we will learn how time is determined, how we can figure out time-zone changes around the world, and something about the instruments the Navy uses for timekeeping.

TIME AND TIMEPIECES

Everyone is familiar with watches and clocks. In the Navy, time and timekeeping are of great importance, both because the routine of shipboard life is often fast-paced, and because time is essential in navigation of the ship. As part of their jobs in most naval ships, the quartermasters go around every couple of days to check and reset all ship's clocks to the correct time, so that all personnel in the ship can be sure they are using an accurate time in their log entries, tactical plots, messages, and all other phases of their daily routine.

In addition to the usual types of watches and clocks, there are more specialized timepieces found on board ship. These are called *chronometers*. A chronometer is a navigational timepiece, designed for extreme accuracy and dependability. It is built to withstand shock, vibration, and temperature variation. It is often mounted in a chronometer box in *gimbals,* which offset ship's motion, thereby keeping the timepiece level at all times. It must be handled with the greatest care, because its accuracy and regularity are essential in determining Greenwich mean time (GMT). This is the basic time used in fixing position by *celestial navigation,* which is finding position by sightings of the sun, stars, planets, and moon.

Radio stations in Washington and Honolulu

broadcast time signals every five minutes, twenty-four hours per day. These signals consist of a series of tones and voice announcements. An example of the voice announcement might be: "This is radio station _____. When the tone returns, the time will be 8:50 A.M. Eastern Standard Time; 8:50 A.M." The ship's chronometer, the most accurate timepiece on board is checked against the time signal by the quartermaster. Any error is recorded, and the navigator must take it into consideration when finding position.

MILITARY TIME: THE 24-HOUR CLOCK

We all know how to tell time by our watches and clocks. We know that the new day begins a fraction of one second after midnight, and concludes twenty-four hours later at midnight. The time between midnight and noon is labeled "A.M."; these letters mean *ante meridiem,* or before the middle of the day (noon). The time between noon and midnight is labeled "P.M.," meaning *post meridiem,* or after the middle of the day. We are used to this system of timekeeping in civilian society, because we can simply look out the window, so to speak, to see if it is morning or afternoon. We do not confuse 5:00 in the evening with 5:00 in the morning, to say nothing of 1:00 in the morning and 1:00 in the afternoon.

But it has long been a custom in the Navy and other military services to tell time by the twenty-four-hour clock. There are several reasons for this. It is done to avoid confusion in message communications, all of which are identified by the date and time at Greenwich. Also, this is the common way to tell time in most European countries, including England, where many of our military customs began. It is also another way to avoid the confusion that might happen if the AM or PM were accidentally left out of directions or orders.

So the Navy, and other military services, use the twenty-four-hour clock. In this way of keeping time, the day begins with a fraction of a second after midnight, 0000 (zero hour), and continues past 0100 (1 A.M.) and 0200 (2 A.M.) toward noon, 1200. The time after noon continues with 1300 (1 P.M.), 1400 (2 P.M.), and so forth until 2400, mid-

night. We do not use the terms "o'clock," A.M., or P.M., and do not use a colon to separate hours from minutes in the Navy. Rather, we speak in terms of "hundred"; for example, 0100 is "zero one hundred," 1000 is "ten hundred," 1800 is "eighteen hundred," and 2130 is "twenty-one thirty."

All NJROTC cadets should learn to use the twenty-four-hour clock. Mathematically, it is very easy to figure out; simply add the P.M. time number to 1200 (noon). For example, 2:25 P.M. becomes 1425, and 10:30 P.M. is 2230. You should memorize the twenty-four-hour clock so it becomes second nature when telling time.

Morning	(A.M.)	*Afternoon*	(P.M.)
2400/0000	12 midnight		
0100	1 A.M.	1300	1 P.M.
0200	2 A.M.	1400	2 P.M.
0300	3 A.M.	1500	3 P.M.
0400	4 A.M.	1600	4 P.M.
0500	5 A.M.	1700	5 P.M.
0600	6 A.M.	1800	6 P.M.
0700	7 A.M.	1900	7 P.M.
0800	8 A.M.	2000	8 P.M.
0900	9 A.M.	2100	9 P.M.
1000	10 A.M.	2200	10 P.M.
1100	11 A.M.	2300	11 P.M.
1200	12 P.M./ noon	2400/0000	12 A.M./ midnight

While 0000 and 2400 are exactly the same time, it is common practice to start each day at 0001 and end it at 2400.

SHIP'S BELL TIME

Another custom on board ship is to indicate time by bells. Before timepieces such as watches or chronometers were common, time on board ship was marked by a so-called hour-glass, which ran out its sand from one side to the other every thirty minutes. The glass would then be turned over to start measuring another thirty minutes, and the bell would be struck so all hands knew a half-hour had passed. It was struck once at the end of the first half-hour, twice at the end of the second, and so on, until eight bells were struck at the end of the fourth hour. After eight bells were struck, the series started over again.

The practice still continues on board many ships, in spite of the use of clocks and watches. The bells are rung in pairs; that is, if there are two or more bells to be rung, they are rung closer together than the odd bell. For example, five bells would sound like "ding-ding, ding-ding, ding." An odd number of bells marks half past the hour, and an even number marks an hour. Bells are rung only from reveille to taps, but not during divine services or when fog requires that the bell be used as a fog signal.

Bells also were related to the watches stood on deck, and for security watches throughout the ship. Everyone has read sea stories or seen movies and television films in which someone reports to the captain or the officer of the deck, "Four bells and all's well." This would indicate on the midwatch, that the security watch had made his rounds at 0200, and, as of that time, the ship was peaceful and secure.

To understand the relationship between naval time, bells, and watches, it will be helpful to review the table on the next page.

TIME AND ARC

From ancient times to the present, people have reckoned time according to the travel of the sun once around the earth each day. Of course, since the time of the medieval astronomer Copernicus in the sixteenth century, we have known that it is really the earth's rotation that makes the sun seem to move. But for navigation, and to make it easier for us to understand how time works, it is best to imagine the earth as standing still at the center of the universe, with the sun, as well as all the other celestial bodies, moving around the earth.

The sun thus appears to make one complete 360° revolution around the earth during each twenty-four-hour day. Actually, as we will see below, on any specific day during the year it will usually take a few minutes more or less than twenty-four hours for the sun to complete its journey. But on the average over a year, we can say that it takes exactly twenty-four hours.

Now, because the sun goes 360° around the earth in twenty-four hours on the average, we can say that there is a definite relationship between *arc* as measured in an east–west direction on the surface of the earth (which we saw in the last chapter is *longitude*) and *time*. If we divide 360° of arc around the earth, or longitude, by 24 hours, we see that it takes the sun one hour to go 15° of arc, or longitude. And, since the sun travels 15° in one hour, it must go 1° (60 minutes of arc) in 4 minutes (1/15 × 60 minutes = 4 minutes). Thus, 1° of longitude can be thought of as being equal to 4 minutes of time. This relationship is of basic importance both in navigation and in keeping time, as we will see.

KINDS OF TIME

The sun is the most convenient reference for reckoning time. Time measured by the sun is *solar time*. Solar time, or sun time, is based on the motion of the sun around the earth. Rotation of the earth on its axis produces apparent motion of the sun around it.

Apparent Time. Time based on the apparent position of the sun from our position is called *apparent time*. If the sun is directly over the meridian we are on, we say that it is noon, local apparent time. When it is directly over the meridian 180° away from ours, it is midnight local apparent time.

If the earth stood still in space, all the days reckoned by apparent time would be exactly the same length. But the earth travels around the sun in an elliptical orbit (like a race track). The earth's axis is inclined with respect to the plane of its orbit around the sun. The earth's speed along its orbit varies with its position in its orbit. Therefore, the time required for a complete rotation of the earth on its axis, relative to the sun, varies according to the position of the earth in its orbit. The length of a day, therefore, reckoned by a complete rotation of the earth with regard to the sun, also varies somewhat. From the standpoint of our calendar, this variation is made up with an extra day in February every fourth year, giving the "leap year" 366 days rather than the usual 365.

Mean Time. It would be confusing if some days

		Morning		Forenoon		Afternoon		Evening		Night	
		Watch		Watch		Watch		Watch		Watch	
Midwatch											
time	bells	time	bells	time	bells	time	bells	time	bells	time	bells
0030	1	0430	1	0830	1	1230	1	1630	1	2030	1
0100	2	0500	2	0900	2	1300	2	1700	2	2100	2
0130	3	0530	3	0930	3	1330	3	1730	3	2130	3
0200	4	0600	4	1000	4	1400	4	1800	4	2200	4
0230	5	0630	5	1030	5	1430	5	1830	5	2230	5
0300	6	0700	6	1100	6	1500	6	1900	6	2300	6
0330	7	0730	7	1130	7	1530	7	1930	7	2330	7
0400	8	0800	8	1200	8	1600	8	2000	8	2400	8

Relationship between ship's time, bells struck, and watches.

had more, and some fewer, hours because of the earth's revolution. To eliminate this confusion, an average solar time is used; this is called *mean solar time*. It is calculated from the motion around the earth of an imaginary sun, which always makes the 360° trip in exactly 24 hours. So when your watch says it is 1200, it is noon by local mean time (LMT)—that is, the *mean* sun is over your meridian, not the *true* sun.

The difference between apparent and mean time is called *the equation of time*. It is tabulated in navigational publications called *almanacs*, and must be taken into account for certain tasks in celestial navigation at sea.

Besides the above kinds of time that are based on the relationship of the earth and the sun, there is one other more modern base for time that is coming into ever wider use because of its extreme accuracy. This is *atomic time*, called *universal coordinated time*, abbreviated as UTC. This time is based on the frequency of vibrations of the radioactive cesium atom. Because cesium is a fairly common element, it is readily available to be used as a time standard everywhere on earth. Since GMT is based on the changing relative motion of the earth and the sun, and UTC is based on the unchanging cesium frequency, GMT and UTC can differ at certain times by as much as nine-tenths of a second. But the difference is usually smaller, and

can be disregarded for most navigational purposes. For more precise needs, the amount of difference at any time is readily available; so the user can easily correct UTC to GMT, or vice versa.

Zone Time (ZT) = Standard Time. Local mean time always differs in different longitudes because it is based on the relationship between your meridian and the mean sun. A slight difference in longitude results in a slight difference in time. Although it is important in determining position, this difference would be entirely impractical in normal living. For example, if we set our watches to local mean time (LMT), we would have to reset them every few blocks on an east–west street. In New York City, for instance, a difference of about nine seconds LMT occurs between one end of 42nd Street and the other end.

To eliminate this problem, *standard time zones* have been established around the world. All clocks and watches within a standard time zone are set to the same time. A difference of one hour takes place between one time zone and the next. Because one hour is 15°, each time zone is based on a division of the globe into 24 zones of 15° each. The standard time-zone system is fixed by international agreement and by law in each country.

The standard time zones begin at the Greenwich meridian (0°). Since the earth rotates toward the east, time zones to the west of Greenwich are earlier; to the east, the zones are later. Every meridian east and west of Greenwich that is a multiple of 15° (15°, 30°, 45°, 60°, and so on) is a standard time meridian. Each standard time meridian is at the center of its time zone, and the zone extends 7°30' (half of 15°) on either side of the meridian. Some standard time zones ashore vary somewhat from this, to make life easier for the people living there. Except for some island groups, however, the time-zone meridians at sea occur every 15° as mentioned. A diagram showing the standard time zones of the world is given on the next page.

Local mean time along each standard time meridian is *zone time,* or standard time for the entire time zone. Zone time in navigation is abbreviated ZT. Each time zone is identified by an alphabetical letter and by a negative or positive number from 1 to 12, east or west of the prime meridian. The number is called the *zone description* (ZD) of the zone. The plus and minus signs indicated in each zone of the map are added to or subtracted from local time to find Greenwich time.

To separate one day from the next, the 180th meridian has been designated the International Date Line. On both sides of the line, the time of day is the same, but west of the line it is one day later than it is to the east.

Daylight savings time is simply zone time set ahead one hour to extend the time of daylight in the evening, usually in summer. This is done strictly for convenience ashore in some localities. Daylight savings time is not used in navigation.

The continental United States has *four standard time zones.* Since North America is west of Greenwich, time zones are described by positive numbers and letters, in sequence from east to west. In the diagram, you will note that Eastern Standard Time (EST) is identified as +5 Romeo (R). This means that Eastern Standard Time plus five hours equals Greenwich ZT; another way of saying this is that Greenwich time is five hours ahead of EST.

Similarly, Central Standard Time is +6 Sierra (S), Mountain Standard Time is +7 Tango (T), and

Pacific Standard Time is +8 Uniform (U). You will note that most of Alaska and Hawaii are in the time zone +10 Whiskey (W).

Zone Time and GMT. Greenwich mean time (GMT) is the ZT at the Greenwich meridian. The Greenwich meridian is the standard time meridian for the time zone numbered 0. It has the zone description letter Zulu (Z). Most information in navigational tables and naval communications uses GMT, so you must know how to convert the time in any zone to GMT.

Remember that the solar day has twenty-four hours, and each time zone represents one hour. Beginning with the 0 zone (Greenwich), time zones run east and west from zone 1 to zone 12. Zones east of Greenwich are minus; those west of Greenwich are plus zones. (Note that the +12 and −12 zones each include only 7½° of longitude.) The zone description (ZD) tells you the difference in hours between your zone time and GMT. In zones east of Greenwich, you must subtract the zone number from the zone time to find Greenwich time. In zones west of Greenwich, you must add the zone number to the zone time to find Greenwich time. This procedure to go from zone time (ZT) to Greenwich time (GMT), or to go from GMT to ZT, can be reduced to the following simple algebraic formulas:

$$GMT = ZT + ZD \qquad ZT = GMT - ZD$$

In using the formulas, you must be careful to remember to use the rule of algebra that two minuses together make a plus. For example, if we were at a position in a time zone east of Greenwich where the zone description was −5, and we wanted to change a GMT of 0600 to our standard zone time, we would set up the formula like this:

$$
\begin{array}{ll}
\text{GMT} & 06\ 00 \\
\underline{-\ \text{ZD}\ -\ (-\ 5)} \\
=\ \text{ZT} & 11\ 00
\end{array}
$$

Standard time zones are also described by letters, as we noted earlier. In writing naval time, it is

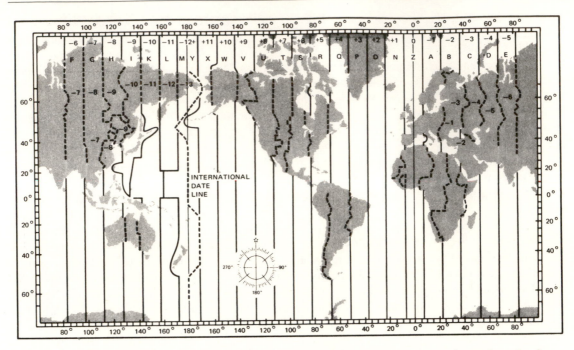

Standard time zones of the world. The prime meridian passes through Greenwich at 0 degrees longitude, and is the central meridian for the Zulu time zone. Zones to the west keep progressively earlier time, and those to the east, later time. The zone description numbers along the top must be added to zone time to find Greenwich time.

generally required to place a time zone's letter after the numbers. For instance, eleven o'clock in the morning in Norfolk, Virginia, zone time, would be written 1100R; 3:30 P.M. in San Diego would be written 1530U. This avoids confusion for the person reading that time.

Date/Time Group. Another aspect of naval time should be described here also. This involves the date, and occasionally the month and the year as well, in naval communications. Messages and other data keep coming twenty-four hours a day, every day of the month, and every month of the year. Therefore, there must be some way to identify exactly when a communication was originated or received. To do so, the Navy uses what is called the date/time group.

Let us assume that a message was originated at 1635Z on 15 April 1996. This would be placed in the message heading as 151635Z APR 96. The first six numbers and letter Z show the date, the time, and ZD for GMT. This part is called the date/time group (DTG). For further clarification, the month and year are also added.

Chapter 2. Study Guide Questions

1. Why do you suffer jet lag if you take a long east–west plane flight?

2. A. What is a chronometer?

B. To what time is the ship's chronometer usually set?

3. What do A.M. and P.M. mean?

4. Why does the Navy use the twenty-four-hour clock?

5. What time would it be on the twenty-four-hour clock for the following times?

A. 8:30 A.M.

B. 5:45 P.M.

C. 11:15 P.M.

D. midnight

6. A. How did telling time by ship's bell originate?

B. What is the maximum number of bells struck?

C. How many bells would be struck by the watch at 0200, 1030, 1600, and 1930?

7. What is the basic relationship between longitude (arc) and time?

8. A. Why does the length of each day vary slightly?

B. How do we make up this variation on the calendar?

9. What is mean solar time?

10. A. How have people made time-setting and time-keeping more practical?

B. How many degrees are in each time zone at sea?

11. How is each time zone identified?

12. How does the International Date Line define the time on each side of the 180th meridian?

13. What is daylight savings time?

14. What are the four standard time zones in the continental United States? Identify each with its numerical and alphabetical ZD.

15. What is the zone description (ZD) of Greenwich?

16. Change the following zone times to Greenwich mean times:

A. 1200 at San Francisco (ZD = +8)

B. 1700 at Norfolk (ZD = +5)

C. 0600 at Rome, Italy (ZD = −1)

17. Change the following Greenwich mean times to zone times at the locations in the previous question:

A. GMT 0800

B. GMT 1600

18. What are the date/time groups for the following:

A. 0835 local time in Norfolk, Virginia, on 23 March 1996?

B. 7:30 P.M. in San Diego, California, on 17 May 1996?

C. The date and time this assignment is due at your location?

Vocabulary

jet lag	local mean time
celestial navigation	(LMT)
chronometer	zone time (ZT)
astronomy	zone description (ZD)
solar time	Greenwich mean time
mean time	(GMT)
apparent time	coordinated universal
gimbals	time (UTC)
rotation (of earth)	date/time group
revolution (of earth)	(DTG)
elliptical orbit	originate (a message)
standard time zone	

Basic Seamanship

Chapter 1.   Marlinspike Seamanship

The first requirement of everyone who sails in the ships of the U.S. Navy is seamanship. Seamanship has three main parts: the art and skill of handling a vessel, skill in the use of deck equipment, and the care and use of various kinds of line, called marlinspike seamanship. On board ship, the people most concerned with seamanship every day are those in the deck department. Sailors who work in the ship's office, radio shack, or engineroom may not be called upon for much seamanship in their normal everyday duties. This does not mean, however, that seamanship is unimportant for them.

Seamanship is the skill that ties every member of the Navy together. Whether one is an admiral or a seaman, one wears a uniform that says he or she is familiar with the art of seamanship. Regardless of what job specialty a sailor selects, that sailor first becomes a *seaman,* and then a technician. The pride with which a person performs seamanship duties will carry over into the specialty ratings.

Many times, especially in smaller ships, everyone must help the deck force. Enlisted persons may have to carry stores on board, assist in replenishment, or help in mooring or unmooring the ship. Officers are expected to be able to supervise all such activities. In emergencies or general quar-

ters, all hands may have to do all manner of seamanship evolutions from manning guns, standing lookout watches, or handling boats, to fighting fires. All departments must keep their spaces (compartments) clean and painted, exercise good safety procedures, and do preventive maintenance of their equipment.

THE FIRST LIEUTENANT

We have already talked some about the first lieutenant in an earlier chapter on shipboard organization. This officer is in charge of the deck department. The title goes back into the early days of British naval sailing ships. Then, the captain was served by a number of lieutenants, each in charge of a division. The first lieutenant was the most senior and knowledgeable in the business of working and maneuvering a man-of-war under sail. He therefore was the specialist in *seamanship.* This title has survived to this day.

The first lieutenant is in charge of deck evolutions and repair and care of the ship's exterior, and in control of the paint, sail, and boatswain's lockers. This officer is in charge of life boats and rafts, life jackets, and other survival equipment. He or she sees that all gear about the weather decks is properly secured. The first lieutenant is in charge of any cargo loading or offloading operations.

Good seamanship is very important to sailors. These Naval Academy midshipmen are learning seamanship on board one of the Academy's sail boats. Many college NROTC units also offer sail training.

To provide him or her technical expertise in deck evolutions, the ship's boatswain (spoken bos'n), a highly qualified warrant or senior petty officer, is the right-hand assistant.

DECK PERSONNEL

The personnel under the first lieutenant who carry out most seamanship duties are members of one or more deck divisions, depending upon the size of the ship. Most large auxiliaries and amphibious ships have three deck divisions. The first division has charge of the forward part of the ship; the second, the ship's boats and boat decks; and the third, the after part of the ship.

On ships having aviation personnel aboard, nonaviation personnel, especially those in the deck department, are traditionally referred to as "blackshoes," while aviation personnel are collectively called "brownshoes." These nicknames refer to the shoe colors of surface line officers who wear black

shoes, as opposed to naval aviators who by custom wear brown shoes and khaki uniforms.

SEAMEN

The seaman apprentice (SA) reporting on board ship from boot camp (recruit training) is usually assigned to one of the deck divisions. These new personnel do the physical work that must be done in any ship in the deck department. This includes upkeep of ship's compartments, living areas, decks, and external surfaces. Also, it includes the deck watches such as helmsman, lookout, messenger under way and in port, and other special watches such as sentry duty and anchor watches. During general quarters, seamen are members of gun crews and damage-control parties. During seamanship tasks, they will operate small boats, booms, cranes, and winches.

Before a seaman apprentice (E-2) can become a striker for advancement to a specialty rating, he or she must first satisfy the requirements for seaman (E-3). To qualify for this rate, the E-2 must prove competent at marlinspike, deck, and boat seamanship. He or she must be able to do these things to the satisfaction of the leading petty officers and division officer, and take a written exam on deck seamanship.

BOATSWAIN'S MATES

The supervisors in deck divisions are boatswain's mates. They direct and train seamen in military duties and in all activities that have to do with marlinspike, deck, and boat seamanship. They also act as petty officers in charge of gun crews and damage-control parties during general quarters. Under way, they stand boatswain's mate of the watch on the bridge; in port they stand petty officer of the watch on the quarterdeck. During replenishment operations under way, boatswain's mates have most of the key jobs at the transfer stations.

The boatswain's mates on board ship have much influence on their enlisted. They spend most of their day supervising seamen. They have the responsibility of training, and working with, almost every new person reporting on board ship. Many

A boatswain's mate striker weaves a fender to protect the sides of his ship. Seamen must be able to do lots of marlinspike seamanship seawork such as this.

The *marlinspike* is a tapered steel tool used for separating strands of rope. It is the basic tool of the seaman, and has become the symbolic "tool of the trade."

Marlinspike seamanship concerns the use and care of fiber line used at sea. It includes every kind of knotting and splicing, as well as all fancywork done with rope, twine, and cord.

It takes knowledge and skill to become proficient in marlinspike seamanship. A good seaman has a real affection for a sound piece of line or a good square knot or splice. One look at the way a person handles a line tells experienced people whether or not that person is a seaman. It is not a difficult art, but it takes time, patience, and practice to learn well. Knowledge of marlinspike seamanship is the real test for deck sailors, and is most important to their chances for advancement in rate.

The rest of this chapter will deal with the types, care, makeup, and use of rope. Many NJROTC cadets will want to try their hand at tying knots, and some may even wish to do some fancy or ornamental work. It can be fun, as well as practical.

Rope is a general term that can be applied to both fiber and wire. In the Navy, though, fiber rope is called *line.* Fiber rope is called rope as long as it is still in its original coil. Once the rope has been uncoiled and cut for use, it is not called rope anymore. Wire rope is called wire rope, or just *wire.*

Most rope used on board ship is made of natural or man-made fiber. Fiber rope is made of nylon or of the fibers of various plants (manila, sisal, hemp, cotton, and flax) which are twisted together in one direction to form yarns or threads. These *yarns* or *threads* are twisted together in the opposite direction to form the strands, which are in turn twisted together in the opposite direction to form the line. General-purpose ropes made in this manner are known as *plain-laid.*

The degree of twist of the strands or the type of lay of the strands will cause the strength of different types of line to vary. For instance, hard twist-

people receive their first impressions of shipboard life in the deck division. The work is often hard, and the hours are long. Seamen are often in the open, exposed to the weather. The life of a deck seaman is demanding, so the leadership of boatswain's mates is very important.

In larger ships, the first lieutenant often has a chief warrant boatswain as an assistant, in addition to deck division officers. In such cases, this officer is called the *ship's boatswain.* The senior chief boatswain's mate will serve as the *leading boatswain's mate,* and assists the ship's boatswain. First-class boatswain's mates serve as division petty officers.

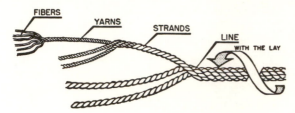

The construction of rope. The fibers of various plants or synthetics are twisted together in one direction to form *yarns*; the yarns are twisted together in the opposite direction to form *strands*; then the strands are twisted together in the opposite direction to form the rope. Rope formed in this way is called *plain-laid* rope.

ing increases the friction that holds the rope together and makes it less likely to absorb moisture. But too many twists reduces the strength of the fibers. Most line used on board ship is three-strand, plain-laid, and has a right-hand twist or lay. *Right-laid* line must always be coiled down right-handed or clockwise.

Single- or *double-braided* rope is also carried on board ship for such things as lines for hoisting signal flags (halyards). Braided rope will not unlay or twist when it is free to rotate on swivels as signal halyards must do. Plain-laid rope will tend to unlay or twist under similar conditions.

Of the natural fibers, *manila* is the strongest and most expensive. It is made from the fibers of the abacá, or wild banana plant, raised chiefly in the Philippines (hence the name, manila). It is reserved for uses such as towing lines, mooring lines, and lines for personnel transfers at sea.

Length of line is normally measured in fathoms (1 fathom = 6 feet). However, *sizes* of lines are identified and measured by circumference.

The largest line used for general shipboard purposes in the Navy is 10-inch, normally referred to as a hawser. A *hawser* is the name given to any rope larger than 5 inches in circumference that is generally used for towing or mooring. Five-inch manila is used for personnel high-line rigs in most cases. Any small stuff less than six-thread is called

by name rather than by the number of threads.

Line less than 1¾ inches in circumference is called *small stuff*, and identified by the number of threads in the line. Twenty-four thread, with about 1¾-inch circumference, is the largest small stuff. Other sizes of small stuff are twenty-one-thread (1½-inch), fifteen-thread (1¼-inch), twelve thread (1⅛-inch), nine-thread (1-inch), and six-thread (¾-inch).

Marline is the most common small stuff referred to by name. It is made of two-stranded, left-laid, tarred hemp. It is not much larger than ordinary household wrapping cord. It is most often used for *serving*, or covering a larger line for protection from abrasion. *Seizing stuff* is similar to marline, though stronger because it is three-stranded and right-laid. *Small white line* is made from cotton or flax and is used for lead lines, signal halyards, and the like. It is like household "clothes line."

Plain-laid, cable-laid, and braided *nylon lines* are much used in the fleet today. Nylon line is more expensive than manila, but it has several advantages. Nylon is nearly three times as strong and lasts five times as long as manila. For these reasons, nylon is often cheaper in the long run, even though its initial cost is greater than that of manila. Nylon has largely replaced manila for mooring and towing lines and for boat falls.

Nylon does not rot or age as rapidly as natural fiber, so it keeps its strength better throughout its life. It is also less bulky, requires less stowage space, and is more flexible, making it easier to handle. Nylon is practically waterproof. It does not decay, and resists marine fungus growths.

Nylon also stretches more than manila under load. For this reason it is not used for transferring people or cargo from ship to ship by highline. It will stretch about 50 percent before breaking, but when it does, it snaps like a rubber band—so it can be very dangerous under heavy strain.

Although *wire rope* has not been in general use for some years, some ships still use it for situations where extra strength is required, such as when storms or high winds are expected. Because such rope tends to form spurs or burrs on the surface over time, since wire strands break, people should always wear heavy leather work gloves when handling this type of line. They should take care not to rub against it with other parts of the body, since the sharp burrs can easily pierce light clothing.

HANDLING FIBER LINE

When preparing to use any line larger than small stuff, it is usually a good idea to lay it out on deck in one of several established ways. Doing so will contribute to ease in handling the line, plus help to avoid kinks in the line as it is run out. It also contributes to the shipshape and seamanlike appearance of the ship or boat.

Coiling down a line means to lay it in circles on the deck, roughly one coil or circle on top of the other. Right-laid line is always coiled down in a clockwise direction and left-laid line in a counter-clockwise direction. Coiling down in the wrong direction results in annoying and possibly dangerous kinks and twists. When a line is coiled down, the end on top is ready for running. Coiling is the fastest way of making up line or wire, and the most common.

Faking down a line is to lay it out in long, flat rows on the deck, one alongside the other. The main advantage of working with line that is properly faked down is that it runs off with little chance of fouling, or kinking. This method is used for readying mooring lines before coming in to a pier.

A third method sailors use in ships and boats for laying down short lengths of line is *flemishing*. To flemish down a line is to lay it down in a flat helical coil on the deck, somewhat like a wound clock spring, with the *bitter end* (end of the line) in the center. The line is laid down loosely, and wound tight to form a "mat" by placing the hands flat on the line and twisting in the direction the line is laid.

Most rope and lines on board ship are stowed in the boatswain's locker. This is a compartment, usually in the forward part of the ship, set aside to hold all the line, wire, and tools used by the deck force.

Faking down a line on the forecastle of a destroyer.

Flemishing down a line. The bitter end is in the center.

Coils of rope are stored on shelves or platforms clear of the deck so they will stay dry. They should not be covered, but should be open to the air, since natural fiber is apt to mildew and rot if damp. Small stuff is stored on a shelf in order of size, with the starting end of the line out for easy reach.

The bitter end of a line should always be *whipped* to prevent it from unlaying, or fraying. A good seaman cannot stand to see a good piece of line frazzled out. To prevent such fraying, a temporary plain whipping can be put on with a piece of small stuff. The whipping line is laid down along the line and bound down with a couple of turns. Then the other end of the whipping should be laid on the opposite way and bound a couple of turns from the bight of the whipping and pulled tight.

A permanent whipping is put on with a palm and needle. A *palm* is a tough piece of leather that fits into the palm of the seaman's hand, serving somewhat the same purpose as a thimble. This is rarely done to line or rope smaller than 1¾ inches, but normally is done with larger lines.

The bitter end of a nylon line is usually secured by taping the end of each strand and then taping all strands together and fusing the end of the line with a hot iron or torch. The heat will melt and fuse the line together.

A good rule to remember with any line is that all loose ends must be cut or tucked. These rules of whipping and tucking are necessary if the ship is to maintain a smart, shipshape appearance. Attention to such detail is important; the ship that takes care of such details usually performs well.

Wet fiber lines should be dried thoroughly before stowing. If this can't be done, the line should be faked out on gratings under cover so it can dry as quickly as possible. All fiber lines shrink when wet and stretch again when dried out. For this reason, wet lines in use should be slackened when the weather becomes damp or lines become wet with rain.

A line with a kink should never be placed under strain. A heavy strain on a kinked or twisted line will cause permanent distortion or damage, seriously weakening the line. When a kink has been forced into each strand, it is impossible to work it out.

Whipping lines. The bitter end of a line should always be whipped (wrapped) to prevent it from unlaying. Whipping is done with a palm and needle.

Line will weaken with use and exposure. It will gradually change its color from yellowish-white to gray. It is necessary to inspect the *inner* part of a line to determine its real condition, however. The strands are unlaid either by hand or with a *fid*, a pointed, round, tapered wooden tool designed for splicing fiber lines. If weakened, the yarns will show bristles and a decrease in diameter. Lines in such weakened condition should not be used, and never for supporting people aloft or over the side.

Natural fiber line under heavy strain will make cracking noises as the strands work against a nearby surface or themselves. When such noises increase in intensity, this is a warning that the line may part. A visible sign of such strain will appear in the form of a steamlike vapor over a weakening area if the line is wet. Nylon may not emit such noises unless against a cleat or bitt, but will stretch and show the steamlike vapor. Fiber line will

HOLD THE STRAND UP WITH
FINGER AND THUMB BEFORE
YOU PULL OUT THE FID

Working the *fid* to separate and splice lines.

stretch very little, even under heavy strain. Natural fiber line will lose about 30 percent of its strength over a two-year period with normal careful use.

KNOTS, BENDS, AND HITCHES

The term "knot" is often used as an all-inclusive term, but experienced seamen distinguish between knots, bends, and hitches.

Knots are used to form eyes or to secure a cord or line around an object such as a package. Generally they are intended to be permanent, so they are hard to untie. *Hitches* are used to bend a line to or around an object such as a ring or stanchion (a metal or wooden pole) or another piece of line, or to form a loop or a noose in a line. *Bends* are used to secure lines together.

Most Navy men and women are expected to know the square knot, bowline, and single and double becket bends, and the round turn and two half hitches. Most also should know the clove hitch. These knots are explained and illustrated here to give you some guidelines to go by in your own seamanship practice. Besides that, it's fun!

To understand these knot-tying procedures, see the figure above, which illustrates a few terms used in describing knot tying.

The *square knot*, also called the reef knot, is the best-known knot for bending two lines together. It can also be made to secure small stuff around a package. It will not slip, but it can jam under heavy strain. It can be loosened by pulling first one and then the other end.

A landlubber trying to tie a square knot often comes out with a *granny knot*. For a square knot, *both* parts of the line must be under the same bight.

Here is the proper way to tie a square knot: Take the end in your right hand, and pass it over and under the part in your left hand. With your right hand, take the end that was in your left, and pass it under and over the part in your left hand.

The *bowline* is one of the most useful knots. It has many variations. The chief use of the bowline is to form an eye, but it also can secure a line to a padeye or other ring, around a stanchion or other object, or to bend two lines together. The bowline neither slips nor jams, but it ties and unties easily. It is the best knot to use for bending a heaving line or messenger to the eye of a hawser because it is quick to tie and easy to get off.

The easiest and most seamanlike method of making a bowline is as follows: Form a bight (loop in the line) and grasp a single part of the line with the left hand, and both parts of the line with the right hand, as shown in the figure opposite. Turn the right hand down, pushing the bitter end through the bight, and then rotate the right hand palm up. With the left hand, form a small loop around the bitter end and grasp both parts of the line where the loop crosses the standing part. Pass the bitter end around behind the standing part and down through the small loop. Tighten the knot as shown in the figure.

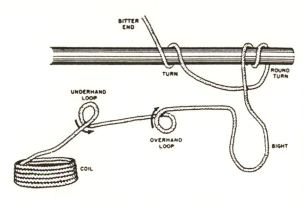

BITTER
END

TURN

ROUND
TURN

UNDERHAND
LOOP

OVERHAND
LOOP

BIGHT

COIL

Terms used in tying knots, bends, and hitches.

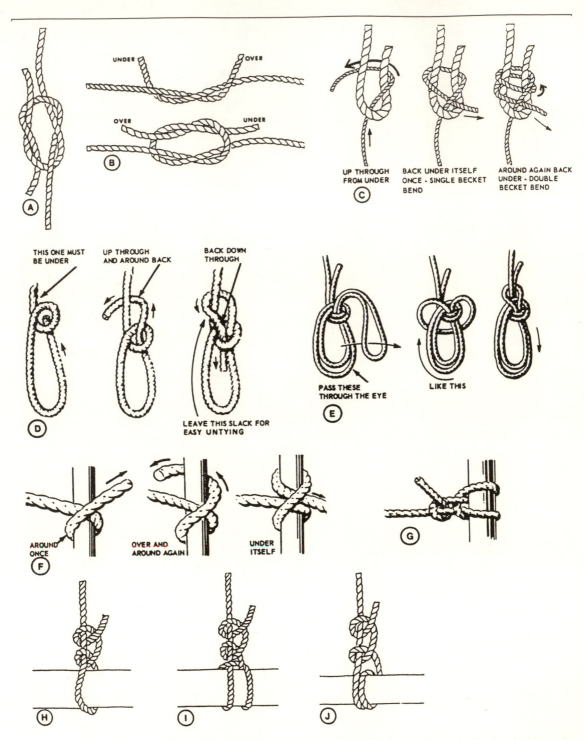

Knots, bends, and hitches. A—Granny knot. B—Square knot. C—Becket bends, single and double. D—Bowline. E—Bowline on a bight. F—Clove hitch. G—Clove hitch and single half hitch. H—Two half hitches. I—Clove hitch with two half hitches. J—Round turn with two half hitches.

The chief value of the *becket bend* is to bend together two lines of different sizes. If there is a great difference in sizes, or the strain on the line is to be great, a double becket bend should be used. A becket bend is as good as a square knot, and much easier to untie after strain.

To fashion a single becket bend, make a bight on one line and run the bitter end of the other line up through it. Pass the end around behind both parts of the bight and back under itself. The third step, to make a double becket, is made by taking another turn around the bight.

The *clove hitch* is the best all-around knot for bending to a ring, spar, or anything else that is round or nearly round. A clove hitch will not jam and will rarely pull out. A slack clove hitch can work itself out, though. For that reason, it is a good idea to put a half hitch on the end of it.

The clove hitch can be easily tied, and it will hold as long as there is a strain on it. Once the strain is taken off, however, the hitch must be checked and tightened to prevent the bitter end from pulling out when the strain is reapplied—again, a good reason to add a half hitch to the clove hitch.

To tie this hitch, take a turn with the bitter end, and pass the end across the standing part, and take another turn. (Notice that both turns go around in the same direction.) Now, pass the end under itself, and the hitch is complete.

Another way to make the clove hitch is to form two underhand loops. Lay the second loop on top of the first. This method is the usual way to form the hitch when it can be slipped over the end of the object to which the line is to be secured.

Since the clove hitch may slide along a slippery spar, the round turn with two half hitches is often used.

The chief advantage of the *round turn and two half hitches* is that it will not slip along the object to which it is secured. If the angle of pull is acute (less than 90°), this hitch should be used. The round turn and two half hitches is especially useful on a spar (pole) because it grips tightly and holds its position.

This hitch is made by taking a round turn and making two half hitches. (The two half hitches actually consist of a clove hitch taken around the line itself.)

Securing for Sea. Knots, bends, and hitches are necessary to ensure the safety of persons working, for many seamanship evolutions, and for securing equipment to prevent damage during rough seas. You can never underestimate the force of the sea!

Lines must be in good shape and strong enough to hold the gear and people who depend on them. For heavy weather, all objects must be lashed tightly against something solid. The lines should be taut so the object will not "work" with the pitch and roll of the ship. Chafing gear should be placed under lines to prevent wearing on sharp corners and rough surfaces. Lines should never be tied to electric cables, small piping, or other movable objects.

Safety first is always the rule when working with lines and wires.

Chapter 1. Study Guide Questions

1. What is the first requirement for personnel who sail in naval ships?

2. A. What is seamanship?

B. Which shipboard department is concerned with seamanship as its primary duty?

3. What is meant by the statement that "one is first a *seaman,* and then a technician"?

4. Which officer is in charge of the deck department?

5. What are the main duties of the ship's boatswain?

6. What must a seaman apprentice accomplish in order to advance to pay grade E-3?

7. What is marlinspike seamanship?

8. A. What is rope?

B. When does the term *line* come into use in the Navy?

C. Of what materials is rope made?

9. What is the most common line used on board ship?

10. A. What is the strongest of the natural fibers?

B. What are its principal uses on board ship?

11. A. How is the length of line measured?
     B. How is the size of line identified?

12. What is the name given to rope larger than 5 inches in circumference?

13. What is line under 1¾ inches in circumference called?

14. What is marline, and what is it used for?

15. What is seizing stuff?

16. A. Why is nylon line in common use in the fleet today?
     B. What is a disadvantage of nylon line?

17. What is the bitter end of a line?

18. Where are most rope and lines stowed in a ship?

19. What is the purpose of whipping a line or rope?

20. Why should loose ends of line be whipped or tucked?

21. A. What is a fid?
     B. What is it used for?

22. What special safety precautions should be observed when handling wire rope?

23. What is the difference between a knot, a bend, and a hitch?

24. What is the best knot for securing small stuff around a package?

25. What is the bight of a line?

26. What is the best knot for bending together two lines of different sizes?

27. A. What is chafing gear?
     B. What is always the rule when working with lines and wires?

Vocabulary

marlinspike seamanship	fishhook (wire rope)
rope	corrosion
line	graphite grease
wire rope	splicing
fiber	rigger's screw
yarn, thread	knots, bends, hitches
strand	sisal
abrasion	hawser
cable	small stuff
clockwise	marline
counterclockwise	serving
halyard	seizing stuff
manila	coiling down
circumference	messenger line
faking down	bight of line
flemishing down	square knot
bitter end	bowline
fid	pitch and roll
tensile strength	chafing gear
galvanize	lash down
spring-lay rope	spurs, burrs

Chapter 2. Ground Tackle and Deck Equipment

Deck equipment consists of all equipment used in deck seamanship. This equipment is normally operated by the deck force. The anchors and chains and all equipment associated with anchoring are fundamental to the business of deck seamanship; they are called *ground tackle* (pronounced tāy'cul). Other deck equipment has to do with mooring the ship, including the deck fittings to which lines are made fast. A third major group of deck equipment is the rigging and booms, which are used to handle cargo.

In this chapter we will discuss some of the basic information about these most important equipments. Different size ships will have different size equipments, but all ships have this basic gear.

GROUND TACKLE

Ground tackle is the equipment used in anchoring and mooring with anchors. It includes anchors, anchor cables and chains, and all chain cable parts such as chain stoppers, shackles, detachable chain links, mooring swivels, and the tools used to work this and other chain parts. It also includes the *anchor windlass,* the machinery used to lift, or weigh, the anchor and its cable.

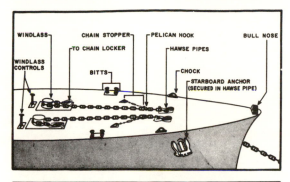

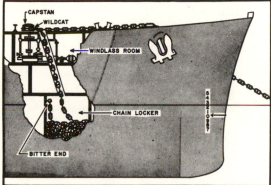

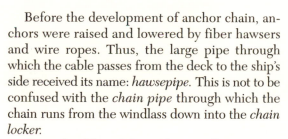

The ground tackle in the forecastle of a typical ship.

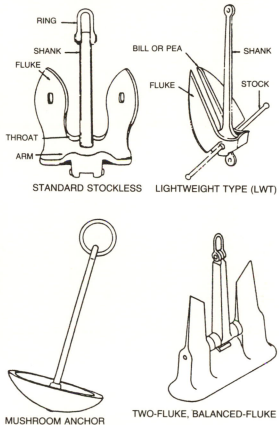

The four major types of anchors used by U.S. naval ships.

Before the development of anchor chain, anchors were raised and lowered by fiber hawsers and wire ropes. Thus, the large pipe through which the cable passes from the deck to the ship's side received its name: *hawsepipe*. This is not to be confused with the *chain pipe* through which the chain runs from the windlass down into the *chain locker*.

Ground tackle and the anchor windlass are very important to a ship. All officers and members of the desk force must know about this gear.

ANCHORS

Anchors used by the Navy today are grouped into four types: the patent or stockless anchors, the mushroom anchor, the lightweight anchors, and the two-fluke, balanced-fluke anchor.

When a ship has one anchor down, she is *an-chored*. When she has two anchors down and swings from a mooring swivel connected to both, she is *moored*. (A ship made fast to a dock with lines or to a buoy with an anchor chain is also moored.) In a Mediterranean moor, a ship usually has the stern moored to a pier, and an anchor out on each side of the bow. An anchor carried aft and used by amphibious ships to pull, or retract, themselves off the beach is called a *stern anchor*.

Most naval ships have *patent* or *stockless anchors* because they are easy to stow and handle. They can be raised directly into the hawsepipe because there is no long stock. Stockless anchors are also called *bower anchors* because they are always carried on and used from the bow. The arms, or *flukes,* of this kind of anchor can swing to either side to permit the anchor to dig into the harbor bottom. The largest stockless anchors weigh 30 tons and are used on aircraft carriers.

The *mushroom anchor* is now being issued to new submarines so they can anchor even when submerged. The mushroom is also used to anchor buoys and torpedo testing barges.

Lightweight (LWT) *anchors* are relatively new, and have been used mostly for small craft until recently. The LWT anchor has a short stock, which makes it easy to stow in the hawsepipe. The LWT anchor tends to bury itself deep in the bottom when under strain, and has better holding power than the stockless anchor. Also, an LWT anchor only half the size of a stockless has the same holding power as a stockless anchor. This makes the cost of the anchor and the gear to handle it much lower. Most new destroyers, frigates, and cruisers have LWT anchors that are bower anchors.

The *two-fluke, balanced-fluke anchor* is used for anchoring some new surface ships and the newest submarines. It is housed in the bottom of the ship. It is used on board some surface ships in place of a bower anchor, in order to prevent interference with the ship's bow sonar dome.

ANCHOR CHAINS AND RELATED EQUIPMENT

Even though it is made up of links, an anchor chain is usually called an *anchor cable* by custom. Modern naval anchor chain is made of high-strength steel links. The size of chain varies according to the size of the ship and her anchors. All links are studded—that is, a solid piece is welded in the center of the link to prevent chain kinking.

To give you some idea of the weight of a large anchor chain, a *single link* of a large aircraft carrier chain weighs about 250 pounds! Most ships are equipped with two anchors and two chains.

The lengths of chain that make up the ship's anchor cable are called *shots.* A standard shot is 15 fathoms, or 90 feet, in length. Shots are connected by *detachable links,* painted red, white, or blue to let the anchor detail know how much chain has run out.

The number of adjacent links painted white in-

dicates the shot number. Each link of the next-to-last shot is painted yellow. The entire last shot is painted red. This is to warn that the chain is out almost to its bitter end.

Shot Number	Color of Detachable Link	Number of Adjacent Links Painted White
1 (15 fathoms)	Red	1
2 (30 fathoms)	White	2
3 (45 fathoms)	Blue	3
4 (60 fathoms)	Red	4
5 (75 fathoms)	White	5
6 (90 fathoms)	Blue	6
And so on.		

On board most ships, standard short *swivel shots* called "bending shots" attach the anchor chain to the anchor. These swivel shots consist of detachable links, regular chain links, a swivel, an end link, and a bending shackle (see the illustration on page 261). The *bending shackle* itself is attached to the anchor shackle.

Chain stoppers are made up of a *turnbuckle* inserted in a short section of chain. A *pelican hook* is attached to one end of the chain, a shackle at the other. They are used for holding the anchor taut in the hawsepipe, or for holding an anchor and its swivel shot when they are disconnected from the chain.

ANCHOR WINDLASS

An *anchor windlass* is the machine used to hoist a bow anchor. A ship with a stern anchor has a stern-anchor winch to hoist it. On board combatant ships the anchor windlass is a vertical type with control, friction brake handwheel, capstan, and wildcat above deck, and an electric and hydraulic drive for the wildcat and capstan below deck. Auxiliary ships have a horizontal windlass that is above deck, with two wildcats, one for each anchor. The *capstan,* or *warping head,* is the line-handling drum on top of the shaft of the anchor windlass. Just below the capstan is the drum or *wildcat,* which contains teeth (whelps) that *engage* (fit in) the links of the anchor chain and prevent it

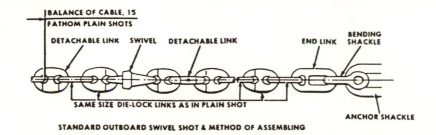

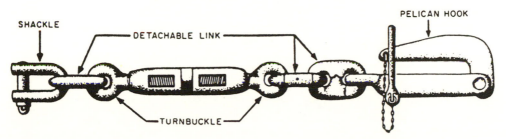

The swivel shot, or bending shot, used to attach the anchor chain to the anchor. The chain stopper (bottom) is used to hold the anchor tight in the hawsepipe, or to hold the anchor if it is detached from its chain for any reason.

from slipping. The wildcat is fitted with a brake to stop the chain at the desired length or scope.

ANCHORING

The first lieutenant is in charge of the *anchor detail* on the forecastle while anchoring and weighing anchor. Either the ship's boatswain or a chief boatswain's mate assists the first lieutenant. A person from the auxiliary machinery division and an electrician's mate, both from the engineering department, are in the anchor windlass room to handle any problems with the equipment. The first lieutenant is in direct contact with the bridge by sound-powered telephone.

Letting Go. In preparing to anchor, all but one of the stoppers are removed, and the brake is released so the anchor is supported only by the remaining stopper. If the ship is anchoring in deep water, the anchor may be walked out slowly by the engine. With all in readiness, the first lieutenant orders all hands (except the person with the sledgehammer to release the last stopper) to stand clear of the chain. This is a safety precaution because nothing will stand in the way of the rapidly moving chain once the stopper is released. On the order "Let go," the pelican hook is knocked open with the sledgehammer.

As the chain runs out, a report is made of the amount, strain, and angle relative to the bow, as: "Thirty fathoms on deck, sir; chain tending at six o'clock; no strain." The word "tend" indicates the direction of the chain relative to the bow, given in terms of clock direction. (Six o'clock would be tending aft, nine o'clock would be tending 270°R on the port beam.) Strain on the chain may be reported as light, moderate, heavy, or no strain.

Scope of Chain. The amount of chain played out (veered) is known as the *scope of chain* used to anchor. Normally a ship anchors in water less than 20 fathoms. Under favorable sea conditions, most commanding officers use a scope of chain that is five to seven times the depth of the water, with six times the depth being a common rule of thumb.

With the chain veered to proper scope, it should hang in a slight *catenary* (downward curve). If too taut, it is apt to drag. Loud rumbles will be heard if it drags on a rocky bottom, and vibrations may be felt on a mud bottom.

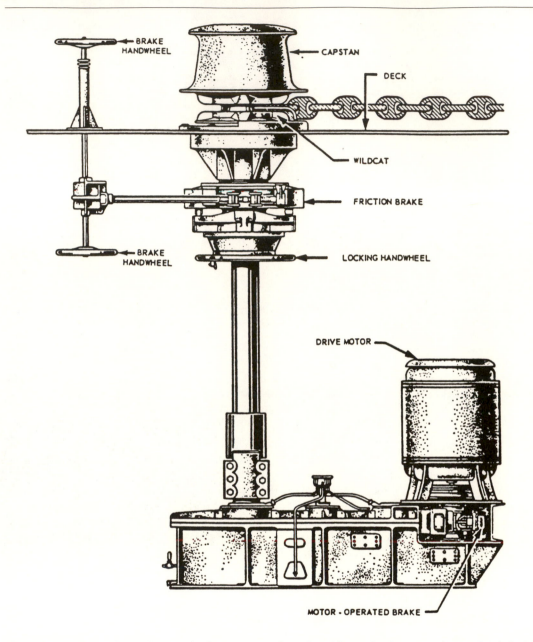

The anchor windlass is the machine used to hoist a bow anchor. The wildcat under the capstan has teeth (whelps) that engage the links of the anchor chain.

Weighing Anchor. Before the anchor is hoisted, the windlass engine is tested. The wildcat is engaged with the shaft, the brake released, a strain taken on the chain, and the stoppers are cast loose.

Just before the ship gets under way, the anchor is usually heaved in to short stay. This is a condition in which there is no more chain out than is necessary to keep from breaking the anchor loose from the bottom. Only the officer of the deck can order heaving to short stay, and only after receiving permission from the captain.

When the ship is ready to get under way, the anchor is heaved in as ordered from the bridge. The amount of chain out is reported to the bridge from time to time, usually when shot markers are at the water's edge. (Examples: "Fifteen fathoms at the water's edge, sir," and when the anchor is at short stay, up and down, aweigh, in sight, and secured for sea and ready for letting go.)

As the chain comes in, it is hosed off to remove mud. Usually, the markings are repainted. Some links of each shot are tested by striking them with a hammer. All links are tested if the chain was subjected to a heavy strain. If a link rings, it is all right; if it sounds flat, it may be damaged, and in this event, it must be marked and the first lieutenant notified immediately.

MOORING

A ship is moored when she is made fast to a mooring buoy, when she is swinging on a bight of chain between two anchors, or when she is secured by lines alongside a pier or another ship. Mooring a ship to a bier, buoy, or another ship, and unmooring, are some of the most basic jobs of the deck department. These tasks require skillful use of mooring lines and deck winches. Deck fittings such as cleats, bitts, bollards, chocks, and towing padeyes are used in the process. Quick, efficient line handling when coming alongside or getting under way is one of the marks of a smart ship.

Deck and Pier Fittings. The fittings used in mooring and unmooring are important to the use of mooring lines. Sailors must know when and how to use these fittings to do a smart job of line handling.

A *cleat* is a device welded to the deck that looks

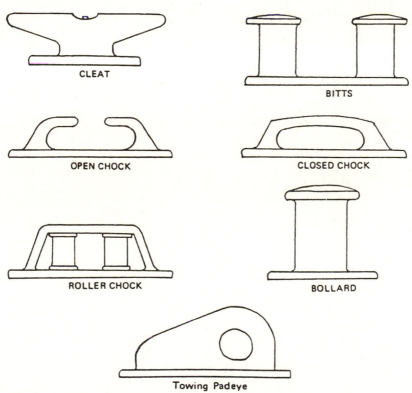

CLEAT

BITTS

OPEN CHOCK

CLOSED CHOCK

ROLLER CHOCK

BOLLARD

Towing Padeye

Deck fittings are needed for the mooring lines. All the fittings shown above are found on board ships except for the bollard, which is a pier fitting. The towing padeye is used as the attachment for a towing hawser.

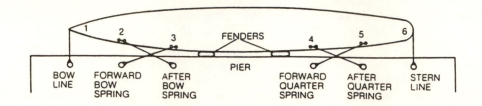

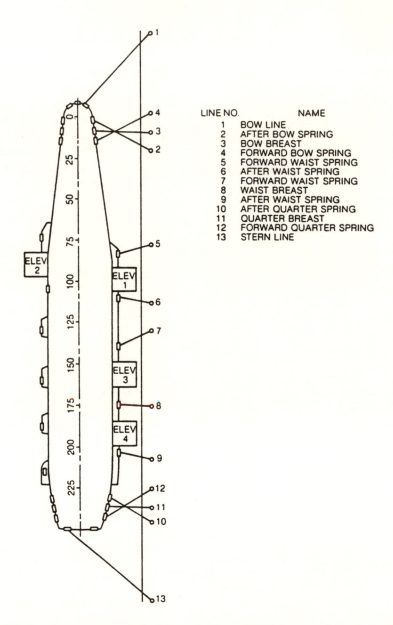

LINE NO.	NAME
1	BOW LINE
2	AFTER BOW SPRING
3	BOW BREAST
4	FORWARD BOW SPRING
5	FORWARD WAIST SPRING
6	AFTER WAIST SPRING
7	FORWARD WAIST SPRING
8	WAIST BREAST
9	AFTER WAIST SPRING
10	AFTER QUARTER SPRING
11	QUARTER BREAST
12	FORWARD QUARTER SPRING
13	STERN LINE

The standard mooring line patterns and their names for a large ship such as a carrier and a small one such as a destroyer.

like a pair of projecting horns. It is used for belaying a line or wire.

Bitts are cylindrical objects made of steel implanted in the deck. They are arranged in pairs, each pair mounted on a separate footing. Usually there is a set of bitts forward and abaft of each chock for use in belaying mooring lines.

A *chock* is a heavy fitting with smooth surfaces through which mooring lines are led. Mooring lines are run from bitts on deck through chocks to bollards on the pier when a ship is moored. Chocks are of three kinds: (1) *open chock*, a mooring chock, open at the top; (2) *closed chock*, a mooring chock closed by an arch of metal across its top; and (3) *roller chock*, a mooring chock that contains a roller for reducing friction.

A *bollard* is a strong cylindrical upright on a pier, around which the eye or bight of a ship's mooring line is thrown.

A *towing padeye* is a large padeye of extra strength that is used in towing operations. It has a hole in the upright plate through which attachments can be made.

MOORING LINES TO A PIER

Ships are moored to piers, wharves, and other ships with a set of mooring lines. In general, they are as light as possible to ease handling. They are also strong enough to take a big strain during mooring, and to hold a ship in place when secured.

Mooring lines are numbered from forward to aft in the order that they are run out from the ship. Ships are normally moored with six lines, though large ships may use seven or eight, aircraft carriers thirteen, and small ships as few as four. In any event, the lines are grouped according to their use as bow, stern, spring, or breast lines.

The *bow line,* line one, is the mooring line that runs through the bullnose or chock nearest the bow or eyes of the ship. On board larger ships this line is led well up the pier to stop the ship from moving aft; similarly the *stern line,* line six, is led down the aft to stop any forward motion of the ship. With destroyers, however, lines one and six lead directly to the pier to serve as breast lines, explained below. Bow *spring lines,* lines two and

three, lead fore and aft at an angle and control the fore-and-aft movement of the ship. Quarter spring lines, lines four and five, do a similar job from the ship's quarter.

Breast lines are at a right angle to the ship and control the distance to that part of the ship from the pier. Breast lines are called bow, waist, or quarter breast lines. If breast lines are used, the numbers of following lines will be changed to follow suit. Refer to the mooring diagrams on page 264 for examples of typical numbering patterns.

The size of mooring line used depends on the type of line and type of ship. Destroyers usually use 6-inch manila or 5-inch nylon. Smaller ships use 5-inch manila or 4-inch nylon, and aircraft carriers use 10-inch manila or 8-inch nylon.

When the ship is secured, the mooring lines are normally *doubled up.* To double up a line, an ad-

When a ship is secured to a pier, the mooring lines are usually *doubled up,* as shown here. Then light line is used to bind the parts together, and conical rat guards are put in place so that rats and mice cannot crawl up the lines onto the ship.

ditional bight of it is passed around the fitting on the pier or other ship to which the line is attached. Then slack is taken out until the two parts of the bight are alongside the original part of the line. Thus, three parts of the line absorb the strain, rather than just one. Often with a line to a pier, the three parts are bound together with small stuff, and a conical *rat guard* is placed about midway up the line, with the open end facing the pier, so that rats and mice cannot crawl up the line onto the ship.

TOWING

Most routine towing in the Navy is handled by harbor tugs, fleet tugs, salvage vessels, and submarine rescue vessels. Such vessels are especially fitted for this task. All ships, however, must be able to tow or be towed in an emergency.

On the stern of the towing vessel, a towing padeye is located on the centerline. The towing assembly has a large pelican hook that is shackled to the towing pad and made fast to a towing hawser.

The hawser is attached to one of the towed ship's anchor chains, which is let out through the bullnose and veered to 20 fathoms.

The length of the towline—hawser and chain—is adjusted to hand in a deep underwater curve called a *catenary*. This catenary helps to relieve surges on the line caused by movements of the two ships. Proper towing technique requires that the towline be of such scope that the two craft are "in step." Both must reach the crest of a wave at the same time, or the towline will be whipped out of the water under terrific strain. Once properly rigged, the towing vessel must barely get under way as the towed vessel begins to move. A sharp start or jerk may part the towing hawser. Speed is gradually increased to about 5 or 6 knots.

CARGO HANDLING

Cargo is loaded or offloaded by ship's gear or dockside winches and floating cranes when in port. At sea the ship's gear is used for underway replen-

Much boom and refueling rigging is being used by this naval oiler during an UnRep of an other ship alongside.

A deck seaman reeves a line through the vang blocks of a boom rigging.

The lower end is fitted with a gooseneck, which supports the boom in a boom step bracket. The free end is raised or lowered and held in position by a topping lift. Booms range in capacity from 5 to 75 tons. When they are used in pairs, the boom lifting cargo from a hold is called the *hatch boom*. The boom that positions cargo over the side to lower it to a dock or boat is called the *yard boom*.

Booms are moved into position, and cargo is moved into and out of holds by running rigging. *Topping lifts* move the boom vertically and hold it at the proper height. Inboard and outboard guys, or *vangs*, move the boom horizontally or hold it in working position over a hatch or dock. The cargo hook is raised or lowered by cargo whips running from winches.

The details of handling booms and running rigging are beyond the scope of this text. But some idea of the many booms and lines it takes to rig for a typical underway refueling can be gotten by looking closely at the picture on page 266. One can quickly see that rigging and running cargo handling gear requires skilled, trained deck sailors.

Chapter 2.   Study Guide Questions

1. What is all of the equipment associated with anchoring called?

2. What is the machinery used to weigh the anchor and its cable called?

3. What is the large pipe through which the cable passes from the deck to the ship's side called?

4. What are the four types of anchors used by the Navy today?

5. A. Explain a Mediterranean moor.
   B. What is a stern anchor used for?

6. What is the most common anchor in use in the Navy today?

7. What are anchors carried on the ship's bow called?

8. What are the advantages of LWT anchors?

9. A. How many fathoms and feet are in a *shot* of chain?
   B. How are shots connected to each other?

ishment (UnRep) either by another ship (ConRep), or by helicopters (VertRep), in which case very little ship's gear will be used. Amphibious and mobile logistic ships have heavy-lift cargo systems. In such ships, deck seamanship is mainly concerned with heavy-cargo handling. Sailors in these ships need to know about all the parts of cargo gear and the various "rigs" for handling cargo.

Rigging. The term *rigging* is used for all wires, ropes, and chains supporting masts or kingposts, and operating booms and cargo hooks. *Standing rigging* includes all lines that support masts or kingposts but do not move, such as stays and shrouds. *Running rigging* includes all movable lines that run through blocks, such as lifts, whips, and vangs.

Booms. A *boom* is a long pole built of steel.

10. What is the identifying color scheme of detachable links and shots?

11. A. What is the line-handling drum on top of the shaft of an anchor windlass called?

B. What part of the windlass system engages the links of the anchor chain to prevent it from slipping?

12. A. How is strain on the chain reported to the bridge?

B. What is the common reference used to describe the direction in which a chain tends?

13. What is the common rule of thumb used to determine the proper amount of chain to be veered in an anchorage?

14. What does it mean to "heave in the anchor to short stay"?

15. Describe the following:

A. Cleat.   C. Chock.
B. Bitts.   D. Bollard.

16. What are names of the lines in a standard six-line moor?

17. What is the purpose of breast lines?

18. Why must all naval ships be prepared to tow or be towed?

19. What names are given to the two booms used to lift cargo from a ship's hold and put it on a pier?

20. What is the purpose of the *outboard guy wires* or *vangs*?

Vocabulary

ground tackle	LWT anchor
mooring	chain shot
anchor windlass	detachable link
hawsepipe	fathom
chain pipe	friction
chain locker	towing padeye
Mediterranean moor	wharf
stern anchor	mooring lines
stockless anchor	forecastle
bower anchor	bullnose, eyes of ship
anchor detail	swivel shot
scope (of chain)	chain stopper
veer (chain)	turnbuckle
catenary	pelican hook
weigh anchor	wildcat
short stay	capstan
deck, pier fittings	towline
cleat	running rigging
bitts	boom
chock	topping lift
bollard	vang
fluke (anchor)	standing rigging
mushroom anchor	

Appendix 1:
First Aid

Everyone in the Navy must know when and how to apply first aid and be prepared to give assistance to persons injured in battle, collision, fire, and other accidents. But first aid should be known by everyone, everywhere; no one knows when or how it will be needed.

First aid is the emergency care given to sick or injured persons before professional medical attention is available. First aid should not take the place of proper medical or surgical treatment. First aid may mean the difference, however, between life and death, between rapid recovery and long hospitalization, or between temporary disability and permanent injury. It is also important, in many cases, to know what not to do.

The purposes of first aid are (1) to save life, (2) to prevent further injury, and (3) to preserve good health and prevent infection.

Each injury or sickness presents its own special problems. But there are some general rules that apply to almost all situations. Among these, remaining calm is the first order. Thereafter, the following rules apply:

1. After finding the extent of the patient's injuries, one should, first, stop severe bleeding; second, restore breathing and if necessary blood circulation by cardiopulmonary resuscitation; and third, treat for shock.

2. Keep the patient lying down in the most comfortable position possible.
3. Avoid touching open wounds or burns unless sterile bandages are not available and it is necessary to stop severe bleeding.
4. Keep movement of the patient to a minimum.
5. Keep the patient comfortably warm.
6. Do not give liquids to an unconscious person.
7. Summon medical help as soon as possible.

In addition to knowing the dos and don'ts of first aid, it is also important to know about the *emergency medical system* (*EMS*) that is now available almost everywhere in the United States, including all military bases and facilities. By dialing the number 911 on the nearest telephone, prompt emergency medical, fire, or police assistance may now be obtained in most urban and many rural areas throughout the country. In the case of a medical emergency, a bystander can often be sent to "Call 911," while someone else knowledgeable in first aid proceeds to render assistance until more qualified help arrives. Qualified medical personnel should always be consulted and, if appropriate, summoned whenever there is a serious injury or accident involving heavy bleeding, severe fractures, stoppage of breath or heartbeat, poisoning, or any other potentially life-threatening situation.

Chapter 1.   Treatment of Principal Injuries

The principal injuries requiring first aid are bleeding, asphyxiation, loss of heartbeat, and shock. Each of these is a common emergency that could confront a person at the scene of an accident.

BLEEDING OR HEMORRHAGE

The blood is circulated throughout the body by means of three kinds of blood vessels. *Arteries* are large vessels that carry blood away from the heart. *Veins* are large vessels that carry blood back to the heart. *Capillaries* are very thin, hairlike vessels that form the connecting network between arteries and veins.

The function of blood is to carry oxygen to the brain and other body tissues. Severe bleeding, therefore, must always be stopped before administering other treatment. Applying artificial respiration is useless if the patient bleeds to death in the meantime. Hemorrhage (escape of blood) occurs whenever there is a break in the walls of blood vessels. In most small cuts, only capillaries are injured. Deeper wounds result in injury to veins or arteries. Life is seldom endangered unless arteries or veins are cut.

The average adult body contains slightly more than five quarts of blood. One pint of blood can usually be lost without harmful effect. This is the amount given by most blood donors. The loss of two pints (one quart) will normally cause shock. As the loss of blood increases, its effect on the system becomes greater. If half the blood in the body is lost, death almost always occurs. Obviously, the control of bleeding is of great importance in first aid.

Capillary blood is usually brick red in color. If capillaries are cut, the blood oozes out slowly. Blood from the veins is dark red. If a vein is cut, the blood escapes in a steady, even flow. If an artery near the surface is cut, the blood will gush out in spurts, pulsed with the heart beats. If the cut artery is deeply buried, there will be a steady stream with minor pulsation effect. Arterial blood is bright red in color.

Arterial bleeding is the most serious because of the rapid loss of blood. It must be stopped, even to the point of ignoring the danger of infection. Prolonged bleeding from any large cut, however, can result in death.

CONTROL OF BLEEDING

The only way to stop serious bleeding is by applying pressure. Usually, bleeding can be stopped if pressure is applied directly to the wound. Should the bleeding occur in an extremity, elevating above the level of the heart, along with the application of pressure, will help as well. If *direct pressure* does not work, the pressure should be applied at the right *pressure point*. (See the figure on page 272.) If severe bleeding cannot be controlled by either of these methods, as a last resort pressure should be applied using a tourniquet.

Because of the threat posed today by the fatal *acquired immune deficiency syndrome (AIDS)*, discussed later in Appendix 2, which can be transmitted by any direct contact with the blood of an infected person, providers of first aid to bleeding victims of any kind are advised to use all possible caution to avoid any such direct contact with the blood of a victim. The rescuer should wear rubber gloves if available, or other waterproof gloves as an alternative, and wash off all bloodstains as soon as possible after rendering first aid with strong soap, water, and disinfectant. Any bloodstained clothing should be removed and discarded. Furthermore, potential rescuers with any type of unhealed wound should avoid personal contact with a bleeding victim, and serve instead as a director of other less susceptible people at the scene.

Direct pressure should be applied with a sterile dressing, clean cloth, or clean article of clothing. The dressing should be folded to form a pad, placed directly over the wound, and fastened with a bandage. (See figure on page 271.)

If bleeding does not stop, try applying direct pressure by hand steadily, for five or six minutes, over the pad. In cases of severe hemorrhage, do not worry about infection. Stop the bleeding even if it takes stuffing the cloth or your hand into the wound.

Bleeding from a cut artery or vein may be controlled by applying pressure to a pressure point. A *pressure point* is a place where the main artery to the injured part lies near the skin surface and over a bone. Pressure at such a point is applied with the fingers or hand; no first aid materials are required. The object is to compress the artery against the bone to shut off the flow of blood from the heart. There are eleven main points on the body where pressure can be used to stop hemorrhage. These points are shown in the figure on page 272 and described briefly below. Note that the correct pressure point is nearest the wound and between the wound and the main part of the body.

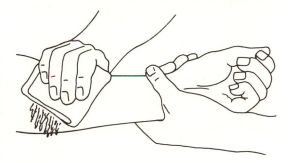

When applying a tourniquet, tie the bandage with an overhand knot, tie a square knot over the stick, and twist the stick to tighten the tourniquet. The tourniquet must be tight enough to stop arterial blood flow to an open wound on a limb, but no tighter than necessary to do that.

A. Bleeding on the face below the eye level may be stopped by pressure to a point on the lower jawbone. To find this point, start at the angle of the jaw and run your finger along the lower edge of the jawbone until you feel a small notch. The pressure point is in this notch.

B. The pressure point for the temple or scalp is just in front of the ear. The pulse can be felt when pressure is applied.

C. For bleeding in the neck area, apply pressure below the wound, just in front of the neck muscle. Press inward and slightly backward, pressing the artery of that side of the neck against the bones of the spinal column. Excessive pressure here should be avoided because of the danger of pressing on the windpipe and choking the person.

D. If bleeding is in the shoulder or upper part of the arm, pressure should be applied with the fingers in back of the collarbone. Press down against the first rib or forward against the collarbone.

E. Bleeding between the middle of the upper arm and elbow can be controlled by pressing on the inner side of the arm, about halfway between the shoulder and elbow. This compresses the artery against the bone of the arm.

F. Bleeding from the lower arm (forearm) can be controlled by applying pressure at the elbow.

G. Bleeding from the hand can be controlled by pressure at the wrist. The arm should also be held up higher than the heart.

H. Bleeding from the thigh may be stopped by applying pressure to the middle of the groin. The artery at this point lies over a bone and quite close to the surface.

I. Sometimes bleeding in the upper thigh can be controlled by heavy pressure in the upper thigh. If this point is used, pressure should be applied with the closed fist of one hand, using the other hand to apply additional pressure.

J. Bleeding between the knee and the foot may be controlled by firm pressure at the knee. If pressure at the side of the knee does not stop the bleeding, hold the front of the knee firmly with one hand, and thrust your fist hard against the artery behind the knee. As a last resort, place a folded compress or bandage behind the knee, bend the leg back, and hold it in place by a firm bandage.

K. The pressure point for bleeding of the foot is at the ankle. Elevating the leg is helpful in controlling this bleeding.

It is very tiring to apply pressure, and seldom can pressure be maintained more than fifteen minutes. If pressure must be continued after that period to control bleeding, it may be necessary to apply a tourniquet. Tourniquets are dangerous, however, and may result in gangrene. They should

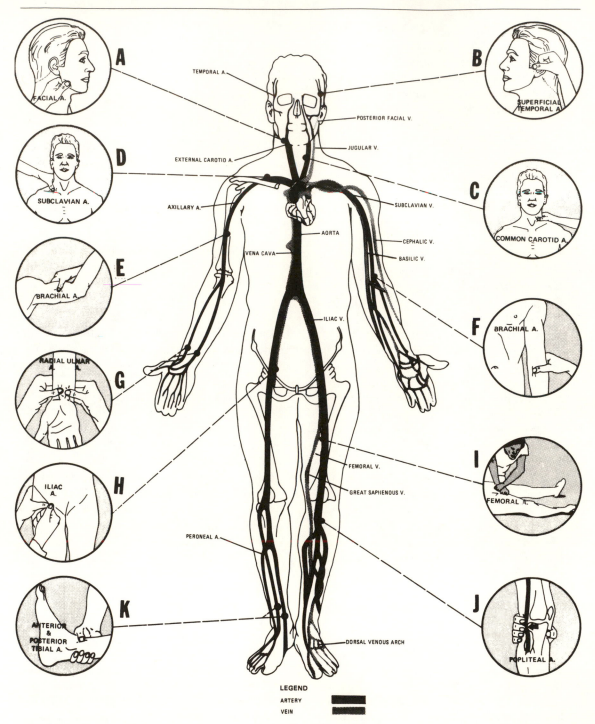

The eleven pressure points. Bleeding can be controlled when pressure is applied at a point where the main artery lies near the surface and over a bone.

only be used as a measure of last resort if all else fails.

A *tourniquet* consists of a pad, a band, and a device for tightening the band so the blood vessels will be compressed. The type found in many Navy first-aid kits consists of a web band, 2 inches wide and 5 feet long, with a buckle for fastening. The tourniquet is applied above the wound, that is, between the wound and the heart. It cannot be used to control bleeding from the neck or body trunk.

A tourniquet can be made from any round smooth pressure object such as a compress, roller bandage, or stone, and with a long flat material for the band, like a belt or stocking. A short stick may be used to twist the band and tighten the tourniquet. Rope, wire, or string should not be used as they will cut the flesh and block capillary action. The figure above shows how to apply a tourniquet.

A tourniquet must be tight enough to stop arterial blood flow to the limb, that is, stop the bleeding, but should not be any tighter than necessary. Once applied, a tourniquet should be released only by medical personnel.

A tourniquet should not be covered with a dressing. If body covering is necessary for warmth, a large *T* should be printed on the victim's forehead or on a medical tag attached to the wrist.

The victim should be kept quiet, warm, and lying down, with the head lower than the feet. He or she should be kept free of excitement and handled carefully. Keeping the patient quiet will hasten the forming of a clot in the wound. Professional medical care is needed as soon as possible.

If bleeding internally, the patient will tend to be thirsty, restless, fearful, and in shock. He or she should not be given anything to eat or drink. Bloody vomit will indicate an internal stomach wound. Treatment for internal bleeding is the same as that for shock, except that stimulants must not be given.

ASPHYXIATION

Persons who have stopped breathing are not necessarily dead, but they are in immediate danger of dying. Life is dependent upon oxygen. Oxygen is breathed into the lungs and then carried by

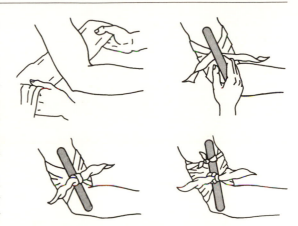

Control of bleeding by direct pressure on the wound with a sterile dressing or clean cloth. The dressing should be folded to form a pad and placed directly over the wound.

the blood to every body cell. The blood can hold only a limited amount of oxygen for a short time.

The heart may continue to beat for some time after breathing has stopped, and the blood may still be circulated to the body cells. For a very few minutes, therefore, there is some chance that the person's life may be saved. A person who has stopped breathing but who is still alive is said to be in a state of asphyxia.

Asphyxiation may result from the following:
- Blocked air passages.
- Lack of oxygen in the air.
- Inability of the blood to carry oxygen.
- Paralysis of the breathing center in the brain.
- Compression of the body.

Blocked air passages occur in cases of drowning, choking, and suffocation. In drowning, the air passages are blocked by water. In choking, they may be blocked by bones, pieces of food, false teeth, or chewing gum. The foreign object becomes caught in the throat and cuts off the air supply. Suffocation may result from a tight band around the neck, a plastic bag over the nose and mouth, or the swelling of membranes in the nose due to breathing in live steam, chemical warfare gases, acid fumes, and so forth.

Insufficient oxygen in voids, tanks, double bottoms, or high altitudes may cause asphyxiation. On shore, cisterns, sewers, silos, or abandoned mines may be poorly ventilated; these places may also have poisonous or explosive gases. No one should enter such places before the air is tested to be sure that it is safe.

Carbon monoxide poisoning is the primary example of asphyxiation due to inability of the blood to carry oxygen. Carbon monoxide combines with certain blood cells very rapidly, preventing the blood from carrying oxygen to the brain, and quickly causing death. Carbon monoxide comes from engine exhaust gases, cooking and heating gases, and sewer gases. Other sources of this deadly gas are burning coal or petroleum-based fuel, and even decaying natural food.

Breathing can be stopped by paralysis of the breathing center in the brain. The most common cause of such paralysis is electric shock. Excessive amounts of alcohol, drugs, or anesthetics, and breathing too much carbon dioxide may cause similar paralysis.

One cannot breath against any great amount of pressure. Accidental burial in dirt or similar material can cause death even though the nose and mouth are uncovered.

Artificial Respiration and CPR

Whatever the cause of asphyxiation, treatment must be started immediately. The process by which persons can be saved after they have stopped breathing is called *artificial respiration,* also known as part of *cardiopulmonary resuscitation (CPR)*. When properly performed, it can save a life.

The purpose of artificial respiration is to force air in and out of the lungs until natural breathing is reestablished. Do not assume that a person's breathing has stopped because he or she is unconscious. If you do not know whether the casualty is breathing, place your hands on his or her sides at the level of the lowest ribs. If the victim is breathing, you will be able to feel the movement. Do not give artificial respiration to a person who is breathing naturally.

Send someone for a medical officer if possible. Do not go if you are alone with the victim. Speed in beginning artificial respiration is essential. Every moment's delay cuts down the victim's chances of survival. Do not move the victim before beginning artificial respiration unless it is necessary for safety, for example, if he or she is in a burning building, gas-filled room, or flooding compartment.

Before starting artificial respiration, remove false teeth, chewing gum, seaweed, froth, mucus, mud, or any other foreign matter from the victim's mouth. Bring the victim's tongue forward. Loosen the clothing around the neck, waist, and chest. Keep him or her sufficiently covered to prevent shock or suffering from exposure. Do not let bystanders crowd around and interfere with the first-aid treatment. Do not try to give an unconscious victim anything to drink.

If the person is a victim of electric shock, the *very first thing* that you *must* do is remove him or her from contact with the electric current. The best method is to open or turn off the electric switch or power. If you cannot locate that, use a belt, a piece of dry line, sound-powered phone cord, or clothing to pull the victim free. Do not use a metal wire or anything that will conduct electricity. Be very careful not to make bodily contact with the victim, or you may become a casualty yourself.

If you suspect that a nonbreathing person is the victim of either choking or drowning, before starting artificial respiration, first perform the standard first aid for a choking victim, called the *Heimlich maneuver* (described in the next section) to clear the airway, and in the case of drowning, to help clear the lungs of water. This will greatly increase the chances of a successful resuscitation.

Methods of Artificial Respiration

The most effective and highly recommended method for most situations is the mouth-to-mouth method of artificial respiration. It is considered the best because it provides for the greatest exchange of air in the victim.

To give *mouth-to-mouth* (or mouth-to-nose) artificial respiration, the following steps should be taken. (See the figure illustrating mouth-to-mouth artificial respiration.)

1. Place the patient on his or her back immediately.
2. Quickly clear the mouth and throat of any obstructions.
3. Tilt the victim's head as far back as possible. Head should be in a "chin up" position and the neck stretched to ensure an open airway.
4. Lift the lower jaw forward; grasp the jaw by placing your thumb into the corner of the mouth; do not hold or depress the tongue.
5. Pinch the nose shut, or seal the mouth, to prevent any air leakage.
6. Blow firmly into the victim's mouth (or nose) until the chest rises. For infants, seal both mouth and nose with your mouth. Blow with small puffs of air from cheeks.
7. Quickly remove your mouth when the chest rises. Listen for exhalation from the victim's lungs. A gurgling sound indicates the jaw is not high enough.
8. Repeat steps six and seven every five seconds (twelve times per minute) for adults, and twenty times per minute for small children. Continue until the victim begins to breathe normally, and under most circumstances, keep trying for at least four hours.
9. Periodically, between breaths, remove air from the victim's stomach by placing your hand on the upper abdomen and firmly pressing the air out.

In some instances, such as when gas masks must be worn in contaminated areas, or when there are facial injuries involving bleeding around the mouth and lips, an alternative method must be used instead of mouth-to-mouth resuscitation. These other methods are much less effective because of the great difficulty in keeping a free and clear airway in the victim. Also, much less air can be provided, and the rescuer is much more apt to become physically exhausted from performing extended lifting.

Of the alternative methods, the *back-pressure armlift* is most commonly used, especially if an assistant is available to hold the victim's head to

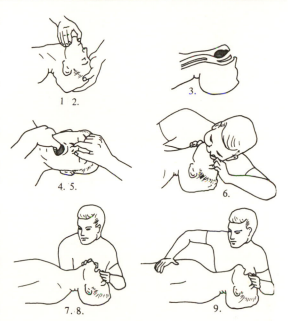

The above steps illustrate the proper method of administering mouth-to-mouth artificial respiration. (The numbers below the drawing are keyed to the steps given in the text.)

maintain an open airway. The steps to use in this method are as follows:

1. Place the patient face down. The assistant should sit at one side and hold the victim's head backward to keep the airway clear. The rescuer kneels at the victim's head, facing toward the feet.
2. If an assistant is not available, fold the victim's arms so one hand is atop the other and under the head. Turn the head to one side, lift the jaw upward and toward you, and hook the jaw over the hands.
3. Place your hands on the victim's back, and the heels of your hands just below his or her armpits. With the tips of your thumbs touching, spread your fingers.
4. Rock forward until your arms are almost vertical. You should allow the weight of the upper part of your body to force a slow, steady, even pressure downward on your hands. This forces

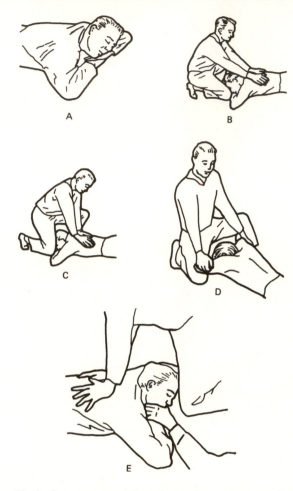

The *back-pressure armlift* method is the most commonly used manual artificial respiration technique, especially if two rescuers are present.

the air out of the victim's lungs. Your elbows should be kept straight. Pressure is exerted almost directly downward on the back.

5. Release the pressure, rock slowly backward, and grasp the patient's arms just above the elbows. Draw the arms upward and backward (toward you) until you feel resistance and tension in the victim's shoulders.

6. Rock forward and drop the arms gently to the ground. This completes the full cycle.

7. Repeat steps three through six at a rate of about twelve to fifteen times a minute. As soon as the victim is breathing, adjust your timing to assist the victim. Do not fight the attempts to breathe. Keep giving artificial respiration in time with the victim's breathing, but in a more relaxed manner, until it is apparent the breathing is steady. Aid may be stopped at this point, but stay in position and remain vigilant until he or she regains consciousness. Keep the patient warm to reduce the effect of shock.

CARDIOPULMONARY RESUSCITATION

Used for sudden cardiac arrest (stoppage of the heart) that often accompanies asphyxiation, drowning, and heart attack, cardiopulmonary resuscitation (CPR) is a temporary method of restoring at least some blood circulation until more advanced life support can be made available. Full CPR involves a combination of mouth-to-mouth artificial respiration and chest compressions.

CPR should not be attempted by a rescuer who has not been properly trained, because serious injury can result if it is not done correctly. Many NJROTC programs will have some sort of formal training programs available either in school or in the community that can provide the necessary training. What follows is a short description of the technique intended to inform you of the general procedure that is followed, and is not intended to be a substitute for the more detailed information and practice on a manikin that formal training programs provide.

The first step in performing CPR is to determine the responsiveness of a victim whose breathing and/or pulse appear to have stopped. This is done by gently shaking the victim's shoulders and asking loudly, "Are you okay?" or words to that effect.

Next, prepare the victim for mouth-to-mouth artificial respiration as described in the preceding section of this text. Look, listen, and feel for breaths by turning your head toward the chest with your ear over the mouth. If no breathing is detected, give two rescue breaths.

If mouth-to-mouth breathing cannot be used

because of a facial injury of the victim, use an alternative method such as the back-pressure arm-lift method.

Check the pulse in the neck by placing two or three fingers into the groove between the Adam's apple and the neck muscle and feeling for it (see the figure below). If there is no pulse, begin chest compressions.

To do compressions, place the heel of your hand that is closest to the head on the victim's sternum (breastbone) about two finger widths above its bottom. Place your second hand on top of the first, and interlock fingers. Keep the interlocked fingers off the chest. Keep your elbows straight, and position your shoulders directly over your hands as shown in the figure. Compress the victim's chest by transmitting your upper body weight directly downward. Compress smoothly and evenly, depressing the sternum 1½ to 2 inches at a time, at a rate of 80 to 100 compressions per minute. After every 15 compressions, deliver two rescue breaths. Recheck for breathing and pulse after every four cycles.

Once begun, it is important to continue CPR until medical assistance arrives or until the victim recovers a pulse and breaths independently. If the victim revives, keep him or her quiet and warm until help arrives.

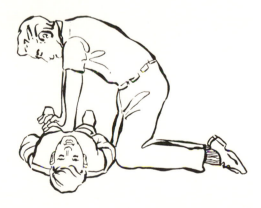

To administer chest compressions during CPR, after locating the proper position, place your hands one over the other and lock fingers as shown.

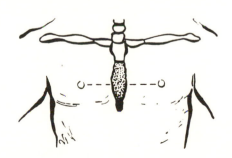

Locate the main arterial pulse in the neck by feeling for it with two fingers as shown.

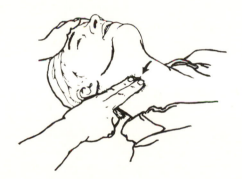

To do chest compressions for CPR, first locate a position about two finger-widths above the bottom of the sternum.

Administer chest compressions during CPR by transmitting body weight directly down along the straightened arms as shown. Don't flex the elbows or rock back and forth.

Drownings are the fourth leading cause of accidental death and the leading cause of respiratory stoppage. In teenage and lower twenties age groups, drowning ranks second only to motor vehicle accidents as a cause of death. Most drowning accidents occur during recreational activities.

Over half of the drownings happen to people who unexpectedly find themselves in the water. Boating accidents are the principal cause, followed by many other nonswimming fatalities. These include falling off a pier while fishing, and slipping into unprotected wells, cisterns, swimming pools, canals, irrigation ditches, or excavations. Careless operation, overloading, and bad weather and water conditions are prime causes of boating accidents. Wading and swimming in unguarded rivers or streams with strong currents are other causes of drownings.

Inability to swim contributes to most accidental drownings. Training in swimming is essential to safe recreational enjoyment of the water. The main factors for prevention of drowning accidents, then, are supervision, protection, and training.

The following are some swimming safety rules:

1. Never swim alone.
2. Adjust slowly to cool or cold water; do not dive in.
3. Swim at a safe pool supervised by lifeguards.
4. Beware of unfamiliar natural swimming areas; they may have treacherous currents, deep holes, debris, or other hazards.
5. Do not swim when overheated or overtired, or immediately after eating a meal.
6. Make sure that the water is deep enough before diving and check to ensure no one is beneath you when you dive.
7. Do not overestimate your swimming ability, especially in distance swimming. If planning a distance swim, have someone accompany you in a boat.
8. When swimming underwater, come up for air as soon as your chest begins to feel tight.
9. Do not dunk or push anyone into the water.

When a person has something lodged in the throat, he or she will start choking and coughing. If the obstruction goes deep enough to block the air passage, the person will die. Each year nearly 2,000 people die due to asphyxia caused by obstruction of breathing. About two-thirds of these deaths are of children under the age of four.

Small children are apt to investigate objects by placing them in their mouths. Also, children cannot chew well until their teeth are developed. The same thing can happen to people with dentures, since the normal chewing sensation is diminished. Obstruction can occur in adults when swallowing unchewed meat or food containing splinters of bone or shell. Alcoholic beverages before a meal decrease sensation in the mouth and reduce normal caution in eating.

Symptoms of choking are violent attempts to clear the throat or to breathe. Often these will be accompanied by the universal signal for choking, the victim's placement of both hands around the neck. The face, neck, and hands will become discolored—at first, flushed, then quickly an ashen gray or white. Breathing is apt to stop, and unconsciousness will quickly follow.

Often a person will be able to cough out the obstruction, but if not, the quickest and most effective life-saving technique, called the *Heimlich maneuver,* is performed as follows:

- Stand behind the victim and wrap both arms around the waist, clasping one hand around your other wrist.
- Place your interlocked hands against the victim's abdomen, just below the breast bone. Press into the abdomen with quick, upward thrusts until the object is forced out by air expelled from the lungs.
- If the victim is lying down, turn the person on his or her side and strike him or her with the flat of your hand on the back between the shoulders.

Never try to dislodge an obstruction from the throat. Doing so only forces the obstruction down deeper. Continue performing the Heimlich maneuver until successful, then if necessary perform artificial respiration or full CPR. Even if first aid treatment is successful, be sure the victim receives medical attention after the choking incident.

SHOCK

Shock is a condition in which blood circulation is seriously impaired. It occurs when the body's blood pressure drops so low that it becomes inadequate to force blood through the vital tissues. Among other things, shock can be caused by extensive loss of blood, severe pain, and heart failure. It is a reaction of the whole body to an injury, regardless of how localized the injury may be.

Blood carries oxygen to all body cells. When shock occurs there is a decrease of blood flow to those cells, and hence a decrease of oxygen to the vital organs like the brain. So you will notice some decreased level of consciousness in a shock victim, due to the reduced oxygen supply to the brain.

Some degree of shock follows all injuries, either immediately or several hours later. It may be slight, lasting only a moment, or it may be severe enough to cause death. Shock often results in death in cases of burns, hemorrhage, poisoning, fractures, and other serious injuries. Signs of shock are sometimes the only outward indication of concussion or internal injury. It is important to remember that *every seriously injured person is likely to develop serious shock.*

In addition to the decreased level of consciousness mentioned earlier, there are a number of other symptoms that clearly identify shock. The pulse is weak and rapid. Breathing is likely to be shallow, rapid, and irregular because poor circulation affects the breathing center in the brain. The temperature near the surface of the body is lowered because of the poor blood flow. The face, arms, and legs feel cold and clammy to the touch. Sweating is probable. The complexion is very pale, and in some cases, there may be a bluish or reddish color to the skin. The pupils of the eyes are often dilated (enlarged).

If otherwise alert, persons feeling the effects of shock may complain of thirst, weakness, faintness, or nausea. They also may be very restless or feel frightened and anxious. As shock deepens, these signs gradually disappear, and they become less responsive to what is going on around them. Even pain may not arouse them. Finally they may become completely unconscious.

Not all of these symptoms of shock are likely to appear in a single case. Most, however, will become apparent during the various stages of a worsening case of shock. Therefore, it is extremely important to recognize the earliest symptoms of shock so action can be taken to prevent a steadily worsening, and eventually irreversible, trend.

TREATMENT OF SHOCK

All injured persons should be treated for shock before being treated for their injury, except in cases where there is severe hemorrhage or asphyxiation. Even if shock has not yet developed, proper treatment may actually prevent it.

Generally speaking, the basic position for treating shock is one in which the head is lower than the feet. The victim's feet should be raised about 12 inches above the head, with the body on a flat but tilted surface. This may be on a cot or stretcher or simply on a naturally sloping ground. The position should enable the blood to flow to the brain.

With some injuries, however, such a position would not be appropriate. For example, if the head is injured, it would be unwise to place the head lower than the rest of the body.

Heat is important in the treatment of shock. The injured person's body heat must be conserved. Exposure to the cold will cause loss of body heat and increase shock. One has to judge the amount of covering to use by considering the weather and general conditions. Often a light covering will be enough to keep the casualty comfortable. Blankets or any dry material will conserve body heat. Artificial heat (hot water bottles or heating pads) should not be used as this will bring blood to the surface and defeat the body's efforts to supply blood to the vital organs and the brain. Wet clothing should be removed and dry covering provided, even on a hot day, because evaporation from wet clothes will cool the victim. The basic rule is to keep the person warm enough for comfort, but not to overheat.

Liquids should be given sparingly, and not at all if medical attention will be available within a short time. If necessary, small amounts of warm water, tea, or coffee may be given if the person is conscious and able to swallow and has not suffered internal injuries. Alcohol must never be given to a person in shock as it diminishes the blood supply to the brain and other vital organs.

Persons in shock tend to feel less pain. Pain is a variable thing, however. Some people feel pain far more than others. Usually a person will feel less pain if rested and relaxed than if tired, tense, and fearful. Pain may cause or increase shock, so relief of some kind should be attempted, preferably without the use of drugs. If injured persons are assured that they will get the best possible treatment, they will normally feel much relief. They should be told of plans to get medical help. Simple adjustment of bandages, slings, or splints, or loosening clothing will often help reduce pain. Ordinarily, drugs are not to be administered by anyone other than qualified medical personnel.

Chapter 1.   Study Guide Questions

1. A. What is first aid?
    B. Who should know first aid?
2. In what order should treatment for main injuries be given?
3. A. What is the emergency medical system (EMS)?
    B. How is it activated?
4. A. How can you tell if an artery is cut?
    B. If a vein is cut?
5. If a person has multiple injuries, why should severe bleeding be stopped first?
6. Before rendering first aid to a bleeding victim, what precaution should a rescuer take? Why?
7. How is a *tourniquet* applied?
8. What are common accidents that can cause asphyxiation?

9. Where are some places that insufficient oxygen may exist, therefore requiring special precautions by people who plan to enter them?
10. What common gas is a major cause of asphyxiation?
11. If the person is the victim of electric shock, what is the very first thing that must be done?
12. A. What is the preferred method of artificial respiration?
     B. How is this done with an adult and an infant?
13. For what purpose is full CPR given?
14. A. When does choking occur?
     B. What is the universal signal for choking?
     C. What quick action must be taken to save the life of a choking victim?
15. A. What is *shock*?
     B. What are the symptoms of shock?
     C. What is the treatment for shock?
16. A. Why must the body heat of an injured person be conserved?
     B. Why should alcohol not be given to a shock victim?

Vocabulary

emergency medical system (EMS)	Heimlich maneuver
	tourniquet
first aid	shock
hospitalization	circulation
disability	symptoms
infection	concussion
patient	compression
artificial respiration	suffocation
asphyxia, asphyxiation	carbon monoxide
hemorrhage	paralysis
arteries	anesthetics
veins	unconscious
capillaries	casualty
tissues	abdomen, abdominal
pressure points	cardiopulmonary
direct pressure	resuscitation (CPR)

Chapter 2.   Wounds, Fractures, and Burns

A *wound* is any injury that causes a break in body tissues. There are two types of wounds, open and closed. An *open wound* is a break in the skin or membrane. A *closed wound* is an injury to underlying tissues without a break in the skin or membrane. The two main dangers of wounds are serious bleeding and infection.

A *fracture* is a broken bone. The severity of the injury depends on the part of the body affected, the type of fracture, and the amount of tissue damaged.

Injuries from heat or cold—exposure to extremes of temperature—can injure the skin, tissues, vital organs, and even the entire body.

DRESSINGS

In general, the term *dressing* means anything used to cover or dress a wound. The sterile pad put directly over the wound is called a *compress*. A *bandage* is used to hold the compress in position. A combined compress and bandage, in which the sterile gauze pad is fastened to a gauze, muslin, or adhesive bandage, is usually called a *dressing*. Most Navy first-aid kits contain both large and small dressings of this kind.

Any part of a dressing that comes in direct contact with a wound should be absolutely sterile. Emergencies may make it impossible to get regular sterile materials. An improvised dressing can be made sterile by boiling it for ten to fifteen minutes. If that is not possible, a freshly washed handkerchief, towel, or shirt may be used.

A compress should be large enough to cover the entire area of the wound and extend about an inch beyond it in all directions. If it is not large enough, the edges of the wound are almost certain to become infected.

Materials that are likely to stick to a wound or that may be difficult to remove, such as absorbent cotton and tapes of any kinds, should *never* be used directly over a wound.

WOUNDS

Wounds usually result from accidents and external physical forces. Some of the most common sources of wounds are car wrecks, falls, and accidents with tools, machinery, and weapons.

There are six kinds of wounds that break the skin:
- Abrasions.
- Incisions.
- Lacerations.
- Punctures.
- Crush wounds.
- Avulsions (severance of limbs or tissue).

Abrasions are caused when the skin is rubbed or scraped off. "Rope burns," "floor burns," and "skinned" knees are common examples. This kind of wound becomes infected easily, because dirt and germs are often ground into the tissues.

Incisions, usually called *cuts*, are wounds made by sharp cutting things such as knives, razors, broken glass, and so forth. Cuts tend to bleed freely because blood vessels are cut straight across. There is relatively little damage to nearby tissues. Of all wounds, incisions are the least likely to become infected because the free flow of blood washes out many germs that cause infection.

Lacerations are wounds that are torn, rather than cut. They have ragged, irregular edges, and torn tissue underneath. These wounds are made by blunt or dull objects or tools such as machinery, barbed wire, and the shrapnel of bombs and hand grenades. They are often complicated by crushed tissues. Lacerations are frequently covered with dirt and grease, so they are likely to become infected.

Punctures are caused by objects that penetrate the tissues. They leave small surface openings. Wounds made by nails, needles, tacks, wire, bullets, and animal bites are usually punctures. Small puncture wounds do not bleed freely. Large ones may cause severe internal bleeding. All puncture wounds are apt to become infected.

Crush wounds may accompany abrasions and lacerations. Bodily impact as the result of an explosion or auto accident, or a heavy blow from something such as a hammer or sledge, bat, brick, or stone can cause crushing wounds. The breakup of body cells will invite infection from any outside source, however slight the break in the skin, and gangrene is a serious danger.

Severance, or *avulsion,* results when tissue is forcibly separated or torn from the victim's body. There will be heavy, rapid bleeding if a limb (hand, arm, foot, or leg) has been torn or cut from the body. Serious accidents with industrial or farm machinery, automobile wrecks, and explosions of any kind may result in such injuries. Modern surgery has been successful in reattaching severed limbs in some instances.

If a wound is fresh, first-aid treatment consists mainly of stopping the flow of blood, treating for shock, and preventing infection. If already infected, first aid consists of keeping the victim quiet while elevating the injured part and applying warm, wet dressings.

If the wound is a puncture wound, and the object is still imbedded in the wound, *do not* attempt to remove it. Doing so may greatly increase the chances of severe hemorrhage (bleeding). Stabilize it with gauze and tape, and wait for medical personnel to remove it.

Large wounds are generally more serious than small ones. They usually involve more severe bleeding, more damage to the underlying organs, and a greater degree of shock. Small wounds, however, are sometimes more dangerous because they may become infected more easily.

The location of the wound is important, especially where it involves serious damage to deeper structures. For example, a knife wound in the chest is likely to puncture a lung, thereby seriously interfering with breathing. Similarly, a knife or bullet wound in the stomach may cause *peritonitis* (a dangerous infection of the abdominal cavity) if vital organs are punctured. The same kind of wound on an arm or leg might be quite minor.

PREVENTING INFECTION

Any break in the skin is serious as it allows bacteria (germs) to enter and grow within the body tissues. This is called *infection*. Infection is especially dangerous in wounds that do not bleed freely, in wounds filled with torn tissue that prevent the entrance of air, and in wounds with crushed tissues.

Serious infection may develop within hours or days following an injury. Symptoms are swelling and redness of the affected part, a sensation of heat around the wound, throbbing pain, tenderness, fever, pus beneath the skin or draining from the wound or swollen lymph glands in the groin (leg infection), armpit (arm infection), or neck (infection in a head wound). Red streaks leading from the wound indicate that the infection is spreading through the lymphatic circulation channels.

The threat of tetanus infection (lockjaw), an often fatal disease involving muscle spasms and convulsions, must never be overlooked. All naval personnel have regular tetanus inoculations and booster shots; most civilians do not, but generally one of the first things a physician does in caring for a wound is give a tetanus immunization.

Minor wounds should be washed immediately with soap and clean water, and patted dry. They should be painted with a mild antiseptic, such as Zephiran or Mercurochrome. If available, a dry sterile bandage or clean dressing should be applied. In small open wounds, sand, wood splinters, and glass fragments often remain near the surface. Objects may be lifted out with the tip of a needle that has been sterilized in rubbing alcohol or in the heat of a flame. Deeply embedded objects should be left for removal by medical personnel.

Large wounds should be treated only by medical personnel. Do not make any attempt to wash or clean a large wound; concentrate on stopping the bleeding. No antiseptic should be applied. Cover the wound with a dry sterile compress and fasten it in place with a bandage.

Puncture wounds are very likely to become infected and develop tetanus unless treatment is given in time. The fishhook is one of the most common objects to penetrate the skin. If only the point enters, it can be easily removed. But, if the barb is embedded in the skin, it would be best to have a doctor remove it. If medical aid is not available, the hook may have to be pushed the rest of the way through so the barb can be cut off the hook. Forcing it through will be painful, but less damaging than tearing the flesh by trying to pull it back with the barb. The danger of tetanus is also great with a nail or barbed wire puncture or laceration.

The infection that must be guarded against with animal bites is called *rabies* (hydrophobia). This disease is caused by a virus present in the saliva of infected animals. The disease occurs most commonly in dogs, but it can be carried by any animal, especially raccoons, skunks, cats, bats, and even farm animals. If rabies develops in a person, it cannot be cured. It is always fatal. A preventive treatment is available that is very effective if it is given within a few days after the bite. Any person bitten by an animal must receive prompt medical attention.

Any animal bite should receive local treatment immediately. The wound and all the surrounding area should be washed carefully with abundant soap and sterile warm water. All saliva from the animal must be removed from the victim's skin to prevent any further contamination. Use sterile gauze to dry the wound, and then cover it with a sterile dressing. Do not use any antiseptic or disinfectant. Be careful that none of the animal saliva comes in contact with an open sore or cut on your own hands.

When a person has been bitten by an animal, every effort must be made to catch that animal so that it can be confined for observation until a diagnosis can be made. If possible, it should not be killed. The symptoms of rabies are not always present in the animal at the time of the bite; however, the saliva may contain the rabies virus. If a suspected rabid animal cannot be caught for observation, immediate preventive treatment must be given to the bite victim.

SPECIAL WOUNDS

Because of their location, chest, abdominal, head, facial, eye, and internal wounds require special first-aid measures.

Chest wounds may involve lung damage and serious interference with breathing. If a lung is punctured, the victim is likely to cough up frothy, bright red blood. First aid for a chest wound is as follows:

- Close the wound at once. If possible, place a dry sterile pad (large enough to cover the wound completely) over the wound. Then place strips of adhesive tape about 2½ inches wide completely over the pad so that it is airtight. This will relieve the victim's breathing difficulties.
- Give oxygen if the apparatus is available and if you know how to use it.
- Treat for shock. Keep the victim warm. It may be necessary to prop him or her up on pillows to assist breathing, even though this is not ordinarily recommended for treatment of shock. Do not give any liquids to a person with a chest wound.

Abdominal wounds are extremely serious since so many vital organs are located there. Abdominal wounds usually cause intense pain, nausea, and vomiting, spasm of the abdominal muscles, and severe shock. Immediate surgery is almost always required, otherwise chances of survival are poor. Give only the most essential first-aid treatment. Keep the victim lying down on the back, possibly with a coat or pillow under the knees if organs are protruding. Concentrate on getting the person to a hospital.

If bleeding is severe, try to stop it by applying direct pressure. Cover the wound with a dry sterile dressing; moisten the dressing with sterile water if intestines are exposed. Fasten the bandage firmly, but with a minimum of pressure. Do not give the victim anything to drink; moisten the lips if the victim complains of great thirst. Make sure the patient is comfortably warm to lessen the effect of shock.

Head wounds must be treated with particular care. There is always the possibility of brain damage. The general treatment for head wounds is the same as for other wounds, with the exception of the following special measures:

- Keep the victim lying flat, the head at the level of the body. Do not raise the feet. If the face is flushed indicating difficulty in breathing, the head may have to be slightly elevated.

- A person with a wound at the back of the head should be kept lying on his side.
- Morphine should never be given to a victim with head injuries.
- If you suspect a neck injury, do not attempt to move the victim. Immobilize the head and neck in the position in which you found the victim, and await the arrival of medical personnel.

Eye injuries and *facial wounds* that affect the eyelids or soft tissues around the eye must be handled very carefully to avoid further damage. If the injury does not affect the eyeball, apply a sterile compress and hold it in place with a firm bandage. If the eyeball appears to be injured, use a loose bandage. Never attempt to remove any object embedded in the eyeball.

There are often small objects lodged on the surface of the eye or on the membrane lining the eyelids in eye wounds. Dirt or any other foreign matter is very irritating to the eye. The proper removal of such objects is very important, as the eye is easily damaged. Fumbling attempts to remove foreign objects can result in harmed vision or even blindness. The following are the steps for removing such objects:

1. Gently pull the lower lid down, and instruct the victim to look up. If you can see the object, try to remove it with the corner of a clean handkerchief or with a small cotton swab. A swab can be made by twisting cotton around a wooden applicator, not too tightly, and moistening it with sterile water. *Caution:* Never use *dry* cotton anywhere near the eye. It will stick to the eyeball, or to the inside of the lids. You will have the problem of removing it as well as the original object.
2. If the object is under the upper lid, turn the upper lid back over a small wooden applicator (or match stick). Tell the patient to look down. Place the applicator lengthwise across the center of the upper lid. Grasp the lashes of the upper lid gently, but firmly, and roll over the applicator. Lift the object out with a moist swab or the corner of a clean handkerchief.
3. If these two actions do not work, try to wash the eye gently with lukewarm sterile water using a sterile medicine dropper or syringe. Have the patient lie down, the head turned slightly to the side of the affected eye. Holding the eyelids apart, direct the flow of water to the inside corner of the eye. Let it run down to the outside corner. Often the foreign material will run with it so it can be removed with the swab or handkerchief.

If these methods do not work, do not make further attempts to remove it. Place a gauze dressing over the eye with a loose dressing and get medical aid.

Internal wounds are often caused by external blows or impacts that do not break the skin. The force from an explosion, for example, often causes internal wounds called *blast* or *concussion injuries*.

The organs most likely to be internally damaged are the lungs and the intestines. The victim will cough up frothy, bright red blood if there is an internal lung wound. The person will have difficulty in breathing and will cough and gasp. The face will be bluish in color if the victim cannot get enough oxygen.

Internal wounds of the intestines usually cause severe pain and cramping. Loose, bloody stools will be passed.

All internal injuries are serious. They require prompt medical attention. There is little first aid that can be done for internal wounds, other than to keep victims lying down and to treat for shock by keeping them comfortably warm. Persons with internal wounds should not be given anything to drink.

FRACTURES

A broken bone is a *fracture*. Fractures of the limbs are most common. The type of fracture, amount of nearby tissue damaged, and the part of the body affected determine the severity of the injury.

Fractures may be classified as either simple or compound. A *simple fracture* is one in which the skin remains unbroken; it is also called a *closed fracture*. A *compound fracture* is one in which the bone protrudes from the skin; it is also called an *open fracture*.

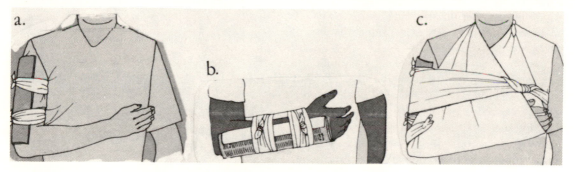

Arm fractures with splints and sling. A. Upper arm break with splint. B. Lower arm break with splint. C. Sling for break in either upper or lower arm.

It is not always readily apparent that a fracture has occurred. The victim may suspect it, however, and may even have heard the bone snap. Some symptoms of a fracture are:

- Pain and tenderness.
- Inability to use the part.
- Creaking or crackling.
- Motion at points other than joints.
- Swelling.
- Deformity.
- Discoloration of skin.

All fractures must be immobilized (splinted) to prevent movement and further injury. *Splints* are devices applied to arms, legs, or trunk to do this. They decrease pain and the likelihood of shock by preventing motion of the broken bone ends and nearby joints. They also protect against further injury during transport. Splints can be made from corrugated cardboard, rolled newspapers, boards, sticks like broomsticks or golf clubs, or rifles. To secure the limb to the splint, belts, ties, neckerchiefs, rope, or strips of cloth may be used.

Splints should be long enough to include the joints above and below the injury whenever possible. They should be wide enough to prevent unnecessary pressure on the injured point or limb. Splints should be padded to reduce discomfort. If the victim complains of numbness or tingling sensations after a splint is tied into place, the ties should be loosened to prevent permanent nerve damage.

Well-padded splints should be placed on closed arm fractures. For upper arm, lower arm, and wrist fractures, the arm should be placed in a sling that both supports the arm and keeps it bound to the chest wall. Elbow breaks should not be bent and placed in a sling; rather, the whole arm should be placed in a splint, and the victim should lie down.

Fractures of the upper leg cause severe pain and shock, and marked disability. The foot is often turned outward and the limb shortened due to overlapping of the bone ends. If the victim is to be transported a short distance on a stretcher, the two legs should be bound together with a blanket between them. If board splints are used, they should be well padded. The outboard one should reach all the way from the armpit to below the foot; the inboard one should extend from the crotch to below the foot. Snug ties should be made all the way up from the ankle to the chest to hold the splints in place.

Breaks of the lower leg or knee are splinted similarly, except that the outboard splint does not need to go above the hip. A person with a broken leg must, of course, lie down.

Open (compound) fractures of the arm or leg should first be covered with a large sterile or clean dressing. The wound should not be cleaned, and no attempt should be made to force the bone back inside the flesh. Bleeding must be stopped before anything else. When splinting, care should be taken that the splint not press against the area of the break.

Fractures of the ankle and foot should be wrapped in large soft dressings and a pillow or small blanket. The patient should lie down with the foot elevated.

Spine and *neck fractures* are extremely dangerous. The backbone and neckbone, called the *spinal column,* are composed of thirty-three bones called *vertebrae.* These vertebrae encase the spinal cord, the basic system of nerves for the whole body. If even one vertebra is fractured or dislocated, the spinal cord may be injured. The slightest movement may cause further damage to the spinal cord and result in paralysis or death.

Movement must be kept to an absolute minimum to prevent additional serious injury to patients with neck and back injuries. In particular, the victim's head should not be bent in any direction. If the victim is lying on his or her back, a small pad may be placed in the space under the neck, but nothing should be placed under the head itself. In general, the patient should be left in the position found, and all other emergencies such as hemorrhage, asphyxiation, and fractures should be treated in place. Only if fire, flooding, gas, or explosion is imminent should the victim be moved. If this is necessary, the entire body should be moved as a whole, avoiding any twisting or turning of the back and neck.

A *dislocation* is a displacement of a bone end from the joint. This may result from a fall or blow. The most common dislocations are those involving a finger, thumb, or shoulder. Less common are those of the elbow, knee, or hip. A dislocation will show up as swelling, deformity, pain, and sometimes, discoloration. Blood vessels and nerves in the vicinity of the joint are very apt to be injured. A dislocation must be treated in the same way as a simple fracture, with splints and immobilization. If proper care is not given, dislocations may occur repeatedly and in response to decreasing amounts of pressure.

A *sprain* is an injury to the soft tissues around joints. Sprains are usually the result of forcing a

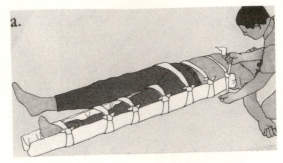
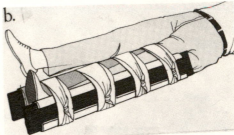

Leg fractures with splints. A. Splints for break in upper leg. B. Splints for break in lower leg. C. Splint for break of knee or knee cap.

limb beyond the normal range of movement. Ligaments, muscles, tendons, and blood vessels are stretched and may be torn. *Chip fractures* (the breaking or chipping of a small fragment from the bone) often go along with sprains.

It is often impossible to tell a sprain from a simple fracture. X-ray is really the only sure way to determine the difference. Sometimes a severe sprain may be even more painful than a break because of the wrenching of the tissues. Ankles, fingers, wrists, and knees are the joints most often sprained. The same symptoms as those for dislocations will show up quickly.

If a victim has sprains of the leg, he or she

should not be allowed to walk. Shoes should be loosened and the leg elevated. Cold, wet packs or a small bag of crushed ice should be placed on the affected area, after the area is protected with a thin towel. The injured joint should not be immersed in ice water or packed in ice. Never soak the joint in hot water.

EMERGENCY RESCUE AND TRANSPORTATION OF THE INJURED

A victim receiving first aid should be moved only if professional medical personnel and equipment are not available, or when the victim might be further endangered by remaining at the site of the injury. In general, the injured should not be moved until hemorrhage is treated and breathing is restored, wounds are dressed, and fractures splinted.

More harm can be done through improper rescue and transportation than through any other emergency assistance. Rescues of persons pinned in a car wreck or collapsed building normally require special tools, equipment, and expertise. People giving first aid in such situations should limit their assistance to emergency care and verbal reassurances, and not make foolhardy rescue attempts that could jeopardize both the victim and themselves.

Immediate rescue attempts may have to be made under the following circumstances:
- Danger of fire or explosion.
- Danger of asphyxia because of gas or lack of oxygen.
- Serious traffic hazards.
- Risk of flooding or drowning.
- Exposure to extreme weather conditions.
- Danger of collapsing walls or ceilings.
- Electrical hazard.
- Pinning by, or entanglement with, moving machinery.

METHODS OF TRANSFER

If a person must be pulled or dragged to safety, he or she should be moved as slowly and gently as possible in the direction of the *long axis* of the body, preferably from the shoulders. If that is not possible, pulling by the feet is acceptable. The body should not be bent or twisted. A better method of transfer is to place a blanket, rug, or piece of cardboard beneath the victim so that it can be pulled with the victim riding on it.

A stretcher is normally available aboard a ship. There are two types in common use: the Army-type "litter" with canvas attached between two sturdy wooden or metal poles, and the Navy *Stokes stretcher*, a wire basket supported by aluminum rods. It will hold a person securely in place even if it is tipped upside down or turned. Padded with blankets and secured with straps, the Stokes basket will prevent almost all movement of the injured person. It is used for transferring injured persons to and from boats, and between ships on a high line. A line can be attached to the head end or by a centered ring, and the injured person can be safely pulled up ladders and through a hatch or open hold, by crew members or a winch.

An injured person usually should lie on his or her back while being moved. If there are no serious wounds or skeletal injuries, then the person should be assisted to walk to safety. Fracture cases should be moved very carefully so the injury will not be made worse. A person with breathing problems due to a chest wound may be more comfortable if the head and shoulders are slightly raised. Patients should be carried feet first if at all possible.

The three-person lift and the fireman's lift are recommended for carrying an injured person. The tied-hands crawl is used to transport a patient under special circumstances.

Three-person Lift. The first person takes head and shoulders of the victim; the second, back and buttocks; and the third, legs and feet. When the first rescuer says, "Ready, lift," all list together and keep the body straight. If the victim has a chest wound, he or she is placed on the stomach. If the person has a stomach wound, he or she should be kept on the back with knees bent.

Fireman's Lift. Turn the patient face down. Kneel over the head, facing the person's shoulders (A). Pass both of your hands under the armpits and

A wounded man in a Stokes stretcher is transferred from a destroyer to an escort carrier by manila highline in the Atlantic during World War II. The wounded man was the captain of a German U-boat that had been sunk by an airplane from the carrier.

lift the patient to his or her knees. Then slide your hands down lower and clasp them around the person's back (B). Raise him or her to a standing position, place your right leg between the person's legs (C), take his or her right wrist in your left hand and swing the arm around the back of your neck, holding the person close to you. Put your right arm between the thighs (D), stoop quickly, pull the person's trunk across your shoulders, and straighten up (E).

To lower the patient, kneel on your left knee. Grasp the victim's left knee with your right hand. Slide him or her around in front of you and down your right thigh into a sitting position. Shift your hands to the head and place the person gently on his or her back.

Tied-hands Crawl. Use this method when you must remain close to the deck, or when you must have both hands free for climbing a ladder. Lay the

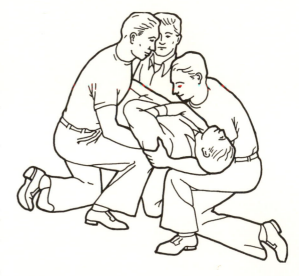

The three-person lift is a recommended method of transporting an injured person.

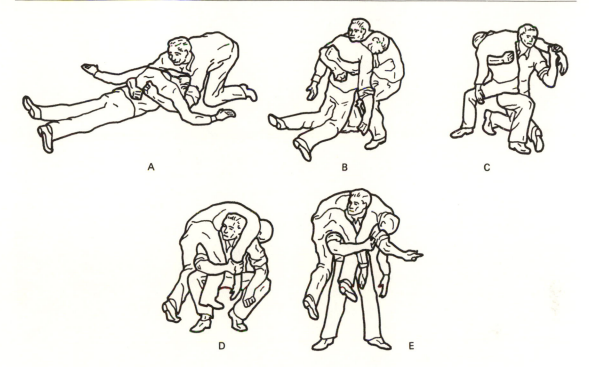

Steps to take in achieving the fireman's lift, a recommended method for lifting and carrying an injured person.

Transport an injured person with a tied-hands crawl when you must remain close to the deck or when you must have both hands free for climbing a ladder.

patient on the back. Lie on your back alongside him and to his or her left. Grasp the right arm above the elbow with your right hand. With your left hand, grasp the same arm below the elbow. Entwine your legs with the victim's and roll over on your chest, pulling the person over onto your back. Now pull his or her free hand (the left one) under your armpit. Tie the wrists together with a handkerchief or any other available material, get up on your knees, and crawl forward.

Chair Carry. If another person is available to help, and a stretcher is not handy, the injured person may be placed on a strong chair. This is good for narrow corridors, or stairs in a building. It is not suitable for neck or back injuries.

Fore-and-aft Carry. This is another two-person technique that can be used if there are no serious injuries to the trunk, back, or neck. It is not suitable for fractures of limbs. One person can lift the person by putting his or her arms under the armpits of the victim and clasping them across his or her chest. The other picks the victim up under each knee. Care must be taken not to twist or jar the patient.

Other lifts, such as the two-handed and four-handed chair seats, are available if the victim's injuries are largely confined to the lower leg, ankle, or foot.

INJURIES FROM HEAT AND COLD

Exposure to extremes of temperature—either heat or cold—can injure skin, tissues, vital organs, or the whole body. These types of injuries are common and require special first-aid treatment.

Injuries from exposure to excessive heat are burns, heatstroke, heat exhaustion, and heat cramps. "Burns" caused by contact with acids, alkalis, and other chemicals are not true *heat* burns, but they will be covered here as well.

Burns and *scalds* are caused by exposure to intense heat, such as fire, bomb flash, sunlight, and hot solids, gases, and liquids. Electric current can also cause burns. Burns and scalds are essentially the same type of heat injury, except for the source of heat. Dry heat will cause a burn; moist heat, such as steam or hot water, will cause a scald. Treatment is the same for both.

CLASSIFICATION OF BURNS

Burns are usually classified according to the depth of injury to the tissues. A burn that reddens the skin is called a *first-degree burn.* A burn that raises a blister is a *second-degree burn.* When the skin is destroyed and the tissues charred or cooked, the injury is a *third-degree burn.*

The size of a burn, however, is usually the most important factor in determining its seriousness. For example, a small third-degree burn in a non-vital area is not as serious as a first-degree or second-degree burn that covers a much larger area. A first-degree burn can cause death if a very large area is burned.

In figuring the extent of burned surface, the *Rule of Nines* is used. (See figure at right.) These figures help determine how much fluid the body would need during the first twenty-four hours after injury. Shock can be expected in adults with burns over 15 percent of the body surface, and

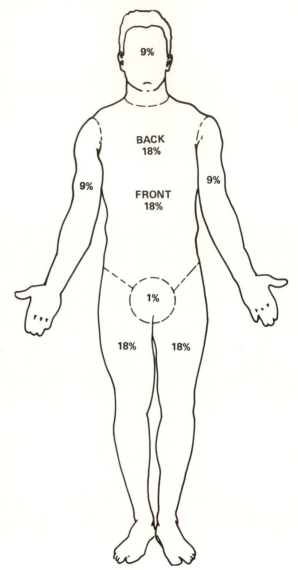

Rule of Nines for estimating percentage of burned area. These figures help determine how much fluid the body would need during the first twenty-four hours after injury. Burns over 15 percent will result in shock, over 20 percent endanger life, and 30 percent will usually result in death.

with burns over 10 percent on small children. In adults, burns covering more than 20 percent of the body endanger life. If more than 30 percent of the body is burned, death will usually occur unless adequate medical treatment is received.

Shock and infection are the main dangers from burns. First-aid treatment must be directed toward relieving pain, combating shock, and preventing infection.

Simple first-degree burns that do not cover a large area may require no more than one or two aspirin tablets to relieve pain. Severe burns cause extreme pain. The pain adds to the severity of shock. If safe to do so, medical personnel may have to give a morphine injection to relieve pain. Ice water gives immediate relief from pain and also seems to lessen the damaging effects of burns. Burns covering less than 20 percent of the body should be soaked in ice water until no pain is felt when the burned area is removed from the water. This may take thirty minutes or more. After this, the burn should be dressed as described below.

Serious shock always accompanies an extensive burn. It is the most dangerous result of the burn. Shock must be treated even before the burn. After relieving the victim's pain, you should place the head slightly lower than the feet. Keep the patient warm enough, but not overheated.

A seriously burned person has an overwhelming need for liquids. Giving liquids in such cases is an important part of the treatment for shock. Give small amounts of sweet tea, fruit juice, or sugar water, if the casualty is conscious, able to swallow, and has no internal injuries. Alcoholic beverages must not be given, as the alcohol will tend to dehydrate the victim even further.

Dressing Burns

Ointments and other medicines should not be put on a burn wound. These may make later treatment by a doctor difficult or impossible. Do not open any blisters and do not allow unsterile objects or material to come in contact with a burn wound. Do not cough or sneeze near the casualty. Keep a piece of sterile gauze over your mouth and nose while working near the burn. Contamination by germs from the mouth and nose is a frequent cause of serious, and even fatal, burn infections.

Usually, first-aid personnel should not attempt to treat the burn. However, if more than three hours will go by before a doctor will be seen, the burn should be dressed. Clothing from around and over the burn area should be cut away. If clothing sticks to the burn wound, do not attempt to pull it loose. Just cut around the part that sticks, and leave it in place. Do not try to remove anything that is sticking to the wound. Never put iodine, alcohol, or any other antiseptic on a burn, as these will cause a medicinal chemical burn and terrible pain.

After removing as much clothing or residue as possible from the burn, a single layer of sterile, fine-mesh *petrolatum gauze* should be laid over the burn wound. Begin at the outside of the wound and work toward the center in a circular manner. Next, place bulky fluffs of gauze over the gauze-covered wound. Use a large padded dressing as the outer layer. Wrap gauze strips smoothly and gently around the dressing. The bandage should give light, even pressure, and should serve to immobilize the injured part. Once the bandage has been applied, it should be left alone.

Burns of the eye require special attention. If they are heat burns caused by exposure to steam, welding arc, sun, or any source of intense heat, they should be treated as follows:

- Cover each eye with a small, thick compress, and fasten the compress in place with a bandage.
- Make sure that the casualty does not rub the eyes.
- Get medical attention as soon as possible.

Chemical Burns

When acids, alkalies, or other chemicals come in contact with the skin or eye, they will probably cause burns through chemical destruction of body tissue.

Common *chemical acids* that cause this kind of injury are nitric acid, sulfuric acid, and hydrochloric acid. *Caustic alkalies,* such as potassium hydroxide (lye), sodium hydroxide (caustic soda, soda lye), and calcium oxide (quicklime), and phenol (carbolic acid) also cause chemical burns. Strong concentrations of bleaches and disinfectants may injure the skin. Chlorine, ammonia, and other industrial gases (whether in liquid or gaseous form) may cause serious chemical burns, as may white phosphorus, used by the Navy for smoke screens.

First-aid treatment for chemical burns is as follows:

- Immediately wash off the chemical that is causing the injury. Flood the affected areas with clean, fresh, cool water in order to dilute and weaken the chemical. The best way is to get under a shower. If a shower is not available, pour as much water over the spot as possible.
- Neutralize any remaining chemical. For acid burns, applying a solution of sodium bicarbonate (baking soda) or some other mild alkali; for alkali burns, apply vinegar, lemon juice, or some other mild acid; for phenol burns, wash the skin with alcohol. Do not attempt to neutralize any chemical unless you are sure what it is.
- Gently wash the area with mild soap and water. Do not break the skin or blisters.
- Treat the victim for shock and pain. From this point onward, treatment is the same as for heat burn.

Chemical burns of the eye should be treated with a steady stream of water from a fountain or faucet so the water flows from the inside corner to the outside corner. Do not use great force with the water flow. If not near a fountain or faucet, have the victim lie down and pour water across the eye in the same manner. If the patient cannot open his or her eyes due to pain, they must be held open so water can be poured across the eyeball.

Another way to help dilute the chemicals in eyes is to repeatedly open and close them in a basin or sink filled with clean water. This water must be changed frequently to prevent burns elsewhere on the face or in the nose.

After washing the eyes as much as possible, cover them with a small, thick compress. Fasten the compress in place with a bandage or eyeshield. Do not use anything except water in treating chemical burns of the eye. Do not try to neutralize the chemical that caused the injury and do not apply any ointment, grease, oil, or salve.

HEATSTROKE AND HEAT EXHAUSTION

Exposure to too much heat may result in either heatstroke (sunstroke) or heat exhaustion. Both are caused by the same external conditions, but constitute different bodily reactions that require different treatments. Desert or jungle heat, exposure to direct rays of the sun, or heat of machinery spaces, foundries, or bakeries may cause these conditions.

Heatstroke is a very serious condition. It results from a failure of the heat-regulating mechanism of the body. The temperature rises to between 105 degrees and 110 degrees F. There is no sweating, and therefore, no cooling of the body. The victim's skin is hot, dry, and red. He may have early symptoms such as headache, nausea, dizziness, or weakness. Very often the first signs are sudden collapse and loss of consciousness. Breathing is likely to be deep and rapid. The pulse is strong and fast. Convulsions may occur.

Heatstroke may cause death or permanent disability. Recovery may be slow and complicated with relapses. The longer the victim remains overheated, the more serious the victim's condition will become. The most important thing is to lower the victim's body temperature. He or she should be moved immediately to the coolest possible shady place. Most clothing should be removed. The victim should be placed on the back with head and shoulders slightly raised. Following this, sponge or spray the victim with cool water, using a fan so the water will evaporate quickly. If the person regains consciousness, he or she should be given cool (not cold) water to drink. No stimulants (coffee or tea) or hot drinks should be given.

With *heat exhaustion*, there is a serious disturbance of the blood flow, similar to that of shock. The bodily reaction is almost directly opposite from that of heatstroke. Through prolonged sweating, the body loses large amounts of salt and water, which probably causes the circulatory disturbance.

Heat exhaustion may begin with headache, dizziness, nausea, weakness, and profuse sweating. The victim may collapse and lose consciousness, but can usually be aroused fairly easily. The body temperature is usually normal or even below normal—even as low as 97 degrees F. (Normal is 98.6 degrees.) As in shock, the pupils of the eyes are usually enlarged. The pulse is weak and rapid. The skin is pale, cool, and sweaty. The condition is sometimes accompanied by severe *heat cramps* in the abdomen, legs, and arms.

First aid for heat exhaustion is much like treatment for shock. The patient should be moved to a cool, shady place without drafts that will cause chill. Clothing should be loosened to make the patient comfortable. He or she should be kept lying down and quiet and comfortably warm, perhaps with a single blanket or poncho. If the victim is conscious and able to swallow, give plenty of warm water to drink. Up to half a teaspoonful of salt should be added to each glass. Replacement of salt and water is the most important part of the treatment and usually brings about a rapid recovery.

COLD INJURIES

Cold injury means the injury of tissue from overexposure to cold. The most severe cold injury is frostbite.

Cold injury should never be treated lightly because of the possibility of tissue loss and nerve damage. Regular activities and duties should not be attempted until the severity of the injury has been determined.

Frostbite is caused by exposure to extreme cold (–20 degrees F and below) for several hours. It may occur in less time if a strong wind is blowing, causing rapid chill. At temperatures from –20 degrees to –60 degrees F or colder, exposed fingers and toes will rapidly freeze, with freezing extending up the arms and legs as exposure is prolonged.

The first symptoms are burning and stinging, and then numbness. Ice crystals in the skin cause a gray or white waxy color. The skin will move over bony ridges. When the part is completely frozen, there are ice crystals throughout the part, indicated by a pale yellow, waxy color. The skin will not move over bony ridges. When the frozen part is thawed, it becomes red and swollen and large blisters develop.

The victim should be moved to a warm place as soon as possible. Before this is done, however, other injuries, if any, should be treated. Great care must be taken when removing clothing to avoid skin breakage, because infection is very possible. Nothing should be rubbed or applied to the frozen parts. They should be thawed rapidly in a water bath of 107 degrees to 109 degrees F, described as "comfortably warm." Warming should not continue beyond the time necessary to complete the thaw. After warming, the parts should be carefully dried. The person should be placed in a bed with sterile sheets covering but not touching the damaged parts. Sterile gauze or cloth pads should be placed between the toes or fingers. Stimulants such as coffee or tea may be given to the victim, but no alcohol and tobacco.

Casualties with frostbitten or frozen feet or legs must be treated as litter patients. No walking should be permitted.

General loss of body heat may result from total immersion in cold water or by prolonged exposure without adequate clothing. In either case, the victim will be pale and unconscious, and may be taken for dead. Breathing is slow and shallow. Pulse may be faint or undetectable. Body tissues feel semirigid, and legs and arms may be stiff.

First-aid treatment consists mainly of bringing the body temperature up to normal. This should be done by wrapping the person in warm blankets. After regaining consciousness, the victim should be given hot coffee or tea and a gentle massage.

Chapter 2.   Study Guide Questions

1. A. What is a *wound*?
     B. What are the two types of wounds?
2. Why should bandages or dressings be sterile if at all possible?
3. What is the usual first aid for a fresh wound?
4. A. What causes *infection*?
     B. What are the symptoms of infection?
5. A. Which types of wounds are most susceptible to infection?
     B. How should minor wounds be treated to prevent infection?
     C. Larger wounds?

6. A. What dangerous infection can be transmitted by dog and other animal bites?

  B. Why is immediate treatment necessary?

7. A. What is the sign of a chest wound with lung damage?

  B. What is the most important first-aid treatment?

8. Why are abdominal wounds so serious?

9. What is the deadly infection that may occur if internal organs are cut or torn?

10. How should a person with a head wound be positioned?

11. What are the two best ways to remove foreign objects from the eye (if they are not embedded in the eyeball)?

12. A. What is a *fracture*?

  B. How are fractures classified?

13. A. What are some common symptoms of a fracture?

  B. What must be done to fractures to prevent further injury?

14. Why are neck and spine fractures so dangerous?

15. What is a *dislocation*?

16. A. What is a *sprain*?

  B. What first-aid treatment should be given for a sprain?

17. A. Under what conditions should movement of an injured person be attempted?

  B. If a person must be pulled or dragged to safety, how should it be done?

18. What types of stretchers are normally available aboard ship? Describe each briefly.

19. What are the recommended lifts for carrying an injured person?

20. What are the principal heat injuries?

21. A. How are burns classified?

  B. What is usually the most important factor in determining the seriousness of a burn?

22. A. Why should ointments or medicines not be put on a burn wound by first-aiders?

  B. Why should antiseptics *not* be put on a burn wound?

23. A. What classes of chemicals cause *chemical* burns?

  B. What are some of the more common types of chemical burns?

24. What is the general first-aid treatment for chemical burns?

25. What is the first-aid treatment for chemical burns of the eye?

26. A. What is *heatstroke*?

  B. What are symptoms of heatstroke?

  C. How should it be treated?

27. A. What is the body's reaction to *heat exhaustion*?

  B. What is the proper first aid for heat exhaustion?

28. What first aid is required for *frostbite*?

Vocabulary

membrane	skeletal injury
wounds	scald
body tissue	Rule of Nines
dressing	blister
compress	ointment
bandage	immunization
abrasion	inoculation
incision	lymph glands
laceration	antiseptic
puncture	rabies
avulsion	petrolatum gauze
gangrene	acid, alkali
peritonitis	neutralize
tetanus (lockjaw)	dilute
deformity	heatstroke
splint	disinfectant
vertebra, -ae	diagnosis
spinal column	surgery
dislocation	fractures
immobilization	nausea
sprain	convulsions
ligaments, tendons	heat exhaustion
Stokes stretcher	frostbite
litter (stretcher)	

Chapter 3.   Poisoning

A *poison* is a substance that causes bodily disturbance, injury, or death, by chemical (rather than mechanical) means. It may be a liquid, solid, or gas. It may be introduced into the body by swallowing, breathing, injection into the muscles or blood vessels, or contact with the skin.

Many substances are harmless if used in the proper way, but they can be poisonous if used in the wrong way or in the wrong amount. Nearly all drugs and medicines are both beneficial and poisonous. Such things as alcohol, coffee, tobacco, and narcotic drugs are poisonous substances for which the human body may develop certain tolerances. Certain plants, plant juices, and fibers are poisonous. And the bites, stings, and wounds inflicted by some reptiles, fishes, and insects are poisonous.

Poisoning can be the result of attempted suicide or homicide, but much more frequently is accidental, the result of an overdose or a mistake. It may be cumulative, that is, suffered as the result of continuous use or exposure in small amounts over a long period of time, as with lead, pollution, and medicines. The effects of this type of poisoning may not always be immediately obvious. For instance, although the drug addict or alcoholic may be able to build a tolerance for drugs that would kill the average person, at the same time he is damaging his heart, kidneys, liver, lungs, and brain. Poisoning is inevitably disastrous to the human body, resulting in loss of mental and physical health, and early death, if not counteracted quickly.

Symptoms of Poisoning

There are some general signs that indicate that a person has been poisoned. Intense pain, nausea, and vomiting are common symptoms. The victim may become delirious, collapse, or become unconscious. Poisoning by caustic acids, alkalies, phenols, and metallic salts is likely to cause corrosion (eating away), swelling, and bleaching of the skin, mouth, and throat. Brown or black stains on the skin and mucous membranes may mean iodine poisoning. Some poisons turn the urine different dark or bright colors.

In almost all cases of acute poisoning, the victim is likely to have trouble breathing. Some poisons cause paralysis, and others cause convulsions. Pupils of the eye may markedly contract (become smaller) or dilate (become larger). The skin will generally turn pale or bluish in color, since shock is always present in poisoning cases. If a person seems to be sick or shows any of the symptoms above, you should look around the immediate area for possible sources of poisoning. An empty poison, medicine, or pill bottle may be the clue that could save the person's life.

The U.S. Public Health Service maintains information about symptoms and treatments for all types of poisons. So do most hospitals, clinics, and fire department paramedic units. Emergency treatment is usually required for poisoning cases. If several people are present, one should notify medical professionals while the others give first-aid treatment. If only one person is present, medical people should be notified as soon as possible. Poison victims should have professional help even if the symptoms of poisoning disappear completely after first aid. Some poisons can cause harmful effects that do not appear immediately.

Effects of Poisons

Another word for poison is *toxin*; another word for poisonous is *toxic*. The action of a poison or the degree of danger from a poison is called *toxicity*. The toxicity of a poison varies greatly, and depends on several factors:

1. *Type of poison and the amount taken.* A few drops of one poison might be immediately fatal, while another might not be harmful unless taken by tablespoonsful.
2. *Weight of the victim.* The less a person weighs, the smaller will be a fatal dose. Infants, young children, and old people are likely to be more affected by poisons.
3. *Condition of the stomach.* Poisons taken on an empty stomach will act more quickly and violently than those taken when the stomach is full.

4. *General health and tolerance level.* A victim may have natural resistance to certain poisonous substances, or resistance built up over time, as in the case of drug addicts and alcoholics.
5. *Physical state of the poison and how it enters the body.* Gases are absorbed more quickly than liquids. Liquids are absorbed more quickly than solids. Inhaled poisons work most quickly. Injected poisons and poisons taken by mouth act more slowly. It is important to know the way a poisoning happened, because proper first aid depends partly on this information.

INGESTED POISONS

There are many substances that are poisonous if *ingested* (swallowed). Proper first-aid treatment is based on which of the four classifications the poison belongs to: *corrosives*, *irritants*, *depressants*, or *excitants*.

Corrosives rapidly destroy, or eat up, the body tissues they contact. They include acids such as hydrochloric and sulfuric; phenols, such as Lysol and creosote; or alkalies, such as lye and ammonia. Iodine is also a corrosive and so are petroleum products. General symptoms of corrosive poisoning include immediate burning pain in the throat and stomach, followed by retching and vomiting. Stomach contents are mixed with dark, colored liquid and shreds of tissues that line the mouth, stomach, and throat. Swallowing is very difficult and so is breathing. The abdomen becomes tender and filled with gas. The body temperature is high, and facial expression shows anxiety and great suffering.

Irritants do not directly destroy body tissues. The cause inflammation of the contact area. Some examples of these are arsenic, phosphorus, zinc sulfate and zinc chloride, and potassium nitrate. Irritants cause faintness, nausea, vomiting, and diarrhea. There is pain with cramps.

Depressants are substances that depress the nervous system. These include the alkaloids such as atropine, morphine and its derivatives, bromides, barbiturates, and alcohol. When swallowed, depressants usually have an initial stimulative effect, but this is soon followed by drowsiness and stupor. Breathing is slow with snoring. The skin is moist, with face and fingers turning a bluish color. Muscles are relaxed and pupils are either very small or very large.

Excitants stimulate the nervous system. Examples are strychnine, camphor, and the fluorides. When swallowed, excitants cause delirium, mental disturbance, and physical restlessness. There is a feeling of suffocation and inability to breathe. Other symptoms are hot, dry skin; rapid weak pulse; convulsions or jerking muscles; and dilated or contracted pupils.

Ingested poisons are treated with emetics, demulcents, and antidotes. *Emetics* cause vomiting; they should be used with irritants, depressants, and excitants. They may not be sufficient to induce vomiting with depressants, so the throat may have to be tickled. They should *never* be used with corrosives, since that will serve to recoat the throat with additional corrosive. Common emetics are salty warm water (2 teaspoonsful per glass), warm water with soapsuds (*not* detergents), or large quantities of warm water.

Demulcents are substances that will calm the stomach and delay absorption of the poison. After a victim has vomited, he should be given a demulcent such as raw egg whites, milk, or a thin paste of cooked starch or flour. Milk will serve to dilute acids, alkalies, and petroleum products.

Antidotes are substances that tend to neutralize or counteract a poison. Milk of magnesia, lime water, or soap in lots of warm water are effective antidotes for acids. Alkalies may be neutralized using vinegar, lemon juice, or grapefruit juice as antidotes.

Basic first-aid procedures for ingested poisons are as follows:
1. Identify the poison.
2. Remove the bulk of the poison from the stomach with emetics, except when the poison is corrosive.
3. Administer the antidote in large quantities, and then repeat with emetics.
4. Give demulcents between doses of the antidote.
5. After the poison has been removed from the

stomach, give the victim epsom salts (½ ounce in half a glass of water). This will speed passage of any remaining portion of the poison through the intestines.

6. Treat the victim for shock. Give stimulants such as strong coffee or tea, but *not* if the poisoning was caused by iodine or strychnine. Do *not* give alcohol as a stimulant.

Inhaled Poisons

Toxic vapors and fumes are a hazard in many industrial operations. Industrial operations include casting, molding, welding, plating, and so on, all common operations in tenders and repair ships and in shipyards. In the Navy, many industrial processes are carried out aboard ships and at shore installations; poisoning by inhalation, therefore, can be a danger.

Inhaled poisons may come from refrigeration machinery, firefighting equipment, paints and solvents, photographic materials, and other shipboard equipment that contains chemicals. Petroleum products—fuel oils and gasoline, in particular—are special hazards.

Other poisonous gases are found in the by-products of exhaust gases from internal-combustion engines, the processing of ores and refining of metals (metallurgy), and even from food spoilage in closed spaces.

Carbon monoxide is probably the most frequent cause of gas poisoning by inhalation. It is colorless, odorless, and tasteless. It gives no warning of its presence. It is present in all exhaust gases of internal-combustion engines (cars). It is in sewer gas and in gas used for heating and cooking. Carbon monoxide is present in dangerous amounts in any poorly ventilated space where fire has occurred. It is so dangerous because it combines very rapidly with red blood cells, preventing them from carrying oxygen.

Before receiving first-aid treatment, a victim of carbon monoxide or any other gas poisoning should first of all be removed immediately to a warm, well-ventilated place free of the gas—not a cold place, as this will cause the patient to collapse. This must be done rapidly as inhaled poisons affect the body very quickly. The rescuer must use protective equipment and observe safety precautions so as not to also become a victim. Oxygen should be administered if an inhalator is available. If breathing fails, give artificial respiration. The victim must be hospitalized because rest is very important for recovery and prevention of serious aftereffects.

Petroleum products (gasoline, benzine, kerosene, naphtha, and many others) give off poisonous fumes. If inhaled, such fumes cause a kind of intoxication similar to that of ingested alcohol. Disorientation is likely, and injuries from falling or slow reactions are common. Lighting a cigarette could result in an explosion if the person is in a vapor-filled room. Unconsciousness and serious depression of breathing are likely, and death from asphyxiation can follow quickly. As the victim begins to recover, he or she is likely to become violent and almost uncontrollable, so must be carefully guarded.

Carbon tetrachloride and other *chlorinated hydrocarbons* are used for solvents, degreasing metal articles, cleaning electrical components, and dry cleaning of clothing. They are extremely dangerous because heat causes them to decompose, forming deadly phosgene gas. Persons who work with these solvents must not drink liquor as this greatly increases their susceptibility to poisoning. The first symptoms of poisoning are extreme nausea and mental confusion.

Freon is a colorless, odorless gas used as refrigerant. It is toxic in high concentrations. Even a small amount of Freon can freeze the delicate tissue of an eye, so medical attention must be obtained quickly to avoid permanent damage.

Hydrogen sulfide smells like rotten eggs. It is flammable and poisonous. The first signs of such poisoning are eye, nose, and throat irritation, and the heavy flow of tears. Breathing is at first deep and gasping, but soon feeble and irregular. Death is caused by paralysis of the brain.

Poisoning by Skin Contact

Poisoning by skin contact is not ordinarily a first-aid problem. It occurs when people are regularly exposed to poisonous agents over a long period of time, so it is normally attended to by a physician. Such poisoning may be very serious and often results in death.

Common agents that can poison through contact are gasoline, benzine, naphtha, and other petroleum products; lead compounds such as those in lead-based paints, arsenic, mercury, some other metals and metallic compounds, and chlorinated solvents such as carbon tetrachloride. There is no real cure for this kind of poisoning, so all safety precautions must be observed when handling these products.

INJECTED POISONS

Although there are a number of substances that are highly poisonous when injected, these are matters more of concern to doctors and psychologists. First aid for drug overdose should follow the general procedures for asphyxiation and shock, and treatments for inhaled, ingested, or injected poisons as applicable. Normally, first aid is concerned only with poison injected through the bites of spiders or snakes, or stings from fish and scorpions.

Spiders are common in almost all parts of the world. Only two spiders found in the United States are known to be poisonous: the black widow and the brown recluse. The female *black widow* has the infamous red hourglass on her underbelly; the male is a small yellow and brown nonpoisonous spider who usually ends up being eaten by his dangerous mate. The black widow makes a messy web in dark corners, under stairways, in woodpiles, and between garage studding across the southern and southwestern United States. She strikes quickly and retreats into her dark home.

The bite of the black widow causes pain almost at once. The pain spreads quickly from the bite to the muscles of the back, shoulders, abdomen, and limbs. The pain is usually accompanied by severe spasms of the abdominal muscles, profuse sweating, nausea, and difficulty in breathing and speaking. Most healthy adult victims recover, but small children, the elderly, or sick people may die.

The *brown recluse* lives mostly in the region east of the Mississippi, in the Middle Atlantic

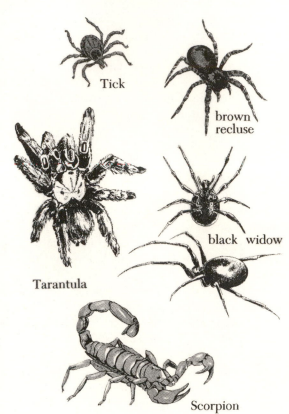

The bites of these American insect-animals may inject poison, disease germs, or infection. The *tick* can carry dangerous Rocky Mountain spotted fever, and the *tarantula* can inflict a severe bite very liable to become infected. The *brown recluse* spider bite causes a painful ulcer and illness. The female *black widow* spider bite and *scorpion* sting can be fatal if not properly treated.

states and Appalachia. The bite causes severe local reaction. The victim develops chills, fever, joint pains, nausea, and vomiting, and often a rash within twenty-four to forty-eight hours. Red blood cells are destroyed in the area of the wound, resulting in an open ulcer within one to two weeks.

Tarantulas, the huge hairy banana spiders of Central America, and large western desert spiders of the same name, do not have a poisonous venom.

But they can cause a severe local wound that is very apt to become seriously infected if not treated immediately.

Scorpions are normally found in the dry deserts of the world, including the United States. Huge black ones are common in the tropics also. A scorpion strikes the victim with a powerful stinger on the end of its tail. It commonly comes out at night and is likely to crawl into the blankets or shoes, striking when the person moves or puts his or her shoes on in the morning. Fatalities have been recorded, usually with the young, old, or ill. The larger the scorpion, the greater the amount of poison and the more serious the effect. Excruciating pain is instantaneous at the site of the wound. This is quickly followed by nausea, vomiting, and abdominal pain. Shock, convulsions, and coma may follow. The leg or arm, if stung, will quickly swell up to large size, with damage to capillaries, and great danger of infection.

First-aid measures for spider bites and scorpion stings are limited. Simply clean the wound and surrounding area with alcohol to rid them of bacteria. Treat victims for shock. Keep them lying down, quiet, and warm. Severe muscle cramps and pain may be relieved by warm-water baths. Do not apply suction and do not cut the wound; it will do no good. Keep the affected part down, below the level of the heart. Ice in a towel or plastic bag may be applied to the sting or bite. Get the victim to a doctor as soon as possible.

Ants, bees, wasps, and hornets may also be poisonous. Death from such poisoning is very uncommon, however, and is the result of acute allergic reaction. Bites and stings from *ticks, fleas, mosquitoes, lice, gnats, chiggers, and other common insects* may cause local irritation but seldom a severe reaction. Ticks, however, may carry the germs of several diseases, including Rocky Mountain spotted fever. If untreated this disease is often fatal. Other insects can also carry deadly diseases; for example, the mosquito can carry malaria and other tropical diseases; fleas or lice on rats can carry bubonic plague and typhus.

If a tick is found attached to the body, do not attempt to rub or pull it off. This will break the head off in the skin and certainly result in infection. Rather, cover the tick with some heavy oil or grease to close its breathing pores; the tick is likely to disengage at once. A warm matchhead applied to the tick's stern may also cause it to disengage. The area must be carefully washed with soap and water after all parts of the tick have been removed.

Minor bites and stings may be treated by cold application, calamine lotion, or a paste of baking soda and water. In case of a bee sting, the stinger should be removed with a disinfected needle or tweezers. Soap and water is always soothing and helpful.

Contact with Poisonous Plants. Contact with plants of the poison ivy group, including poison oak and poison sumac, can result in an often severe reaction. These plants cause an acute rash that is characterized by redness, blisters, and itching. It can be extremely serious if in the eyes, where it will cause intense burning and swelling of the surrounding tissues. If the case is severe, the victim may develop a high fever and become quite ill. The rash will usually begin itching within a few hours.

This group of poisonous plants has three smooth, glossy leaflets at the end of each stem; all have small, yellowish-white berries when mature. Barely touching the leaves will cause them to bleed a white milky fluid. Walking through a patch of poison ivy will cause a mist of this juice, almost like an aerosol, to float in the air as leaves and stems are broken. If a weed patch containing these plants is burned, the smoke will carry the juices through the air. *Poison ivy* grows almost everywhere in the United States except California. *Poison oak* grows in California and in parts of nearby states. *Poison sumac* grows in most of the eastern third of the country, especially in low areas.

SNAKEBITE

There are two classes, or families, of poisonous snakes in the United States. The *pit viper* family is abundant and spread widely throughout most of the country. These include the thirteen species of rattlesnakes, the copperhead, and water moccasin (cottonmouth). The pit vipers have long fangs and

COMMON POISON IVY

- Grows as a small plant, a vine, and a shrub.

- Grows everywhere in the United States except California and parts of adjacent states. Eastern oak leaf poison ivy is one of its varieties.

- Leaves always consist of three glossy leaflets

- Also known as three-leaf ivy, poison creeper, climbing sumac, poison oak, markweed, picry, and mercury.

WESTERN POISON OAK

- Grows in shrub and sometimes vine form.

- Grows in California and parts of adjacent states.

- Sometimes called poison ivy, or yeara.

- Leaves always consist of three leaflets.

POISON SUMAC

- Grows as a woody shrub or small tree from 5 to 25 feet tall.

- Grows in most of eastern third of United States.

- Also known as swamp sumac, poison elder, poison ash, poison dogwood, and thunderwood.

The three plants of the United States that are poisonous to the touch are *poison ivy, poison oak,* and *poison sumac.* All cause acute rash characterized by redness, blisters, and itching and can have very serious results if in the eyes.

thick, stocky bodies with blunt, diamond-shaped heads. They have a "pit" between the eye and the nostril on each side, with slitted eyes and elliptical pupils. The venom of these snakes is *hemotoxic,* that is, it affects the blood and circulatory system.

Pit viper bites are extremely painful and characterized by rapid swelling. One or two puncture marks are usually easy to see. The skin will discolor rapidly around the puncture holes. The victim will soon show general weakness, severe headache, rapid pulse, nausea and vomiting, shortness of breath, dimness of vision, and shock. Bleeding will occur from the internal organs and capillaries,

which will show up in the body's waste material.

The *coral snake* is the only member of the short-fanged *cobra* family of poisonous snakes in the United States. Africa, Asia, and Australia have many others, such as the cobras, kraits, and mambas. The venom of these snakes is an extremely potent *neurotoxin* (poisonous to the nervous system). The coral snake is small, only about 3 feet long. It has red, yellow, and black rings around the body, with the red and yellow adjoining and always has a black nose. It is found on the coastal plains from North Carolina, through Florida, along the Gulf Coast, and up the Mississippi Valley to southern Indiana. Coral snakes are sometimes confused with other similarly colored snakes. An easy way to tell the difference at a quick glance is given in the following rhyme:

Red and yellow
Kill a fellow.
Red and black
Venom lack.

The bite of the coral snake causes only mild burning pain and local swelling at the wound. Irregular heartbeat, general weakness, and shock occur quickly. Severe headache, dizziness, mental confusion, incoherent speech, and unconsciousness will follow. Bodily coordination will fail, and often there will be muscular twitching. There will be a numbness and tingling of the skin, especially the lips and soles of the feet, and excessive sweating. Breathing will become labored and respiratory paralysis is likely.

First Aid for Snakebite

The first advice to give the snakebite victim is to lie down and keep calm. Encourage the victim, reminding him that few people actually die of snakebite. Try to identify and kill the snake if at all possible so proper antivenin can be given, preferably by medical personnel.

The objectives of first aid are to reduce circulation of blood through the bite area, to delay absorption of venom, and to sustain respiration. Try to keep the bitten limb, usually hand or leg, below

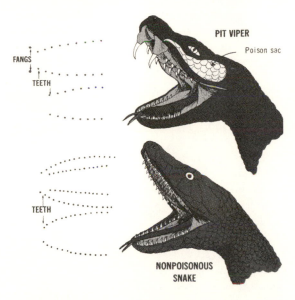

FANGS

TEETH

PIT VIPER

Poison sac

TEETH

NONPOISONOUS
SNAKE

Different characteristics of pit viper family and nonpoisonous species. With the exception of the coral snake, all poisonous snakes native to the United States are pit vipers with fangs, triangular-shaped heads, slit eyes, three rows of overlapping scales beneath the eyes, and a "pit" or depression between each eye and nostril.

the victim's heart. For a pit viper bite, apply a tourniquet between the bite and the heart, tight enough to restrict the flow of blood in the veins but not in the arteries. For a coral snake or another of its family, the tourniquet must be tight enough to stop arterial flow as well. There will be some oozing from the wound if the tourniquet is properly placed.

Using the sharp blade from a snakebite kit, or a sterile knife, a trained rescuer may make an incision and perform suction. This is necessary if more than an hour is going to pass before a pit viper bite can be medically treated and must be done almost immediately with a neurotoxic venom. An incision not more than ½ inch long and ¼ inch deep should be made through each fang hole. Cuts should be lengthwise along the arm or leg, with care not to injure tendons, muscles, blood vessels, or nerves. *Suction* can then be performed by suction cup, or

by mouth, and continued for at least thirty minutes. The sooner suction is started, the better. Fluids sucked into the mouth should not be swallowed, although they are harmless to the first-aider, if he does *not* have any cuts in the mouth or lips.

The Armed Forces provide an antivenin kit that neutralizes the venom of hemotoxic snakes of North and South America. Antivenins have been developed for the venoms of most snakes around the world with the exception of the king cobra and some sea snakes. Antivenin must be given as soon as possible, normally within fifteen minutes. This is best done by a physician since there may be reactions to the serum. It should be given as first aid, however, if medical assistance is not going to be quickly available, and it is necessary to save the victim's life.

Victims should be treated for shock. They should be kept lying down, quiet, warm, and as comfortable as possible. It may be necessary to give artificial respiration and heart massage. Cases are on record where people have been kept alive as long as two hours after they became unconscious and have then been saved by antivenin injection.

Morphine should not be given for pain when the venom affects the nervous system. Alcohol should not be given, since it speeds circulation. Ice packs should not be used. If the victim is alone and must walk to aid, he or she should perform all the first aid possible before walking *slowly* for help.

Poisoning by Fish and Sea Animals

Most fish can inflict puncture wounds by spines, fins, or gills. Some others can give stings of varying severity. The reactions to these wounds will vary from one individual to another, depending on the amount of venom injected or contacted.

A number of fish are sharp spined, most of which have venom. Examples of these are catfish, both freshwater and saltwater, and the deadly scorpionfishes, toadfish, and weeverfish of shallow, brackish, coastal waters and inlets. There are no known antidotes for these fish stings, and they can be fatal.

The Portuguese man-of-war and species of the jellyfish family have long tentacles covered with stingers. Ammonia water, vinegar alcohol, or a soothing lotion should be applied to such stings. Artificial respiration is sometimes necessary, as well as treatment for shock. Coming into contact with a Portuguese man-of-war while swimming is apt to cause panic, paralysis, and pain. These stings will not kill in themselves but may result in drowning.

Stingray wounds are almost always the result of stepping on a ray in shallow water. The ray defends itself by slamming its barbed tail into the foot or lower leg. The wound should be immediately washed out with cold salt water. That will clear out most of the toxin and cause the blood vessels to constrict and slow down circulation. It is painful and apt to become infected without care, but the venom itself is not deadly.

PREVENTION OF ACCIDENTAL POISONING

Accidental poisoning is most common with children. Effective prevention is, in most cases, a matter of being careful, and keeping poisonous substances out of the reach of children. Swallowing, or ingesting, poisons is the most common serious hazard. Often, aspirin and other home medicines are found in large quantities around homes. The toxic effect of these and other chemicals like cosmetics, cleaning products, furniture polish, insecticides, and paints is seldom understood by adults, and almost never by children. It is not practical to eliminate such things from the home, but it is possible to keep them out of the reach of children.

Accidental poisoning by drugs and chemicals could be almost eliminated if people would simply take time to read the labels, and keep them out of reach. Leftover pills and medicines should be flushed down the toilet (not thrown in the trash).

It is important that a poisonous substance taken from its original container not be placed in another container without proper markings. It is common for unsuspecting persons to misuse chemical poisons that have been left out in cups or bowls or in unmarked containers.

Contaminated air can often be corrected simply by providing ample ventilation. Chemicals that cause fumes, or sprays, can be used more safely outdoors. If inside use is necessary, read and follow all safety measures. Covers and caps should always be replaced securely on chemicals so they will not evaporate into the air or spill if tipped.

While most ingestion of poisons occurs in homes, it can also happen outdoors. Eating poisonous berries, leaves, and roots, as well as toadstools, which are often confused with mushrooms, can result in serious illness or death. A simple rule to follow is to *never* eat wild foods without positively identifying them.

Everyone should take protective measures when in areas where poisonous insects, snakes, plants, or marine life could be encountered. Insecticides and repellents will reduce or control insects. As poison ivy can grow almost anywhere, all play areas should be cleared of such plants. Protective boots and caution where stepping or placing hands are recommended when in snake-infested areas. Similarly, use care and common sense when walking in shallow water and swimming where poisonous sea life might exist. Most animals will avoid contact with people unless provoked, threatened, or injured, and will strike or bite only as a last resort.

Chapter 3.   Study Guide Questions

1. A. What is a *poison*?
   B. How may it be introduced into the body?
2. What are the signs that a person has been poisoned?
3. What are the four classifications of ingested poison? Describe each briefly.
4. A. How are ingested poisons treated?
   B. What is the action of each of these treatments?
5. Why is carbon monoxide so dangerous?
6. A. What are the names of the two poisonous spiders found in the United States?
   B. How is the black widow easily identified?

C. Where is this spider found in the United States?

7. What is the first-aid treatment for spider bites and scorpion stings?

8. What is good first-aid treatment for minor bites and stings of insects and bees?

9. A. What are the three common poisonous plants in the United States?

B. Where are these plants found?

C. How can one be poisoned by these plants?

10. A. What are the two classes of poisonous snakes in the United States?

B. Name the common poisonous snakes in the United States.

11. What are the objectives of first aid for snakebite victims?

12. What parts of fishes can produce painful or even poisonous puncture wounds?

13. A. What is the particular danger about being stung by a Portuguese man-of-war or a jellyfish while swimming?

B. How might a wound be inflicted by a stingray?

14. A. What are the two most effective ways of preventing ingestion or other contact with poisons in the home?

B. What common household items not generally considered poisons may be lethal if ingested by children?

15. What is the commonsense rule one should use with wild foods such as berries, leaves, and mushroom-type fungi?

Vocabulary

poison, toxin	antidote
tolerance	stimulant
cumulative	metallurgical process
delirious	collapse
paramedic unit	naphtha
poisonous, toxic	intoxication
toxicity	spasm
ingestion	black widow
inhalation	brown recluse
injection	tarantula
corrosives	scorpion
irritants	fatality
depressants	poison ivy
excitants	hemotoxin
dilated pupils	neurotoxin
emetics	viper
pulse	venom
demulcent	insecticide

Appendix 2: Principles of Health Education

Health education is also of great concern in today's world. The Navy and the other armed services stress the good health and well-being of all their members.

A few health problems are unique to the military, but most can happen to people anywhere.

Cleanliness, good habits, and common sense—things that are just as important in a high school as they are in a ship—can help alleviate health problems. This appendix covers some basic information on human growth and development, personal health care, and matters of health and safety.

Chapter 1. Human Growth and Development

Human growth is the way in which our bodies and minds develop. When this development is complete, a person has matured, or reached *maturity.*

Human growth, from birth to maturity, involves many changes in the body. It also involves changes in the way we think. Sometimes this growth happens quickly, and sometimes more slowly. Each person grows at his or her own speed. But every healthy person grows in the same basic way.

People's growth patterns are different because of heredity and environment. *Heredity* includes the traits we get from our parents when we are born. *Environment* is the effect that the world has upon the human body and mind *after* we are born. Both of these affect growth and development. An example of this is the trend over the centuries toward larger size. This is thought to be a result of better living conditions and diet.

The rate of growth differs from one person to the next. Some children grow very fast at a certain age, while others may not. This is no real cause for worry. A wide range of growth rates is normal. What is often called a "normal" growth rate is really only an *average* growth rate.

There are two periods of rapid growth. One of these occurs immediately after birth. In the first year, the average baby grows about 50 percent in

The rate of growth differs a lot from one young person to another. A wide range of physical growth during adolescence is normal.

size, and its weight triples. The other time is during *puberty,* which is when sexual development begins.

Puberty usually occurs at nine to thirteen years of age with girls, and from eleven to fifteen years with boys. Boys tend to be slightly taller and heavier than girls during the first nine or ten years of life. Then girls briefly take the lead in growth. As a boy enters puberty about age thirteen, his growth rate gets faster again. The average girl reaches adult size at about age seventeen, while an average boy does so at eighteen or nineteen. Growth stops when the bones no longer grow. The body will continue to fill out and strengthen until about age twenty-five. "Filling out" means the development of muscles and other tissue.

Predicting how big a child will grow to be as an adult is difficult. Adult height is usually about twice the height reached by age two. In other words, a child who is 3 feet tall at age two will probably be about 6 feet tall at maturity.

The whole process of growing up is called *maturation.* There are two kinds of maturity: physical and emotional. *Physical maturation* refers to the appearance and body shape of the adult male or female, and the ability to have babies. Measuring *emotional maturity* is hard because there are no clear physical signs (such as bone growth).

EMOTIONAL GROWTH

Emotional growth is related to physical growth, but other things come into play. Most of these come from a person's environment. The *environment* includes such things as the family and community life, school, and work. All are important to emotional growth, and each person is affected differently by them.

Individuals may grow up physically much sooner than they mature emotionally. This is usually true for young people in today's society. Our society does not make the average young person take on adult responsibilities at the same time he or she reaches physical maturity. This often leads to a lack of understanding between young people and older, emotionally mature adults.

Persons of fifteen or sixteen can often become emotionally mature earlier if their environment has forced them to take on adult responsibilities. A death or tragedy in the family can sometimes cause this. In primitive societies, for instance, boys have been hunting for food and building shelters for years before they reach eighteen; girls have been doing household chores since eight or nine, and are expected to take on home and child-bearing responsibilities by age fourteen or fifteen. But our society requires much more education, training, and experience before young people take on adult roles. Very few teenagers have had enough education or experience to take on the modern world. They must get more schooling, job training, and the maturity to earn a living and support a family of their own.

On the other hand, some persons can stay very immature emotionally—even after they have reached physical maturity. For some men and women, the pressures of life may cause them to shy away from adult responsibilities. They may never reach emotional maturity. Fortunately, most people do achieve emotional maturity when they leave home and school and move on to their life's

By the time young men and women are in their senior year in high school, most will have completed much of their physical—but not probably their emotional—growth. These high school seniors talk with a midshipman at the Naval Academy about his school.

A person's family is important in developing his or her emotional maturity. The personalities and attitudes of parents are very important. You can see that there is parental love, support, and understanding for this young midshipman who has just entered the Naval Academy.

work. They have families of their own and become productive members of society.

THE FAMILY AND EMOTIONAL MATURITY

The family is important in developing emotional maturity. Emotional problems don't happen all-of-a-sudden. They often go back to early childhood. Even things that happen in the first weeks and months of a baby's life are very important to later emotional growth.

A person's parents are particularly important. Growing children need healthy and happy home lives. The increase of divorce and broken homes in the United States in recent years has increased the social problems of youth today, for instance. Children need to take part in family life and discuss their problems freely. Relationships with other children in the family are also important.

When children become teenagers, family relations change, and hard feelings sometimes develop. Teenagers have a natural desire to be independent. At the same time, they should look to parents for support and advice. If parents fail to understand both needs—independence, as well as support and advice—trouble can develop. If parents don't give emotional support, young persons may feel no one cares about them. Since they need someone, they often look to the advice of equally confused teenagers.

It is a difficult time for parents too. They must encourage their children to take on responsibility. But, at the same time, parents should not force their children into situations for which they are not yet ready.

Chapter 1.   Study Guide Questions

1. Why is health education just as important to civilians as to service personnel?

2. A. What is human growth?

 B. What causes individual growth patterns to vary?

3. When do the two periods of rapid human growth occur?

4. What are the two kinds of maturity?

5. A. Why do most individuals mature *physically* sooner than they mature *emotionally* in our society?

B. What may cause emotional maturity to occur sooner?

6. Why is the family important in developing emotional maturity?

7. Why are there often bad feelings between parents and teenagers?

Vocabulary

cleanliness

environment

human growth

heredity

puberty

maturation

physical maturity

emotional maturity

traits

Chapter 2. Health and Hygiene

Health is complete physical and mental well-being and freedom from disease. Health and happiness go together. Healthy minds and bodies make us feel well and happy. The body does many things almost automatically to keep itself healthy. But individuals must learn important rules to help their bodies along.

The human body is the most complicated machine there is. On the other hand, it needs less upkeep than any metal machine, and lasts much longer—now more than seventy years on the average. It can adjust to most situations better than any other machine. It only needs air, water, and food, and good treatment. Each individual must learn how to take care of his or her own "machine" so it will work well and feel good.

Good health is no accident. Each person can have good health by paying attention to personal hygiene, a balanced diet, plenty of fresh air and exercise, good posture, and proper rest.

The Navy trains its personnel in how to do their military and professional duties. But the ability to perform well depends on their physical and mental condition. Good health and a cheerful attitude make the job easier. These are each person's responsibilities.

Sailors in our Navy today are living better and safer and healthier than most of the people in the world. Even the smallest ship provides good meals, comfortable berthing spaces, medical and dental attention, laundry service, hot and cold running water, and sanitary living conditions. Naval hospitals are among the best in the world. It's almost impossible not to be healthy in the Navy. But a few people will always manage. They will be the ones with athlete's foot, ringworm, impetigo, or persistent colds. These sailors make things difficult for their shipmates.

Personal Hygiene

Hygiene is the science of health. It is the study of those things that affect both physical and mental health. Personal hygiene involves many things, such as cleanliness, good diet, regular sleep, exercise, and emotional attitudes. Every person should develop habits of good personal hygiene.

It is in the home that these habits are developed. Children learn by watching their parents and older brothers and sisters. If the family practices good personal hygiene, the child will develop good habits.

Cleanliness

Never forget that keeping clean and keeping healthy are very nearly the same. Sometimes it is hard to keep clean, especially in dirty or hot places. But the effort is worthwhile. Dirt breeds germs, and germs cause illness, skin irritations, and infections. Take a shower daily in warm weather or when you are sweating heavily. In cool weather, once every other day may be often enough—but wash your hands with hot water and soap before

Sailors in our Navy live better and are safer and healthier than most of the people in the world. This sailor is working in the deck force of a salvage ship operating in tropical waters.

every meal. Shampoo your hair at least once or twice a week. The salt from perspiration (sweat), dirt, dust, and dead skin collect on the surface of the body. Keeping your skin clean, your hair washed, and your nails cut cleans up areas where dirt is apt to build up.

It is best not to go outside right after a hot bath or shower in very cold weather. The skin's pores are open, and the sudden change could cause you to catch a cold.

An important part of cleanliness is changing into clean clothing. You should change your underclothing every day after showering. Put talcum powder on parts of your body where clothing is tight. This will keep your skin dry and free from itching.

Bed linens—sheets or mattress cover, pillow case, and blanket—should be clean. Linens should be changed at least weekly. It feels so good to "crawl into" nice clean sheets—and it certainly is healthy.

FOOT CARE

Most trouble with feet comes from fallen arches or athlete's foot. If a person's arches need support, special supports should be put into the shoes.

Most people with foot trouble got it during their teenage years, when their feet were growing rapidly. Properly fitted shoes and socks are important in good foot care. The inside of the shoe should be about a quarter-inch longer and wider than the foot.

Improperly fitted socks and socks with holes can cause blisters. Shoes and socks should be changed daily. Ingrown toenails can be prevented by cutting the nails straight across.

To help avoid athlete's foot, shower shoes should be worn when taking showers, even in the home if someone else is infected. Care of the feet after showering is important. Dry your feet thoroughly to prevent growth of the fungus of athlete's foot. It is wise to put foot powder between your toes. Remember: if your feet hurt, you hurt all over. Sore feet affect your posture. If you have to do some marching, sore feet will ruin your whole day.

EXERCISE AND CONDITIONING

Mild exercise for a few minutes every day is important for your efficiency. Work out a system of conditioning exercises and follow it every day. These should include warming-up exercises like the ones athletes do to prepare their muscles, joints, and body for activity. These exercises include standing, kneeling, sitting, and lying prone. Then do limbering exercises: body stretching, twisting, bending, and running in place.

Bones and muscles need exercise to develop properly and to hold the body in good shape.

Bones and muscles need exercise to develop properly and hold the body in good shape. These young women are having fun while doing some exercises during an NJROTC miniboot camp.

Healthy people can stay in condition through exercise and physical training. Exercise can prepare a person for the day's activity. It is also relaxing, and helps a person forget the strains of the day. Free exercises, or exercises of the whole body, stretch all of the muscles. Deep breathing exercises should also be done with other exercises.

Here is a plan for conditioning exercises:

1. Arm exercises—extension of arms and shoulders.
2. Trunk turning—for waist.
3. Leg raising—for pelvic regions or balance.
4. Trunk sideward bending—for extension of lower back and thighs.
5. Bending and twisting neck and chest—for loosening neck and chest.
6. Trunk forward bending—for extension of lower back and thighs.
7. Trunk lowering—trunk straight from head to hips for posture.
8. Sit-ups—for abdominal muscles.
9. Correctional exercises—include work where there is a deficiency in strength.
10. Stepping—for legs, rhythm, balance, and agility.
11. Breathing—for tapering off in effort and relaxation.

All applicants for the Naval Academy and NROTC must pass a physical aptitude examination (PAE) as part of the tests for admission. The examination tests coordination, physical strength, speed, agility, and endurance. It is used to predict a candidate's ability to handle the Navy's physical education program.

Exercise helps to develop good posture. It helps you to move easily and gives your muscles a chance to relax and contract. Good posture is needed in both sitting and standing. For good posture, keep the head erect, shoulders back, chest out, and stomach in. This puts the spinal column into line. When people sit or stand incorrectly, they get tired easily. If you tire quickly, or have aches and pains, the chances are that your posture is poor. Good posture can correct the problem.

REST AND SLEEP

The body must have rest and sleep. Otherwise it will become overtired and unable to fight off disease. Night is the normal time for best rest and sleep, for there is less noise, light, and activity then. Thus the mind and muscles relax quickly after a day's work.

Have a regular time to go to bed. This prepares the body for better rest. Remember, for good study habits you need to have a regular time for best results. In the same way, regular sleeping hours allow the body to refresh itself for the next day.

DIET AND DIGESTION

In the old days of "iron men and wooden ships," disease killed more men than cannonballs did. Not until World War II did combat cause more deaths than disease in the U.S. Army and Navy. Sailors in the old days lived for months in damp and cold ships. They ate salted or rancid meat and moldy or wormy bread. They drank foul-smelling water, and bathed—if at all—in cold salt water.

Today, naval food is good and wholesome, and provides a well-balanced diet. There is no good reason why the diet in every U.S. home cannot be just as good and wholesome. The person who eats hamburgers, hot dogs, or "junk" foods at every meal is missing out on a lot. But, more important, he or she probably is not getting a properly balanced diet.

Work and exercise use up the body's energy. This must be replaced by food. Bones and muscles need foods high in *protein* and *calcium* for growth and repair. Thus a balanced diet should include protein from meat and fish for building body tissues. *Carbohydrates* come from sugar and starchy foods such as bread and pasta. There are two sorts of carbohydrates: simple and complex. Simple carbohydrates are in sweets such as candy, and tend to turn into fat. Complex carbohydrates are in whole-grain products and are very good for you. Both kinds give the body quick energy. *Fats,* such as oil, butter, or margarine, as well as excess carbohydrates, are a source of energy that can be stored for later use.

Minerals and vitamins are needed for your blood and general health. If your diet is balanced, you don't need to take extra vitamin tablets or iron pills. In fact, overdoing it on vitamins may do more harm than good.

Your body must get enough liquids each day. The basic liquid is water, and it is usually recommended that a person drink six to eight glasses a day. You may need less if you drink milk or fruit juices. Alcoholic beverages, soft drinks, tea, and coffee have little food value, and can damage the body if used too much.

According to current governmental guidelines, a healthy diet should include the daily servings listed below from each of the six basic food groups, as identified by the U.S. Department of Agriculture:

1. *Vegetables*. Three to five servings. Includes dark green and dark yellow vegetables, potatoes.
2. *Fruits*. Two to four servings. Includes citrus fruits, juices, berries, and grapes.
3. *Breads and cereals*. Six to eleven servings. Includes all products made with whole grains or enriched flour or meal, like whole-wheat bread, pasta, and ready-to-eat cereals.
4. *Milk products*. Two to three servings. Includes whole, skim, and low-fat milk, evaporated dry milk, ice cream, yogurt, ice milk, and cheeses. Fortified (with vitamins A and D) skim and low-fat milk provide the same nutrients as whole milk products, but with fewer calories.
5. *Meat, poultry, fish, and beans*. Two to three servings. Includes beef, veal, lamb, pork, poultry, fish, shellfish, beans or peas, eggs, nuts, and peanut butter.
6. *Fats, sweets, and oils*. Includes butter, margarine, oils, sugar, honey, syrups, candy, soft drinks, and salad dressings. Since all these foods provide calories but relatively few nutrients, there is no suggested number of servings per day. Overuse can lead to health problems.

Three meals a day is the normal eating routine. It is best to eat meals at regular times so the body's digestive system gets used to a routine. Snacks between meals should be kept to a minimum. Avoid sweets, overeating, and eating too much fatty "junk" food. Obesity (grossly overweight condition) from bad eating habits is a very common health problem in the United States today, especially among teenagers.

ORAL HYGIENE—DENTAL CARE

Three dental diseases are most often seen by the Navy's dental personnel. These are tooth decay (*caries* or *cavities*), reddening of the gums around the tooth (*gingivitis*), and a disease of the gums and bone surrounding the teeth (*pyorrhea*). All of these diseases can cause you to lose your teeth. All of them can be prevented or controlled by proper oral hygiene.

Tooth decay can be greatly reduced by carefully brushing your teeth and by cutting down on sweets. Sugar causes tooth decay; the more sugar you eat in *any* form, the more cavities you'll have. At the first sign of decay, see the dentist. Go to the dentist for a thorough checkup every six months. Frequent checkups and regular brushing will help you keep healthy teeth and gums.

Many dental disorders begin with the buildup of plaque on the teeth. *Plaque* is a thin film containing bacteria. It forms on the tooth surface, and, if not removed, it hardens into *tartar,* a yellowish coating. Tartar encourages tooth decay, and looks ugly. The main purpose of oral hygiene is to remove this plaque. Plaque between teeth is removed by using dental floss, using an up-and-down motion. Brushing your teeth completes the removal procedure. When you brush, direct the bristles of your toothbrush toward the tooth roots and where teeth and gums meet. Short back-and-forth strokes should be used to clean all sides of the tooth. Use a scrubbing motion to clean chewing surfaces. Plaque is constantly reforming on teeth. Thus it is best to brush the teeth after each meal. But at least brush in the morning after breakfast, and in the evening before going to bed. Many dentists recommend brushing the tongue and gums as well.

Proper brushing will (a) remove food and other deposits from the teeth, between the teeth, and from the gums; (b) help the circulation in the gum tissues; (c) toughen or harden the gums.

Normal healthy gums are pale pink in color, are firm, and fit firmly against the tooth. If tartar and food particles are allowed to accumulate, the gums will become swollen or puffy, reddish in color, and loose around the teeth. They are likely to bleed easily when touched. These are symptoms of *gingivitis.*

If gingivitis has been present for some time, pockets will form between the tooth and gum. The mouth will become sore and bleed easily. Teeth will become loose, and even get to the point where they fall out because of bone decay. *Pyorrhea* is the disease one step beyond gingivitis. Poor mouth hygiene will result in these dental diseases.

Have two or more toothbrushes, so at least one is always dry for use. If the bristles become soft or bent, the brush should be thrown away. Medium stiffness is best for toothbrush bristles.

INFECTIOUS DISEASE AND INOCULATIONS

Personal hygiene is of great importance in the Navy. People live close together on board ship, so cleanliness and good personal hygiene are essential for the well-being of the entire crew. Dirt breeds disease.

When persons are ill, they should not come to school and pass the germs around. The same commonsense rules hold true in civilian life as on board ship in the Navy. Most schools now have full-time public health nurses. If you become ill when in school, report to the nurse immediately. The nurse can take the necessary action to have you taken home or get other medical attention.

Today, few high school students come down with the "childhood diseases" that used to sweep through every school once or twice a year. Mumps, measles, chicken pox, scarlet fever, whooping cough, and even more serious diseases such as typhoid fever, smallpox, diphtheria, and polio used to be common, and feared by everyone. Today, inoculations (shots) are available to all children, either in preschool clinics, public health programs, or the schools themselves. If any child is not inoculated against these diseases, it is a matter of negligence on the part of parents. In fact, in many cities and schools it is unlawful not to be inoculated against these diseases. Such inoculations must be done for the health of all the people.

The Navy requires all of its personnel to have inoculations. In addition to the usual shots required for most citizens, the Navy has to see that its personnel are protected from diseases that are common in foreign areas, particularly the tropics. Some of these are typhus, bubonic plague, cholera, smallpox, and yellow fever. Inoculations for infectious influenza (flu) are also given.

Sexually Transmitted Diseases (STDs). For many years sexually transmitted diseases were not mentioned in polite society. This did not prevent people at every level—from royalty to riff-raff— from getting them. STDs are no longer such hush-

hush subjects. They should not be, because they are a big problem among young people in the United States. This makes it a matter of great public concern.

Sexually transmitted diseases are serious infections that, in all but the rarest instances, are caught through sexual intercourse. Preventing these diseases depends almost completely on limiting sexual contact—no sexual contact, no STDs.

If signs of STD infection do appear, it is absolutely vital for the person to get medical care immediately. Many types of these diseases can be cured if proper treatment is given at the first sign of infection. The effects on the future well-being of the individual who does not cure an STD case can be tragic—inability to bear children, birth of deformed or mentally diseased children, heart disease, blindness, insanity, and death are some of the possible consequences. An STD *must* receive professional medical attention; it will not go away by itself. The longer the disease remains untreated, the more serious the effect on a person's health.

Acquired Immune Deficiency Syndrome (AIDS). In recent years an even worse kind of sexually transmitted disease than the older kinds discussed above has arisen. Called acquired immune deficiency syndrome (AIDS for short), it is caught mostly by direct sexual contact, but sometimes by injection by an infected needle or blood transfusion. Eventual death from inability to fight infection usually results from the disease. There is no known cure.

When the AIDS virus enters the bloodstream, there are several possibilities. Some people may remain well for some time, but even so, they are able to infect others. They have human immunodeficiency virus (HIV). Others may develop a disease that is less serious than AIDS called AIDS-related complex. But in most people, once they are infected with the AIDS virus, it destroys the protective immune system. This allows other germs and cancers that ordinarily would never get a foothold to cause "opportunistic" diseases such as pneumonia and tuberculosis that eventually result in death. The AIDS virus may also attack the nervous system, causing damage to the brain.

Some symptoms and signs of AIDS include unexplained weight loss, a persistent cough, fever, and shortness of breath. Multiple purplish blotches and bumps may appear on the skin. Brain damage caused by AIDS may take years to develop, and the symptoms may show up as memory loss, indifference, loss of coordination, partial paralysis, or mental disorder.

Currently, an estimated 1.5 million people in the United States are infected with the AIDS virus. Victims include both homosexual and heterosexual men and women, teenagers, and children.

Although the AIDS virus has been found in several body fluids, including tears and saliva, no instance of transmission from casual contact such as shaking hands, hugging, kissing, crying, coughing, or sneezing has been reported. There are no known cases of AIDS transmission by insects such as mosquitoes, or by contact with domestic animals such as dogs and cats. AIDS is caught by direct sexual contact with infected persons or by direct blood contact mainly through sharing infected needles or contaminated blood transfusions. So the best way to avoid AIDS is to avoid illicit drug use and casual sex, especially with multiple partners and homosexual or bisexual individuals.

Chapter 2. Study Guide Questions

1. What is meant by the term *health*?
2. Upon whom does the responsibility of keeping healthy fall?
3. Why are sailors in our Navy healthier today than ever before?
4. What is involved with personal hygiene?
5. Why is cleanliness important for health?
6. How often should a person bathe or shower?
7. A. Why is foot care important?
B. How should the feet be cared for after showering?
8. Why is exercise important for the body?
9. What is a usual cause of tiring quickly, or having common aches and pains?

10. Why are regular hours for sleep helpful for good health?

11. A. Why is a balanced diet important?

B. Why should eating simple carbohydrates be carefully limited?

12. What are the six basic food groups recommended by experts in nutrition?

13. What are the three most common dental diseases?

14. A. What are *plaque* and *tartar*?

B. Why is proper tooth brushing important?

15. Why is personal hygiene important in the Navy?

16. A. Why are *inoculations* important?

B. Why must the Navy give a group of special inoculations to its personnel?

17. Why must sexually transmitted diseases be medically treated at the first signs of infection?

18. A. What is AIDS?

B. How is it best avoided?

Vocabulary

hygiene	nutrition
health	oral hygiene
posture	infectious disease
medication	inoculation
perspiration	permissiveness
limbering exercises	supervision
abdominal muscles	penicillin
digestion	sexual intercourse
balanced diet	sexually transmitted
protein	disease (STD)
carbohydrate	AIDS

Chapter 3. Drugs, Alcohol, and Tobacco: Use and Abuse

The abuse of drugs is a matter of great concern to all society. Especially in the military, where people greatly depend on each other for safety and survival, drug abusers cannot be tolerated.

In this chapter we will discuss some of the history of drug use, terms used in regard to drugs, and possible effects of drug abuse.

EARLY HISTORY

Drugs that affect behavior have been known all through history. Even primitive people used drugs in religious rites or to prepare warriors for battle. The Chinese knew of marijuana as far back as 2700 B.C.; they may have used opium to dull the senses of attacking troops in the Korean War in the early 1950s.

From earliest days, there has been a proper use of some drugs for medicinal purposes. Ancient Egyptians used opium to relieve pain and to induce sleep. It was used in the early Christian era in Mediterranean countries for the same purpose, and to relieve symptoms of cough and diarrhea. Opium was used in medieval Europe to treat hysteria.

By the eighteenth century, opium was used by doctors in the American colonies as a pain reliever for cancer, gallstones, dysentery, toothache, epileptic spasms, and pains of childbirth. Some of these uses continue today.

NONMEDICINAL USE

Since earliest times, nonmedicinal opium smoking has been a means of escape for people who are unable to cope with the realities of life. Such persons seek relief from anxiety, gloom, despair, boredom, and loneliness.

In the 1800s two opium derivatives, morphine and codeine, were discovered. Morphine became popular among opium users, as well as some doctors, because it is about ten times more potent than opium. Unfortunately, it is easy to become addicted to these powerful opium derivatives.

A big factor in the growth of narcotic abuse was the invention of the hypodermic syringe and needle in 1843. Brought to the United States in 1856,

Most illegal drugs are smuggled into the United States by crime syndicates. The Coast Guard seized this freighter, which was attempting to smuggle marijuana from South America to the Gulf Coast.

it was used to give morphine to wounded soldiers in the Civil War. Many soldiers came home addicted to the drug. By 1880, the use of the needle by addicts was widespread.

Because of its medicinal use, opium and its derivatives were available in any drugstore. There were no controls. Many people became addicted by using the drug for medicinal purposes. Then, in 1898, another derivative was discovered: heroin. First it was used as treatment for morphine addiction, just as morphine had been used to treat the opium habit. Heroin, however, proved to be even more addictive and dangerous.

By 1900 doctors began to realize the destructive nature of the drug, especially in the form of heroin. At first the public had felt sorry for the victims and blamed the drug. Now they saw addiction as an illness or a vice. By 1909 a direct association between addiction and crime had been confirmed. The U.S. government stepped in to pass laws against importing these drugs except for medicinal use.

Now addicts were cut off from all legal sources of drugs, so the underworld market began to grow.

Prices on black-market narcotics rose, and addicts were forced into criminal activities to support their habit. Illegal drug dealing grew, as did drug-related crime. As dealing in illegal drugs became more profitable for crime syndicates, they encouraged addicts to become pushers. This would increase the market, and provide addicts with a source of money to support their own habit. But addicts did not make good pushers. They could not be depended upon to make payments as their own habit became worse. So pushers became middlemen. Laws were passed to control both addicts and pushers.

In 1929 the U.S. government opened federal drug rehabilitation centers at Forth Worth, Texas, and Lexington, Kentucky. The extreme difficulty of rehabilitation from drugs became known to the public. This, together with a tough crackdown on drug dealing, reduced the number of addicts to about 60,000 by the time the United States entered World War II in 1941.

During the war, people did not think much about the drug problem. In fact, the number of addicts decreased until by 1957 there were fewer than 45,000 reported in the United States. About that same time, however, younger people began becoming involved with narcotics. Stiffer laws were passed, and penalties were increased. Despite the efforts of law enforcement agencies, and attempts at drug education in schools, the problem grew rapidly. It continues to grow, especially in the junior-high age group.

Today the drug problem is a serious matter of national concern. Crime, broken homes, child abuse, unemployment, and automobile accidents, all may result from drug use. Increases in drug-related hospitalizations, deaths, suicides, vandalism, and birth defects are other effects of drugs.

These are serious problems facing all Americans. Minds weakened by drugs do not have the will to resist the pressures of modern life. Attempts to liberalize drug laws and ease drug penalties go against the best interests of the United States. Stamping out drug abuse could be a matter of national survival.

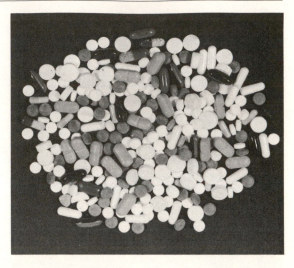

Many drugs taken by abusers come in the form of pills or capsules. Stimulants such as amphetamines and depressants of the barbiturate group are commonly taken in this way. These drugs are dangerous to the body and often lead to death from overdose.

Obtaining Illegal Drugs

Despite strict laws on dangerous drugs, there is a ready supply of them on the illegal drug market. They are obtained in several ways.

Smuggling. This is illegal importing of drugs. It is usually done by ship or aircraft from foreign countries. Heroin, for example, is completely outlawed in the United States and most other countries. It can only be brought in by smuggling. Most marijuana and cocaine in the United States is also smuggled in. Crime syndicates run most smuggling operations.

Illicit Operations. This refers to the making of drugs by criminals. Most of these drugs are chemically inferior, and some are contaminated. Another illicit operation is the "front" or phony company set up to buy drugs from legal manufacturers.

Bulk Peddlers. These individuals are the supply points for the pushers. They buy from criminal manufacturers, smugglers, and other sources and distribute to pushers.

Fraud. This means obtaining drugs from a doctor or pharmacist by forging or altering a prescription.

Illegal Sales. Most druggists and doctors are honest, but some have been caught using their position to make money by selling drugs illegally. This violates the public trust.

Drug laws vary from state to state. The federal law on drugs is the Comprehensive Drug Abuse Prevention and Control Act of 1970. The criminal penalties under the act vary, according to the drug involved. Making or selling illicit drugs is punishable by as much as fifteen years in prison, depending upon the kind of drug. If a person is involved with five or more other persons in illicit drug dealing, the mandatory sentence is not less than ten years, and as much as life imprisonment. In recent years many states and localities have enacted even tougher antidrug laws including "drug free zones" around schools, within which penalties for anyone caught dealing drugs are very severe.

These laws are apparently not tough enough, however, for some are still willing to chance arrest because of the large profits they can make. In the meantime, a terrible toll of young lives is being taken.

WHAT IS DRUG ABUSE?

The word *drug* refers to a wide variety of substances. Drugs include aspirin, penicillin, antihistamines, and antacids commonly used for medication—and also illegal substances such as marijuana, LSD, cocaine, and heroin. Alcohol and tobacco are also classified as drugs.

Medicinal drugs are necessary to treat disease and relieve pain. Without the proper use of medicinal drugs, there would be much more pain, suffering, and death in the world today. *Drug abuse* (sometimes called *substance abuse*) refers to the illegal or improper use of drugs or other substances for inappropriate reasons.

It is difficult to understand how people with common sense would destroy their health or avoid healthy adjustment to the world around them by drug or other substance abuse. But too many young people are doing so. Those who abuse drugs fall into the following three categories.

Situation Users. These persons misuse drugs in a particular situation or at certain times. These may be people who want to sleep but can't, people who want to stay awake even though they are tired, or people who think they can pep themselves up for a test or athletic event.

Spree Users. These people think they can get excitement from a mind-altering drug or inhalant. Sometimes the "high" lasts for an extended time, such as a night or a weekend. These people sometimes "overdose" or mix drugs with alcohol, and seriously damage their minds or even kill themselves as a result. Many are involved in automobile accidents and kill not only themselves, but innocent persons.

Hard-core Users or Addicts. These victims of drug abuse have become dependent on drugs. Their whole lives involve the drugs to the point where family, friends, school, jobs, and other things in normal life are no longer important. They have become drains on society and dangers to the community. They often get into crime and pushing to "feed" their habit.

Even if some people who are situation or spree users avoid long-term effects, many others will end up as hard-core users. That is the nature of addiction. The fact is that all addicts were, at one time, situation or spree users. All of them once thought they would never become addicts.

REASONS TO AVOID DRUG ABUSE

Unquestionably, the main reason to avoid situation or spree misuse of drugs or other substances is the danger of becoming a hard-core addict. There is no way for anyone to know when dependency will take over. But there are other reasons to avoid *any* use, even situation or spree misuse.

1. *Drug abuse is medically unwise.* It is dangerous to health. Overdoses can kill. In fact, death or serious illness from overdose occurs most often with situation or spree users. The hard-core user has less resistance to sickness and disease than the normal, healthy person. Disease germs causing hepatitis, lockjaw (tetanus), blood poisoning, and blood clots can easily come from unsterile needles used to inject drugs. In recent years, many intravenous drug users have gotten AIDS (acquired immune deficiency syndrome—usually fatal) from using contaminated needles. And sooner or later probably *all* drug abusers will use an unsterile needle.

2. *Drug abuse will ruin personal appearance.* Long-term drug use will change one's appearance, producing glazed eyes, a sickly complexion, a generally unhealthy look. The hard-core user usually will not bother with personal hygiene, and physical and mental breakdown will occur.

3. *Drug abuse is expensive.* Cigarette smokers can easily spend dollars a day for their habit. But hard drug users may spend as much as $100 or more a day to keep their habit going. In most cases, crime is the only way to get this much money.

4. *Drug abuse endangers safety.* Those who use drugs are more likely to have accidents than those who do not. People under the influence of drugs often don't care about their personal safety or that of others. Drugs can also make people think they can do superhuman things:

walk on water, drive at great speed, float in the air out of windows, or balance on roof tops. The result is disaster.

5. *Drug abuse is illegal.* It is against the law in every state and every country, and carries heavy penalties. The spree or situation user is breaking the law—just the same as the hard-core user—when "experimenting" with drugs. Arrest can spell disaster for the experimenter. It causes embarrassment, school problems, and family problems. If a person gets a police record, many careers are closed or restricted to him. A Naval Academy or NROTC midshipman found guilty of any involvement with drugs, for exmaple, will immediately be dismissed. A drug arrest for even a first offense can have lasting effect on one's life.

6. *Drug abuse is antisocial.* Many people experiment with drugs thinking it will make them popular, or put them with an "in" group. It may seem exciting and different from the "straight" world. But the user's social contacts soon become limited to other abusers, pushers, and dealers. Pushers and dealers are the scum of the earth, for they prey on the weaknesses of their fellow human beings. The world can be a wonderful place, full of opportunity and enjoyment for a young person. But the drug abuser can't be a part of that world.

7. *Drug abuse is illogical.* Drug abuse appeals to uncontrolled emotions, not to the sensible mind. It is not a need, but a bad personal choice that the user makes. For this mistake, the user will suffer both physically and mentally. Becoming a user is voluntary. It just doesn't make sense to do something that is so destructive to yourself.

8. *Drug abuse can mean long suffering for the user and the user's family.* It can lead to legal, health, financial, and family problems. The effects are long-term. A criminal record or a broken family is a long-lasting thing. In addition, there is now strong evidence that the newborn children of abusers tend to be physically and mentally deficient. Babies of addicted mothers are themselves addicts at birth, are often premature, and

may die. There is growing evidence that use of even relatively mild drugs such as marijuana has much more serious long-term effects on your mind and body and future children than was thought even a few years ago.

These are some of the reasons for avoiding any abuse of drugs. In spite of these reasons, however, many young people today do experiment with drugs. Here are some of the "reasons" they have given for drug abuse:

- "I just wanted to get away from this lousy world."
- "For kicks, what else?"
- "I wanted to expand my mind."
- "My friends are doing it."
- "I was just curious."
- "I just wanted to relax."
- "I wanted to feel good."
- "Because my parents told me not to."

Do these "reasons" make good sense? They are *excuses,* and very poor ones, for wanting to experiment with drugs, not *reasons.* If you want to change yourself or the world, experimenting with dangerous drugs is not the way to do it. You can easily lose control, and drugs will come to control your life.

DEPENDENCY AND ADDICTION

Every drug has its own effect upon the user. Much research is being done on this subject, and there have been many findings. Some definitions will be helpful at this point.

Addiction is a state produced by the repeated abuse of a drug. Its characteristics are:

- An overpowering desire or "need" to keep taking the drug, and desire to get it by any means.
- A tendency to have to increase the dose each time to get the same "high."
- A psychological and physical dependence on the effects of the drug.

Habituation is a state that includes:

- A desire to keep taking the drug for the temporary sense of well-being that it produces.
- No strong tendency to increase the dose.
- Some degree of psychological dependence, but little or no physical dependence.

- A bad effect on the individual but less effect on society as a whole.

Drug dependence is the need of a person to use a drug on a regular basis. Dependency is different for different drugs.

Physical dependence happens when the body adapts to the presence of a drug. The body then develops a need for the drug. Once such dependence has been established, the body may react severely if the user stops taking the drug. Such symptoms are collectively called *withdrawal,* and they may occur when a user tries to stop taking the drug altogether, or when the effects of a previous dose start to wear off.

Psychological dependence is an attachment to a drug that satisfies some emotional need of a person. Psychological dependence does not necessarily mean physical dependence.

Tolerance is the tendency for the body to "get used to" the drug. This causes the user to keep increasing the dosage to get the same effect.

The term *hooked* applies to physical addiction, which almost always leads to terrible results.

One can become dependent on such substances as alcohol, tobacco, or even the caffeine in coffee or soft drinks, in addition to the more dangerous drugs.

There are different ways in which a person can become dependent on drugs. Any use of drugs can lead to continued use of them. Therefore, you must avoid *all* ways of using dangerous drugs, for the sake of health and safety.

TYPES OF DRUGS

Drugs may be divided into five general categories:
- Stimulants.
- Depressants.
- Hallucinogens.
- Deliriants.
- Narcotics.

Stimulants. These speed up the central nervous system. They cause a temporary sense of well-being and self-confidence. They temporarily increase alertness, curb the appetite, and reduce depression. The most abused stimulant drugs are *cocaine* (coke or crack) and the *amphetamines*: amphetamine or "bennies," dextroamphetamine or "dexies," and methamphetamine or "speed." As a group, stimulants are known as "uppers." They are usually taken as pills, but can be taken by sniffing or injection.

Amphetamines stimulate the areas of the nervous system that control the blood pressure, heart rate, and breathing, all of which increase when the drug is taken. Amphetamines can keep the body in a "high" state for long periods of time. They are not addictive, but can create a psychological dependence in a few weeks.

Amphetamine abusers are talkative, excitable, and restless. Long-term heavy users are irritable and unstable. They may break down completely. Going off the drug can result in deep and suicidal depression. Many medical authorities believe that amphetamines are more harmful to the body than any other drug.

Cocaine has become common on the drug scene in the United States in recent years. It has an intense, addictive, and stimulating effect. Cocaine also has many other extremely harmful side effects, especially in its purer form, called *crack*. Even a small one-time dose of crack cocaine can kill a person. Permanent brain damage can result, and nerve structure can be altered. Transmission of nerve signals can be blocked, causing heart failure. It can induce epileptic seizures in a person with no previous signs of epilepsy. Overdoses cause extreme agitation, fast irregular breathing, possible convulsions, respiratory arrest, and death. Long-term effects from repeated usage of any form of cocaine include weight loss, heart damage, and depression leading to suicidal tendencies. Because it is some 90 percent pure, and it is usually smoked, crack cocaine is one of the most highly addictive substances known. Using crack just one time can result in addiction for many people.

Depressants. Some depressants are called *sedatives* or *tranquilizers*. They relax the central nervous system. Controlled medical usage is for treatment of epilepsy, high blood pressure, insomnia, and mental illness, if it does not kill them outright.

Commonly abused depressants include the *bar-*

biturates, such as phenobarbital, pentobarbital, secobarbital (Seconal), and amobarbital, among others. In drug talk they are called "downers." They have many other names, such as goof-balls, red devils, yellow jackets, phennies, and blue heaven. The abuse of barbiturates is highly dangerous. Many accidents are caused by abusers who have slow and erratic reactions. Fatal overdoses are possible when abusers become confused about how many pills they have taken. Mixing alcohol with barbiturates causes many deaths among youths every year.

Opiates are depressants. These include the opium derivatives such as *heroin, morphine,* and *codeine.* Such names as stuff, junk, horse, morph, and smack apply to this group. Morphine and codeine have some medicinal value as pain relievers, but heroin has no medicinal value whatsoever. The opiates cause both physical and psychological dependence. The body develops a *need* for the drug. Because the user's tolerance keeps increasing, he or she must keep taking larger and larger doses. Because opiates are usually injected, there is great danger from contaminated injections and overdoses. In New York City alone, more than a thousand deaths occur each year from these causes.

The depressant user acts a lot like an alcoholic drunk. This individual is confused, has slurred speech, and staggers around in a dreamlike state. The ability to think, concentrate, or work is impaired. The person's behavior is irrational. Withdrawal is dangerous. Heroin addicts will suffer chills, muscle aches and jerks, severe abdominal pains, and frightful hallucinations about twelve to sixteen hours after their last "fix" or injection.

Hallucinogens. These drugs distort the way the abuser sees reality. They can cause wild dreams and weird visions. They can also cause extreme and dangerous behavior. Effects vary widely among individuals. There may be sensations of lightheadedness and emptiness, and the body may seem to float. Time seems to race, stop, slow down, or even go backward. A person may cry, laugh, or feel no emotion at all. One may feel alone and cut off from the world. This may lead to anxiety, fear, and panic. Colors become intense, shapes and spaces look distorted, and objects (tables, chairs, books) are thought to have emotions.

Hallucinogens include *marijuana* (grass, pot), *hashish* (hash), *lysergic acid diethylamide* (LSD), *mescaline, peyote, psilocybin,* and *dimethyltryptamine* (DMT), among others. LSD and marijuana have been studied extensively by medical laboratories, but new information keeps coming in as long-term research projects are concluded. The long-term bad effects of these drugs are still not fully known. Psychological dependence can result from their use, though physical addiction does not. Persons involved with either of these drugs may progress to other kinds, especially heroin.

The psychological effects of marijuana include distortions of hearing, vision, and sense of time. A person "high" on marijuana usually has a feeling of quietness and tends to withdraw into oneself. Heavy use causes a person to lose all desire to work or compete. A few inhalations on a strong marijuana cigarette, or "joint," can intoxicate one for several hours. It has been found that the active ingredient in this drug remains in the body tissues of users for several months after only a single use of this drug. Other recent studies indicate that long-term usage can damage the human reproductive system, resulting in birth defects, hyperactivity, and learning disabilities in the children of those who use it.

LSD is an extremely potent drug that causes weird sensations to the abuser. One ounce of LSD is enough to provide 300,000 average doses. Each dose is a tiny speck, whose effect lasts from eight to twelve hours. It is usually swallowed on wafers, sugar lumps, or candy. Hallucinations are a part of an LSD "trip." Emotions may range from bliss to sheer horror. A "good trip" consists of pleasant feelings and views; a "bad trip" or "bummer" provides terrible images that arouse dread and terror. Panic sometimes follows if the abuser cannot "turn off" the drug's action.

Flashbacks are common with LSD; that is, days or even months later the "trip" may recur, causing the person to believe he is losing his mind. There is strong evidence that LSD has caused permanent mental derangement, and that it may cause inher-

Marijuana is a widely found plant of the cannabis or wild hemp family. It is generally grown in countries with warm climates, then smuggled into the United States. But it is often found growing here also.

itable defects in children of abusers. Suicides, suicide attempts, violent assaults, and murders have been committed under the influence of LSD. Accidental deaths have occurred with LSD users who have walked into traffic or jumped from high windows, feeling they were invulnerable.

A common hallucinogen used by some young people in recent years is *angel dust* (phencyclidine, PCP). It comes in tablets, capsules, or powder for swallowing or sniffing. It impairs thinking and concentration, and often causes extreme worry about death. It is often produced in makeshift laboratories in highly contaminated form, and may result in permanent brain damage.

Deliriants. These substances cause mental confusion when inhaled. They include such things as aerosol products, airplane glue, lighter fluid, paint thinner, gasoline, cleaning fluid, and spray can propellants. Inhalation or "sniffing" causes nausea, dizziness, shakiness, and muscle spasms. The effect is a "high" dreamlike state, sleepiness, and disorientation. Such drugs are extremely dangerous to the experimenter. Fatal accidents have repeatedly occurred due to asphyxiation and suffocation.

Narcotics. The term *narcotic* refers to opium and to the pain-relieving drugs made from opium. These drugs are depressants, but are in a separate category because they cause physical addiction. Cocaine, even though a stimulant, is also included in this category. The group includes opium, heroin, percodan, demerol, morphine, codeine, and cocaine.

Heroine accounts for about 90 percent of the narcotic addiction cases in the United States. It is the most dangerous of the narcotic drugs. It is almost impossible to cure a heroin addict. Tolerance builds up quickly, causing the abuser to need more and more of the drug. Sickness from withdrawal and overdose is common. Serious overdose will cause death just minutes after injection. Even without an overdose, the life of a heroin addict may be shortened by fifteen to twenty years.

Once a person is hooked on heroin or other narcotics, getting a regular supply becomes the main goal of his or her life. The need to get money for drugs keeps addicts from continuing their education or job. Addicts will usually steal or deal drugs to sustain their habit. Female addicts often turn to prostitution to support the habit. An addict lives only to support his or her addiction.

ALCOHOL ABUSE

As serious as the "drug scene" is, alcohol is the number-one drug problem in the United States today. Most people, however, do not think of alcohol as a drug. This is probably because of its widespread use in our society. Throughout history, alcoholic drinks have been used with meals, at social gatherings, in religious ceremonies, and in celebration. Alcohol does have some acceptable uses—but it also can be abused.

Alcohol is a depressant. It produces lightheadedness if consumed in small amounts. But alcohol also slows down the central nervous system, so the good feeling at the beginning quickly wears off. Large amounts of alcohol over a long period of time cause anxiety. Just as with other dangerous drugs, it may cause physical or psychological dependence. This dependence is an illness called *alcoholism.*

Alcohol is a natural substance formed by sugar

and yeast. *Ethyl alcohol* is the form of alcohol found in beer, wine, and liquor. It slows activity of the brain.

Alcohol is absorbed directly into the stomach lining. It does not have to be digested like food does. Therefore, it takes effect very fast. Once it enters the bloodstream, it goes through the entire body. Its effects continue until it is completely used up. The length of time the effects remain depends on the size of the person. The average 150-pound person needs at least an hour to go through the effects of one drink (one shot of whiskey, one beer, or five ounces of wine). If a person has six drinks, it will take six hours or more to "sober up."

A person becomes intoxicated or "drunk" when the alcohol level in the bloodstream becomes high. Intoxication has several stages. The first stage is a "happy" relaxed state in which the person likes to talk, and be with people. There is some loss of judgment and coordination, however. Later, an individual may become excited and be unable to think or keep control. If the person keeps drinking, he or she becomes confused and moody, and finally may go into a stupor or coma. A drinker who has had too much alcohol at one time may even die from respiratory paralysis.

Alcoholism is the condition of a person who has become dependent upon alcohol. An alcoholic uses alcohol to ease personal problems. Such a person has lost control of the drinking habit. Drinking then dominates all other aspects of life.

The disease goes through stages. Early signs may be an increase in drinking to escape problems. Too much "party drinking" can also be an early sign. Soon the body begins to show tolerance, and more alcohol needs to be drunk for the same effect. Now the person has trouble stopping drinking "in time" to avoid getting drunk. Later signs may include drinking alone and drinking during the early part of the day. By this time, the individual probably feels guilty about the problem and tries to hide it. Finally, drinking becomes the primary goal in life, and the body is physically dependent on alcohol.

Alcoholism causes poor health, in one form or another. Alcohol is a major factor in heart disease, birth defects leading to mental retardation, and cancer. In a recent year, statistics from the National Institute on Alcohol Abuse and Alcoholism showed these facts:

- About 100 million Americans drink alcoholic beverages. About 13.3 million of these people are alcoholics, including 3.3 million youths aged fourteen to seventeen. About one-third of the alcoholics are women.
- More than 200,000 deaths a year are caused by drinking.
- About 10,000 alcoholics commit suicide annually.
- Drunk drivers cause 800,000 auto accidents and account for 25,000 deaths annually.
- More than one-fourth of the admissions to mental institutions are alcohol-related.
- An alcoholic is about five times more likely to die of disease, accident, or violence than the average person.
- About 35 percent of U.S. high school students get drunk at least four times a year. About 5 percent get drunk once a week.
- Between 30 and 40 percent of delinquent children come from alcoholic homes.
- Alcoholism costs Americans over $40 billion a year in lost work, medical expenses, and accidents.

Other horrible statistics could be quoted. But these are enough to show how big the problem is. If the statistics are astounding, the list of unreported or uncategorized figures would be just as tragic: unhappy marriages, divorces, poor families, deprived or displaced children, and disciplinary actions by school, civil, and military authorities.

Young persons are especially tempted to over-indulge, thinking that they must do so to be "one of the gang." Such behavior shows not how manly or womanly they are, but how immature they are. The mature person knows his or her limit and never goes beyond it.

Many experts believe that alcoholism can be treated, but never fully cured. Several things are known about the treatment of the disease:

- The alcoholic must honestly admit the problem and face it.

- The alcoholic must stop drinking, totally.
- The alcoholic needs help from family and friends, and professional help is usually required.

The drinking of alcoholic beverages has long been an accepted social custom. But society has always been intolerant of those who drink too much. Laws on drunken conduct and driving are generally very severe. Millions of people can drink some alcoholic beverages without becoming addicted. Only about one in fifteen becomes an alcoholic, but many of the others are "problem drinkers." As with any drug, not using *any* is the best solution. Otherwise, moderation is the key.

TOBACCO

The health hazards of using tobacco have received more and more attention in recent years. The effects can be very severe.

Nicotine is the main active ingredient in tobacco smoke. In small quantities it acts as a stimulant to the nervous system. In larger quantities, it can cause shortness of breath, coughing, vomiting, and diarrhea, especially in people having low tolerances for nicotine. Large doses act as a depressant, and can cause convulsions, respiratory slowing, coma, and even death. Nicotine is absorbed very fast by the lungs. It reaches the brain only eight seconds after one inhales a puff of tobacco smoke.

Besides nicotine there are several other harmful ingredients in tobacco smoke, particularly cigarettes. These include gases such as carbon monoxide, ammonia, and hydrogen cyanide, and particles called "tar," which cause a yellow stain on many smokers' teeth. Tar is actually made up of a number of substances, many of them cancer-causing. Among these are numerous hydrocarbons and other compounds, even some that are radioactive. Research has shown that more than 4,000 compounds are formed by the burning of tobacco and paper in a typical cigarette.

Regular use of tobacco is linked to birth defects and a variety of serious diseases, including nicotine dependence, emphysema (shortness of breath), lung-tissue damage, heart disease, and lung can-

cer. In a recent year it was estimated that smoking tobacco caused some 80,000 deaths from lung cancer, 22,000 deaths from other cancers, and 225,000 deaths from various heart and blood diseases. Once a person starts smoking tobacco regularly, it is very hard to stop. There are various withdrawal symptoms that last several days to weeks. These include nausea, headache, sleepiness by day and insomnia by night, irritability, and inability to concentrate.

Obviously, the best thing is to avoid using tobacco altogether, which is what more and more smart people are opting to do nowadays.

CLOSING THOUGHTS

We have given a brief account of drug history and abuses, the kinds of drugs, and the destructive effects of drugs. You probably have some ideas of your own on the subject. In today's schools, you probably have already faced the problem, one way or another.

Some young people defend the use of drugs, even if they have decided not to try drugs themselves. They say it is a person's "right" to use drugs, regardless of the law. Others look the other way, saying it is none of their business. Some are afraid to say anything about it at all. Let us look at these and other typical thoughts.

What about those of the older generation who warn about drugs, but then use alcohol and tobacco themselves? Well, they probably wish they had never started, and want to save the younger generation from their pain and anguish. Why not be smarter than they were, and seek to have a long, healthy life?

How can anyone defend marijuana by saying that it is no worse than alcohol? Alcohol is now the nation's number-one problem. Why develop another problem at least as bad as this?

It has been argued that hallucinogens "expand the mind." Actually they produce illusions and distortions. They cause the senses to distort reality, so mental work on problems becomes more difficult—or even impossible. Why not change reality for the better, so problems can be solved?

Some have said that stimulants increase your

mental abilities—more alertness for tests, more zip for athletics, etc. Actually, they draw on the body's reserve energy. If you use them too much, you will exhaust your mind and body. Why not build your abilities by *natural* means? That way, what you do will really be your *own* accomplishment.

Some have said that depressants slow the world down and make problems smaller. Actually, they slow the abusers down, not the world. They dull the abusers' senses and make them less effective, less able to respond to normal demands and emergencies. Isn't it silly to think that by not caring you will either solve problems or make them go away?

It is often said that trying "just once" never hurt anyone. This is *not* so. The law makes few exceptions for the first error. Most addicts started by trying "just once." Why should you think you are smarter or luckier than those other poor souls who got hooked? There is no way to predetermine how the first use of an illegal drug or other substance will affect you. It may range from almost no effect, to violent reaction, addiction, or even death. Is it smart to take that kind of chance?

Is drug use in your school none of your business? How can that be so, when it involves criminals and criminal acts, and affects the security, safety, and good health of you and your classmates? Doesn't it concern you that your life may be endangered by some drunk or doped-up person the next time you ride your bicycle or drive your car on the street? The U.S. Constitution does *not* give lawbreakers the right to deprive law-abiding citizens of their health and happiness.

And remember this too. Drug abuse has particularly important consequences for the armed forces. Therefore, under military law, drug abuse is "conduct prejudicial to good order and discipline." Abusers will be disciplined at Captain's mast or tried by courts-martial. Dishonorable discharge and extended imprisonment are possible punishments in such cases. At the least, confirmed users are discharged.

It must be so. Far more than civilians, those in military service have to depend on each other. The lives of all hands in a naval ship or an aircraft may depend on the alertness of one person and his or her assignment. No commanding officer can entrust his or her unit, ship, or plane to an individual who may be under the influence of drugs or ill from hangover or withdrawal symptoms, or may have a drug flashback in a moment of tension or combat. The safety of the ship depends on the top performance of everyone in the crew. Preserving the independence of the United States does too.

Chapter 3.   Study Guide Questions

1. What are the two basic uses for drugs?

2. Over the centuries, what kinds of people have used opium, and why?

3. A. What are the three main opium derivatives, or opiates?

   B. Which is the strongest and most addictive?

4. With the strict drug laws, who became involved in the illegal drug traffic, and why?

5. What do statistics show to be some of the social problems caused by drug abuse in the nation today?

6. How do most heroin, cocaine, and marijuana enter the country?

7. A. What is the federal law on illegal drug activities?

   B. What are the penalties authorized by the law?

8. What are the three categories into which drug abusers fall? Briefly describe each.

9. What are eight practical reasons to avoid any kind of drug abuse?

10. What are some of the current findings concerning long-term drug abuse?

11. What is addiction?

12. A. What are the two types of drug dependence?

   B. What is the main characteristic of each?

13. What is drug tolerance?

14. A. What are the five general categories of drugs?

   B. What is the effect of each on the human body? List one or two of the principal drugs within each category.

15. Why does one category of drugs get the name *hallucinogen*?

    B. What do recent studies concerning the long-term effects of hallucinogens seem to indicate?

16. What are "flashbacks," and what drug is known for causing them?

17. What is meant by the term *withdrawal*?

18. Which drug is the number-one drug problem in the United States today?

19. A. How long does it take an average person to go through the effects of one drink?

    B. What is the condition of the body when a person becomes intoxicated?

20. A. What is physical and/or psychological dependence on alcohol called?

    B. What are the steps toward alcohol dependence?

21. What three things are necessary for the treatment of alcoholism?

22. What are some of the harmful substances in tobacco smoke?

23. Why is experimentation with drugs dangerous?

24. Why is the use of drugs in your school and community everyone's business?

25. Why is the use of drugs totally unacceptable in the Navy and other military services?

Vocabulary

derivatives
hypodermic needle
addiction
prescription
narcotics
depressant
birth defect
inhalation
illusion
mental derangement
concentration
overdose
hallucinogen, -ation
deliriant
opiate
irritable
crime syndicate
drug trafficking
smuggling
illicit operations
fraud

pharmacist
tranquilizer
drug, drug abuse
irrational
withdrawal
distortion
illogical
intoxication
habituation
drug dependency
drug tolerance
caffeine
stimulant
alcoholism
stupor, coma
statistics
intolerant
moderation
anguish
rational
symptom

Appendix 3:
Text of the Declaration of Independence

When in the Course of human events, it becomes necessary for one people to dissolve the political bands which have connected them with another, and to assume among the powers of the earth, the separate and equal station to which the Laws of Nature and of Nature's God entitle them, a decent respect to the opinions of mankind requires that they should declare the causes which impel them to the separation.—We hold these truths to be self-evident, that all men are created equal, that they are endowed by their Creator with certain unalienable Rights, that among these are Life, Liberty and the pursuit of Happiness.—That to secure these rights, Governments are instituted among Men, deriving their just powers from the consent of the governed.—That whenever any Form of Government becomes destructive of these ends, it is the Right of the People to alter or to abolish it, and to institute new Government, laying its foundation on such principles and organizing its powers in such form, as to them shall seem most likely to effect their Safety and Happiness. Prudence, indeed, will dictate that Governments long established should not be changed for light and transient causes; and accordingly all experience hath shewn, that mankind are more disposed to suffer, while evils are sufferable, than to right themselves by abolishing the forms to which they are accustomed. But when a long train of abuses and usurpations, pursuing invariably the same Object evinces a design to reduce them under absolute Despotism, it is their right, it is their duty, to throw off such Government, and to provide new Guards for their future security.—Such has been the patient sufferance of these Colonies; and such is now the necessity which constrains them to alter their former Systems of Government. The history of the present King of Great Britain is a history of repeated injuries and usurpations, all having in direct object the establishment of an absolute Tyranny over these States. To prove this, let Facts be submitted to a candid world.—He has refused his Assent to Laws, the most wholesome and necessary for the public good.—He has forbidden his Governors to pass Laws of immediate and pressing importance, unless suspended in their operation till his Assent should be obtained; and when so suspended, he has utterly neglected to attend to them.—He has refused to pass other Laws for the accommodation of large districts of people, unless those people would relinquish the right of Representation in the Legislature, a right inestimable to them and formidable to tyrants only.—He has called together legislative bodies at places unusual, uncomfortable, and distant from the depository of their public Records, for the sole purpose of fatiguing them into compliance with his measures.—He has dissolved Representative Houses repeatedly, for opposing with manly firmness his invasions on the rights of the people.—He has refused for a long time, after such dissolutions, to cause others to be elected; whereby the Legislative powers, incapable of Annihilation, have returned to the People at large for their exercise; the State remaining in the meantime exposed to all the dangers of invasion from without, and convulsions within.—He has endeavoured to prevent the population of these States; for that purpose obstructing the Laws for Naturalization of Foreigners; refusing to pass others to encourage their migrations hither, and raising the conditions of new Appropriations of Lands.—He has obstructed the Administration of Justice, by refusing his Assent to Laws for establishing Judiciary powers.—He has made Judges dependent on his Will alone, for the tenure of their offices, and the amount and payment of their salaries.—He has erected a multitude of New Offices, and sent hither swarms of Officers to harass our people, and eat out their substance. He has kept among us, in times of peace, Standing Armies without the Consent of our legislatures.—He has affected to render the Military independent of and superior to the Civil power.—He has combined with others to subject us to a jurisdiction foreign to our constitution, and unacknowledged by our laws; giving his Assent to their Acts of pretended Legislation:—For quartering large bodies of armed troops among us:—For protecting them, by a mock Trial, from punishment for any Murders which they should commit on the Inhabitants of these States:—For cutting off our Trade with all parts of the world:—For imposing Taxes on us without our Consent:—For depriving us in many cases, of the benefits of Trial by Jury:—For transporting us beyond Seas to be tried for pretended offenses:—For abolishing

the free System of English Laws in a neighbouring Province, establishing therein an Arbitrary government, and enlarging its Boundaries so as to render it at once an example and fit instrument for introducing the same absolute rule into these Colonies:—For taking away our Charters, abolishing our most valuable Laws and altering fundamentally the Forms of our Governments:—For suspending our own Legislatures, and declaring themselves invested with power to legislate for us in all cases whatsoever.—He has abdicated Government here, by declaring us out of his Protection and waging War against us.—He has plundered our seas, ravaged our Coasts, burnt our towns, and destroyed the lives of our people.—He is at this time transporting large Armies of foreign Mercenaries to compleat the works of death, desolation and tyranny, already begun with circumstances of Cruelty & perfidy scarcely paralleled in the most barbarous ages, and totally unworthy the Head of a civilized nation.—He has constrained our fellow Citizens taken Captive on the high Seas to bear Arms against their Country, to become the executioners of their friends and Brethren, or to fall themselves by their Hands.—He has excited domestic insurrections amongst us, and has endeavoured to bring on the inhabitants of our frontiers, the merciless Indian Savages, whose known rule of warfare, is an undistinguished destruction of all ages, sexes and conditions. In every stage of these Oppressions We have Petitioned for Redress in the most humble terms: Our repeated Petitions have been answered only by repeated injury. A Prince, whose character is thus marked by every act which may define a Tyrant, is unfit to be the ruler of a free people. Nor have We been wanting in attentions to our British brethren. We have warned them from time to time of attempts by their legislature to extend an unwarrantable jurisdiction over us. We have reminded them of the circumstances of our emigration and settlement here. We have appealed to their native justice and magnanimity, and we have conjured them by the ties of our common kindred to disavow these usurpations, which would inevitably interrupt our connections and correspondence. They too have been deaf to the voice of justice and of consanguinity. We must, therefore, acquiesce in the necessity, which denounces our Separation, and hold them, as we hold the rest of mankind, Enemies in War, in Peace Friends.—

WE, THEREFORE, the Representatives of the UNITED STATES OF AMERICA, in General Congress, Assembled, appealing to the Supreme Judge of the world for the rectitude of our intentions, do, in the Name, and by the Authority of the good People of these Colonies, solemnly publish and declare, That these United Colonies are, and of Right ought to be FREE AND INDEPENDENT STATES; that they are Absolved from all Allegiance to the British Crown, and that all political connection between them and the State of Great Britain, is and ought to be totally dissolved; and that as Free and Independent States, they have full Power to levy War, conclude Peace, contract Alliances, establish Commerce, and to do all other Acts and Things which Independent States may of right do.—And for the support of this Declaration, with a firm reliance on the protection of divine Providence, we mutually pledge to each other our Lives, our Fortunes and our sacred Honor.

Appendix 4: Text of the Constitution of the United States

We the People of the United States, in Order to form a more perfect Union, establish Justice, insure domestic Tranquility, provide for the common defence, promote the general Welfare, and secure the Blessings of Liberty to our selves and our Posterity, do ordain and establish this Constitution for the United States of America.

ARTICLE I.

SECTION 1. All legislative Powers herein granted shall be vested in a Congress of the United States, which shall consist of a Senate and House of Representatives.

SECTION 2. The House of Representatives shall be composed of Members chosen every second Year by the People of the several states, and the Electors in each State shall have the Qualifications requisite for Electors of the most numerous Branch of the State Legislature.

No Person shall be a Representative who shall not have attained to the age of twenty five Years, and have been seven Years a Citizen of the United States, and who shall not, when elected, be an Inhabitant of that State in which he shall be chosen.

Representatives and direct Taxes shall be ap-portioned among the several States which may be included within this Union, according to their respective Numbers, which shall be determined by adding to the whole Number of free Persons, including those bound to Service for a Term of Years, and excluding Indians not taxed, three fifths of all other Persons. The actual Enumeration shall be made within three Years after the first Meeting of the Congress of the United States, and within every subsequent Term of ten Years, in such Manner as they shall by Law direct. The Number of Representatives shall not exceed one for every thirty Thousand, but each State shall have at Least one Representative; and until such enumeration shall be made, the State of New Hampshire shall be entitled to chuse three, Massachusetts eight, Rhode-Island and Providence Plantations one, Connecticut five, New-York six, New Jersey four, Pennsylvania eight, Delaware one, Maryland six, Virginia ten, North Carolina five, South Carolina five, and Georgia three.

When vacancies happen in the Representation from any State, the Executive Authority thereof shall issue Writs of Election to fill such Vacancies.

The House of Representatives shall chuse their

Speaker and other Officers; and shall have the sole Power of Impeachment.

SECTION 3. The Senate of the United States shall be composed of two Senators from each State chosen by the Legislature thereof, for six Years; and each Senator shall have one Vote.

Immediately after they shall be assembled in Consequence of the first Election, they shall be divided as equally as may be into three Classes. The Seats of the Senators of the first Class shall be vacated at the Expiration of the Second Year, of the second Class at the expiration of the fourth Year, and of the third Class at the Expiration of the sixth Year, so that one third may be chosen every second Year; and if Vacancies happen by Resignation, or otherwise, during the Recess of the Legislature of any State, the Executive thereof may make temporary Appointments until the next Meeting of the Legislature, which shall then fill such Vacancies.

No Person shall be a Senator who shall not have attained to the Age of thirty Years, and have been nine Years a Citizen of the United States, and who shall not, when elected, be an Inhabitant of that State for which he shall be chosen.

The Vice President of the United States shall be President of the Senate, but shall have no Vote, unless they shall be equally divided.

The Senate shall chuse their other Officers, and also a President pro tempore, in the Absence of the Vice President, or when he shall exercise the Office of President of the United States.

The Senate shall have the sole Power to try all Impeachments. When sitting for the Purpose, they shall be on Oath or Affirmation. When the President of the United States is tried the Chief Justice shall preside: And no Person shall be convicted without the Concurrence of two thirds of the Members present.

Judgment in Cases of Impeachment shall not extend further than to removal from Office, and disqualification to hold and enjoy any Office of honor, Trust or Profit under the United States: but the Party convicted shall nevertheless be liable and subject to Indictment, Trial, Judgment and Punishment, according to Law.

SECTION 4. The Times, Places and Manner of holding Elections for Senators and Representatives, shall be prescribed in each State by the Legislature thereof; but the Congress may at any time by Law make or alter such Regulations, except as to the Places of chusing Senators.

The Congress shall assemble at least once in every Year, and such Meeting shall be on the first Monday in December, unless they shall by Law appoint a different Day.

SECTION 5. Each House shall be the Judge of the Elections, Returns and Qualifications of its own Members, and a Majority of each shall constitute a Quorum to do Business; but a smaller Number may adjourn from day to day, and may be authorized to compel the Attendance of absent Members, in such Manner, and under such Penalties as each House may provide.

Each House may determine the Rules of its Proceedings, punish its Members for disorderly Behaviour, and, with the Concurrence of two thirds, expel a Member.

Each House shall keep a Journal of its Proceedings, and from time to time publish the same, excepting such Parts as may in their Judgment require Secrecy; and the Yeas and Nays of the Members of either House on any question shall, at the Desire of one fifth of those Present, be entered on the Journal.

Neither House, during the Session of Congress, shall, without the Consent of the other, adjourn for more than three days, nor to any other Place than that in which the two Houses shall be sitting.

SECTION 6. The Senators and Representatives shall receive a Compensation for their Services, to be ascertained by Law, and paid out of the Treasury of the United States. They shall in all Cases, except Treason, Felony and Breach of the Peace, be privileged from Arrest during their Attendance at the Session of their respective Houses, and in going and returning from the same; and for any Speech or Debate in either House, they shall not be questioned in any other Place.

No Senator or Representative shall, during the Time for which he was elected, be appointed to any civil Office under the Authority of the United States, which shall have been created, or the Emoluments whereof shall have been encreased during such time; and no Person holding any Office under the United States, shall be a Member of either House during his Continuance in Office.

SECTION 7. All Bills for raising Revenue shall originate in the House of Representatives; but the Senate may propose or concur with amendments as on other Bills.

Every Bill which shall have passed the House of Representatives and the Senate, shall, before it become a Law, be presented to the President of the United States; If he approve he shall sign it, but if not he shall return it, with his Objections to that House in which it shall have originated, who shall enter the Objections at large on their Journal, and proceed to reconsider it. If after such Reconsideration two thirds of that House shall agree to pass the Bill, it shall be sent, together with the Objections, to the other House, by which it shall likewise be reconsidered, and if approved by two thirds of that House, it shall become a Law. But in all such Cases the Votes of both Houses shall be determined by Yeas and Nays, and the Names of the Persons voting for and against the Bill shall be entered on the Journal of each House respectively. If any Bill shall not be returned by the President within ten Days (Sundays excepted) after it shall have been presented to him, the Same shall be a Law, in like Manner as if he had signed it, unless the Congress by their Adjournment prevent its Return, in which Case it shall not be a Law.

Every Order, Resolution, or Vote to which the Concurrence of the Senate and House of Representatives may be necessary (except on a question of Adjournment) shall be presented to the President of the United States; and before the Same shall take Effect, shall be approved by him, or being disapproved by him, shall be repassed by two thirds of the Senate and House of Representatives, according to the Rules and Limitations prescribed in the Case of a Bill.

SECTION 8. The Congress shall have Power To lay and collect Taxes, Duties, Imposts and Excises, to pay the Debts and provide for the common Defence and general Welfare of the United States; but all Duties, Imposts and Excises shall be uniform throughout the United States;

To borrow Money on the credit of the United States;

To regulate Commerce with foreign Nations, and among the several States, and with the Indian Tribes;

To establish an uniform Rule of Naturalization, and uniform Laws on the subject of Bankruptcies throughout the United States;

To coin Money, regulate the Value thereof, and of foreign Coin, and fix the Standard of Weights and Measures;

To provide for the Punishment of counterfeiting the Securities and current Coin of the United States;

To establish Post Offices and post Roads;

To promote the Progress of Science and useful Arts, by securing for limited Times to Authors and Inventors the exclusive Right to their respective Writings and Discoveries;

To constitute Tribunals inferior to the supreme Court;

To define and punish Piracies and Felonies committed on the high Seas, and Offences against the Law of Nations;

To declare War, grant Letters of Marque and Reprisal, and make Rules concerning Captures on Land and Water;

To raise and support Armies, but no Appropriation of Money to that Use shall be for a longer Term than two Years;

To provide and maintain a Navy;

To make Rules for the Government and Regulation of the land and naval Forces;

To provide for calling forth the Militia to execute the Laws of the Union, suppress Insurrections and repel Invasions;

To provide for organizing, arming, and disciplining, the Militia, and for governing such Part of them as may be employed in the Service of the United States, reserving to the States respectively, the Appointment of the Officers, and the Authority of training the Militia according to the discipline prescribed by Congress;

To exercise exclusive Legislation in all Cases whatsoever, over such District (not exceeding ten Miles square) as may, by Cession of Particular States, and the Acceptance of Congress, become the Seat of the Government of the United States, and to exercise like Authority over all Places purchased by the Consent of the Legislature of the State in which the Same shall be, for the Erection of Forts, Magazines, Arsenals, dock-Yards, and other needful Buildings;—And

To make all Laws which shall be necessary and proper for carrying into Execution the foregoing Powers, and all other Powers vested by this Constitution in the Government of the United States, or in any Department or Officer thereof.

SECTION 9. The Migration or Importation of such Persons as any of the States now existing shall think proper to admit, shall not be prohibited by the Congress prior to the Year one thousand eight hundred and eight, but a Tax or duty may be imposed on such Importation, not exceeding ten dollars for each Person.

The Privilege of the Writ of Habeas Corpus shall not be suspended, unless when in Cases of Rebellion or Invasion the public Safety may require it.

No Bill of Attainder or ex post facto Law shall be passed.

No Capitation, or other direct, Tax shall be laid, unless in Proportion to the Census or Enumeration herein before directed to be taken.

No Tax or Duty shall be laid on Articles exported from any state.

No Preference shall be given by any Regulation of Commerce or Revenue to the Ports of one State over those of another; nor shall Vessels bound to, or from, one State, be obliged to enter, clear or pay Duties in another.

No Money shall be drawn from the Treasury, but in Consequence of Appropriations made by Law; and a regular Statement and Account of the Receipts and Expenditures of all public Money shall be published from time to time.

No Title of Nobility shall be granted by the United States: And no Person holding any Office of Profit or Trust under them, shall, without the Consent of the Congress, accept of any present, Emolument, Office, or Title, of any kind whatever, from any King, Prince, or foreign State.

SECTION 10. No State shall enter into any Treaty, Alliance, or Confederation; grant Letters of Marque and Reprisal; coin Money; emit Bills of Credit; make any Thing but gold and silver Coin a Tender in Payment of Debts; pass any Bill of Attainder, ex post facto Law, or Law impairing the Obligation of Contracts, or grant any Title of Nobility.

No State shall, without the Consent of the Congress, lay any Imposts or Duties on Imports or Exports, except what may be absolutely necessary for executing its inspection Laws: and the net Produce of all Duties and Imposts, laid by any State on Imports or Exports, shall be for the Use of the Treasury of the United States; and all such Laws shall be subject to the Revision and Controul of the Congress.

No State shall, without the Consent of Congress, lay any Duty of Tonnage, keep Troops, or Ships of War in time of Peace, enter into any Agreement or Compact with another State, or with a foreign Power, or engage in War, unless actually invaded, or in such imminent Danger as will not admit of delay.

ARTICLE II.

SECTION 1. The executive Power shall be vested in a President of the United States of America. He shall hold his Office during the Term of four Years, and, together with the Vice President, chosen for the same Term, be elected, as follows

Each State shall appoint, in such Manner as the Legislature thereof may direct, a Number of Electors, equal to the whole Number of Senators and Representatives to which the State may be entitled in the Congress: but no Senator or Representative, or Person holding an Office of Trust or Profit under the United States, shall be appointed an Elector.

The Electors shall meet in their respective States, and vote by Ballot for two Persons, of whom one at least shall not be an Inhabitant of the same State with themselves. And they shall make a List of all the Persons voted for, and of the Number of Votes for each; which List they shall sign and certify, and transmit sealed to the Seat of the Government of the United States, directed to the President of the Senate. The President of the Senate shall, in the Presence of the Senate and House of Representatives, open all the Certificates, and the Votes shall then be counted. The Person having the greatest Number of Votes shall be the President, if such Number be a Majority of the whole Number of Electors appointed; and if there be more than one who have such Majority, and have an equal Number of Votes, then the House of Representatives shall immediately chuse by Ballot one of them for President; and if no Person have a Majority, then from the five highest on the list the said House shall in like Manner chuse the President. But in chusing the President, the Votes shall be taken by States, the Representation from each State having one Vote; a quorum for this Purpose shall consist of a Member or Members from two thirds of the States, and a Majority of all the States shall be necessary to a Choice. In every Case, after the Choice of the President, the Person having the greatest Number of Votes of the Electors shall be the Vice President. But if there should remain two or more who have equal Votes, the Senate shall chuse from them by Ballot the Vice President.

The Congress may determine the Time of chusing the Electors, and the Day on which they shall give their Votes; which Day shall be the same throughout the United States.

No Person except a natural born Citizen, or a Citizen of the United States, at the time of the Adoption of this Constitution, shall be eligible to the Office of President; neither shall any person be eligible to that Office who shall not have attained to the Age of thirty five Years, and been fourteen Years a Resident within the United States.

In Case of the Removal of the President from Office, or of his Death, Resignation, or Inability to discharge the Powers and Duties of said Office, the Same shall devolve on the Vice President, and the Congress may by Law provide for the Case of Removal, Death, Resignation or Inability, both of the President and Vice President, declaring what Officer shall then act as President, and such Officer shall act accordingly, until the Disability be removed, or a President shall be elected.

The President shall, at stated Times, receive for his Services, a Compensation, which shall neither be encreased nor diminished during the Period for which he shall have been elected, and he shall not receive within that period any other Emolument from the United States, or any of them.

Before he enter on the Execution of his Office, he shall take the following Oath or Affirmation:— "I do solemnly swear (or affirm) that I will faithfully execute the Office of the President of the United States, and will to the best of my Ability, preserve, protect and defend the Constitution of the United States."

SECTION 2. The President shall be Commander in Chief of the Army and Navy of the United States, and of the Militia of the several States, when called into the actual Service of the United States; he may require the Opinion, in writing, of the principal Officer in each of the executive Departments, upon any Subject relating to the Duties of their respective Offices, and he shall have Power to grant Reprieves and Pardons for Offences against the United States, except in Cases of Impeachment.

He shall have Power, by and with the Advice and Consent of the Senate, to make Treaties, provided two thirds of the Senators present concur; and he shall nominate, and by and with the Advice and Consent of the Senate, shall appoint Ambassadors, other public Ministers and Counsuls, Judges of the supreme Court, and all other Officers of the United States, whose Appointments are not herein otherwise provided for, and which shall be established by Law: but the Congress may by Law vest the Appointment of such inferior Officers, as they think proper, in the President alone, in the courts of Law, or in the Heads of Departments.

The President shall have Power to fill up all Vacancies that may happen during the Recess of the

Senate, by granting Commissions which shall expire at the End of their next Session.

SECTION 3. He shall from time to time give to the Congress Information of the State of the Union, and recommend to their Consideration such Measures as he shall judge necessary and expedient; he may, on extraordinary Occasions, convene both Houses, or either of them, and in Case of Disagreement between them, with Respect to the Time of Adjournment, he may adjourn them to such Time as he shall think proper; he shall receive Ambassadors and other public Ministers; he shall take Care that the Laws be faithfully executed, and shall Commission all the Officers of the United States.

SECTION 4. The President, Vice President and all civil Officers of the United States, shall be removed from Office on Impeachment for, and Conviction of, Treason, Bribery, or other high Crimes and Misdemeanors.

ARTICLE III.

SECTION 1. The judicial Power of the United States, shall be vested in one supreme Court, and in such inferior Courts as the Congress may from time to time ordain and establish. The Judges, both of the supreme and inferior Courts, shall hold their Offices during good Behaviour, and shall, at stated Times, receive for their Services, a Compensation, which shall not be diminished during their Continuance in Office.

SECTION 2. The judicial Power shall extend to all Cases, in Law and Equity, arising under this Constitution, the Laws of the United States, and Treaties made, or which shall be made, under their Authority;—to all Cases affecting Ambassadors, other public Ministers and Consuls;—to all Cases of admiralty and maritime Jurisdiction;—to Controversies to which the United States shall be a Party;—to Controversies between two or more States;—between a State and Citizens of another State;—between Citizens of different States;—between Citizens of the same State claiming Lands under Grants of different States, and between a State, or the Citizens thereof, and foreign States, Citizens or Subjects.

In all Cases affecting Ambassadors, other public Ministers and Consuls, and those in which a State shall be Party, the supreme Court shall have original Jurisdiction. In all the other Cases before mentioned, the supreme Court shall have appellate Jurisdiction, both as to Law and Fact, with such Exceptions, and under such Regulations as the Congress shall make.

The Trial of all Crimes, except in Cases of Impeachment, shall be by Jury; and such Trial shall be held in the State where the said Crimes shall have been committed; but when not committed within any State, the Trial shall be at such Place or Places as the Congress may by Law have directed.

SECTION 3. Treason against the United States, shall consist only in levying War against them, or in adhering to their Enemies, giving them Aid and Comfort. No Person shall be convicted of Treason unless on the Testimony of two Witnesses to the same overt Act, or on Confession in open Court.

The Congress shall have Power to declare the Punishment of Treason, but no Attainder of Treason shall work Corruption of Blood, or Forfeiture except during the Life of the Person attainted.

ARTICLE IV.

SECTION 1. Full Faith and Credit shall be given in each State to the public Acts, Records, and judicial Proceedings of every other State. And the Congress may by general Laws prescribe the Manner in which such Acts, Records and Proceedings shall be proved, and the Effect thereof.

SECTION 2. The Citizens of each State shall be entitled to all Privileges and Immunities of Citizens in the several States.

A Person charged in any State with Treason, Felony, or other Crime, who shall flee from Justice, and be found in another State, shall on Demand of the executive Authority of the State from which he fled, be delivered up, to be removed to the State having Jurisdiction of the Crime.

No Person held to Service or Labour in one State, under the Laws thereof, escaping into another, shall, in Consequence of any Law or Regulation therein, be discharged from such Service or Labour, but shall be delivered up on Claim of the

Party to whom such Service or Labour may be due.

SECTION 3. New States may be admitted by the Congress into this Union; but no new State shall be formed or erected within the Jurisdiction of any other State; nor any State be formed by the Junction of two or more States, or Parts of States, without the Consent of the Legislatures of the States concerned as well as of the Congress.

The Congress shall have Power to dispose of and make all needful Rules and Regulations respecting the Territory or other Property belonging to the United States; and nothing in this Constitution shall be so construed as to Prejudice any Claims of the United States, or of any particular State.

SECTION 4. The United States shall guarantee to every State in this Union a Republican Form of Government, and shall protect each of them against Invasion; and on Application of the Legislature, or of the Executive (when the Legislature cannot be convened) against domestic Violence.

ARTICLE V.

The Congress, whenever two thirds of both Houses shall deem it necessary, shall propose Amendments to this Constitution, or, on the Application of the Legislatures of two thirds of the several States, shall call a Convention for proposing Amendments, which, in either Case, shall be valid to all Intents and Purposes, as Part of this Constitution, when ratified by the Legislatures of three fourths of the several States, or by Conventions in three fourths thereof, as the one or the other Mode of Ratification may be proposed by the Congress; Provided that no Amendment which may be made prior to the Year One thousand eight hundred and eight shall in any Manner affect the first and fourth Clauses in the Ninth Section of the first Article; and that no State, without its Consent, shall be deprived of its equal Suffrage in the Senate.

ARTICLE VI.

All Debts contracted and Engagements entered into, before the Adoption of this Constitution, shall be as valid against the United States under this Constitution, as under the Confederation.

This Constitution, and the Laws of the United States which shall be made in Pursuance thereof; and all Treaties made, or which shall be made, under the Authority of the United States, shall be the supreme Law of the Land; and the Judges in every State shall be bound thereby, any Thing in the Constitution or Laws of any State to the Contrary notwithstanding.

The Senators and Representatives before mentioned, and the Members of the several State Legislatures, and all executive and judicial Officers, both of the United States and of the several States, shall be bound by Oath or Affirmation, to support this Constitution; but no religious Test shall ever be required as a Qualification to any Office or public Trust under the United States.

ARTICLE VII.

The Ratification of the Conventions of nine States, shall be sufficient for the Establishment of this Constitution between the States so ratifying the Same.

done in Convention by the Unanimous Consent of the States present the Seventeenth Day of September in the Year of our Lord one thousand seven hundred and Eighty seven and of the Independence of the United States of America the Twelfth In witness whereof We have hereunto subscribed our Names,

	Go. Washington—Presidt. and deputy from Virginia
New Hampshire	John Langdon
	Nicholas Gilman
Massachusetts	Nathaniel Gorham
	Rufus King
Connecticut	Wm. Saml. Johnson
	Roger Sherman
New York	Alexander Hamilton
New Jersey	Wil. Livingston
	David Brearley
	Wm. Paterson
	Jona. Dayton
Pennsylvania	B Franklin
	Thomas Mifflin
	Robt. Morris
	Geo. Clymer

	Thos. FitzSimons
	Jared Ingersoll
	James Wilson
	Gouv. Morris
Delaware	Geo. Read
	Gunning Bedford jun.
	John Dickinson
	Richard Bassett
	Jaco. Broom
Maryland	James McHenry
	Dan of St. Thos. Jenifer
	Daniel Carroll
Virginia	John Blair
	James Madison Jr.
North Carolina	Wm. Blount
	Richd. Dobbs Spaight
	Hu Williamson
South Carolina	J. Rutledge
	Charles Cotesworth Pinckney
	Charles Pinckney
	Pierce Butler
Georgia	William Few
	Abr. Baldwin

In Convention Monday, September 17th 1787.
Present
The States of
New Hampshire, Massachusetts, Connecticut, Mr. Hamilton from New York, New Jersey, Pennsylvania, Delaware, Maryland, Virginia, North Carolina, South Carolina and Georgia.
Resolved,

That the preceeding Constitution be laid before the United States in Congress assembled, and that it is in the Opinion of this Convention, that it should afterwards be submitted to a Convention of Delegates, chosen in each State by the People thereof, under the Recommendation of its Legislature, for their Assent and Ratification; and that each Convention assenting to, and ratifying the Same, should give Notice thereof to the United States in Congress assembled. Resolved, That it is the Opinion of this Convention, that as soon as the Conventions of nine States shall have ratified this Constitution, the United States in Congress as-

sembled should fix a Day on which Electors should be appointed by the States which shall have ratified the same, and a Day on which the Electors should assemble to vote for the President, and the Time and Place for commencing Proceedings under this Constitution. That after such Publication the Electors should be appointed, and the Senators and Representatives elected: That the Electors should meet on the Day fixed for the Election of the President, and should transmit their Votes certified, signed, sealed and directed, as the Constitution requires, to the Secretary of the United States in Congress assembled, that the Senators and Representatives should convene at the Time and Place assigned; that the Senators should appoint a President of the Senate, for the sole Purpose of receiving, opening and counting the Votes for President; and, that after he shall be chosen, the Congress, together with the President, should, without Delay, proceed to execute this Constitution.

By the Unanimous Order of the Convention
Go. Washington—Presidt.
W. Jackson Secretary

ARTICLES IN ADDITION TO, AND AMENDMENTS OF, THE CONSTITUTION OF THE UNITED STATES OF AMERICA, PROPOSED BY CONGRESS, AND RATIFIED BY THE SEVERAL STATES, PURSUANT TO THE FIFTH ARTICLE OF THE ORIGINAL CONSTITUTION.

AMENDMENT I.

Congress shall make no law respecting an establishment of religion, or prohibiting the free exercise thereof; or abridging the freedom of speech, or of the press; or the right of the people peaceably to assemble, and to petition the Government for a redress of grievances.

AMENDMENT II.

A well regulated Militia, being necessary to the security of a free State, the right of the people to keep and bear Arms, shall not be infringed.

AMENDMENT III.

No Soldier shall, in time of peace be quartered in any house, without the consent of the Owner, nor in time of war, but in a manner to be prescribed by law.

AMENDMENT IV.

The right of the people to be secure in their persons, houses, papers, and effects, against unreasonable searches and seizures, shall not be violated, and no Warrants shall issue, but upon probable cause, supported by Oath or affirmation, and particularly describing the place to be searched, and the persons or things to be seized.

AMENDMENT V.

No person shall be held to answer for a capital, or otherwise infamous crime, unless on a presentment or indictment of a Grand Jury, except in cases arising in the land or naval forces, or in the Militia, when in actual service in time of War or public danger; nor shall any person be subject for the same offence to be twice put in jeopardy of life or limb; nor shall be compelled in any criminal case to be a witness against himself, nor be deprived of life, liberty, or property, without due process of law; nor shall private property be taken for public use, without just compensation.

AMENDMENT VI.

In all criminal prosecutions, the accused shall enjoy the right to a speedy and public trial, by an impartial jury of the State and district wherein the crime shall have been committed, which district shall have been previously ascertained by law, and to be informed of the nature and cause of the accusation; to be confronted with the witnesses against him; to have compulsory process for obtaining witnesses in his favor, and to have the Assistance of Counsel for his defense.

AMENDMENT VII.

In Suits at common law, where the value in controversy shall exceed twenty dollars, the right of trial by jury shall be preserved, and no fact tried by a jury, shall be otherwise re-examined in any Court of the United States, than according to the rules of the common law.

AMENDMENT VIII.

Excessive bail shall not be required, nor excessive fines imposed, nor cruel and unusual punishments inflicted.

AMENDMENT IX.

The enumeration in the Constitution, of certain rights, shall not be construed to deny or disparage others retained by the people.

AMENDMENT X.

The powers not delegated to the United States by the Constitution, nor prohibited by it to the States, are reserved to the States respectively, or to the people.

AMENDMENT XI.

The Judicial power of the United States shall not be construed to extend to any suit in law or equity commenced or prosecuted against one of the United States by Citizens of another State, or by Citizens or Subjects of any Foreign State.

AMENDMENT XII.

The Electors shall meet in their respective states and vote by ballot for President and Vice-President, one of whom, at least, shall not be an inhabitant of the same state with themselves; they shall name in their ballots the person voted for as President, and in distinct ballots the person voted for as Vice-President, and they shall make distinct lists of all persons voted for as President, and of all persons voted for as Vice-President, and of the number of votes for each, which lists they shall sign and certify, and transmit sealed to the seat of the government of the United States, directed to the President of the Senate;—The President of the Senate shall, in the presence of the Senate and House of Representatives, open all the certificates and the votes shall then be counted;—The person having the greatest number of votes for President, shall be the President, if such number be a majority of the whole number of Electors appointed; and if no person have such majority, then from the persons having the highest numbers not exceeding three on the list of those voted for as President, the House of Representatives shall choose immediately, by ballot, the President. But in choosing the

President, the votes shall be taken by states, the representation from each state having one vote; a quorum for this purpose shall consist of a member or members from two-thirds of the states, and a majority of all the states shall be necessary to a choice. And if the House of Representatives shall not choose a President whenever the right of choice shall devolve upon them, before the fourth day of March next following, then the Vice-President shall act as President, as in the case of the death or other constitutional disability of the President—The person having the greatest number of votes as Vice-President, shall be the Vice-President, if such number be a majority of the whole number of Electors appointed, and if no person have a majority, then from the two highest numbers on the list, the Senate shall choose the Vice-President; a quorum for the purpose shall consist of two-thirds of the whole number of Senators, and a majority of the whole number shall be necessary to a choice. But no person constitutionally ineligible to the office of President shall be eligible to that of Vice-President of the United States.

AMENDMENT XIII.

Section 1. Neither slavery nor involuntary servitude, except as a punishment for crime whereof the party shall have been duly convicted, shall exist within the United States, or any place subject to their jurisdiction.

Section 2. Congress shall have power to enforce this article by appropriate legislation.

AMENDMENT XIV.

Section 1. All persons born or naturalized in the United States and subject to the jurisdiction thereof, are citizens of the United States and of the State wherein they reside. No State shall make or enforce any law which shall abridge the privileges or immunities of the citizens of the United States; nor shall any State deprive any person of life, liberty, or property, without due process of law; nor deny to any person within its jurisdiction the equal protection of the laws.

Section 2. Representatives shall be apportioned among the several States according to their respective numbers, counting the whole number of persons in each State, excluding Indians not taxed. But when the right to vote at any election for the choice of electors for President and Vice President of the United States, Representatives in Congress, the Executive and Judicial officers of a State, or the members of the Legislature thereof, is denied to any of the male inhabitants of such State, being twenty-one years of age, and citizens of the United States, or in any way abridged, except for participation in rebellion, or other crime, the basis of representation therein shall be reduced in the proportion which the number of such male citizens shall bear to the whole number of male citizens twenty-one years of age in such State.

Section 3. No person shall be a Senator or Representative in Congress, or elector of President and Vice President, or hold any office, civil or military, under the United States, or under any State, who, having previously taken an oath, as a member of Congress, or as an officer of the United States, or as a member of any State legislature, or as an executive or judicial officer of any State, to support the Constitution of the United States, shall have engaged in insurrection or rebellion against the same, or given aid or comfort to the enemies thereof. But Congress may by a vote of two-thirds of each House, remove such disability.

Section 4. The validity of the public debt of the United States, authorized by law, including debts incurred for payment of pensions and bounties for services in suppressing insurrection or rebellion, shall not be questioned. But neither the United States nor any State shall assume or pay any debt or obligation incurred in aid of insurrection or rebellion against the United States, or any claim for the loss or emancipation of any slave; but all such debts, obligations and claims shall be held illegal and void.

Section 5. The Congress shall have power to enforce, by appropriate legislation, the provisions of this article.

AMENDMENT XV.

Section 1. The right of citizens of the United States to vote shall not be denied or abridged by the United States or by any State on account of race, color, or previous condition of servitude.

SECTION 2. The Congress shall have power to enforce this article by appropriate legislation.

AMENDMENT XVI.

The Congress shall have power to lay and collect taxes on incomes, from whatever source derived, without apportionment among the several States, and without regard to any census or enumeration.

AMENDMENT XVII.

The Senate of the United States shall be composed of two Senators from each State, elected by the people thereof, for six years; and each Senator shall have one vote. The electors in each State shall have the qualifications requisite for electors of the most numerous branch of the State legislatures.

When vacancies happen in the representation of any State in the Senate, the executive authority of such State shall issue writs of election to fill such vacancies: *Provided,* That the legislature of any State may empower the executive thereof to make temporary appointments until the people fill the vacancies by election as the legislature may direct.

This amendment shall not be so construed as to affect the election or term of any Senator chosen before it becomes valid as part of the Constitution.

AMENDMENT XVIII.

SECTION 1. After one year from the ratification of this article, the manufacture, sale, or transportation of intoxicating liquors within, the importation thereof into, or the exportation thereof from the United States and all territory subject to the jurisdiction thereof for beverage purposes is hereby prohibited.

SECTION 2. The Congress and the several States shall have concurrent power to enforce this article by appropriate legislation.

SECTION 3. This article shall be inoperative unless it shall have been ratified as an amendment to the Constitution by the legislatures of the several States, as provided in the Constitution, within seven years from the date of the submission hereof to the States by the Congress.

AMENDMENT XIX.

The right of citizens of the United States to vote shall not be denied or abridged by the United States or by any state on account of sex.

Congress shall have power to enforce this article by appropriate legislation.

AMENDMENT XX.

SECTION 1. The terms of the President and Vice President shall end at noon on the 20th day of January, and the terms of Senators and Representatives at noon on the 3d day of January, of the years in which such terms would have ended if this article had not been ratified; and the terms of their successors shall then begin.

SECTION 2. The Congress shall assemble at least once in every year, and such meeting shall begin at noon on the 3d day of January, unless they shall by law appoint a different day.

SECTION 3. If, at the time fixed for the beginning of the term of the President, the President elect shall have died, the Vice President elect shall become President. If a President shall not have been chosen before the time fixed for the beginning of his term, or if the President elect shall have failed to qualify, then the Vice President elect shall act as President until a President shall have qualified; and the Congress may by law provide for the case wherein neither a President elect nor a Vice President elect shall have qualified, declaring who shall then act as President, or the manner in which one who is to act shall be selected, and such person shall act accordingly until a President or Vice President shall have qualified.

SECTION 4. The Congress may by law provide for the case of the death of any of the persons from whom the House of Representatives may choose a President whenever the right of choice shall have devolved upon them, and for the case of the death of any of the persons from whom the Senate may choose a Vice President whenever the right of choice shall have devolved upon them.

SECTION 5. Sections 1 and 2 shall take effect on the 15th day of October following the ratification of this article.

SECTION 6. This article shall be inoperative unless it shall have been ratified as an amendment to the Constitution by the legislatures of three-fourths of the several States within seven years from the date of its submission.

AMENDMENT XXI.

SECTION 1. The eighteenth article of amendment to the Constitution of the United States is hereby repealed.

SECTION 2. The transportation or importation into any State, Territory, or possession of the United States for delivery or use therein of intoxicating liquors, in violation of the laws thereof, is hereby prohibited.

SECTION 3. This article shall be inoperative unless it shall have been ratified as an amendment to the Constitution by conventions in the several States, as provided in the Constitution, within seven years from the date of the submission hereof to the States by the Congress.

AMENDMENT XXII.

SECTION 1. No person shall be elected to the office of the President more than twice, and no person who has held the office of President, or acted as President, for more than two years of a term to which some other person was elected President shall be elected to the office of the President more than once. But this Article shall not apply to any person holding the office of President when this Article was proposed by the Congress, and shall not prevent any person who may be holding the office of President, or acting as President, during the term within which this Article becomes operative from holding the office of President or acting as President during the remainder of such term.

SECTION 2. This Article shall be inoperative unless it shall have been ratified as an amendment to the Constitution by the legislatures of three-fourths of the several States within seven years from the date of its submission to the States by the Congress.

AMENDMENT XXIII.

SECTION 1. The District constituting the seat of Government of the United States shall appoint in such manner as the Congress may direct:

A number of electors of President and Vice President equal to the whole number of Senators and Representatives in Congress to which the District would be entitled if it were a State, but in no event more than the least populous State; they shall be in addition to those appointed by the States, but they shall be considered, for the purposes of the election of President and Vice President, to be electors appointed by a State; and they shall meet in the District and perform such duties as provided by the twelfth article of amendment.

SECTION 2. The Congress shall have power to enforce this article by appropriate legislation.

AMENDMENT XXIV.

SECTION 1. The right of citizens of the United States to vote in any primary or other election for President or Vice President, for electors for President or Vice President, or for Senator or Representative in Congress, shall not be denied or abridged by the United States or any State by reason of failure to pay any poll tax or other tax.

SECTION 2. The Congress shall have the power to enforce this article by appropriate legislation.

AMENDMENT XXV.

SECTION 1. In case of the removal of the President from office or of his death or resignation, the Vice President shall become President.

SECTION 2. Whenever there is a vacancy in the office of the Vice President, the President shall nominate a Vice President who shall take the office upon confirmation by a majority vote of both houses of Congress.

SECTION 3. Whenever the President transmits to the President pro tempore of the Senate and the Speaker of the House of Representatives his written declaration that he is unable to discharge the powers and duties of his office, and until he transmits to them a written declaration to the contrary, such powers and duties shall be discharged by the Vice President as Acting President.

SECTION 4. Whenever the Vice President and a majority of either the principal officers of the executive departments or of such other body as Congress may by law provide, transmit to the President pro tempore of the Senate and the Speaker of the House of Representatives their written declaration that the President is unable to discharge the powers and duties of his office, the Vice President shall immediately assume the powers and duties of the office as Acting President.

Thereafter, when the President transmits to the President pro tempore of the Senate and the Speaker of the House of Representatives his written declaration that no inability exists, he shall resume the powers and duties of his office unless the Vice President and a majority of either the principal officers of the executive department or of such other body as Congress may by law provide, transmit within four days to the President pro tempore of the Senate and the Speaker of the House of Representatives their written declaration that the President is unable to discharge the powers and duties of his office. Thereupon Congress shall decide the issue, assembling within forty-eight hours for that purpose if not in session. If the Congress within twenty-one days after receipt of the latter written declaration, or, if Congress is not in session, within twenty-one days after Congress is required to assemble, determines by two-thirds vote of both Houses that the President is unable to discharge the powers and duties of his office, the Vice President shall continue to discharge the same as Acting President; otherwise, the President shall resume the powers and duties of his office.

AMENDMENT XXVI.

SECTION 1. The right of citizens of the United States, who are 18 years of age or older, to vote shall not be denied or abridged by the United States or any state on account of age.

SECTION 2. The Congress shall have the power to enforce this article by appropriate legislation.

Appendix 5: Origins of Selected Naval Terms

ABOVE BOARD—meaning to have nothing concealed. Originally, nothing concealed below deck on a ship.

ADMIRAL—a high-ranking officer. The title may be traced to the Arabic *Amir-al-Bahr,* meaning commander of the seas. *Bahr* was subsequently dropped, and the Romans called their sea commanders *admirati.* The term was introduced into Europe during the Crusades.

AHOY—a nautical greeting. Originally a dreaded way cry of invading Vikings.

AIGUILLETTE—an ornamental cord or braid worn on the shoulder of a military uniform. Probably based on the practice of the aide to a superior knight carrying around the rope and pegs for tethering the knight's horse, leading to the rope becoming the badge of one near the leader. Another tradition relates that it was the rope of the provost marshall used to hang the condemned.

ANCHOR—a heavy weighted object used to moor a ship in place. Derived from an early Greek word for hook.

AYE AYE—a nautical phrase used for acknowledging an order. Probably based on the Old English term for "yes," based in turn on the Latin verb *aio,* to affirm.

BOAT—a small watercraft. Derived from the Anglo-Saxon word *bat,* meaning a boat, small ship, or vessel.

BOATSWAIN—an officer or petty officer in charge of the deck crew. Based on the Middle English *botswein.* *Bot* referred to a ship, and *swein* meant a boy or servant.

BRIG—a ship's jail. In the eighteenth century, a brig was a small two-masted sailing ship of the type often used by pirates in the Mediterranean. Because the English naval hero Lord Nelson used a brig in battle for relieving his ships of prisoners, sailors began to call a prison anywhere by the name brig.

BUMBOAT—a small boat used to peddle provisions offshore to large ships. Probably derived from boomboat, signifying boats permitted to lie at booms.

BY AND LARGE—a term meaning generally speaking or under all conditions. Derived from the sailing terms "by the wind" (close hauled) and "sailing large" (running free).

CAPTAIN—the commander of a boat or ship. From the Latin word *capitaneus,* meaning head or chief.

CARGO—freight carried by a ship. From the Latin word *cargo* or *carga,* meaning a load or freight.

CHAINS—a platform near the bow of a ship from which a sounding lead is lowered to obtain water depth. Derived from platforms on a sailing ship's side supported by chains, which was where rigging to support the ship's mast was secured.

CHART—a nautical map. From the Latin word *charta*, and the Greek *charte*, a kind of papyrus.

CHIT—a permission slip, note, voucher, or receipt. From the Hindu word *chitti*, brought to England by the British East India Company.

COXSWAIN—a person in charge of the crew of a small boat. Based on the Middle English *cock*, a small boat, and *swein*, a servant.

CRUISER—a fast warship of medium tonnage with a large cruising radius and less firepower and armor than a battleship. Derived from the *crusal*, a fast light vessel used by pirates in the Mediterranean.

DERRICK—a large crane used for hoisting heavy objects. Derived from the name of Thomas Derrick, an executioner of the time of the English Queen Elizabeth, whose favorite method was to hang condemned individuals from a rope at the end of a spar.

DINGHY—a small rowboat. Based on the Indian word *dinghey*, brought back to England by the British East India Company.

ENSIGN—a national flag displayed on a ship or aircraft. From the Norman word *enseigne* meaning flag.

EYES OF THE SHIP—the openings on the bow through which the anchor cable is run. Loosely based on the eyes of figureheads carved in the bow of sailing ships.

FATHOM—a nautical unit of length equal to 6 feet. From the Anglo-Saxon *faehom*, the Dutch *vadem*, and Latin *patene*, meaning the act of stretching out two arms' width as a rough measure of 6 feet.

FLEET—a collection of vessels. From the Anglo-Saxon *floet* and Old Spanish *flota*.

FORECASTLE—the front portion of a ship. Derived from the practice in the Middle Ages of building towers of wood to fight from on the front and rear of warships of the day.

FRIGATE—a warship of intermediate size between a cruiser and a destroyer. Originally a class of Mediterranean warships that used both oars and sails.

FURL—to roll up and secure a sail or flag to a pole or mast stay. Based on the Old English *furdle*, meaning to make up a bundle.

GALE—a strong wind. From the Old Norse *galem*, and Danish *gal*, meaning mad or furious.

GANGWAY—a passage or opening on the side of a ship through which people may walk. From the Anglo-Saxon *gang*, to go, make a passage in, or through.

GUNNEL, GUNWALE—the upper edge of a boat's side. Derived from the custom of firing guns over planking which had been reinforced by "wales," derived from the Anglo-Saxon *wala*, meaning strips or ridges.

HAWSEPIPE—a pipe in the bow of a ship through which the anchor chain is led. Derived from *hawse*, an old term for throat.

HORSE LATITUDES—either of two belts of latitudes between about 30 and 35 degrees north and south of the equator, characterized by frequent calms and light winds. The name originated in the nineteenth century, when numerous horses were transported from Europe to the Americas. When the ships carrying them were becalmed, voyage durations increased, causing many of the horses to die and be thrown overboard. Their carcasses often floated for some time.

KNOT—a unit of nautical speed equal to one nautical mile per hour. Derived from the practice in days of sail of determining speed by casting overboard a float to which a line with knots every 47 feet was attached. The number of knots that would run out every 28 seconds as measured by a sand-glass was equal to the speed in nautical miles per hour.

LIEUTENANT—one of two ranks held by lower-ranking naval officers. Derived from a French word meaning "in lieu of" or "one who replaces." Originally it referred to the immediate replacement for the ship's captain, called the first lieutenant, now the executive officer.

LUCKY BAG—a small compartment or locker where loose articles of clothing or other belongings are stowed. Originally the term referred to a bag kept by a ship's master-at-arms into which these items were placed and kept until brought to the mainmast once a month, whereupon their owners would claim them at the cost of a few lashes for their carelessness in leaving them lying about.

MASTER-AT-ARMS—a naval petty officer who performs police functions. Evolved from the English sea corporal, whose department included custody of all the ship's small arms and swords.

MESS—a ship's crew's dining compartment. Derived from the Middle English *mes*, meaning a dish.

MIDSHIPMAN—a naval cadet. Originated from days of sail when boys or young men were stationed amidships during battle to carry messages, bring up ammunition, and relay messages to the gundecks.

MOOR—to secure a vessel by means of cables or anchors. Derived from the Dutch word *marren,* to tie or fasten.

OAR—a pole with a flat end used to propel or in some cases steer a vessel. Derived from the Middle English *ayr,* of the same meaning.

OFFICER—one who holds a commission in the armed forces. Derived from the Latin *officium,* meaning agent or official.

PORT—the left side on board a ship or boat. Originally *larboard,* or loading side, changed to port in the 1840s because of too much tendency to confuse it with starboard, the designation for the right side.

QUARTERDECK—the portion of the deck of a ship set aside for ceremonies and honors. Originally, a portion of a sailing ship's deck that covered a quarter of the ship, and from which the ship was conned or controlled.

QUARTERMASTER—a naval petty officer who assists with the navigation of the ship. Originally, a petty officer assigned to look after the food, clothing, equipment, and quarters of troops assigned to ships. In later years after most ships no longer carried troops these petty officers were reassigned to navigational duties, but in other services the word still has its original meaning.

RUDDER—the device that steers the vessel through the water. Derived from the Anglo-Saxon *rother,* that which guides.

SAILOR—one who serves in a navy or earns a living by working on board a ship. Derived from the Middle English *saylor,* of the same meaning.

SCUTTLEBUTT—a nautical term for a drinking fountain, or rumors. Derived from the cask containing drinking water in days of sail, around which the crew used to gather and talk shop.

SEA—any large body of salt water. Derived from the Greek *seio,* or tossed-about water.

SHIP'S BELLS—a system of bells to mark the passage of time during a four-hour watch, struck each half-hour, from one through eight strokes. The time interval was originally based on the time it took for sand to run through a half-hour glass, before the clock was invented.

SHIPSHAPE—neat and clean. Originally a ship that was ready for sea with all lines neatly coiled and all loose geared properly stored.

SICK BAY—the infirmary of a ship. Originally called "sick berth," but later modified to "bay" after the introduction of rounded bows about 1811.

SKIPPER—the master of a ship. Derived from the Scandinavian *schiffe,* meaning ship, or the Dutch *schipper,* meaning captain.

SMOKING LAMP—in days of sail, an oil lamp aboard ships used by sailors to light their pipes. The term is now symbolic, used to indicate when a ship's crew is allowed to smoke, as for example, "The smoking lamp is now lit in all authorized spaces."

STARBOARD—the right side on board a ship or boat. Originally based on the right side of a ship where the steering gear was traditionally located, called the "steer board." The practice originated with the Vikings, whose steering oars were always placed on the right quarter.

THREE SHEETS TO THE WIND—to be drunk or otherwise out of control of oneself. Based on the loss of control a sailing ship would suffer if the ropes called sheets controlling the sails on her three masts were to be inadvertently released in a high wind and allowed to flail about, thus causing the ship to be tossed about on the sea.

TYPHOON—a hurricane in the Pacific ocean. Based on the Chinese *t'ai-fun,* or great wind.

WARDROOM—the officer's dining and lounge area aboard ship. Originally in the English navy a compartment near officers' quarters used to stow valuables taken from prizes. When empty, it was used by junior officers for lounging and for meals. In time the compartment was designated to be used solely for the officers' messroom.

WEIGH—to lift. Derived from the Anglo-Saxon *woeg,* to lift the anchor.

Adapted from *Naval Ceremonies, Customs, and Traditions,* Annapolis, Md.: Naval Institute Press, 1980.

Glossary

AMPHIBIOUS INVASION—an attack launched from the sea by naval forces embarked in ships or craft.

ARMAMENT—weapons of a ship or an aircraft.

AUXILIARY MACHINERY—all machinery other than the main engines on board a ship. On a sailboat, its motor or other secondary propulsion machinery.

AUXILIARY SHIP—a naval vessel designed for and used in other than combat roles, such as a tug or supply ship.

BALLAST WATER—water temporarily placed in a ship's empty cargo or fuel tanks to enhance stability.

BALLISTIC MISSILE—a missile that goes on a free-falling path after a powered and guided ascent.

BATHYSCAPHE—a small manned research vessel designed to operate at extreme ocean depths.

BATHYTHERMOGRAPH (BT)—a temperature and depth-sensing device used to record water temperatures at various depths.

BINNACLE—the stand for a magnetic compass.

BITTS—a pair of short stubby posts on board a ship, used to secure mooring lines.

BLOCK AND TACKLE—a set of pulley blocks and ropes or cables used for hoisting heavy objects.

BLOCKADE—a naval operation wherein ships are prevented from entering or leaving certain ports or areas.

BOLLARD—a single post on a pier, used in securing a ship's mooring lines.

BOOST—Broadened Opportunity for Officer Selection and Training program, San Diego, California.

BOYCOTT—to abstain from using, buying, or dealing with, as a protest.

BROADSIDE—simultaneous firing of all main battery guns on one side of a warship.

CALL BOOK—a book kept by the night watch of a ship or shore station containing the phone numbers and locations and wake-up times for the on-coming watch.

CAPSTAN—a rotating winch that raises an anchor or other heavy weight.

CATAMARAN—a boat with two parallel hulls.

CATAPULT—a device for launching aircraft from a ship's deck, which takes the aircraft from a standing start to flying speed.

CELESTIAL NAVIGATION—finding a ship's position by means of observations of the sun, moon, planets, and stars.

CHAIN OF COMMAND—the succession of people through which command is exercised.

CHOCK—a metal fitting on board a ship, through which mooring lines are passed.

CHRONOMETER—a precise timepiece used for recording the exact times of celestial observations at sea.

CLEAT—an anvil-shaped deck fitting for securing lines on a boat, ship, or pier.

CNET—Chief of Naval Education and Training, headquartered at Pensacola, Florida.

COLLATERAL DUTY—a duty or task done in addition to a main job or duty.

COMBAT INFORMATION CENTER (CIC)—the section of a ship or patrol aircraft with personnel and equipment to collect and organize tactical information.

COMBAT SYSTEMS—any electronic equipment, weapons, or sensors related to a ship's offensive or defensive capabilities.

COMMODORE—an officer commanding two or more ships, or a convoy of merchantmen; a naval rank between captain and admiral.

CONTINENTAL SHELF—the sea bottom from the shore to a depth of 200 meters (100 fathoms).

CONVOY—a group of merchant ships or naval auxiliaries, or both, usually escorted by warships and aircraft.

CORIOLIS EFFECT—a tendency due to the earth's rotation that makes moving objects tend to curve clockwise in the Northern Hemisphere.

CRUISE MISSILE—an air-breathing surface-to-surface guided missile.

CRYPTOGRAPHIC—pertaining to coded communications or data.

DAMAGE CONTROL—measures or equipment used to limit damage to a ship from enemy action, fire, flooding, and smoke.

DESERT—to be absent from a military command without authority, with no intent to return.

DISPLACEMENT—the weight of water taken up by a ship's hull, in tons.

DOG WATCH—one of two watches, 1600–1800 or 1800–2000, used to rotate the watch every twenty-four hours.

EMBARGO—a government-ordered stoppage of foreign trade in a particular type of goods or commodity.

ENDURANCE—maximum time or distance a ship or aircraft can operate without replenishment.

ESTUARY—an area of the sea that extends inland to meet the mouth of a river, influenced by both current and tides.

FIRE MONITOR—a cannon-like firewater nozzle on a tug or fireboat.

GARRISON—a military post, or the troops stationed there.

GENERAL MESS—the compartment in which the ship's crew eats and lounges. On a shore station, called the *mess hall*.

GROUND TACKLE—any equipment having to do with a ship's anchors, anchor cable, or handling gear.

HALYARD—any line used to raise or lower a sail.

HAWSEPIPE—heavily built pipes in a ship or boat hull through which an anchor cable runs on its way from the deck to the water.

HAWSER—a thick line used for towing or high-line transfer.

HEAVY WEATHER—stormy weather conditions or high seas.

HELM—the steering on board a ship or boat. The position is manned by the *helmsman*.

HULL NUMBER—the identification number or letter painted on a ship's hull.

HYDROFOIL—a surface craft designed to be propelled over the water by use of submerged foils.

IMPRESSMENT—the forcing of a person to act as a crewmember of a ship, especially a warship, against his will.

LEE—the side of a ship or shore away from the direction from which the wind is blowing.

LEE HELM—in older ships, the station on the bridge from which engine orders are sent to the engine-room(s). Manned by the *lee helmsman*.

MAINMAST—the second mast of a ship with two or more masts, except when the first is taller.

MARLINSPIKE SEAMANSHIP—skill with rope, line, and other deck gear.

MEAN TIME—time based on the relationship of the mean sun with the earth; i.e., a make-believe sun that travels around the earth at the equator at a constant speed of 15° per hour.

MILITARY PARITY—equality in all aspects of conventional and nuclear war-fighting capability.

MISSION—the objective or purpose of a military organization or operation.

NROTC—Naval Reserve Officer Training Corps.

OBA—oxygen breathing apparatus, a self-contained mask plus a vestlike apparatus used to supply oxygen to a wearer in a contaminated space.

OCS—Officer Candidate School, Newport, Rhode Island.

PHASED ARRAY RADAR—a radar that uses electronics instead of a rotating dish to send out and receive radar pulses and target echoes.

PONTOON—any watertight structure used to float something.

PRIVATEER—a private commerce raider who attacks enemy shipping for personal gain, similar to a mercenary in land warfare. Traditionally commissioned by a *letter of marque* by the host government.

QUARANTINE—similar to a blockade, except that only ships with designated contraband are prevented from entering or leaving a designated port or area.

RAKING FIRE—gunfire along the length of a ship, fired from a point either directly ahead or astern.

RANGE OF GUNS—the distance a projectile from a gun can be fired.

RANK—relative position of authority among officers and petty officers.

RATE—level of proficiency within an enlisted rating, similar to a pay grade.

RATING—general grouping of enlisted personnel by job specialty.

REGULATIONS—a body of written rules for conduct and procedures in a military organization.

REPAIR PARTY—a group of specialists organized to control damage and make repairs throughout a ship during battle.

REPLENISHMENT—the process or procedure of supplying fuel, food, stores, ammunition, and personnel to combatant ships under way.

SALVAGE—to save or recover material or ships that have been wrecked, sunk, or damaged.

SEA LANE—a route of travel across an ocean or other large body of water. See also *Sea lines of communication.*

SEA LINES OF COMMUNICATION—the sea routes of travel, supply, and transport between two points on an ocean or other large body of water. See also *Sea lane.*

SEAMANSHIP—skill in handling a boat or ship, or in doing those things related to the job of a seaman.

SEA POWER—the ability of a country to use and control the sea, and to prevent its use by an enemy.

SHOAL WATER—shallow water.

SHORE PATROL—naval personnel ashore on police duty. Called *military police* (MPs) in the army and the air force.

SHORT STAY—position of an anchor cable straight up and down, or nearly so, with the anchor barely holding the bottom.

SHOT (OF ANCHOR CHAIN)—a 15-fathom section of anchor chain, joined to the next shot by a detachable link.

SIDE BOYS—nonrated sailors (either male or female) stationed in two ranks at a quarterdeck to render honors to an arriving or departing official.

SMOKE SCREEN—a mass of dense smoke used to conceal a maneuver at sea.

SOLAR TIME—time based on the relationship of the sun with the earth.

SQUALL—a short but intense windstorm.

STANDARD TIME—a 15°-wide sector or zone of the earth in which the same time is kept by all in it. Uses as a basis the relationship of the mean sun with the central meridian of the zone.

STATEROOM—an officer's living quarters on board ship.

TRUE BEARING—a bearing using true north as the reference.

UNDERWAY REPLENISHMENT (UnRep)—replenishment by use of ships while under way.

USNA—U.S. Naval Academy, Annapolis, Maryland.

VEER—to let out, as in veering anchor chain; a clockwise change in wind direction.

VERTICAL ENVELOPMENT—a tactical maneuver in which troops are air-dropped or landed by helicopter to attack an enemy's rear or flanks.

VERTICAL LAUNCH SYSTEM (VLS)—missile-launching tubes mounted vertically within a ship's hull.

VERTICAL REPLENISHMENT (VertRep)—replenishment by use of helicopters.

WAR OF ATTRITION—a lengthy war in which both sides concentrate on reducing the other's forces rather than capturing territory.

WARDROOM—the compartment on board a naval ship where the officers eat and lounge.

WATERLINE—the line on a ship's hull to which she sinks in the water.

WEIGH ANCHOR—to lift or hoist an anchor off the bottom.

Bibliography

BOOKS

Bearden, Bill, revisor. *The Bluejackets' Manual,* Twenty-first Edition. Annapolis: Naval Institute Press, 1990.

Bradford, James C., editor. *Command Under Sail: Makers of the American Naval Tradition,* 1775–1850. Annapolis: Naval Institute Press, 1985.

Bureau of Naval Personnel. *Naval Orientation,* NAVPERS 16138F. Washington, D.C.: Government Printing Office, 1988.

Calkins, Carroll C., editor. *The Story of America.* Pleasantville, N.Y.: The Reader's Digest Association, Inc., 1975.

Chalker, Edsel O. *Leadership Education I.* Air Force Junior ROTC text. Maxwell Air Force Base, Alabama: Air Training Command/Air University, 1979.

Crenshaw, Capt. R. S., Jr., USN (Ret.). *Naval Shiphandling,* Annapolis: Naval Institute Press, 1975.

Cross, Wilbur. *Naval Battles and Heroes.* New York: American Heritage Publishing Company, Inc., 1960.

Engle, Eloise, and Arnold S. Lott. *America's Maritime Heritage.* Annapolis: Naval Institute Press, 1975.

Ferguson, John H., and Dean McHenry. *The American System of Government,* Sixth Edition. New York: McGraw-Hill, 1961.

Fincher, Ernest B. *The Government of the United States,* Second Edition. Englewood Cliffs, N.J.: Prentice-Hall, 1971.

Hobbs, Richard R. *Marine Navigation: Piloting and Celestial and Electronic Navigation.* Annapolis: Naval Institute Press, 1990.

Leadership Support Manual, NAVPERS 15934B, Washington, D.C.: Government Printing Office, 1968.

Lyon, Jane D. *Clipper Ships and Captains.* New York: American Heritage Publishing Co., Inc. 1962.

Mack, VAdm. William P., USN (Ret.), and LCdr. Royal Connel, USN. *Naval Ceremonies, Customs, and Traditions.* Annapolis: Naval Institute Press, 1980.

Miller, Nathan, *The U.S. Navy: An Illustrated History.* New York and Annapolis: American Heritage Publishing Company, Inc., and Naval Institute Press, 1977.

Naval Education and Training Program Development Center, Pensacola. *Human Behavior and Leadership,* NAVEDTRA 10058-B. Washington, D.C.: Government Printing Office, 1977.

Naval Education and Training Program Development Center, Pensacola. *Naval Orientation,* NAVEDTRA 16138-G. Washington, D.C.: Government Printing Office, 1977.

Naval Education and Training Program Development Center, Pensacola. *Quartermaster 3 & 2,* NAVEDTRA 10149-F. Washington, D.C.: Government Printing Office, 1988.

Noel, Capt. John V., Jr., USN (Ret.). *Knight's Modern Seamanship,* Seventeenth Edition. New York: Van Nostrand Reinhold Co., 1984.

Potter, E. B., editor. *Sea Power,* Second Edition. Annapolis: Naval Institute Press, 1981.

Potter, E. B. *The Naval Academy Illustrated History of the United States Navy.* New York: Thomas Y. Crowell Company, 1971.

Snouck-Hurgronje, Jan, editor. *Ship Organization and Personnel.* Annapolis: Naval Institute Press, 1972.

Staton, Thomas F. *How to Study,* Fifth Edition. Montgomery, Ala.: 1968.

Sutton, Felix. *The American Revolution*. New York: Wonder Books, Inc., 1963.

Training Publications Detachment, Naval Training Command, Pensacola. *Basic Military Requirements*, NAVTRA 10054-D. Washington, D.C.: Government Printing Office, 1988.

Training Publications Division, Naval Personnel Program Support Activity, Washington, D.C. *Seaman*, NAVPERS 10120-F. Washington, D.C.: Government Printing Office, 1988.

Training Publications Division, Naval Personnel Program Support Activity, Washington, D.C. *Quartermaster 1 & C*, NAVTRA 10151-D. Washington, D.C.: Government Printing Office, 1988.

Webster's New Geographical Dictionary. Springfield, Mass.: G. & C. Merriam Co., 1980.

Booklets and Pamphlets

Annapolis, The United States Naval Academy Catalog, 1994–95. Annapolis: U.S. Naval Academy, 1994.

Anne Arundel County Office of Drug and Alcohol Programs. *A Drug Education Handbook*. Annapolis, Md.: Anne Arundel County School Board, 1990.

Chief of Naval Education and Training. *Regulations Governing Administration of the Naval Junior Reserve Officers' Training Corps (NJROTC)*, CNET Instruction 1533.9B. Pensacola: CNET Code N-161, 27 February 1976.

Freed, Alvyn M. *T.A. for Teens*, Rolling Hills Estates, Calif.: Jalmar Press, 1976.

Harris, Sydney J. *Winners and Losers*. Allen, Tex.: Argus Communications, 1968.

McCain, John S., Jr., USN. *The Expanding Scope of Sea Power*, NAVPERS 15233. Washington, D.C.: Bureau of Naval Personnel, General Military Training Branch, undated.

Naval Air Basic Training Command. Programmed Text, *Relations with Seniors* (CNABT P-639). Pensacola: Naval Air Station, 1968.

Naval Air Basic Training Command. Programmed Text, *Techniques of Leadership* (CNABT P-668). Pensacola: Naval Air Station, 1966.

Naval Sea Systems Command. *Building Destroyers for the United States Navy*. Washington, D.C.: Naval Sea Systems Command, 1975.

Naval Sea Systems Command. *Building Patrol Frigates for the United States Navy*. Washington, D.C.: Naval Sea Systems Command, 1974.

NJROTC, A Navy Program for High School Students, NAVEDTRA 37076. Pensacola: Director of Naval Educational Development, 1976.

Surgeon General of the United States. *Acquired Immune Deficiency Syndrome, Report on*. Washington, D.C.: Government Printing Office, 1989.

United States Navy Recruiting Command. *How to Display and Respect the Flag of the United States*, RAD 74967. Washington, D.C.: Government Printing Office, 1974.

Index

The **Naval Institute Press** is the book-publishing arm of the U.S. Naval Institute, a private, nonprofit society for sea service professionals and others who share an interest in naval and maritime affairs. Established in 1873 at the U.S. Naval Academy in Annapolis, Maryland, where its offices remain today, the Naval Institute has more than 85,000 members worldwide.

Members of the Naval Institute receive the influential monthly magazine *Proceedings* and discounts on fine nautical prints and on ship and aircraft photos. They also have access to the transcripts of the Institute's Oral History Program and get discounted admission to any of the Institute-sponsored seminars offered around the country. Discounts are also available to the colorful bimonthly magazine *Naval History*.

The Naval Institute's book-publishing program, begun in 1898 with basic guides to naval practices, has broadened its scope in recent years to include books of more general interest. Now the Naval Institute Press publishes about 100 titles each year, ranging from how-to books on boating and navigation to battle histories, biographies, ship and aircraft guides, and novels. Institute members receive discounts of 20 to 50 percent on the Press's nearly 600 books in print.

Full-time students are eligible for special half-price membership rates. Life memberships are also available.

For a free catalog describing Naval Institute Press books currently available, and for further information about joining the U.S. Naval Institute, please write to:

Membership Department
U.S. Naval Institute
118 Maryland Avenue
Annapolis, Maryland 21402-5035

Telephone: (800) 233-8764
Fax: (410) 269-7940